Practical PHP
and MySQL®

NEGUS LIVE LINUX SERIES

Practical PHP and MySQL®

Building Eight Dynamic Web Applications

Jono Bacon

PRENTICE HALL

Upper Saddle River, NJ ■ Boston ■ Indianapolis ■ San Francisco
New York ■ Toronto ■ Montreal ■ London ■ Munich ■ Paris ■ Madrid
Cape Town ■ Sydney ■ Tokyo ■ Singapore ■ Mexico City

The publisher offers excellent discounts on this book when ordered in quantity for bulk purchases or special sales, which may include electronic versions and/or custom covers and content particular to your business, training goals, marketing focus, and branding interests. For more information, please contact:

> U.S. Corporate and Government Sales
> (800) 382-3419
> corpsales@pearsontechgroup.com

For sales outside the United States, please contact:

> International Sales
> international@pearsoned.com

Visit us on the Web: www.prenhallprofessional.com

Library of Congress Cataloging-in-Publication Data

Bacon, Jono.
  Practical PHP and MySQL : building eight dynamic web applications / Jono Bacon.
     p. cm.
  Includes index.
  ISBN 0-13-223997-3 (pbk. : alk. paper) 1. PHP (Computer program language) 2. MySQL (Electronic resource) 3. Web site development. I. Title.
  TK5105.888.B325 2007
  005.13'3—dc22
                              2006027701

ISBN 0-13-223997-3
Text printed in the United States on recycled paper at R. R. Donnelley in Crawfordsville, Indiana.
Third Printing: March 2008

To my family for their never-ending support...

Contents

Foreword

Listen to podcasts by Jono Bacon and friends at LUG Radio (www.lugradio.org) and you get a sense of both the spirit and thoughtfulness Jono brings to the open source community. At one moment they speak seriously about hurdles in contributing code to free software projects, while the next they offer a Monty Python-like discussion on which Linux distribution each of them most resembles.

Practical PHP and MySQL reflects Jono's commitment to the spirit of making open source subjects accessible to everyone. The book carefully walks you through the code for eight useful, dynamic Web applications. Projects are presented in a playful way, like the forum project that touts horror movies that make you "hide behind the couch." And everything in the book can be run live, modified, saved, and reused from the included live CD.

Although the tools you need to create Web content are readily available from the open source community, having a skillful guide like Jono Bacon to help you create dynamic Web applications from those tools is a real treat. The results form a foundation for developing your own blogs, forums, shopping carts, and other Web destinations that should significantly cut your startup time.

I am thrilled to have Jono Bacon's *Practical PHP and MySQL* as one of the first books in the Negus Live Linux Series. Its content perfectly suits the goals of the series to put quality free and open source software covering various topics into peoples' hands so they can quickly get high-quality results. I hope you enjoy learning from this book as much as I have.

—Christopher Negus
   Series Editor, Negus Live Linux Series

About the Author

Jono Bacon works for Canonical as the Ubuntu community manager and is an established speaker, author, and regular contributor to the Open Source community. As an author, Bacon co-authored *Linux Desktop Hacks* and the *Official Ubuntu Book*, and has written more than 400 published articles in more than 14 publications. Bacon has also contributed as a columnist for *Linux Format*, *Linux User & Developer*, and *PC Plus*, and is an O'Reilly Network weblog author.

In addition, Bacon is a regular contributor to Open Source in a range of projects, a lead developer on the Jokosher (www.jokosher.org) project, and one of the co-founders of the popular LUGRadio (www.lugradio.org) podcast—a show with more than 15,000 listeners and an annual event that pulls visitors from around the world.

Acknowledgments

Writing thank-you lists is always hard, because I always end up leaving out some-one important. I want to give thanks to the following people for their incredible sup-port and help:

Susan Curtis, John and Pauline Bacon, Simon and Martin Bacon,
Banger and Frankie, Prentice Hall (Debra Williams-Cauley, Songlin Qiu),
LUGRadio (Stuart Langridge, Matthew Revell, Adrian Bradshaw),
OpenAdvantage (Paul Cooper, Elliot Smith, Scott Thompson), #php,
#mysql, and #lugradio on Freenode, the LUGRadio community,
Kai "Oswald" Seidler, and many more.

Introduction

Everyone is going nuts about the Web. Ever since we started getting creaky old modems installed in our homes and businesses, the Web has become an increasingly dominant part of our lives. With it we explore, shop, diagnose, entertain, amuse, communicate, collaborate, and more. The Web is no longer a novelty item that the few use to stretch their technical muscles; millions of people all over the world are living their normal lives, with the Web playing a central role.

The popularity of the Web means interesting things for developers such as you. The Web has not only presented a means to develop information-rich resources such as IMDB, Wikipedia, and so on, but the Web also provides a real opportunity to create online applications for doing everyday things, such as managing contacts, balancing accounts, selling products or services, creating content, expressing opinions, chatting, and much more. A worldwide audience awaits, and if you have the technical chops, you can tap into this audience.

This is where PHP and MySQL swirl into play. In recent years, PHP and MySQL have come together to form a unique and awesomely powerful platform. With their roots in Open Source, these entirely free tools can be used to create hugely functional, stable, enterprise-class Web sites. We can wax lyrical about PHP and MySQL later, so let's talk about what this book can do for you.

A Different Approach

If you walk into the vast majority of bookstores and look for programming books, they all use approximately the same format. These books tend to progressively and linearly ramble through the subject and present a series of facts. This approach is

1

not too dissimilar to learning at school, where you are trained to retain facts and skills, and it is up to you to apply those facts and skills to real-world scenarios.

Well, that's all very dull isn't it? Whenever I want to learn something, I want to dig in straight away and get at the core of the subject and its application. When I learned to play guitar, I wanted to play songs, not learn music theory; when I learned to drive, I wanted to go places, not drive at 30 mph down a village road. This book takes exactly that approach. Instead of teaching random programming facts, you get to roll up your sleeves and start writing applications straight away.

This book starts with a brief introduction to the technology and then gives you a quick primer in core PHP and MySQL skills—just enough to get you started writing an application. After this short primer (because no one likes reading primers), you get straight into writing an application. This way, you don't have to wade through 200 pages of reading before you can get started writing an application.

After the primer in Chapter 2, you get to the applications. I have prepared a menu of applications for your esteemed delectation:

- Chapter 3, "Running the Projects." The Live CD that accompanies this book contains software projects, applications, and the LAMPP server. This chapter provides information about the CD contents and how you operate the disc on your computer.

- Chapter 4, "Building a Weblog." Plug into the weblog culture by creating a weblog system. Here you can add posts, have your readers submit comments, create different categories, and much more.

- Chapter 5, "Discussion Forums." Create a discussion forums Web site with all the bling of the circus. You add forum categories, different forums, threads and messages, user accounts, forum administration, and more.

- Chapter 6, "Creating a Shopping Cart." Open an online shop with this project, in which you add support for products, create a shopping cart, take payment via checks/PayPal, support different accounts, and more.

- Chapter 7, "Building an Online Auction Site." Auction sites present an interesting challenge, and in this chapter, you learn to support multiple accounts, write a bidding engine, support uploaded images, add auction summaries, and more.

- Chapter 8, "Creating a Web-Based Calendar." Don your orange sunglasses and prepare to write the word *Beta* everywhere as you write an AJAX-driven calendar. Here you learn how AJAX works, create a calendar interface, support different events, set up user logins, and more.

- Chapter 9, "FAQ Content Management System." In this chapter, you create a Content Management System (CMS) for FAQs. Features include different privilege levels for users, topic ownership, a submissions system, comment support, and more.
- Chapter 10, "Building a Re-Usable Project." In this application, you create an independent component that could be dropped into any Web site. This is useful if you want to create projects for other developers to download and use. This chapter discusses how to create a portable component and integrate it into a separate site easily.
- Chapter 11, "Building a News Web Site." This project solidifies much of the previous knowledge in the book and also looks at categorization, search support, and the use of the HTML_QuickForm PEAR extension.
- Appendix A, "Web Site Design." In this chapter you create a static Web site and add features such as a FAQ page and an About page, and design the pages with Cascading Style Sheets (CSS).

As each project progresses, you learn more and more skills that are useful in a wide variety of PHP and MySQL Web applications.

WHAT YOU NEED TO USE THIS BOOK

If you are keen to get started, all you need is an enthusiasm to learn and a computer running Linux, Windows, Mac OS X, or Solaris. Each of these different operating systems supports PHP and MySQL, and as is explained later in the book, you can fast-track installation of the required software by using an awesome tool called XAMPP.

In addition to this core platform, it is recommended that you take plenty of time to learn the different skills involved. Learning to code is like baking a cake—sometimes it takes shorter or longer for concepts to bake in your head and solidify. Concepts that may seem obvious to some take a little longer to sink in with others, and you should allow yourself plenty of time to learn these different skills at your own pace.

Finally, it is recommended that you have a look around the Internet and join up on some of the PHP/MySQL discussion forums and mailing lists. This will give you a great support mechanism when you don't understand certain concepts or need more help.

CONVENTIONS

This book has a few different style conventions that are useful in helping you develop the applications. Take a moment to get a quick understanding of these conventions.

First, there are some type conventions:

- `Monospaced text`. This style is used for technical items such as a command, keyword, or function.

- *Italic text*. Italic text is used for words being defined and filenames.

Throughout the book, you will find literally hundreds of code snippets that are used to build your applications. They look like this:

```
if(x ==y) {
    echo "hello world";
}
```

In some of the code snippets, you will see bold text like this:

```
if(x ==y) {
    echo "hello world";
    echo "this is extra code that has been added"
}
```

The bold line indicates a new line or a new section of code that is being added to the snippet. The non-bold text gives an easy way of double-checking that the new chunks of code are going in the right place.

ONWARD

You are at the beginning of an exciting journey, and in the tradition of the rest of the book, I don't want to waste any of your time unnecessarily. Sit down, plug yourself in, and get ready to rock your world with PHP and MySQL. Avast!

CHAPTER 1

A New Approach

Learning how to program has always been tough. Although a mind-boggling array of documentation, tutorials, Web sites, videos, books, and other resources is available, learning to program is still fundamentally difficult, particularly if you don't wear sandals and a ponytail.

One of the main reasons learning to code is so difficult is that code is typically taught in an unnatural way. Most books and tutorials seem to follow a clear-cut path of explaining the minor details of the language and then continuing to build upon each detail to cover more complex concepts. This kind of tuition is akin to cramming for exams—it is difficult to remember all of the separate bits of information in the right order and how they relate to each other.

This book is different. Although most books follow the path just discussed, this book shakes up things and changes the recipe. Instead of blinding you with 300 pages of science, this book focuses primarily on a number of real-world projects, which you will write yourself. These projects span a range of Web applications, and by learning how to write these different applications, you will gain not only a better understanding of PHP and MySQL, but also you will get a stronger sense of how to write *real* applications.

The projects that you will work on in this book include the following:

- Generic Web site
- Weblog
- Auction site
- Shopping cart
- Discussion forums

- Frequently Asked Questions (FAQ) management site
- News site
- Independent PHP application
- Simple AJAX calendar

Each project provides the opportunity to learn new skills and focuses on specific challenges.

THE TECHNOLOGY

It should come as no surprise that the technology being used to build the Web applications in this book uses PHP and MySQL. If you picked up this book in the ASP section of your bookstore, I am afraid someone has played a cruel joke on you.

When put together, PHP and MySQL offer a compelling framework in which you can develop powerful and flexible Web applications. The reason they work well together is that each provides a comprehensive part of the Web development toolkit. In building any Web application, the first thing you need is some form of language in which to write dynamic pages and create features to handle dates, process data, connect to resources, manage users, and perform other tasks. PHP steps up to solve this problem. PHP is an incredibly flexible language with a huge array of functionality for solving common Web development challenges, many of which are covered in the projects in this book. The second requirement is to have somewhere to store the oodles of data that you will be displaying, updating, removing, modifying, and otherwise showing off. A solution for this challenge is to use a database, and MySQL provides a reliable and easy-to-use database that is well supported and flexible.

Before looking at the architecture of how the Web works, however, this chapter explores the tools of the trade in more detail.

PHP

PHP is a popular high-level scripting language used by a range of organizations and developers. Originally developed as a small Perl project by Rasmus Lerdorf in late 1995, PHP was intended as a means to assist in developing his home page, and as such he named it Personal Home Page (PHP) Tools.

When Lerdorf was contracted to work for the University of Toronto to build a dial-up system for students to access the Internet, he had no means of connecting Web sites to databases. To solve this problem, the enterprising Lerdorf replaced his

Perl code with a C wrapper that added the capability to connect his Web pages to a MySQL database. As his small project grew, he gave away his changes on the Internet as an Open Source project and cordially received improvements from other programmers with an interest in PHP. The language was later renamed to the current recursive acronym PHP: Hypertext Preprocessor by Zeev Suraski and Andi Gutmans after they rewrote the parser in 1997. The software continued to develop and now forms the comprehensive PHP platform we know today.

PHP provides a solid and well-defined programming language that includes support for object-orientated programming, conditions, file handling, arithmetic, and more. The language that PHP forms is similar in semantics to that of a shell scripting language combined with the easier bits of the C language.

PHP subscribes to the batteries-included philosophy of programming languages and includes extensive support for a huge range of needs, such as cookies, forms, sessions, include files, network sockets, e-mail, LDAP, IRC, and more. Database support covers not only MySQL but many others, including but not limited to PostgreSQL, Oracle, MS SQL, dBase, Sybase, and DB2. This flexible database support is useful if you ever need to port your application to a different database.

In addition to PHP's capability as a Web scripting language, PHP also can be used as a shell scripting language. This means that you can use a single language to write Web applications and create shell scripts to manage your computers. You can even use PHP for creating desktop applications. Although this usage was typically one for the wiry-haired and zany part of the PHP demographic, more and more developers are using it.

PHP also extends its batteries-included philosophy and includes support for third-party functionality via the PHP Extension and Application Repository (PEAR) library. PEAR works in a similar fashion to Perl CPAN modules and provides additional functionality that is easily available via a number of independent modules built to solve specific problems. These special modules can be included in your application to access this special functionality easily. For example, if you need to send e-mail using your Web application, you can use the special PEAR mail functionality that extends the included PHP mail support. This makes PHP better at supporting third-party extensions and has resulted in a huge number of freely available PEAR modules.

MySQL

MySQL is a powerful and comprehensive relational database server, which was originally developed by David Axmark, Allan Larsson, and Michael "Monty" Widenius. The commercial company they founded, MySQL AB, develops and markets

MySQL and associated products. Although the MySQL software originated as an Open Source project, its creators were confident that they could run a business using the product as a base. This business enables the developers to work full time on the software, which in turn benefits both the Open Source community and commercial users of MySQL. Both the open and commercial MySQL variants are functionally the same; the only difference in the software is how it is licensed. (Companies must buy a license if they want to deploy MySQL commercially in a closed source application.) MySQL has enjoyed enormous popularity, and its customers include Yahoo! Finance, MP3.com, Motorola, NASA, Silicon Graphics, and Texas Instruments.

MySQL is a full-featured database and uses open standards, such as the ANSI SQL 99 standard, for communicating with databases with Structured Query Language (SQL). This standard provides a means to insert, update, and query information in the database by using an industry standard language. This standard language is used across database products, and like other products, MySQL supports a number of additional SQL statements. As well as being a standardized database, MySQL is also multi-platform. This means that in addition to Linux, MySQL also runs on other operating systems, such as Windows, Mac OS X, or BSD and UNIX variants.

The database itself includes an interactive command-line client, which allows you to communicate with the server. Although this client is useful, it's a bit scary for new users who are unfamiliar with command-line zen. Fortunately, a number of graphical and Web-based clients can avoid the command-line encounter. (This book uses the Web-based phpMyAdmin client extensively.) MySQL also has support for a number of programming languages to access and query the database. This includes languages such as PHP, Python, Perl, C, C++, and Java, among others. Although you may wish to initially use only PHP to query the database, multi-language support is useful if you need to write modules and applications in different languages in the future.

HOW THE DYNAMIC WEB WORKS

At its most fundamental level, the PHP and MySQL system provides a means to allow dynamic content to be distributed to a networked device. This can be Uncle Bob connecting to your Web site, a delivery service connecting wirelessly to its tracking network, or you accessing your e-mail via the Web. Each of these different solutions uses essentially the same software components that access each other over different hardware contexts. The technical description for the type of programming you are engaging in with PHP and MySQL is called *client/server development*.

To fully understand this concept, this chapter offers several examples and explains how information is bounced between parts of the Web.

Imagine a Web site, any Web site. Go on—be exciting and imagine you are an undercover spy who just so happens to have a Web site with your favorite spy-related stuff. Assume that this Web site displays HTML code (the basic code that a Web browser understands) and nothing else. The page contains only a list of spy-related text, and there is no interactivity. You simply connect to www.thewebaddress-ofthesite.com, and the Web site displays the information. Figure 1-1 shows the kind of interaction involved with this example.

FIGURE 1-1

How a Web browser connects to a Web site

In this example, the client connects to the Web server (in this case, an Apache server) and requests an HTML page. When the client has connected, the Apache server returns the requested page to the client. In this example, the Apache server acts as a middleman for taking the requests and sending the responses back to the client.

Figure 1-2 demonstrates the slightly more complex example of how an HTML input form works.

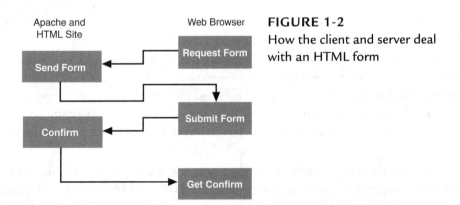

FIGURE 1-2

How the client and server deal with an HTML form

If you start at the bottom-right corner of this diagram, you can see that the very first part is that the Web browser requests the HTML form. The Apache server then responds and sends the form back to the browser. Next, the user fills in the form and submits it back to the Apache server. Apache then sends a confirmation page back to the client. By following the direction of the arrows, you can see how the process works and how information is sent between the client and the server.

The next example, shown in Figure 1-3, demonstrates what happens when you roll a database server into the mix. In this case, you not only are filling in the form but you want to store the contents of the form in the database. For this to happen, you need to include one extra step when the Web site receives the contents of the form. The Web site must send out a confirmation page and put the data in the database. Because putting the data in the database is a one-way process, no two-way arrow is included in this figure.

The model shown in Figure 1-3 is virtually the same as before but with the extra stage added. In addition to putting information into a database, you also need to be able to retrieve information from the database to display the results. In Figure 1-4, you get the client to request a form, fill in the request details (such as a search form), and then query the database for the results and return them to the client.

FIGURE 1-3
When a database is thrown in, the information flow is a little different.

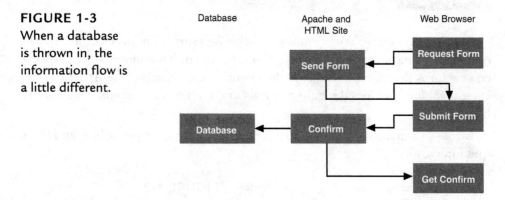

In this example, you begin by requesting the form from the server. The server sends the form back to the browser, and the user fills in the information he needs and submits the form. Next, the server receives the search string and requests from the database the items that match the search term. The database then finds the data and returns the relevant results to the server, which in turn sends the results to the client.

The client/server examples described here use a fairly loose definition of the different components (such as the database, server, and browser) in the models shown. The reason for this is so that you can concentrate on how data flows between the different major parts of the client/server system.

This last example (as shown in Figure 1-5) explains in detail how each step works in terms of these components.

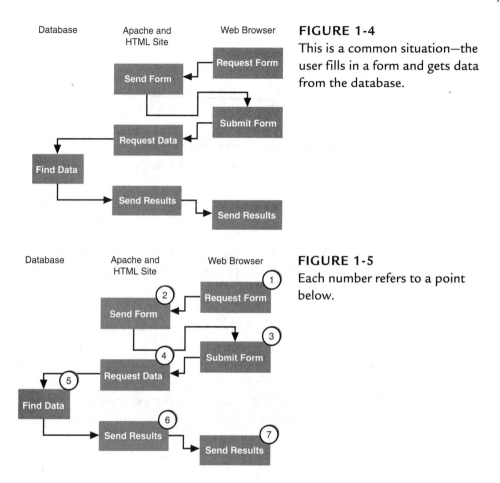

FIGURE 1-4
This is a common situation—the user fills in a form and gets data from the database.

FIGURE 1-5
Each number refers to a point below.

1. The user types a Web address in a Web browser (the client) to access the site. This connection also requests the HTML page containing the HTML form.

2. The browser connects to the Apache server, which has the HTML and PHP files that form the Web site. Apache services the request (by following the rules in its configuration file to find the relevant page and send it back) and sends the client the Web page containing the HTML form.

3. The user fills in the form (in the Web browser) and submits the form to the server.

4. The Apache server receives the submitted form and loads the relevant file to handle the form submission. This file contains PHP code that is used to connect to the database. This PHP code is passed to the PHP interpreter by Apache and run by the interpreter. PHP connects to the MySQL database (which may be on the same computer or another one; it doesn't matter

which). When connected to the MySQL database, a request is made for the information by using SQL, which is a language designed for communicating with databases.

5. The MySQL database receives the SQL request and finds the information. When the information is located, the result is sent back to the PHP script that made the request.

6. The PHP script receives the result from the MySQL server and constructs an HTML page with the results included before sending it back to the Web browser client.

7. The Web browser receives the HTML result of the query and displays it to the user.

Throughout this process, you'll want to bear in mind a few key items. It is recommended that you read the following key points and then review the preceding process to clarify any confusion.

To begin, the Web browser understands hypertext only; it does not understand PHP. (Of course, the former is the assumption that one makes for all Web browsers because they all are built to understand hypertext. Some browsers may understand scripting languages such as JavaScript, but that example is out of the scope of this discussion.) All communication to and from the Web browser is done in hypertext (hence converting the results of the MySQL query to hypertext in Step 6). Another point is that PHP is tightly linked with Apache on the server, and all database connections/queries are executed by PHP. This tight integration involves the PHP process being closely linked to Apache for high performance. PHP can be thought of as the middle ground for accessing databases, files, XML, and so on, and this middle ground sends everything out of the machine via Apache. MySQL should be thought of purely as a data storage device that is useful only when something else connects to it to add, remove, update, or request information. You can consider MySQL as the equivalent of a hard disk for a computer; a hard disk is useful only if there is software to access it and store data on it. PHP is the metaphorical equivalent to this "software."

SUMMARY

As with learning anything, PHP and MySQL development has a number of underlying concepts that need to be understood before you hit the nitty-gritty of the subject. The major concepts have been discussed in this chapter to provide a solid foundation.

The next chapter moves on and teaches the core principles of PHP and MySQL. You will discover the fundamental language bits and pieces, and then get straight to writing an application. With each application, you will explore new concepts and skills, and push your knowledge further, while always writing relevant Web applications.

CHAPTER 2

Getting Started with PHP and MySQL

As the proud owner of *Practical PHP and MySQL* or a prospective owner rifling though it in a bookstore—you will be pleased to know that this book consists of a number of real-world Web applications that are built from scratch. Although the main focus of the book is to teach you how to create these applications, it is important to review some of the introductory aspects of learning PHP and MySQL. This chapter provides a quick primer.

The intention of this chapter is not to be exhaustive, but to provide a solid introduction to PHP and MySQL—enough to get you started writing applications. Many PHP and MySQL books spend most of the time discussing abstract concepts that don't relate in any way, and you can often see the eyes of the readers physically glazing over with sheer, unadulterated boredom. As a man who objects to any kind of retina glazing, you won't find this kind of content here. The grand plan is to show you enough of PHP and MySQL to get started and then get on with the interesting stuff: writing applications.

This chapter discusses core PHP language fundamentals such as loops and variables and then moves on to cover how to create a database and access it from PHP. The chapter concludes with coverage of sessions, a key technology used in most Web applications. Although this chapter provides an introduction to these concepts, the real action happens inside the applications you will write. Each project provides a means to explore further into the many aspects of programming PHP and MySQL Web applications, and the general ethos is of learning by doing instead of learning by reading.

SETTING UP PHP AND MySQL

When I started teaching people how to use PHP and MySQL, I would typically teach it within the safe confines of a computer lab, complete with a network of perfectly set up and configured machines. My students would come to the course, learn how to use the software, and leave incredibly excited about the potential that PHP and MySQL gave them. Then, a few days later, I would start getting e-mails detailing problems they were facing when installing PHP, MySQL, and Apache on Windows, Linux, or Mac OS X. Although the computer lab was great for teaching the software, the course back then did not cover installation—yet it was evidently such a hurdle.

The problem is that PHP, Apache, and MySQL are really difficult to set up on Windows. They are much easier to set up on Linux because the major distributions typically include MySQL, Apache, and PHP packages, but on Windows it is a royal pain in the nether region. Back then, I was somewhat stumped about what to do— teaching the installation side of the software could take up a substantial amount of time on the course.

Then, in a fit of pure genius, my colleague and friend Elliot Smith discovered XAMPP (www.xampp.org/). XAMPP provides a complete PHP, Apache, and MySQL Web development environment that can be installed by downloading, unzipping, and running the software. XAMPP makes the installation dramatically easier, and the software also includes a raft of additions and extras that are genuinely useful, including PHP extensions, a Web front-end for MySQL (which is used throughout the book), and more. XAMPP is freely available for Windows, Linux, Mac OS X, and Solaris.

It is recommended that you use XAMPP for setting up the software if you have never done it before. The following sections cover how to set up XAMPP on Windows and Linux.

Setting Up XAMPP on Windows

To begin, download the latest XAMPP installer from www.xampp.org/. Double-click the installer and follow the instructions. After installation, load the XAMPP Control Panel by clicking Start > Programs > XAMPP.

Setting Up XAMPP on Linux

To begin, download the latest XAMPP release from www.xampp.org/. Next, copy the installation file to /opt and then unzip it. If you don't have an /opt directory, create it with 'mkdir /opt' as the superuser. If you don't have sudo installed on your computer, you can become the superuser by running 'su' and entering your super-user password.

To copy the file to /opt:

```
foo@bar:~$ sudo cp xampp-linux-x.x-x.tar.gz /opt
```

To move to /opt and unzip the file:

```
foo@bar:~$ cd /opt
foo@bar:/opt$ sudo tar zxvf xampp-linux-x.x-x.tar.gz /opt
```

A stream of files is now unpacked into a directory called lampp. Currently, all of this unpacking has been done as the superuser, yet you will want your normal user account to be able to write to the htdocs directory, so change the permissions on the directory:

```
foo@bar:/opt$ sudo chmod -R a+rw /opt/lampp/htdocs
```

You are now all set to run XAMPP:

```
foo@bar:/opt$ sudo /opt/lampp/lampp start
```

You can also stop XAMPP:

```
foo@bar:/opt$ sudo /opt/lampp/lampp stop
```

You can now save your PHP code in /opt/lampp/htdocs and access your new XAMPP server in your Web browser at http://localhost/.

 NOTE

XAMPP Control Panel for Linux

Rather disappointed with the nice graphical XAMPP Control Panel for Windows, I wrote one in Python for Linux, and it is now included with the official XAMPP release. You can find it in /opt/lampp/share/xampp-control-panel. Just run it like this:

```
foo@bar:/opt/lampp/share/xampp-control-panel$ sudo ./xampp-
control-panel
```

GETTING STARTED WITH PHP

PHP and HTML are good friends. Working side by side, the PHP and HTML pals are so reliant on each other that it is virtually impossible to tear them apart. Whenever you do any kind of Web development, you use PHP and HTML interchangeably on the vast majority of scripts that you write. Both your HTML and PHP code will reside in any files that end in *.php*.

To begin, you'll create a simple page that contains some HTML. Create a new file, and call it 1.php. Add the following code in the file:

```
<!DOCTYPE HTML PUBLIC "-//W3C//DTD HTML 4.01 Transitional//EN"
"http://www.w3.org/TR/html4/loose.dtd">
<html>
<head>
   <title>Tough first script</title>
</head>
<body>
   <h1>The very first script</h1>
   <p>
   This is the first script!
   </p>
</body>
</html>
```

In this example, you are writing some HTML to construct a simple Web page. This HTML first selects a suitable DOCTYPE (the dialect of HTML to use) and then goes on to set the title of the page (the text in the window border) with the <title> tag. Next, a large heading with the <h1> tag is added before then supplying the memorable words This is the first script! inside a paragraph (indicated by the <p> and </p> tags). If you have a burning ambition to change the memorable words to something else, so be it.

NOTE

Running Your Code

When you create the files that store your code, make sure to place them in the directory that your Web server reads for files. This directory is typically called htdocs. If you are using XAMPP, this directory is called /opt/lampp/htdocs on Linux, and in Windows it is the htdocs directory inside the directory where you installed it.

To run your code, remember that http://localhost points to this htdocs directory. As such, if you want to access 1.php, go to http://localhost/1.php in your Web browser.

You may have noticed that this code has been stored in a file that has a .php extension instead of the .htm or .html extension. This is because all PHP scripts that you will use are ultimately converted into text that the Web browser can understand. You should *always* remember that the Web browser has no idea what PHP is. The Web browser understands text, HTML, and CSS only. It is the Web server that runs PHP that does the job of processing the PHP before sending the text, HTML, or CSS back to the browser.

Add a PHP block into your code:

```
<!DOCTYPE HTML PUBLIC "-//W3C//DTD HTML 4.01 Transitional//EN"
"http://www.w3.org/TR/html4/loose.dtd">
<html>
<head>
   <title>Tough first script</title>
</head>
<body>
   <h1>The very first script</h1>
   <p>
   This is the first script!
   </p>
   <p>
   <?php

       echo "This is PHP code";

   ?>
   </p>
</body>
</html>
```

In this example, you created another paragraph block and added a PHP block inside it. If you run the script again, you will see another line of text that displays in your Web browser.

QUICK TIP

In this book, the code shown in bold represents new code that is added to your script.

When you want to use PHP code, encase the PHP commands within the `<?php` and `?>` tags. These two tags indicate the start and end points of a PHP block, and anything between these tags will be fed to the PHP interpreter and digested. You can think of these tags behaving in a similar way as the HTML `<!-` and `->` comment tags, where everything inside those tags is considered a comment.

Remember how the Web browser doesn't understand PHP? To demonstrate this, look at the source code in your Web browser (usually by clicking View > Source Code). As you can see, there is no PHP in there. What happens is that the PHP interpreter on the server reads any PHP commands, executes them, and spits out HTML as the final output. In this example, the PHP echo command was used to send the contents within the double quotes to the Web browser. Each command in PHP ends in a semi-colon (;), and you can see it at the end of the echo command.

NOTE

Using HTML Within PHP

You can use HTML tags within the PHP echo statement. The purpose of an echo statement is to send information to the browser, and if you want to embed HTML tags or other content (such as CSS or JavaScript) that is readable by Web browsers, you are free to do so. For example, change the preceding echo line to this:

```
echo "This is <strong>PHP</strong> code";
```

In this line, you are using the HTML <strong> tag to make a part of the echo statement bold. This is an incredibly useful and often used feature in PHP.

Remember that you can only put HTML tags inside legitimate PHP commands. You can't just dump HTML inside a PHP block like this:

```
<?php
    <strong>Boogaloo with my didgeridoo</strong>
?>
```

Everything inside the <?php and ?> tags is expected to be PHP, and the <strong> tags are HTML (not PHP).

Using Variables

Variables are the bread and butter of any programming language. A **variable** is a small portion of memory that stores a particular piece of information. Imagine for a second that you have a cardboard box and a pen in your hand. You now decide to store your favorite CD in the box. To better remember what is in it later, you write 'favealbum' on the front of the box. You now know that if you look at the box and see 'favealbum,' you will remember that you have your slightly embarrassing Leprechaun Hits Volume 1 CD in there.

This is exactly how variables work, except that a variable stores information. In your program, you can create a variable to store some information and then reference what is in that variable by the name of the variable itself. This is best explained with an example.

Create a new file called `simplevariable.php` and add the following code:

```
<?php

    $monkeys = 10;

    echo "Number of monkeys: " . $monkeys;

?>
```

All variables in PHP begin with a dollar sign ($). In the preceding example, you first create a variable called $monkeys and then used the = sign to set this to the value 10. This is the common way to create a variable in PHP; you simply pick a variable name out of thin air (in this example, my love of monkeys has been indulged) and then set the variable to store a particular value. With $monkeys created, you can now read the code and mentally replace $monkeys for the value 10 when you see it.

One important note at this point, particularly for those of you with prior experience in other programming languages, is that you do not need to indicate what type a variable will be in PHP. In other languages (such as C/C++), you would need to indicate that a variable containing a number is an integer variable. PHP is different and figures out what the type is when you use the variable.

With the variable set, it is then used in the next line in which the echo command is used to first display Number of monkeys: and then the value of $monkeys is displayed next to it. When you run the script, you should see the following output:

```
Number of monkeys: 10
```

This echo line uses a technique called **concatenation**. This bizarre-sounding act provides a simple method of stringing together bits of text (called strings) with the contents of variables. To do this, you use the . symbol (called the **concatenation operator**) to glue together whatever is on the left and right sides of the dot, or period. In the preceding code, the part on the left side is the text Number of monkeys: and the part on the right is the contents of the $monkeys variable.

Concatenation is an important but often slightly confusing topic. It does take a little while to get used to, particularly when using more complex examples. As an example of this, change the echo line above to the following line:

```
    echo "You have " . $monkeys . " monkeys!";
```

In this line, you used the concatenation operator twice to glue an additional part onto the line. If you read the line from left to right, you can see how You have is then glued to the value of $monkeys (10), which is then glued to monkeys.

PHP as a Simple Calculator

When you have the ability to create variables, you also have the ability to perform some simple mathematic calculations on them. For those of you who shudder at the thought of math, fear not; you will explore some of the common mathematical uses you will need in PHP.

To begin, create a new file called `simplemath.php` and add the following code:

```php
<?php

    $cds = 50;
    $tapes = 60;

    $total = $cds + $tapes;

    echo "You have " . $cds . " cds and " . $tapes
. " tapes with " . $total . " items!";

?>
```

In this example, you first created two variables, called $cds and $tapes, that have numbers stored in them. (If you are reading this book in 2020, tapes were items that stored music on them, a bit like your AstroDisks.) The sixth line of code then uses the + sign to add the $cds and $tapes variables together and stores the result in the $total variable. The final `echo` line then concatenates all of the variables into a single line that explains how many CDs and tapes there are and the total number of items available.

A number of symbols can be used when performing math. Some of the most common are covered in Table 2-1.

TABLE 2-1 Math Operators in PHP

OPERATOR	DESCRIPTION	EXAMPLE
+	Addition	$total = $cds + $tapes;
–	Subtraction	$total = $cds – $tapes;
*	Multiplication	$total = $cds * $tapes;
/	Division	$total = $cds / $tapes;

One of the great benefits of PHP has been its batteries-included approach to functionality. To help solve a range of problems, a number of facilities and functions are built right into PHP. For example, some numbers don't divide easily. Imagine that you need to split a range of news stories across a number of different pages. To calculate how many pages you need, you can take the number of stories and the number of entries you want on each page and then divide the number of stories by this page size. The result of the calculation will give you how many pages you need.

Add the following code to a new file called `simplemath2.php`:

```php
<?php

    $stories = 43;
    $pagesize = 8;

    $pages = $stories / $pagesize;

    echo "You will need " . $pages . " pages";

?>
```

When you run this script, you will see the result is 5.375 pages. Obviously, this is no good because you need a whole number. To solve this problem, you can use the `floor()` function to round the value down or the `ceil()` function to round up.

NOTE

Functions? Huh?

If you are new to functions, they are fairly straightforward to understand. A **function** is a chunk of code somewhere else that does something for you. For example, the `floor()` function rounds something down for you. Somewhere, deep in the PHP machine, a chunk of code actually does the work of rounding the value down. You can reference this functionality with the function name: `floor()`.

To use a function, specify the name of the function and then include brackets at the end. The brackets are used pass information to the function. For example, `floor()` is pretty useless unless you send the function a value to convert. You put this value inside the brackets. These values are called **parameters**.

We will cover functions and how to roll your own later in this chapter.

Try the following code in `simplemath3.php` to see how this works:

```php
<?php

    $stories = 43;
    $pagesize = 8;
```

```
$pages = $stories / $pagesize;

echo "Rounded down: " . floor($pages)
. " Rounded up: " . ceil($pages);
```

```
?>
```

To use these handy functions, you put the variable you want to convert between the brackets in the function.

> ### NOTE
>
> **No Batteries Required**
>
> As you learned in Chapter 1, PHP is very much a batteries-included language and includes a huge range of functions that solve a huge range of common challenges. Throughout this book, you will learn to use a range of functions that are common in typical programming situations.
>
> To find out more about a function, just visit www.php.net. Add the function after a slash, such as www.php.net/floor, to find out more about `floor()`.

Arrays

One of the most useful types of variable is an **array**. This special variable gives you the ability to store more than one piece of information in a single variable. Imagine that you are storing a list of your favorite choices in a program. You may want to store the following choices:

Favorite	Choice
Color	Blue
Food	Mexican
Pastime	Swimming
Music	Metal

In this list of things to store, a clear relationship exists between the item on the left and the item on the right. This is called a **key-value pair**, or an **associative array**. With one of these pairs, you have a key (such as Color) and a value that the key is set to (such as Blue). Arrays are perfect for storing these relationships.

There are a few methods of creating arrays. The first is to use the following format:

```
$arr['Color'] = "Blue";
$arr['Food'] = "Mexican";
```

In this example, you created a new array called $arr. Inside the brackets, you specified the key that you wanted to set in the array and then passed the value in the same way you created a normal variable. In the preceding two lines, you created two entries in the array.

If you would prefer to use a function to create the array, use the following format:

```php
$arr = array("Color" => "Blue", "Food" => "Mexican");
```

In this example, you used the array() function to specify the key and then the matching value is specified after the => symbol. Commas separate each of the different entries in the array.

Arrays are used extensively when dealing with database information. You store information from the database record in a row, and the key will be the field name. This will make far more sense later when you connect to MySQL and bring some data into PHP.

Loops

When you code in any programming language, it's helpful to shut your eyes and think of an imaginary stylus that moves through your program, pointing at the current line of code. This stylus will start at the top of the script and move down, reading each instruction in turn.

When this imaginary stylus hits a loop statement, the code in the loop section will be repeated as long as a specific rule is adhered to. This rule is called a **loop condition**. Loops are useful for such purposes as looping through rows from a database, creating numbered lists, and more.

The for Loop

One of the most useful loops is the for loop. To see this in action, create a new file called forloop.php and add the following code:

```php
<?php

for($i=1; $i<10; $i++) {
   echo $i . "<br />";
}t

?>
```

When you run this example, you should see the numbers 1 to 9 displayed each on a separate line. The for loop is dependent on the three conditions inside the brackets. These conditions are:

$i = 1;   This part is where the loop begins. In this case, the loop begins
             with 1.

$i<10;   This is where the loop finishes looping. In this example, the loop
             will continue while $i is less than (indicated with the < operator)
             10. This is why the loop loops until 9; the number 9 is less than
             10, but the number 10 is not 10. If you wanted to loop from 1
             to 10, you would change the operator to less-than-or-equal-to, or
             $i<=10.

$i++   This final part determines how much the loop will increment each
             time. In this example, $i++ is shorthand for $i = $i + 1. This
             means that the loop will increment by 1 each time.

The for loop is particularly useful for repeating between a defined range of values. For example, you could use a for loop to populate a drop-down box that is used
to select the day part of a date of birth. You would use it to loop between 1 and 31 to
fill the box with possible day values.

The while Loop

The other type of loop that is used extensively in PHP is the while loop. A while is
particularly useful because it simply keeps looping while the loop condition is true.
This is commonly used to iterate through database records.

The while loops are difficult to demonstrate because they are most typically
used in real-world examples that uses code not yet covered in this book. To provide
a simple example, however, add the following code into a file called whileloop.php:

```php
<?php

$age = 1;

while($age < 18) {
    echo "You are age " . $age . " and still not an adult<br />";
    $age++;
}

echo "You are now an adult!";

?>
```

In this example, you first created a variable, called $age, that is set to 1. You
then created a while loop that repeated the code between the { and } brackets while
$age is less than 18. Inside the while loop, a line is printed out indicating the cur-
rent age, and then the $age variable is incremented by 1 each time with the $age++
line. With this value increasing each time, the loop will loop 17 times. The loop will

not loop 18 times because 18 is not less than 18; it is equal to 18. Finally, a line is displayed to indicate that adulthood has been reached.

An important point to note is what would happen if you left off the $age++ line. If you create a while loop in which it loops while a particular condition is set, but that condition never changes, an infinite loop will occur. This is never a good thing, and you should always check your loop to ensure that it will eventually end when you want it to. If you are running your scripts on somebody else's server and get into an infinite loop, you may get some angry emails. Always check that the while has some means of ending.

You will revisit while loops later when you explore other facets of PHP programming, particularly database development.

⚠ WARNING

Be Careful!

One common mistake you can make with a while loop is to set the loop condition to something that doesn't change, and as such, causes the while loop to loop forever. This is known as an **infinite loop**. For example—don't run this—here is an example of an infinite loop:

```php
<?php
$age =1;
while($age == 1) {
echo "Argh! Infinite loop!";
}
?>
```

Here, the loop cannot break out of the of $age being set to 1 and as such loops forever. This causes an insane slowdown on your computer, and you will probably need to restart your Web server or XAMPP if you are using it.

Ask Questions of Your Code

One of the most fundamental purposes of a programming language is to check a particular condition and respond where necessary. A good example of this is if you were to type an age into a Web form, and you wanted to return a response based on the user's age. For example, you may want to respond to the user differently if she is a child as opposed to an adult. This is a common theme among Web sites containing content that may be unsuitable for minors; the user is prompted to enter her age and is denied access if the age is below a certain threshold.

NOTE

Horrifically Ageist?

You may have noticed that many of the examples here are age related. This can mean one of two things: I am either horrifically ageist or about to have a mid-life crisis. Well it's neither, drama fans. Age is just a great subject for sample programs.

There are two major types of conditional to explore here: the `if` and `switch` blocks. The `if` statement is useful for asking a single question of a particular condition, whereas a `switch` is useful for checking whether a particular value meets any one of a number of options.

The if Statement

The `if` statement is used extensively throughout PHP development. You use `if` to check conditions across different pages in a variety of different ways. To get started, you'll first create a very simple example. Add this code to a file named `if1.php`:

```php
<?php

$age = 21;

if($age == 21) {
    echo "Congratulations!";
}

?>
```

In this example, you first created a variable called `$age` and set it to 21. You then used the `if` statement to check if `$age` is equal to 21 and if it is, the text `Congratulations!` is displayed in the browser. The magic in this statement happens between the brackets. You may have noticed that two equals signs are used instead of a single equals sign. This is important. When you use two equals signs in your code, you are comparing the values on either side. In the preceding example, the use of the two equals signs compares the `$age` variable and the value 21. If you use a single equals sign, the variable on the left is set to the right value.

In the previous example, the `if` check was fairly straightforward. The problem with the previous example, however, is that it only caters for a match. In many cases, you need to check when the `if` does not match.

To achieve this, you can bolt on an `else` to the `if` block. This small addition will execute some code when the `if` doesn't match.

TIP

Always Check for the Equals Signs

When you are new to a language, subtleties such as the == or = issue can often trip you up. When you get errors in your code, always check to see that you have used the correct equals signs.

Add the following code to `if2.php`:

```php
<?php

$age = 21;

if($age < 18) {
    echo "Congratulations! You are a kid";
}
else {
    echo "Just a normal age";
}

?>
```

In this example, you changed the `if` condition to check a range. In the condition (within the brackets) the `if` checks to see whether the value of the `$age` variable is less than 18. If it is, the `if` code is executed; if not, the `else` code is executed.

The switch Statement

Although the `if` statement is incredibly useful, it is only really practical for making comparisons against single values. If you want to make a series of choices available, you would need to resort to a number of `if` statements to check whether each choice has been selected. A `switch` prevents having all multiple `if` statements and provides a single, clean method of achieving this.

Add the following code to `switch.php`:

```php
<?php

    $choice = 2;

    switch($choice) {
        case 1:
            echo "You picked choice #1 - well done!";
        break;

        case 2:
            echo "You picked choice #2 - well done!";
```

```
        break;

    case 3:
        echo "You picked choice #3 - well done!";
        break;

    default:
        echo "You did not pick a valid choice!";
        break;

    }

?>
```

In this example, you first create a variable, called $choice, that is set to 2. This variable is then fed into a switch statement that analyzes $choice. Within the switch block are a series of case entries. The first case (case 1:) is applied if the value of $choice is 1. If it is, the code between the case and the break statement is executed. The other two case statements apply if $choice is equal to 2 or 3 respectively. Finally, in all other cases, the default section will be executed.

The switch statements are very useful in examples such as this, when you need to check whether the value is equal to a variety of different conditions.

Using Functions

Earlier you learned how to use the floor() and ceil() functions. These small but useful facilities in PHP provide a handy method of solving specific, directed problems. In the case of floor(), if your problem is that you need to round something down, floor() comes leaping to your assistance and provides a simple means of converting the value.

PHP includes functions for a huge range of problems. Areas such as file handling, arithmetic, validation, forms, XML, networking, and more are packed with hundreds of functions for a wide variety of tasks. These functions have been designed by the PHP developers to provide an easy way of solving these specific tasks.

Although these functions exist in the PHP language, you also have the ability to create your own functions. Rolling your own functions is typically useful when you have specific processing that needs to be applied to something in your project. For example, you may need to take a base price and then automatically add onto other various costs until you reach your final price.

```php
<?php

function calculatePrice($price) {
    $manufacturingcosts = 10.50;
    $pretax = $price + $manufacturingcosts;
    $tax = ($pretax / 100) * 20;
    $total = $pretax + $tax;

    return $total;
}

echo calculatePrice(304);

?>
```

In this example, you created a function to add two primary costs onto the price. First was a stock 10.50 manufacturing cost. Second was the 20% needed for the tax office.

The first step is to create the outer shell of the function. On the first line, you use the function keyword to create a new function called calculatePrice(). Inside the brackets of the function, you include $price. This refers to a single parameter that is being used by the function. This parameter is a channel in which you can feed data into the function. When you actually use the function later in the example, you will replace this parameter with whatever data you want to be processed.

Between the { and } brackets is the main body of the function. This is where the actual processing occurs. Looking at the costs to add on, the first cost is manufacturing. To achieve this, you first create a new variable called $manufacturingcosts and set this to 10.50. The next line creates a new variable called $pretax and adds the value that is being passed into the function ($price) and the $manufacturing-costs variable.

The next step is to calculate the right amount of tax. To do this, a new variable called $tax is created, and then the calculation in brackets is made, the total of which is divided by 20 to determine the final amount. This amount is then added to the $pretax variable.

The final part of the function is the return $total line. The purpose of this line is to specify which variable contains the result that the function has processed. By using the return keyword, the function can now be used like any other function in PHP and will output the processed data as you would expect. This return line simply sends back the result to the line that called the function.

Finally, the function is executed by passing 304 as the value to it. The result of the function is echoed out to the screen. The result of 377.4 is then displayed; 377.4 is the value that was returned with the return line.

Working with Forms

If you do any kind of Web development, you will come across forms in your daily programming. These unsuspecting creatures reside on Web pages, suck information from you through your fingers, and are then processed by a script on the server.

Dealing with forms involves two processes. First, the displayed form needs to capture all the relevant information. Second, you read in the form and process it when the user clicks the Submit button.

The first step is performed with HTML, to use the wide range of HTML form elements to produce the form on the page. To get started, add the following code to form1.php:

```
<form action="form1.php" method="POST">
   Username <input type="text" name="username"><br />
   Password <input type="password" name="password"><br />
   <input type="submit" name="submitbutt" value="Login!"><br />
</form>
```

In this example, you create a simple form that contains three different elements. These elements work together to create a login form.

On the first line, is the opening <form> tag. This tag takes two primary attributes. The first (action) needs to know the location of the script that will process the form. In this example, the action contains the name of the file with the form in it (form1.php), so the code to process the form is assumed to be in the same file.

The second attribute (method) can contain either GET or POST. This refers to how the data will be transferred to the action script. These two types of method are very different:

- **POST**: When you use the POST method, the data entered into the form is transferred to the action behind the scenes. The user has no visual cue as to what the data is; it will be transmitted non-visually. Although you cannot see it, there are still methods of accessing POSTed data, so it should not be considered 100% secure.

- **GET**: When you use the GET method, the data from the form is appended to the end of the URL as a series of variables. For example, if you were to fill in the preceding form and use the GET method, you would see http://localhost/form1?username=jono&password=secretpass&submitbutt=Login%21 in the address bar of your browser, assuming you typed jono and secretpass into the form. When you use the GET method, be careful that no sensitive information is displayed in the URL, such as a password!

After the <form> tag has been displayed, the next step is to display each form element. The majority of form elements are added with the <input> tag and then relevant options are selected with the type attribute in the <input> tag.

The first field added is a normal text box. This provides a single line box in which the user can type some text. To select this type of element, use the text setting in the type attribute. You also should give the tag a name attribute. You will use the value of the name attribute to refer to the contents of the box later.

The second field added is a password box. When you use password in the type field of the <input> tag, the box behaves the same as a text box, but it disguises the data the user enters with stars or circles.

The final box added uses the submit type. This provides a clickable Submit button that can be used when the user has clicked the form. The additional attribute passed to this tag is value; this pre-fills the widget with data. In the case of the Submit button, the value attribute changes the text displayed on the button.

NOTE

Web Editors

A number of Web editors help you to write HTML more efficiently. A good example is a tool called Bluefish (http://bluefish.openoffice.nl) available for Linux. With it you can use toolbar buttons to add form elements easily. A number of handy editors like this are available all operating systems, such as SciTE (http://www.scintilla.org/).

Processing the Form

Displaying a form and not processing it is just short of useless. To do anything useful with the form data, you need to hook up the form to some PHP that can process the data.

To process a form, follow these steps:

1. Determine whether the submit button variable exists. If the user has clicked the button, you can make the assumption that the form has been displayed and that the Submit button has been clicked.

2. If the Submit button has not been clicked, you should assume the form has not been displayed yet, so you display it.

3. If the Submit button has been clicked, you then process the form.

To demonstrate how this process works, create a new file called form2.php and add the following code:

```php
<?php

if($_POST['submitbutt']) {
    echo "username: " . $_POST['username'] . "<br />";
    echo "password: " . $_POST['password'] . "<br />";
}
else {
?>

<form action="form2.php" method="POST">
    Username <input type="text" name="username"><br />
    Password <input type="password" name="password"><br />
    <input type="submit" name="submitbutt" value="Login!"><br />
</form>

<?php
}

?>
```

When understanding this code, it helps to put yourself in the position of the PHP interpreter and assume you have never sent the page before. The very start of this example contains the if statement. This line checks to see if the Submit button has been clicked. This is determined by checking if there is a GET variable with the same name as the Submit button (submitbutt).

In PHP, a number of special commands can be used to access certain types of variables. In this particular example, you are using $_POST['submitbutt'] to refer to the submitbutt POST variable. If you were to use GET as the method, you also could use $_GET['submitbutt'].

NOTE

Super What?

The $_GET and $_POST features in PHP are known as **superglobals** in PHP lingo and they are used to access different types of information. As an example, $_GET is used to access GET variables.

The if line simply checks to see if this variable exists. If the variable exists, the contents of the other GET variables are then displayed on the screen by referencing them in the same way. If the variable does not exist, you need to assume the form has not been displayed yet, and the else is run. You can see how to actually break out of PHP mode to display the form and then return back to PHP mode at the bottom of the code to close off the `else` block with the final } bracket. This is the common way in which forms are displayed and processed. Using this method means that you can keep your form processing and form tags on the same page for ease of access.

To clarify this, these are the steps in which the form is processed:

1. The page is loaded and a check is made to see if the `submitbutt` POST variable is present. Because you have not even seen the form yet, the answer is no and so the code in the `if` block is skipped.

2. The `else` is executed, and the form is displayed.

3. The user enters some information and clicks the Submit button. The browser then checks the action and accesses that page using the POST method. Because the action specifies the same page name, the page is reloaded.

4. The page reloads, and the `if` again checks if there is a `submitbutt` POST variable. This time there is, so the `if` code is executed and the username/password details are displayed.

ROLLING IN MYSQL

At this point in your adventure into PHP and MySQL, the MySQL side of the bargain has remained errant. Up until now, the focus has been on learning the core fundamental features behind the PHP language, but it is now time to shift this focus. It is now time for MySQL.

A typical database consists of a number of different parts. These different parts are outlined in Figure 2-1.

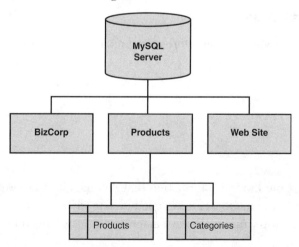

FIGURE 2-1
How a database works

The top level is the main MySQL Server. The server contains all of the other parts in the diagram. Many people get confused by the term *server* and think that it must be some kind of hardware. The word *server* actually has a dual meaning, referring to both hardware designed to serve things and software designed to serve things. In the case of MySQL, we are referring to a software server.

Within the MySQL server, you then may have a number of databases. This is another area in which newcomers to database development sometimes get confused. When you use MySQL, you can actually have a number of databases within the same server; you are not limited to just one. As such, you could run a single MySQL installation on a computer and run databases for your main company, a products database, and your Web site.

To now shift the focus to a specific database inside the server, you can see a number of tables. Each database stores its data in a series of tables that can relate to each other in different ways. Table 2-2 shows a typical table from a database.

TABLE 2-2   An Example Database Table

FORENAME	SURNAME
Craig	Tucker
Lee	Jordan

Every table consists of rows and columns. In database parlance, columns are referred to as **fields**, and rows are referred to as **records**. When you create database tables, you define what kinds of information you want to store in your fields (the columns), and then each entry in the database is stored as a record (the rows).

An Example: Product Database

In this example, you will create a database that stores product information. The kind of information you want to store includes:

- Product name
- Category
- Price
- Product description

This content is very typical of the kind of information that you usually want to put in a database. Before you create any database, it is a good idea to write down the kind of data that you need to deal with; this makes it easier when designing your tables.

Designing the Table Structure

With a clear understanding of the kind of data that needs to be stored, the next step is to develop a table structure that is suitable for storing the data sensibly and without reproducing data unnecessarily.

> **NOTE**
>
> **Learning Database Theory**
>
> It should be noted that database design is a huge subject, and there simply isn't the space in this book to provide a thorough explanation of database design theory and referential integrity. If you are new to database design and would like to understand how to design a solid database structure, consult your local bookstore and take a look at one of the many books on the subject.

In this example, you will use two tables to store the data: a products table and a categories table. The products table will contain the following fields:

- id
- cat_id
- product_name
- description
- price

Whenever you create a table, it is essential that you have a means of pulling out a unique record. To do this, you need to be able to identify certain fields, or groups of fields, that can assist you in adding uniqueness when pulling out a specific record. For example, if you were storing a list of customers, you might think that you could reference a unique record by searching for the name. This would not work, however; a number of people share the same name and, hence, are not unique. Another option is to search for the name AND the postal code. Again, this would not work because there may be more than one person with the same name living in the same postal code. This may be unlikely, but the point is that you should not base this uniqueness judgment on likeliness—it absolutely *must* be unique.

The solution to this problem is to create an additional field that contains a unique ID number for that record. Each time a new record is added to the database, this number will be increased by 1, and as such you will have this unique ID by which you can reference each record. MySQL includes support to make this unique number very easy to implement. In the field list for the previous products table, the very first field (the id field) stores this unique number. This unique field (be it a unique number or some other unique field such as a username) is called a **primary key**. You will use primary keys throughout the book.

The second field in the previous list is cat_id. This field is called a **foreign key** and will be matched to the primary key of the categories table, discussed next. The other fields in the table contain generic information about different aspects of the product.

The categories table contains a series of fields that pertain to the different types of product categories. This table includes the following fields:

- id
- category

As you can see, this table is rather simple, because the aim of the table is simply to provide a means to store information about the category. In this simple example, you will just store the name of the category in the table as well as its primary key field.

How the Tables Relate to Each Other

With the two tables designed, it now makes sense to discuss how they relate to each other. The relationship that is created between the two tables is performed by matching certain types of information. In these two tables, this match is made between the id field in the categories table and the cat_id field in the products table. If both fields contain the same number, a relationship exists.

When you add records to the products table, instead of adding the text name of the category in the cat_id field, you instead store the id value associated with the relevant category. For example, if the first category in the categories table is Swimming and has an id of 1, you would store the number 1 in the cat_id field of the products table for a swimming-related product. Later, when you write code to pull information from the database, you can make use of these different relationships to pull different types of information.

At this point, you may be wondering what the benefits are of separating this information into separate tables. Why not just include the name of the category in the field? There are various practical reasons for this separation, as follows:

- The first benefit becomes obvious when you want to change the name of the category. If you wanted to broaden the category from Swimming to Water Activities, for example, you would need to go through each record and change the field manually. If you used two tables to separate the data, you would need to change only a single record to adjust the category, and then the changes would be reflected in all related records.

- If you use separate tables, you can associate more information with the category. There is no reason you could not add extra fields in the `categories` table later to add features such as a description of the category, category icon, translated definitions, and more.

- A big reason for extracting data into separate tables is ease of use. If you have a single table with a huge number of fields, it looks a lot more complex and difficult to deal with. It is better to have a number of simple, smaller tables.

- If you spread your data across a number of smaller tables, your database will perform more efficiently, because it will not need to trudge through endless amounts of irrelevant data.

Separating your information into different tables has a number of benefits, and it is certainly the *right* way to develop database-driven applications. You will see many examples of how this separation of data across tables works throughout the book.

Creating the Database

The next step is to actually turn this theory into something you can see, touch, and work with. To do this, you need to make use of your database client. In this example, you will make use of phpMyAdmin, a tool included with XAMPP, to create the database.

First, open your Web browser and connect to phpMyAdmin by accessing http://localhost/phpmyadmin/. A login screen displays in response. If you have only just installed MySQL, or XAMPP, use the username `root` with no password. If you are working on a shared computer, change your root password by first connecting to the server with the following command:

```
mysql -u root mysql
```

Now issue the following SQL query

```
SET PASSWORD FOR root@localhost=PASSWORD('chinnyraccoon');
```

Obviously, replace the password in the parentheses with your own password.

After you have logged into phpMyAdmin, you will see a frame on the left side of the screen that is used to list databases and tables (nothing will be selected currently). In the main body of the screen is a box in which you can type a database name to be created (see Figure 2-2). In this box, type productsdb and click the Create button. You now see the productsdb database appear in the left frame. Ordinarily, your tables are listed under the database name on the side, but no tables have been created yet.

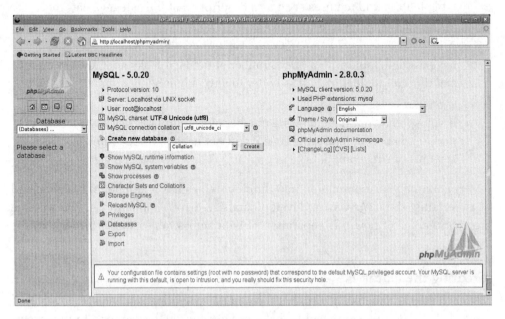

FIGURE 2-2 Creating a new database is simple in phpMyAdmin.

Creating the Tables

In the main body of the screen is a box that you can use to create a table. In this box, type the name products and give it 5 fields. You will then be presented with the table design screen. As shown in Figure 2-3, there are five rows with a number of different boxes to configure each field in the table. The majority of these boxes will be irrelevant in this simple example.

Before you create the fields, it's necessary to discuss the concepts of *types* in MySQL. In any kind of database programming, the kind of information you store inside the database has different characteristics depending on what type of information it is. For example, if you store a float in a database (a **float** is a number with a decimal place, such as 21.45), more memory is required to store this type of information than storing an integer (a whole number, such as 35). In addition to this, different numbers of have different ranges. For example, the TINYINT type in MySQL can store any whole number between −128 and 127. As a contrast, the BIGINT data type can store anything from −9223372036854775808 to 9223372036854775807.

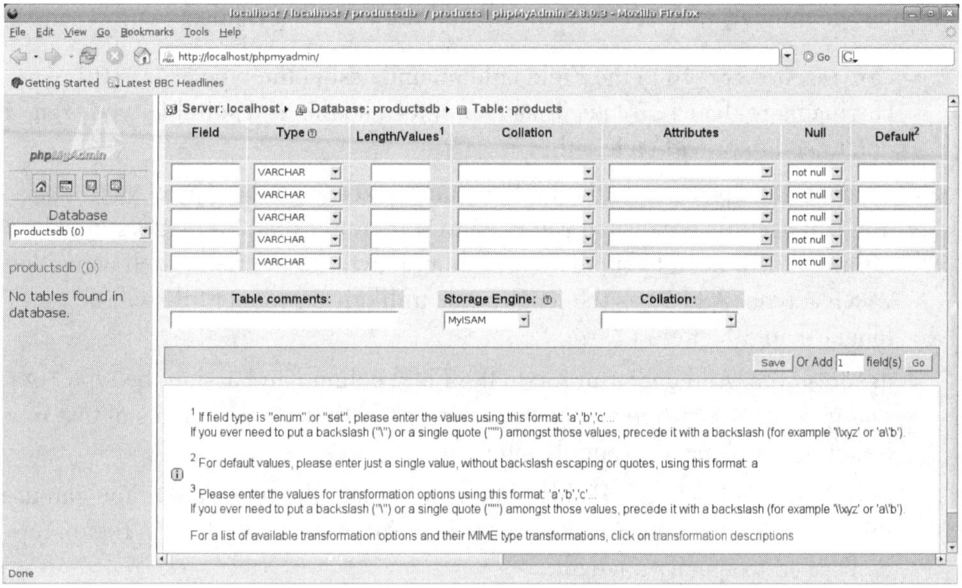

FIGURE 2-3 The table design screen has a lot of options; use the scroll bar to move along them.

In terms of memory usage and performance, there is the difference between storing a 1-byte value with TINYINT and storing an 8-byte value with BIGINT. Throughout this book, you will be using the major MySQL types extensively, and each example will explain why the relevant data type has been selected. This should give you a solid, practical idea of how different data types should be used.

Without further ado, it's time now create the tables. In the first row of the Field column, add id as the name of the field. In the second column (Type), select the data type as MEDIUMINT; this will provide access for up to 8388607 products. Remember that this id column requires a unique value for each product, so you need to ensure that the data type is large enough to cater for the potential number of products you will need. Continue along the row, and then select the Extra box and select auto_increment from it. This option automatically fills the id field for you when you add a record. With this option enabled, each new record is given a value in the id column that is 1 larger than the id in the previous record. With auto_increment set, you can effectively ignore the id field and it will look after itself. The final option to set is the first radio button (it has an icon of a small key and a table). By selecting this option, you are making the field the primary key, and the database will not allow a duplicate value in this field. If you combine this option and auto_increment as done here, you can be assured that you will have a reliably unique primary key.

Now, go through each row in turn and add the following fields:

- cat_id: Add cat_id to the Field column and assign the type of TINYINT. Having more than 127 categories is unlikely, so this is a suitable type. You don't need to provide a length.
- product: Add product to the Field column and assign the type of VARCHAR. You can use this type when you need to store fewer than 255 letters in the field. You will need to supply a maximum length for the field when using the VARCHAR type. Add 50 as the length; it is unlikely a product title will be longer than 50 letters in size.
- description: Add description to the Field column and assign the type TEXT. You can use TEXT when you need to store potentially large chunks of text in a field. You don't need to supply a length.
- price: Add price to the Field column and assign the type FLOAT. You can use this type when you need to store numbers with a decimal place in them. You don't need to specify a length.

When you have configured your fields, click the Save button, and your table is created. One of the most useful benefits of using phpMyAdmin is that the SQL that is generated when you do something is always shown to you. This gives you a fantastic idea of how SQL works by just having a casual look at the generated code when you use phpMyAdmin. This SQL code will not make much sense right now, but have a look over it to get a gist of what SQL looks like. SQL is used extensively in the many projects later in the book, so it is advised you get used to reading through SQL as soon as possible.

The generated SQL should look fairly similar to this:

```
CREATE TABLE 'products' (
'id' MEDIUMINT NOT NULL AUTO_INCREMENT ,
'cat_id' TINYINT NOT NULL ,
'product' VARCHAR( 50 ) NOT NULL ,
'description' TEXT NOT NULL ,
'price' FLOAT NOT NULL ,
PRIMARY KEY ( 'id' )
);
```

If you read the SQL from top to bottom, you will see how it is similar to English. Although you will rarely write SQL manually to create tables (you normally just create them in a client such as phpMyAdmin), the syntax to create a table is fairly straightforward.

Now you need to create the second table. To do this, click the perfectproducts link in the left frame. In the main body of the page, you can now create a new table called `categories` and give it 2 fields. In the table design screen, add the following fields:

- `id`: Add if to the Field column and assign the type `TINYINT`. Now select `auto_increment` from the Extra box and then select the Primary Key option in the column with the small key icon at the top.
- `category`: Add `category` to the Field column and assign the type `VARCHAR`. Set the length to 30.

When you have added these fields, click the Save button. You are finished.

Adding Data to the Tables

With the tables complete, you are ready to load them with data. You will begin by doing this manually in phpMyAdmin, but as you work through the book, you will create forms to automate how the data is added to different tables.

First, you'll add some data to the `categories` table. You need to add some categories first so that you can reference the relevant categories in the `products` table. To add data, select the `categories` table from the tables list in the left frame. You should now see a number of tabs appear in the main body of the screen at the top. Click the Insert tab. You are taken to a screen in which you can add data into the table, as shown in Figure 2-4.

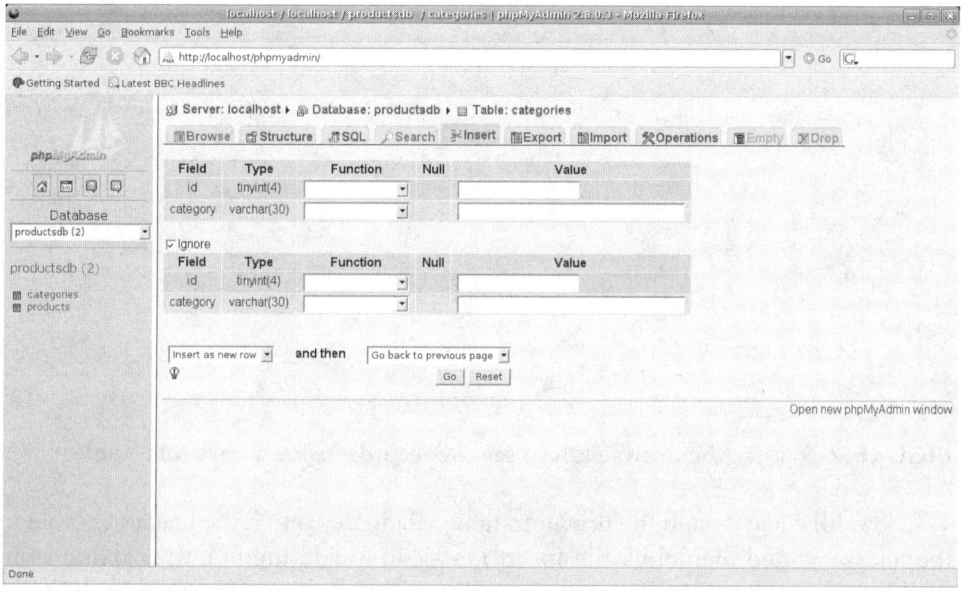

FIGURE 2-4 You can insert data two records at a time.

When adding information, you are given two sets of forms to add two records into the table at a time. You don't need to use both, but it is handy to have two forms at the same time when entering test information, as you are doing here.

When you add the data, you don't need to use any of the Function options. Also, remember to not add anything into the `id` field; `auto_increment` will deal with that for you. All you need to do is fill in a category in the Category field. Add the following categories one at a time:

- Swimming
- Soccer
- Baseball
- Cricket

When you have added these records, click the Browse tab in the main body of the page. You now see the table with the `id` values automatically filled in, as well as the categories that you added (see Figure 2-5).

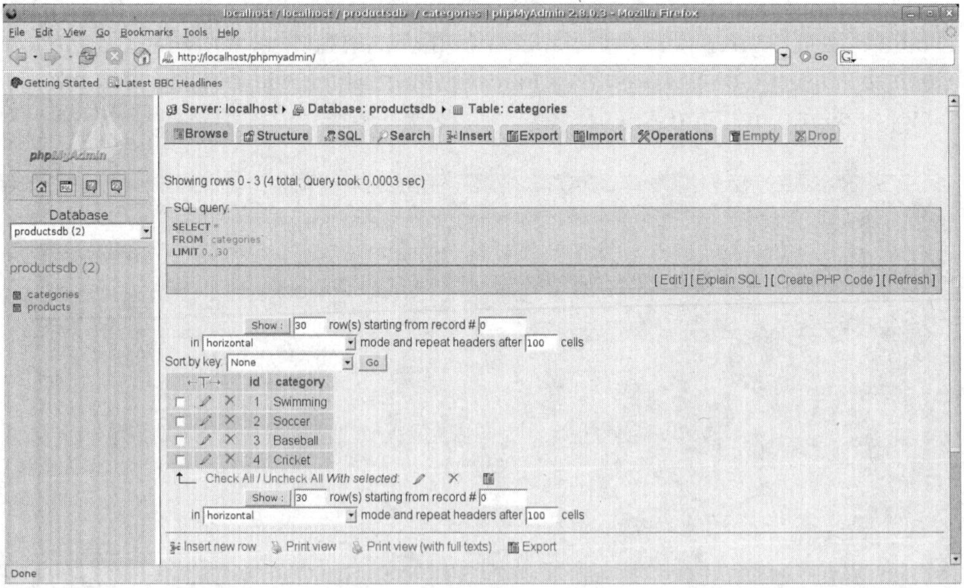

FIGURE 2-5 Click the Browse tab to see the records inside a particular table.

Now, fill some data in the `products` table. To do this, click the `products` table in the left frame and then click the Insert tab again to add the following information into the form:

- In the first record, add 1 into the `cat_id` box (this puts this record in the `Swimming` category) and then add any swimming-related product that you can think of. (Be imaginative; it is always fun add some kind of ludicrous product that gives you a chuckle when you deal with the record.) Add the price as a proper price (such as 21.99), but do not add the currency symbol.

- For the second record, add 3 to the `cat_id` box (this puts this record in the `Baseball` category). Again, add fun product and add a normal price.

Feel free to add some more products, but remember to use the `id` from the `categories` table in the `cat_id` field. This will ensure you are relating the two tables properly.

Connecting to MySQL in PHP

With some core PHP experience and a database development behind you, now is the time to perform the all-important step of hooking the two together and connecting to the database in PHP. This involves you creating the database connection, then issuing a SQL query, and finally dealing with the results of the query in a way that makes sense in your Web application.

To actually connect to MySQL, PHP provides built-in support to make the connection, perform queries, and deal with the results. To do this, a number of PHP functions, prefixed with `mysql_`, make the magic happen. Although these functions are very useful, there may a case in the future when you want to be able to use any one of a number of databases with your Web application. With this requirement, you would need to use a third-party database abstraction library, such as PEAR::DB or ADODB. If you know you will be using MySQL for a specific project, however, the `mysql_` range of functions is perfectly suitable.

Making the Connection

The first step is to actually make a connection to the database. This connection is used to communicate with the database when sending queries and data back and forth. To do this, you need to write some PHP that will pass the relevant authentication details to MySQL and, if you are authorized, give you a connection.

Create a new file called `dbconnect.php` and add the following code:

```
<?php

$dbhost = "localhost";
$dbuser = "root";
$dbpassword = "";
```

```
$dbdatabase = "productsdb";

$db = mysql_connect($dbhost, $dbuser, $dbpassword);
mysql_select_db($dbdatabase, $db);

?>
```

The first four lines in the code create some variables that contain the relevant pieces of information that are required to connect to a database. It is important to remember that these four lines literally are just set a bunch of variables; no connection is made at this point. You can call these variables what you like, but you will need to provide legitimate information for the host, username, password, and database that you are using on the MySQL server.

After you set the variables, you can make the connection. This happens with the $db = mysql_connect($dbhost, $dbuser, $dbpassword) line. This line uses the mysql_connect() function to pass the host, username, and password variables to the MySQL server and put the result of the connection in the $db variable. You then use the $db variables as a pointer to the main connection. To keep the code simple, this example does not involve any error checking; often you would check to see if the connection is suitable and possibly display a suitable error message. Some programmers feel this is unnecessary as you will get a PHP error message anyway if the connection is rejected, but if you implement your own errors, you can format and reference your errors in a nicer way.

When the connection has been made, you need to select the database that you want to use (remember, MySQL can have a number of different databases). This is performed with the mysql_select_db() on the next line. Here you specify the variable with the chosen database and also specify the connection ($db) that the database should be selected from.

At this point, you are now connected. Any other MySQL-related connections on this page will be applied to the connection that has just been created.

NOTE

Database Connections Are Per Page

The database connection you made does not span across other pages. You need to include the connection details on each page that needs to access MySQL. Of course, ways of making this more efficient will be covered later in the book.

At this point, you are ready to start playing with the database on this page.

Querying the Database

When you want to get, set, or update information in the database, you use SQL queries. You experimented with SQL a little earlier when you created your tables in phpMyAdmin. Take a deep breath, as now you will be writing specific SQL queries by hand. Don't worry; that doesn't sound nearly as scary as you may think.

Beneath the `mysql_select_db` line, add the following code (shown in bold):

```
$db = mysql_connect($dbhost, $dbuser, $dbpassword);
mysql_select_db($dbdatabase, $db);

$sql = "SELECT * FROM products;";
$result = mysql_query($sql);
```

The first line (the `$sql` line) simply sets another variable, but this one contains the SQL for the query that you want to send to MySQL. SQL is a very simple and effective language, and you will be using it throughout the book—with each piece of SQL being fully explained as you go along. In this particular line, you are selecting all the rows from the `products` table. You can read the SQL line from left to right to understand how it works:

First select (SELECT) everything (*) from (FROM) the products table (products) and then end the query (;).

Every SQL statement should end with a semi-colon. Although you do not need to explicitly add a semicolon in your PHP scripts, it is good form to do so. It just keeps you in the habit of adding a semi-colon, particularly if you use the command-line MySQL client.

> ### NOTE
> **Other Clients**
>
> There are a number of ways to talk to MySQL. Some of these are Web-based (such as phpMyAdmin), some are graphical desktop applications (such as the MySQL Control Center), and some are command-line based (such as the `mysql` command).

At this point, the SQL has not actually been sent to the server; you have merely created a variable that contains the query. The next line actually sends the query to the database. The `mysql_query()` function is used to send the SQL (in the `$sql` variable) to the database, and the results of the query is placed into the `$result` variable.

Iterating Through the Results

Inside $result lies the holy grail, the motherland that is the result of your query. Although $result contains the results, you can think of it as a big conjoined mess of results. In its current form, $result is not all that useful, and to be really practical you need to iterate through each row from the query. If you loop through each row, you can then display the relevant information on the page. This is the grand plan.

Add the following code beneath the mysql_query line in your file:

```
$sql = "SELECT * FROM products;";
$result = mysql_query($sql);

while($row = mysql_fetch_assoc($result)) {
    echo $row['product'];
}
```

In this chunk of code, you are using a while loop to iterate through each row in the result set. This is performed by adding a loop condition that extracts each row from $result by using mysql_fetch_assoc and then putting the row into the $row variable.

The purpose of the mysql_fetch_assoc() function is to make an associative array out of the results. This provides you with a convenient key-value (explained in the "Arrays" section earlier) means of pulling out information. As such, if you need to access the contents of the product field in the current row, you would use $row['product'].

Consistency Across Pages with Sessions

One of the biggest challenges when doing any kind of Web development is maintaining state across pages in a stateless Web. This grandiose statement basically translates into "sharing information across different pages." The reason for this difficulty is that each Web page you create essentially functions as an individual program. When you build Web applications that span a number of different pages, there is no implicit means of sharing information across these pages other than using the GET and POST variables. Sessions change all of this.

Sessions offer a surprisingly simple and efficient means of literally sharing variables across different pages. This is achieved with a number of PHP functions that give you the ability to enable a page with sessions, create session variables, and use these session variables in your scripts. Sessions can be used to share any PHP variables you like across different pages.

Creating the Session

To use sessions, first add the `session_start()` function at the very beginning of each page for which you want to use sessions. It is critically important that `session_start()` is right at the beginning—no fancy HTML, no picture of your Aunt Maud, and not even white space should come before it.

To demonstrate the importance of this, create a new file called `sessions.php` and add the following code:

```
<?php
session_start();
?>
```

When you run the script, you will not see anything; the session support has been happily built into your page. Now adjust the code and put a single white space before the `<?php` tag:

```
 <?php
session_start();
?>
```

When you make this tiny change, you are given a particularly venomous error message:

```
Warning: session_start() [function.session-start]: Cannot send session
cookie - headers already sent by (output started at
/opt/lampp/htdocs/sites/startingchapter/sessions.php:1) in
/opt/lampp/htdocs/sites/startingchapter/sessions.php on line 3
```

The reason it is so important to not have anything before `session_start()` is that the sessions framework makes use of the HTTP headers that form the mechanics of the Web page. These special headers are pre-pended to each Web page and as such, if you add any content before `session_start()`, the script will be trying to send out content (such as the white space), then the headers, and then the main content. This is not the way the Web works and, hence, PHP will shout at you in the form of the previous warning message.

> ### NOTE
>
> #### All About Headers
>
> Every Web page on the Internet has some information called **headers** that is invisible to most users. Headers store a number of pieces of information that browsers care about. Here are some example headers:
>
> ```
> GET / HTTP/1.
> Host: www.yourfavewebsite.org
> Connection: close
> Accept-Encoding: gzip
> Accept: text/xml,application/xml,application/xhtml+xml,
> text/html;q=0.9,text/plain;q=0.8,image/png,*/*;q=0.5
> Accept-Language: en-gb,en;q=0.5
> Accept-Charset: ISO-8859-1,utf-8;q=0.7,*;q=0.7
> User-Agent: Mozilla/5.0 (X11; U; Linux i686; en-GB;
>  rv:1.8.0.3) Gecko/20060523 Ubuntu/dapper Firefox/1.5.0.3
> Referer: http://www.someotherwebsite.net/
> ```
>
> Beneath the headers lies the content. When you add content to the page, the headers are added automatically. As such, when data is added to the page, the headers are also sent and cannot be modified after they have been sent.
>
> When you use sessions, the sessions system modifies some of these headers, and this is why you must add session_start() before any data is added to the page.

Using Session Variables

Before you use a session variable, you need to register it. This is achieved with the rather predictably named session_register() function. To use it, specify the name of the variable to create inside the brackets. To demonstrate this, add the following line of code to sessions.php after session_start():

```
session_register("userid");
```

This line registers with the session handling system that the userid variable can be shared across pages. The next step is to actually set this variable to something useful. Add this line next:

```
$_SESSION['userid'] = 10;
```

In this line, you are using the special $_SESSION superglobal to reference the userid variable. The $_SESSION syntax should look fairly familiar, as you used $_GET and $_POST earlier to access GET and POST variables respectively.

To test whether your session variable is accessible on the second page, create a file called `sessions2.php`, and add the following code:

```php
<?php

session_start();

echo "The userid session variable is: " . $_SESSION['userid'];

?>
```

Remember to visit `sessions.php` first (so the variable is set) and then visit `sessions2.php` to see that the variable is shared across the pages. To access the session variables, you simply include `session_start()` on the page and then refer to the variable with `$_SESSION`.

The session information is available while the browser is open. When the browser window is closed, the session information is lost. Although this is often a suitable means of destroying a session, sometimes you need to forcibly destroy the session data on command. To do this, you can use the following command:

```php
session_destroy();
```

All the session variables are then suitably deleted.

SUMMARY

This chapter explored some of the core concepts that need to be understood before you can move on and start writing applications. Instead of spending hours covering every nuance of PHP and MySQL, you have learned the fundamentals needed to move on, and each application will present news skills, techniques, and ideas.

As with any programming language, or natural language for that matter, practice really does make perfect. Just reading how to do something in PHP and actually understanding it are often two separate things. A great way to get accustomed to the language is to create lots of little scripts that test different aspects of the language. These scripts are useful not only for learning, but also they can be a great reference point further down the line when you have forgotten how to do something.

CHAPTER 3

Running the Projects

This book is crammed full of projects, lots of delightfully delicious projects that show you how to do interesting things with PHP and MySQL. Within each project are pages and pages of source code that gradually build up each project. Although you are more than welcome to sit there and carefully type each line as you go, we figured you might want to just run the projects right away and see how they work. Sound good? Well, you will be pleased to see that the shiny disc wedged into the book provides you with hours of project-running enjoyment!

So what is on the disc? Well, the disc is called a Live CD, and it provides you with a simple and easy means of running a complete operating system on your computer without touching your existing hard disk in any way. The way it works is that you pop the disc in the drive and boot from it. The computer then pretends that the CD is a hard disk and runs the operating system like any other. This means that you can play around with the system as much as you like, and it won't touch your precious hard drive. Cool, huh?

ABOUT THE DISC

With most programming books, you often get a disc that contains the code from the book. This handy supplement saves hours of laborious copying of code from the book to your computer. Despite saving hours of typing, the code-on-the-disc approach still makes the assumption that you actually have the software required to run it. As such, if you know you want to learn something (such as PHP and MySQL), but you don't have the PHP and MySQL software to run the code, you are stumped.

Not so with this book. The Live CD not only contains the code for each of the projects, but also includes a complete development environment in which to run the code. You get PHP and MySQL, as well as Apache, phpMyAdmin, Mozilla Firefox, PEAR modules, and much more—all neatly contained on the Linux operating system.

Now, we know what you are thinking—"Oh, I need to go out and buy a new hard disc, or I need to partition my existing disk, or I need to …" Relax. There is no need to buy a new hard disk, no need to partition, and no need to worry. The entire system runs from the CD.

Live CDs: A New Approach

In recent years, the Live CD has really taken off. The idea is simple: You take an operating system (usually Linux), and instead of running it from a hard drive, you run it from a CD or DVD. This provides a number of benefits. First, you can try out an operating system without actually installing it. When you run the disc included with this book, it won't ever touch your hard drive. Because the system runs from the CD, you can play around with it, break things, and experiment. Not only is your hard drive completely safe, but you can also reboot the CD to get the original system back at any time. Second, a Live CD provides a great way to "take your system" with you; just put the disc in a drive of any computer and reboot to run it.

Starting the System

Not all computers automatically attempt to boot from the CD/DVD drive when starting. If you turn on your computer and see the CD/DVD drive light flicker, the computer is looking for something to boot. In this case, put the Live CD in and reboot to get started!

If the light did not flicker, you may need to enable booting from the CD/DVD drive in your computer's BIOS. To access the BIOS setup, your computer will have a particular key or key combination to press to enter it. Common keys are F12 and Del. I recommend that you refer to the manual for your computer or motherboard to find out how to boot from the CD/DVD drive.

For best results, find a computer that has lots of RAM. Because a Live CD is a read-only medium, areas that need to be written to for running the Linux system are stored in RAM. So, for example, the live CD will boot faster and run better on a computer with 1GB or more of RAM than it will on a computer with 256MB of RAM.

When your system is enabled to boot, pop the disc in the drive and reboot. After a few seconds, the screen shown in Figure 3-1 should appear.

Press Enter to the start the system. Soon, you'll see the desktop boot and the splash screen appear, as shown in Figure 3-2.

FIGURE 3-1   The bootup splash screen, lovingly customized for the book!

FIGURE 3-2   The desktop loading

Finally, double-click the Start XAMPP icon. XAMPP starts in a terminal window, as shown in Figure 3-3.

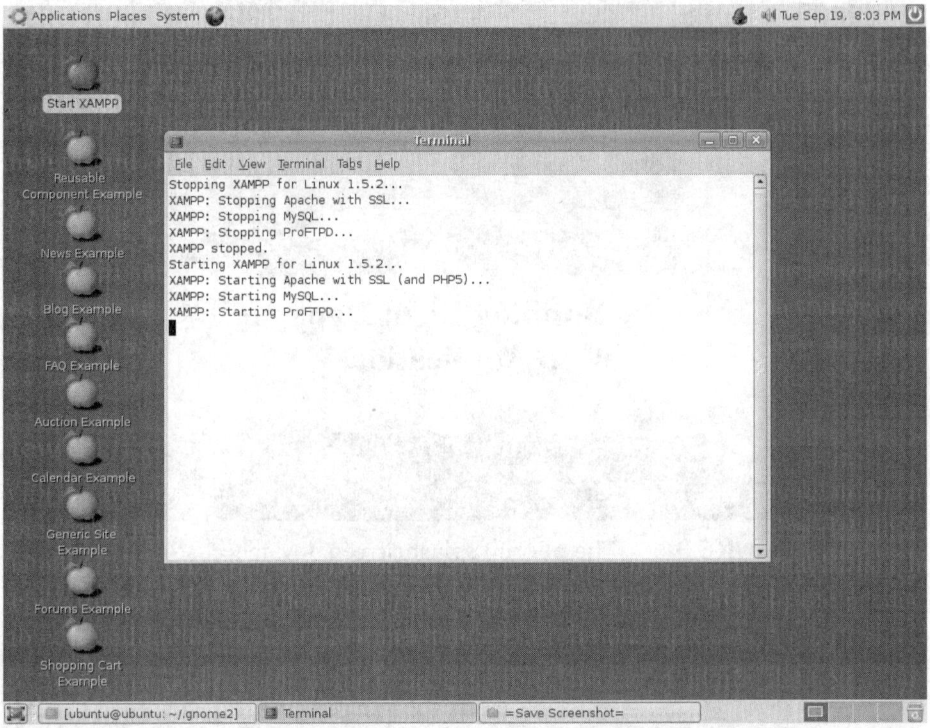

FIGURE 3-3   Firing up XAMPP

RUNNING THE APPLICATIONS

Running the different applications included with the disc is simple—just double-click one of the icons on the desktop to access that particular application. When you double-click an application icon, Firefox opens and displays the application that icon represents in the window. As an example, double-clicking the Forums icon causes the Forums application to appear, as shown in Figure 3-4.

If you want to play with the source code to the applications, double-click the Bluefish icon. When it loads, use the side panel to load the project that you want to develop. Remember, all projects are stored in /opt/lampp/htdocs/sites, so be sure to choose the right project inside that directory. Later, you can run the code from those project directories by entering http://localhost/sites in the location box of your Web browser on your Live CD.

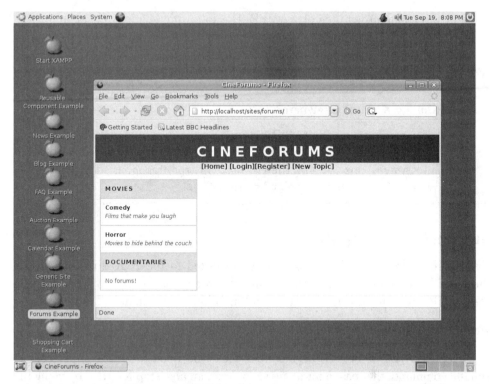

FIGURE 3-4 Loading an application is as simple as double-clicking an icon.

USING XAMPP

Other than the operating system included on the Live CD, the most critical piece of software is XAMPP. The XAMPP project provides the core pieces of software required for LAMP development (Apache, MySQL, and PHP) in a single download-able archive. As such, you can go to the XAMPP Web site (http://www.xampp.org), download the latest version to your computer, unzip it, and run it; you now have a complete LAMP system set up to do your development. This saves the hours of tweaking and configuration and frustration with the non-trivial installation of the separate Apache, MySQL, and PHP components.

Not only does XAMPP ease the installation of these components, but it also includes a huge array of additional software, including phpMyAdmin (used to cre-ate databases easily), PEAR modules (additional features in PHP), graphics libraries, documentation, and much more. XAMPP really does provide a compre-hensive and complete Web development platform.

Although you can just boot from the Live CD, start XAMPP, and access your applications straight away in the Web browser, it will be useful to have a look at some of the common features of XAMPP. The following sections cover these features, so you can get to know the system.

> ### NOTE
>
> **Running XAMPP Elsewhere?**
>
> If you want to run the XAMPP included on the disc on a different operating system, you can find a file called lampp.tgz in /opt. Just copy that file to a Linux system, unzip it, and then run /opt/lampp/lampp, as shown in the following "Starting and Stopping" section.

Starting and Stopping

XAMPP installations in Linux are always installed to the /opt directory. Inside the XAMPP directory is the lampp command, which can be used to start and stop the XAMPP system. To start XAMPP, run the following command:

```
foo@bar: /opt/lampp $ sudo /opt/lampp/lampp start
```

Because XAMPP provides system services, you need to be the super-user to run the command, the reason for using sudo. You can also stop XAMPP by using the following:

```
foo@bar: /opt/lampp $ sudo /opt/lampp/lampp stop
```

You can stop and start XAMPP by using restart (this is the command that the Start XAMPP icon on the desktop runs):

```
foo@bar: /opt/lampp $ sudo /opt/lampp/lampp restart
```

This command actually has a huge range of features available, and you can see them all by running the command without any options:

```
foo@bar: /opt/lampp $ sudo /opt/lampp/lampp
```

Table 3-1 provides a list of some of the commands that may be of particular interest for starting and stopping specific components.

When the XAMPP system is started, you can use the Web browser to view the running server by visiting http://localhost. When you visit that page, you will see a number of included Web pages that are part of the XAMPP system. These pages provide a number of small example applications, links to other parts of the system, and information about the running.

TABLE 3-1   Options for starting and stopping different LAMPP components

OPTION	DESCRIPTION
lampp startapache	Starts only Apache
lampp startmysql	Starts only MySQL
lampp stopapache	Stops only Apache
lampp stopmysql	Stops only MySQL
lampp restartapache	Stops and then restarts Apache
lampp restartmysql	Stops and then restarts MySQL

Accessing phpMyAdmin

Included with XAMPP (and on the Live CD) is a powerful Web-based database editor called phpMyAdmin, available from http://localhost/phpmyadmin/. phpMyAdmin will be used extensively throughout the book.

Switching PHP Versions

One of the nicest features in XAMPP is that it includes both PHP4 and PHP5 with the release (in the future it will no doubt include PHP5 and PHP6). This makes testing your application with different versions of PHP simple. Simply restart XAMPP with the version you want to use.

To switch versions, pass the version to the lampp program. So, to start PHP4, run the following:

```
foo@bar:/opt/lampp$ sudo /opt/lampp/lampp php4
```

To start PHP5, run the following:

```
foo@bar: /opt/lampp $ sudo /opt/lampp/lampp php5
```

These commands restart Apache with the version of PHP that you want to use. You can also check which version of PHP you are running by using the following:

```
foo@bar: /opt/lampp $ sudo /opt/lampp/lampp phpstatus
```

Backing Up

There are also techniques available for backups. After you create the backup archive, you can copy it to the hard disk or a network server so you can keep the backup permanently. (Remember that after you reboot, any changes you make will disappear from the Live CD if you don't somehow back those changes up to another medium.) First, use the build XAMPP backup script. Make sure XAMPP is running and then run the following:

```
foo@bar: /opt/lampp $ sudo /opt/lampp/lampp backup
```

This command backs up the databases and Web pages and then puts them in a single script that you can run to restore the system. This script will be stored in /opt/lampp/backup. To restore the backup, install a free XAMPP and run the following script, making sure to replace the filename for the filename of your backup script:

```
foo@bar: /opt/lampp/backup $ sudo /opt/lampp/backup/xampp-backup-00-00-00.sh
```

The second technique backs up the entire XAMPP directory. To do this, first shut down the XAMPP server by using lampp stop and then go to the /opt directory and zip it up:

```
foo@bar: /opt $ sudo tar zcvf lamp.tgz lampp
```

To restore it, make sure you are on a Linux system and run the following:

```
foo@bar: /opt $ sudo tar zxvf lamp.tgz
```

SUMMARY

The Live CD included with the book provides a simple and easy way to get started running the applications that you will write throughout the book. This disc is a great example of how innovative open source software, such as the Ubuntu Live CD, XAMPP, and the different LAMP components, make Web development easier and more efficient. This is far nicer than a book with a drab floppy disk that contains a few scant source code files.

The disc provides a great opportunity just in running the applications. But it is also recommended that, when going through each of the projects, you carefully follow how the code is built up—building up the source files manually by entering the code is essential when learning PHP and MySQL. The aim of this book is not to get you to read a chapter and follow the code with your finger, but to instead write code, run it, fix errors, and learn as you go. Just reading code and not actually typing it and running it nearly always results in a less than great learning experience; instead, in this book you learn by doing.

So, as much as this Live CD is a fantastic time-saver, don't let it replace the essential act of typing code from the book, running it, and fixing errors. That is where the real learning happens.

CHAPTER 4

Building a Weblog

One of the most talked about Internet phenomenon in recent times is that of the Weblog (often shorted to *blog*). The concept of a blog—and the subsequent art of blogging—is that you provide your own online diary or journal in which you can scribe your thoughts for the world to see. The actual content that you pour into your blog is completely up to you, and the blog can be as formal, or informal, as you like. If you want to tell the world that your milk went bad and you need to pick up some from the store, a blog is where you write all about it.

The blog-reading public is not just obsessed with milk-longevity-related shenanigans, though. Although typically used as a vehicle to communicate thoughts online, blogs have also become a primary means by which various people connected to a hobby or project share what they are working on. This has been particularly popular with Open Source developers who use their blogs to give their readers a sneak peak of what's to come in the software they hack.

Although the basic function of a blog is to store a series of blog posts (often called *entries*), many blogs also include other features:

- **Commenting.** Readers of the blog can often leave comments. This can add real value to a blog, and conversations often strike up over varying subjects.

- **Categorization.** Blogs are often separated into different categories. This gives the blog author the ability to file entries into a specific section. This also allows readers to read only the category that interests them.

- **Archives.** Most blogs have some means of archiving and accessing previous entries. With blogs becoming as relevant a medium as "normal" Web sites, being able to access earlier entries is important.

In this project, you will build a blog that incorporates all of the preceding features. Aren't you lucky?

PROJECT OVERVIEW: BLOGTASTIC USE CASE

The blog application created in this chapter is rather niftily titled Blogtastic. To get an overview of how to build the blog, here is a simple use case that demonstrates how typical users would interact with the application. Use cases are very handy for helping to visualize exactly how different interactions and content should be presented to users. The following is a synopsis of the use case for the Blogtastic application:

John visits Pauline's blog and, naturally, wants to see Pauline's latest entry. John is interested in reading the blog entry but would also like to see if any comments have been posted in response to the entry. If the blog entry has comments, the names of the commenters are added to the bottom of the blog, so John can see who posted each comment.

To access the blog and any corresponding comments, John clicks the title of the blog entry, and that specific entry (with comments) is displayed. In case John wants to leave a comment, a form for him to express his views is conveniently available on the same page. John fills outs the form and clicks the Submit button, after which the page is reloaded with John's comment added. John then whiles away the afternoon perusing through older blog entries in the archived entries page.

Later that day, Pauline decides she wants to add a new blog entry. Pauline visits a special page on the Web site where she can log in. As the blog's author, some additional options are made available only to her. Pauline can add a new blog entry to a specific category, or she can even add a new category. Pauline adds a new entry and then realizes she made a mistake. Fortunately, a special Edit button that she—and only she—can see displays on the page. Pauline uses this button to correct her mistake and avoid looking silly in front of John. Pauline secretly thinks she is better than John.

This is a typical example of a blog, and in this project, you will pour all of the preceding functionality into Blogtastic to match this use case.

NOTE

Take Your Time

Because this is the first database-driven project in this book, progress through the chapter at a pace that is comfortable to you. If you come across any concepts you don't understand, take a moment to stop, visit Google, and do some research to clear up the misunderstanding before you continue. When learning a new technology, never plough on if you don't understand the concepts; you will only dig a bigger hole to fall into.

BUILDING THE DATABASE

The first step in the Blogtastic project is to build the database. To begin, create a new database in phpMyAdmin called *blogtastic*. Within this database, create four tables:

TABLE NAME	WHAT THE TABLE STORES
categories	Different blog categories
entries	Blog postings
comments	Comments on blog entries
logins	Usernames and passwords

The schema of the tables is shown in Figure 4-1.

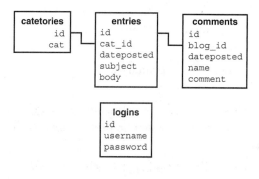

FIGURE 4-1

Even for a simple application such as a blogging engine, careful database design will save a lot of work in the long run.

Figure 4-1 shows how the four tables relate to each other. The first relationship is between the blog category (the *categories* table) and the blog entry (the *entries* table). To reference the correct category, the same id from the *categories* table is stored in the cat_id field of the *entries* table. In database parlance, the id field is known as the *primary key*, and the cat_id field is known as the *foreign key*. If these two values match, an explicit connection exists between the tables. In other words, if you know the id of the category (stored in cat_id), you can run a query to pull out the other category information (such as the name of the category) using that id. The second relationship—between the *entries* table and the *comments* table—works in exactly the same way; the id field from the *entries* table is connected to the blog_id in the *comments* table. This connects each comment with the correct blog entry.

The final table is the *logins* table, which has no relationship to the others; the table is used simply for logging each user into the application.

Implementing the Database

With the database design laid out, you can create the database tables. In phpMyAdmin, follow the steps discussed in Chapter 2 to add new tables, using these details:

The *categories* Table

- id. Make this a TINYINT (this type is used because there will not be many categories) and turn on auto_increment in the Extras column. Set this field as a primary key.
- cat. Make this a VARCHAR. Because a category title longer than 20 letters is unlikely, set the size to 20.

The *entries* Table

- id. Make this an INT (several blog entries are possible) and turn on auto_increment. Set this field as a primary key.
- cat_id. Make this a TINYINT (the same type as the primary key it references—id in the *categories* table).
- dateposted. Use the DATETIME type. This data type stores the current date and time in the international ISO standard format, which is pretty clunky, but you can format the date later in PHP.
- subject. Make this a VARCHAR. Unless your blog title is extremely long, set the length of this field to 100.
- body. Make this a TEXT field. If you ever want to store very large areas of text, the TEXT type is a good choice. You don't need to specify a length.

The *comments* Table

- id. Make this an INT (several comments are likely). Turn on auto_increment and set this field as a primary key.
- blog_id. Make this an INT (the same type as the id field in the *entries* table, to which it is related).
- dateposted. Use the DATETIME type.
- name. Make this a VARCHAR. Because comment titles longer than 50 characters is unlikely, set the length to 50.
- comment. This is the main body of the comment. Set to the TEXT type.

The *logins* Table

- id. Make this a TINYINT (there will be very few logins; possibly only one). Turn on auto_increment and set this field as a primary key.
- username. Make this a VARCHAR and give it a length of 10. (Enforcing a maximum length for the username is a common practice.)
- password. Make this a VARCHAR and give it a length of 10. (As with usernames, enforcing a maximum length for a password is a common practice.)

Inserting Sample Data

With the tables created, insert some initial data into them so that you can test the code as you write it (again using phpMyAdmin). Remember that when you are adding data to any of these tables, do not fill in a number in the id column; this value will be handled by auto_increment.

Because this is the first project in the book, sample data has been add to the tables for you to ensure that everything connects as expected. As you work through the book and understand the database concepts in better detail, you can add additional sample data.

Sample Data for the *categories* Table

Add the following categories in this order: Life, Work, Music, and Food.

Sample Data for the *entries* Table

Add the information in Table 4-1 to the *entries* table.

Both entries reference the Life entry in the *categories* table, via the cat_id. In the dateposted field, use the Function combo box to select the NOW option, which fills the field with the date and time you add the entry to the table.

TABLE 4-1 The sample data for the entries table enables you to follow along with the rest of this chapter's samples.

CAT_ID	DATEPOSTED FIELD	SUBJECT	BODY
1	Select NOW from the function box	Welcome to my blog!	This is my very first entry in my brand-new blog.
1	Select NOW from the function box	Great blog!	I have decided this blog is: Really cool!

Sample Data for the *comments* Table

Add the information in Table 4-2 to the *comments* table.

TABLE 4-2 The comments table has just a few sample comments, used for demonstration purposes.

CAT_ID	DATEPOSTED FIELD	SUBJECT	BODY
1	Select NOW from the function box	Bob	Welcome!
1	Select NOW from the function box	Jim	Hope you have lots of fun!

In this table, reference the first blog entry (the one with the 'Welcome to my blog!' subject) by supplying a value of 1 to the `blog_id` field.

Sample Data for the *logins* Table

In this table, add a single entry with a username and password of your choice. This example includes a username of "jono" and a password of "bacon".

STARTING TO CODE

Start out by creating your project configuration file. This configuration file makes customization of the blog easy, for you or for other users who run it.

Create a new directory in *htdocs* on your computer. Inside this directory, create a new file called *config.php* (as shown in Example 4-1):

EXAMPLE 4-1 Using a configuration file makes customization and personalization a piece of cake.

```php
<?php

$dbhost = "localhost";
$dbuser = "root";
$dbpassword = "";
$dbdatabase = "blogtastic";

$config_blogname = "Funny old world";

$config_author = "Jono Bacon";

$config_basedir = "http://127.0.0.1/sites/blogtastic/";

?>
```

NOTE

Configuration Files for Distributed Applications

If you plan on writing a Web application that you intend to distribute so that others can download, install, and run it, easy configuration is essential. This is where a standard configuration file is useful. Settings that the user may want to tweak can be kept out of the main code.

Most of this file is simple configuration. The first four lines should look familiar to you; they are the normal database settings. You can change these to match your own database setup.

Below the database settings, another three variables are set. The first one ($config_blogname) sets the name of the blog. The second variable ($config_author) enables the user to set his name as the author. The final variable ($config_basedir) refers to the location of the blog, in URL form. This variable is particularly important and is used later in various parts of the code, specifically to redirect to different pages.

TIP

You may have noticed that three of the configuration variables begin with "config." This distinguishes these variables from other, non-configuration-related variables in your code and is a great way to remember what a particular variable is associated with.

Designing a User Interface

In the previous chapter, you created a generic Web site and made use of a number of include() and require() functions to separate different parts of the site. This application uses the same concepts to provide a consistent look and feel.

NOTE

The stylesheet.css File

This project uses the stylesheet.css file created in Appendix A. Copy the file to the current project directory to apply the stylesheet to the project.

Creating the Header File

Create a file called *header.php* and add the code shown in Example 4-2.

EXAMPLE 4-2 This simple header file will be used across all pages.

```php
<?php
require("config.php");
?>
<!DOCTYPE HTML PUBLIC "-//W3C//DTD HTML 4.01 Transitional//EN"
"http://www.w3.org/TR/html4/loose.dtd">
<html>
<head>
<title><?php echo $config_blogname; ?></title>
<link rel="stylesheet" href="stylesheet.css" type="text/css" />
</head>
<body>
<div id="header">
<h1><?php echo $config_blogname; ?></h1>
[<a href="index.php">home</a>]
</div>

<div id="main">
```

There are a few important points to note about this code. Here, a PHP block is opened at the top to include the *config.php* code in the page. The require() function—as opposed to include()—has been used here, because *config.php* is essential to the correct behavior of this page. If *config.php* does not exist, the entire application breaks down during any database work.

Most of the HTML in this code should look fairly straightforward, but you might have also spotted a small chunk of PHP in the <title> tag. In the title, the contents of the `$config_blogname` variable from *config.php* is displayed (refer to Example 4-1); this adds the blog name for the blog in the title bar of the browser window. This variable's value is also repeated inside the first `<div>` within the `<h1>` tag. This provides some basic (very, very basic!) branding.

The final addition to the code is a link beneath the `<h1>` tag to the main page (*index.php*, which you'll create shortly). To keep this project simple, links to different parts of the site will appear in this header `<div>`. The last line of code opens the main `<div>` in similar fashion to the Web site created in Appendix A.

Creating the Footer File

With the yin of the header file complete, it is now time to create the yang of the footer file. Create a new file called *footer.php* that looks like Example 4-3.

EXAMPLE 4-3 Like the header file, this footer will be shared across all pages.

```
</div>

<div id="footer">
&copy; <?php echo $config_author; ?>
</div>
</body>
</html>
```

The first line of the file ends the main `<div>` that was opened at the end of the header file (see Example 4-2 for the opening of this `<div>` tag). After this, you create a footer `<div>` to contain a copyright symbol (achieved with the special `&copy;` markup) and then add a small PHP block to (again) display the contents of a variable from the *config.php* file. This gives the site suitable credit for whoever runs it.

You can test that your header and footer files work by creating a file called *index.php* and adding the code in Example 4-4.

EXAMPLE 4-4 With a header and footer, actual site pages become very simple.

```
<?php

require("header.php");

require("footer.php");

?>
```

When you access the *index.php* page in your browser, you should see the simple design shown in Figure 4-2.

FIGURE 4-2 With a little configuration and a little HTML, the skeleton of the application is in place.

Displaying a Blog Entry

You are now ready to begin crafting some code that actually resembles a blogging application. With your database already loaded with sample content, the first logical step is to display the contents of the most recent blog entry. This involves creating a simple SQL query and then displaying the results of the query (the latest entry) on the page.

Before you create the query, however, you need to add he code to connect to the database. Within this particular application, database access occurs on every page; therefore, adding the database connection code to the main *header.php* file makes sense. This file is included in every page, so it is a logical home for the connection code.

After the `require("config.php")` line of *header.php*, add the following lines (which were explained in Chapter 2):

```php
<?php
require("config.php");
$db = mysql_connect($dbhost, $dbuser, $dbpassword);
mysql select db($dbdatabase, $db);
?>
```

Building the Query

To build the SQL query, think about the kind of information you want the database to return. For the latest blog entry, you want all the information from the *entries* table (such as the subject, body, and date the blog was posted), but you also need to get the category to which the entry belongs.

The name of the category isn't stored in the *entries* table, however; only the cat_id is. With this in mind, you need to ask for all the information from the *entries* table and also ask for the category name in which the category id matches the cat_id from the *entries* table.

Here is the SQL you need:

```
SELECT entries.*, categories.cat FROM entries, categories
  WHERE entries.cat_id = categories.id
  ORDER BY dateposted DESC
  LIMIT 1;
```

One of the great benefits of SQL is that you can read it fairly easily from left to right. Additionally, if you lay out your SQL on separate lines, you easily see the four main parts of the SQL query:

1. The command (first line)
2. The conditions under which the command is executed (second line)
3. Any ordering requirements (third line)
4. Any limits (fourth line)

If you read the SQL from the beginning to the end, this is what happens:

Select (SELECT) every field from the *entries* table (entries.*) and the cat field from the *categories* table (categories.cat) with the condition (WHERE) that the cat_id field from the *entries* table (entries.cat_id) is equal to (=) the id field from the *categories* table (categories.id). Order the results by (ORDER BY) the dateposted field in descending order (DESC) and only show a single result (LIMIT 1).

The aim of the query is to limit the results that come back and return only the last entry that was added to the database. Without the ORDER BY clause, the query would bring back every entry in the order that it was added. By adding the ORDER BY line, the results come back in descending date order (the last date is first). Finally, to return only the latest entry (which is the first result from the query), you use LIMIT 1 to return only a single record.

To run the query in your Web application, you need to first construct the SQL query code inside a variable and then send it off to the database. When you get the data back, you can access the row(s). Between the two require lines, add the following code to the *index.php* file:

```php
<?php

require("header.php");

$sql = "SELECT entries.*, categories.cat FROM entries, categories
  WHERE entries.cat_id = categories.id
  ORDER BY dateposted DESC
  LIMIT 1;";
$result = mysql_query($sql);
$row = mysql_fetch_assoc($result);

require("footer.php");

?>
```

The first added line constructs the SQL query and stores it in a variable called $sql. To actually send the data to the MySQL server, use the mysql_query() function, which puts the result of the query in the $result variable. On the final line, the mysql_fetch_assoc() function pulls the row out of $result and stores it in an array.

A QUICK NOTE...

Because only one row is coming back, there is no need to use a while() loop to iterate through the rows returned from the query. Recall that more details on iterating through results are found in Chapter 2.

Displaying the Entry

With the query result stored in the $row array, you just need to crack open the array, pull out the data, and display it on your Web page. Refer to each field inside the square brackets in the array (such as $row['subject'] for the subject field).

Add the following code after the mysql_fetch_assoc() line:

```php
$row = mysql_fetch_assoc($result);
echo "<h2><a href='viewentry.php?id=" . $row['id']
  . "'>" . $row['subject'] .
    "</a></h2><br />";
echo "<i>In <a href='viewcat.php?id=" . $row['cat_id']
```

```
   ."'>" . $row['cat'] .
      "</a> - Posted on " . date("D jS F Y g.iA",
strtotime($row['dateposted'])) .
      "</i>";
echo "<p>";
echo nl2br($row['body']);
echo "</p>";

require("footer.php");

?>
```

This code creates a second-level heading tag and, within it, a link to a page called *viewentry.php* (which will be created later to view specific blog entries). To show a blog entry, the page needs to be passed the id of the specific blog entry to display. To achieve this, you add a question mark to the end of the filename and then add the variable (such as id=1). This process results in a link such as *viewentry.php?id=1*.

Instead of hard coding the value of the variable, however, use the contents of $row['id'] (from the query) as the value. After you close the first part of the link tag, append the subject from the query and then add the closing link tag. You will see a number of these long, concatenated link tags in your programming, which can be better understood with the aid of a table.

Table 4-3 shows how the HTML is gradually built, step by step. Remember that the . glues these different parts together.

TABLE 4-3 It's often easiest to view long strings of code as a series of individual parts. On each line, the bolded text results from the code in the Code column.

CODE	HTML OUTPUT
`<h2><a href='viewentry.php?id=`	**`<h2><a href='viewentry.php?id=`**
`$row['id']`	`<h2><a href='viewentry.php?id=`**`1`**
`'>`	`<h2><a href='viewentry.php?id=1`**`'>`**
`$row['subject']`	`<h2><a href='viewentry.php?id=1'>`**`Wel-come to my blog!`**
`</a></h2>`	`<h2><a href='viewentry.php?id=1'>Wel-come to my blog!`**`</a></h2>`**

On the second line of code, another link is built in the same way; this link points to a page called *viewcat.php*. Instead of the entry id being passed as a variable, the category id is passed.

Next, the date is displayed. If you output an unformatted date from the database, the date would look something like this:

```
2005-08-01 18:02:32
```

Notice that the preceding result is not in the most useful of formats. Use `strtotime()` and `date()` to clean this up for human consumption.

The `strtotime()` function converts the date into a UNIX timestamp. This timestamp refers to the number of seconds since 12:00 a.m. on January 1, 1970. The time is known as the *Epoch*, and when you have this number of seconds, you can then feed it into the `date()` function to format those seconds into something more useful.

The `date()` function converts this number of seconds into a readable date, using several special format symbols (`D jS F Y g.iA` in this example). Each of these symbols formats a particular part of the date and time. You can find out more about these and other symbols in the PHP manual entry for dates at `http://www.php.net/date`.

Table 4-4 gives an example for 2:35 p.m. on April 6, 2005.

TABLE 4-4 Each letter represents a portion of the date, as well as how to format that date.

DATE() SYMBOLS	DATE
D	**Wed**
D j	Wed **6**
D jS	Wed 6**th**
D jS F	Wed 6th **April**
D jS F Y	Wed 6th April **2005**
D jS F Y g	Wed 6th April 2005 **2**
D jS F Y g.	Wed 6th April 2005 2**.**
D jS F Y g.i	Wed 6th April 2005 2.**35**
D jS F Y g.iA	Wed 6th April 2005 2.35**PM**

Finally, in the last bit of the code, the body of the blog entry is presented. The first of these three lines opens a paragraph tag, and the second actually outputs the content of the blog posting. You need to pass the contents of the database entry through n12br(). This useful little function converts any empty lines into legitimate HTML <br /> tags. The final line closes off the paragraph tag. See the final result in Figure 4-3.

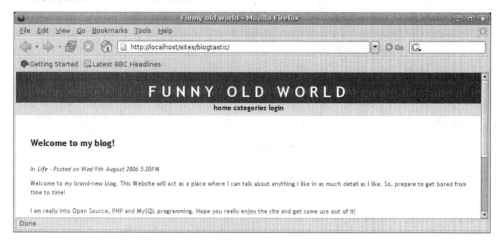

FIGURE 4-3 Your blog entry is ready for the world to see.

Adding a Comments Summary

One of the planned features for this blog is the capability for visitors to add comments to a blog entry. These comments should be visible on the *viewentry.php* page, linked via the subject of the blog (which you just added to *index.php*).

When comments are posted to a blog entry, it's helpful to provide a comments summary. When comments have been posted, you can display the number of comments and the names of the posters. It's also useful to have the names of the posters double as hyperlinks; that is, when you click the poster's name, the application jumps to that poster's comment on the *viewentry.php* page.

After the code already in place in *index.php*, add the following lines:

```php
echo n12br($row['body']);
echo "</p>";

echo "<p>";

$commsql = "SELECT name FROM comments WHERE blog_id = " . $row['id'] .
           " ORDER BY dateposted;";
$commresult = mysql_query($commsql);
$numrows_comm = mysql_num_rows($commresult);

require("footer.php");

?>
```

This chunk of code creates a new paragraph tag, and then a new SQL query to select the `name` field from the *comments* table, where `blog_id` contains the `id` of the current blog entry (stored in `$row['id']`). The entire query is ordered by date (using the `dateposted` field). This query is then executed with the `mysql_query()` command, and the result is stored in `$commresult`.

On the final line, a new function called `mysql_num_rows()` is used to count how many rows are returned from the query, and this number is stored in the `$numrows_comm` variable. The `mysql_num_rows()` function is incredibly useful, because you can use it to determine how to format the comments summary. If no rows are returned, display `'No comments'`; if 1 or more results are returned, display the posters' names:

```
$commsql = "SELECT name FROM comments WHERE blog_id = " . $row['id'] .
            " ORDER BY dateposted;";
$commresult = mysql_query($commsql);
$numrows_comm = mysql_num_rows($commresult);
if($numrows_comm == 0) {
  echo "<p>No comments.</p>";
}
else {
  echo "(<strong>" . $numrows_comm . "</strong>) comments : ";
  $i = 1;
  while($commrow = mysql_fetch_assoc($commresult)) {
    echo "<a href='viewentry.php?id=" . $row['id'] ."#comment" . $i .
            "'>" . $commrow['name'] . "</a> ";
    $i++;
  }
}
echo "</p>";
```

In this block of code, an `if` statement is used to check if `$numrows_comm` has 0 rows. If it does, `No comments` is echoed to the screen. If `$numrows_comm` is not equal to 0, control moves into the `else` statement.

Inside the `else`, an `echo` line prints a bracket and then, in bold typeface, outputs the number of rows stored in `$numrows_comm` and finally outputs a closing bracket and the word `comments`. If there were two comments, the output would be

(2) comments

The next step is to display each comment, as well as a link to that comment, using an anchor.

The anchors used in *viewentry.php* are in the form #comment1, #comment2, and so on. To add these numbered anchors in *index.php*, start at 1 and increment each time a comment link is output.

ALL ABOUT ANCHORS

Anchors are handy methods of linking to different parts of a single page. To reference an anchor, you add the name of the anchor to the URL. As an example, linking to *example.php#theory* jumps to the theory anchor on the *example.php* page. At some point in *example.php*, there should be something like this:

```
<a name="theory">
```

Now, when *example.php#theory* is referenced, the page will jump to that tag.

Back in the code, you'll see that a variable called `$i` is created and set to 1. Next, a `while` loop iterates through the rows. A link to *viewentry.php* is created, and `id=[<entry-id>]` is added to each. In addition to the `id` being appended, the comment anchor (such as `#comment1`) is added, using `$i`. Finally, the value of `$i` is increased by 1, ready for use on the next link. The completed output should look something like this (obviously with different names if you have added different comments):

```
(2) comments : Jim Bob
```

NOTE

If you are using the sample detail discussed earlier in the chapter, you will continue to see "No comments" because no comments are associated with the second blog entry. To resolve this, use phpMyAdmin to add some records to the *comments* table and specify a value of 2 in the `blog_id` field.

You can see the comments shown in Figure 4-4.

Displaying Previous Blog Entries

It is often convenient to see the last five or so blog entries, so that if a user misses a few entries, she can access them easily without having to dig through the archives.

First, create the query. Luckily, this query is the same as the one you used to find the latest blog entry—the only difference being that instead of limiting the results to a single entry, you limit the result set to five entries. Do this by changing the `LIMIT 1` line to `LIMIT 1, 5`. This ensures that you get records 0 to 4.

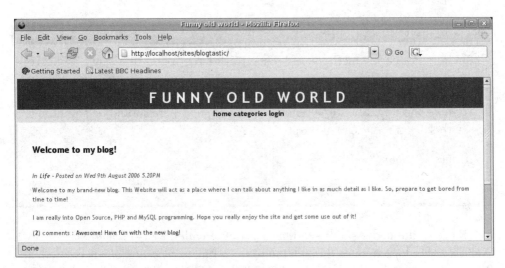

FIGURE 4-4 Displaying comments on the front page shows visitors that your blog entries cause discussion and debate.

> **TIP**
>
> When you use LIMIT, the first record returned is marked as the zeroth. As such, LIMIT 1,5 returns the first record through to the fifth. LIMIT 0, 1 is synonymous with LIMIT 1.

Add the following code to your page:

```
echo "</p>";
$prevsql = "SELECT entries.*, categories.cat FROM entries, categories
  WHERE entries.cat_id = categories.id
  ORDER BY dateposted DESC
  LIMIT 1, 5;";
$prevresult = mysql_query($prevsql);
$numrows_prev = mysql_num_rows($prevresult);
```

This query counts the number of rows returned so you can display the relevant information. Now, add the code to display the results:

```
$numrows_prev = mysql_num_rows($prevresult);

if($numrows_prev == 0) {
  echo "<p>No previous entries.</p>";
}
else {
```

```
echo "<ul>";

while($prevrow = mysql_fetch_assoc($prevresult)) {
    echo "<li><a href='viewentry.php?id="
. $prevrow['id'] . "'>" . $prevrow ['subject']
. "</a></li>";
  }
}

echo "</ul>";
```

If no rows were returned in the query, the text No previous entries. is displayed. If rows are returned, the else block is executed and the previous entries are displayed in an unordered list.

Inside the else block, use a while loop to iterate through the results from the query to create the blog entry subjects with the <li> and </li> tags. The subject is linked to *viewentry.php* with the relevant id appended as a variable in the link. The end result is shown in Figure 4-5.

FIGURE 4-5 Including previous blog entries shows visitors that your blog gets updated frequently.

> ### NOTE
>
> **Ordered and Unordered Lists**
>
> Within HTML, Web developers often use ordered and unordered lists to create bullet points. To create a *numbered* list, you use the <ol> and </ol> ordered list tags. To create an unnumbered bullet point list, use the unordered <ul> and </ul> tags.
>
> List items are placed inside <li> and </li> tags. An example of an unordered list is shown as follows:
>
> ```
> <ul>
>     <li>One item</li>
>     <li>Another item</li>
> </ul>
> ```

VIEWING SPECIFIC ENTRIES

When *index.php* was created, three distinctive sections were added to the page:

- Main blog entry
- Number of comments
- Previous blog entries

In the main blog entry and previous entry sections, you link to another page called *viewentry.php*. The *viewentry.php* page has a number of important features:

- The page displays the contents of the blog entry.
- The page uses virtually the same code from *index.php*.
- The need to create the anchors that were added to the comment names (and links) in *index.php*.
- The page provides a form to post comments about the blog entry.
- The form is displayed, and when the user fills it in, the comment is added to the database.

This page is an important step in building the blog, so without further ado, it's time to get going and do some coding!

Validating the Request URL

The first step for the *viewentry.php* page is to ensure it's requested with valid date. Whenever you work on a Web project, it is important to verify that any changeable information (such as the ID of an entry or comment) is legitimate. This verification process is known as *validation*. In this project, validation is applied to only the variables that are added to the address of the site. These variables are visible, and the user can change them by editing the address in the browser.

> ## NOTE
>
> **Validation, Step by Step**
>
> The reason you will validate only GET variables, and not other types of information, is to make validation easier to learn. This application introduces some basic concepts and keeps things simple. Later projects in the book explore validation in more detail, and you can return to earlier projects and apply these skills later.

Although GET variables can be set to letters or numbers, virtually every GET variable in this book is set to a number. When you created *index.php* and the links to *viewentry.php*, each of them included a GET variable that contained a numeric id.

To validate a numeric variable, feed it into a block of code that runs some simple tests. Add the following code to the beginning of *viewentry.php*:

```php
<?php

require("config.php");

if(isset($_GET['id']) == TRUE) {
  if(is_numeric($_GET['id']) == FALSE) {
    $error = 1;
  }

  if($error == 1) {
    header("Location: " . $config_basedir);
  }
  else {
    $validentry = $_GET['id'];
  }
}
else {
  $validentry = 0;
}
```

The first line includes *config.php*. Unlike the previous example, *header.php* has not been included (yet). If validation fails, you'll redirect users to another page, so there's no need to show the HTML in *header.php* until these tests have passed.

The next line is the first if condition. The isset() function checks to see if the GET variable exists. If it does, isset() returns TRUE; if not, validentry is set to 0.

> ## NOTE
>
> **Redirection Fun and Games**
>
> *Redirection* is when you automatically jump to another page on the Web site. There are two main methods of redirecting to a page:
>
> - Use JavaScript. The problems with this technique are that not all browsers fully support JavaScript, and users and network managers can also turn off JavaScript.
>
> - Use HTTP headers. Use the HTTP headers that are present in every Web page to change the current page. This technique is supported by every browser, but it can occur only before any data is sent to the client. This same restriction applies to sessions when you use `session_start()` at the beginning of a page.
>
> As a general rule, use HTTP headers for redirection, because of its availability in all browsers and ease of use.

Assuming a variable is being sent, a check is made to ensure the value is numeric; if someone sets the variable to "bananas," for example, this is obviously incorrect. The `is_numeric()` function tests the GET variable; if the result is `false`, error is set to 1.

> ## NOTE
>
> **The Nasty World of SQL Injection**
>
> One of the risks of using GET variables is SQL injection. Imagine that you have a SQL statement such as the following:
>
> ```
> SELECT * FROM entries WHERE id = <id value>
> ```
>
> and where `<id value>` is, you add the value from the GET variable:
>
> ```
> $sql = "SELECT * FROM entries WHERE id = " . $_GET['id'];";
> ```
>
> This code assumes that the value of id is numeric. If you don't check for this, a malicious user could try to inject SQL code into the query. Imagine what would happen if the user added `1; DROP DATABASE blogtastic;`. The following SQL is now executed:
>
> ```
> SELECT * FROM entries WHERE id = 1; DROP DATABASE blogtastic;
> ```
>
> This code would result in a lost database (assuming the user had appropriate permissions)! To protect against this risk, always ensure that numeric GET values are actually numeric.

Next, if error is indeed equal to 1 (indicating a non-numeric value), the header() command redirects to the main page. The header() command is passed the Location header and the full location to redirect to (such as Location: http://localhost/blogtastic/). In the code, the "Location:" text is added, and then the location is picked out of the config_basedir variable from *config.php*.

> ### TIP
>
> When using the Location header, you will need to provide a complete URL such as http://www.foo.com/—as opposed to www.foo.com or foo.com.

If error is not set to 1, the validentry variable is set to the value of the GET variable. With this validation in place, the code below the header() function runs only with a valid GET variable.

> ### NOTE
>
> **Don't Confuse the User with Errors**
>
> When an invalid variable is detected, this script redirects to a legitimate page instead of displaying an error message. When considering the usability of your Web application, it generally makes sense to redirect rather than report an error. Error messages are rarely useful to users, and anyone who has the knowledge to adjust the GET variable on the URL is probably fully aware that they are tampering with the application instead of using the application. Automatically redirecting avoids potentially confusing the user with error messages.

Showing the Entry

With the validation complete, you can display the blog entry. This code looks very similar to the code on *index.php*. First, add the header HTML:

```
require("header.php");
```

You now need to determine which type of query to run. Inside the validation checking code, validentry is set to either 0 (if no variable was supplied) or to the ID of the entry to view.

If `validentry` is set to anything other than 0, the query is simple—ask for that specific blog entry. If the value is 0, however, the query should load the latest blog entry (the same behavior as *index.php*):

```
require("header.php");
if($validentry == 0) {
  $sql = "SELECT entries.*, categories.cat FROM entries, categories " .
         " WHERE entries.cat_id = categories.id " .
         "ORDER BY dateposted DESC " .
         " LIMIT 1;";
}
else {
  $sql = "SELECT entries.*, categories.cat FROM entries, categories " .
         "WHERE entries.cat_id = categories.id
 AND entries.id = " . $validentry .
         " ORDER BY dateposted DESC LIMIT 1;";
}
```

Send the query to to the database with the `mysql_query()` function:

```
else {
  $sql = "SELECT entries.*, categories.cat FROM entries, categories " .
         "WHERE entries.cat_id = categories.id
 AND entries.id = " . $validentry .
         " ORDER BY dateposted DESC LIMIT 1;";
}
$result = mysql_query($sql);
```

Now you can present the results to the user. This code is virtually identical to the code that you wrote on *index.php* to present the blog entry. The only real difference is that the subject of the entry is not linked to anything.

```
$result = mysql_query($sql);

$row = mysql_fetch_assoc($result);
echo "<h2>" . $row['subject'] . "</h2><br />";
echo "<i>In <a href='viewcat.php?id=" . $row['cat_id'] ."'>" .
    $row ['cat'] ."</a> - Posted on " .
    date("D jS F Y g.iA", strtotime($row['dateposted'])) ."</i>";
echo "<p>";
echo nl2br($row['body']);
echo "</p>";
```

The main blog entry section is now complete.

Showing Blog Comments

To display the comments, first create a SQL query that will get the comments for the current blog entry:

```
echo "</p>";

$commsql = "SELECT * FROM comments WHERE blog_id = " . $validentry .
        " ORDER BY dateposted DESC;";
$commresult = mysql_query($commsql);
$numrows_comm = mysql_num_rows($commresult);
```

You count the number of rows again with mysql_num_rows() and use the value to determine if any comments have been posted. If numrows_comm is equal to 0, the text No comments is displayed; otherwise, the else block of code is executed.

```
$numrows_comm = mysql_num_rows($commresult);

if($numrows_comm == 0) {
  echo "<p>No comments.</p>";
}
else {
  $i = 1;

  while($commrow = mysql_fetch_assoc($commresult)) {
    echo "<a name='comment" . $i . "'>";
    echo "<h3>Comment by " . $commrow['name'] . " on " .
        date("D jS F Y g.iA",
  strtotime($commrow['dateposted'])) . "</h3>";
    echo $commrow['comment'];
    $i++;
  }
}
```

Inside the else, you perform two basic functions: display each comment and then create an anchor on each one that can match up with the anchors referenced by *index.php*.

At the top of the else block, you first set i to 1; this variable is used as a counter to implement the anchors. Next, the while loop iterates through each comment from the query and creates the anchor. A link is created with a name attribute set to the text comment, with the value of i appended (resulting in, for example, comment2). The main comment fields are then displayed in a similar way to the main blog entry. Finally, the i variable is incremented by 1, preparing for the next comment's output.

Build the Comment Form

Allowing a user to add comments involves three distinct actions:

- Display the form for adding comments.
- Process the form and add its data to the database after the user clicks the Submit button.

■ Reload the page and show the new comment.

QUICK NOTE...

This functionality is a little more complex than the previous sections, largely because you need to add some code to various parts of the page, instead of just adding one line at a time to the end of your page.

First, add the main form shown in Figure 4-6.

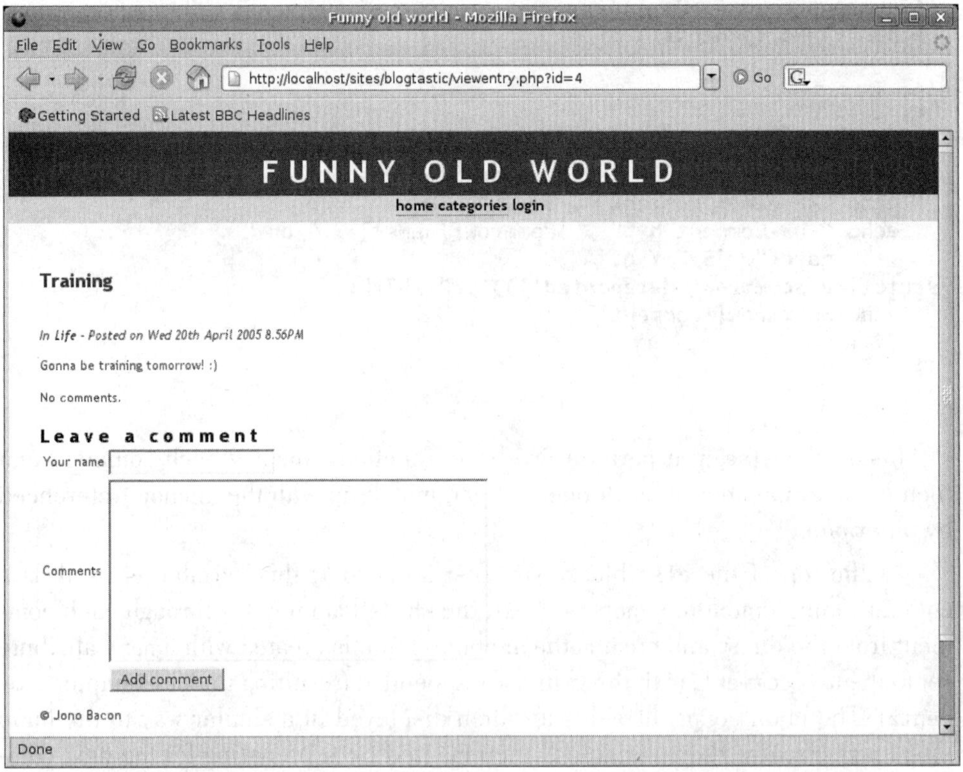

FIGURE 4-6 Forms are useful for allowing users to contribute comments.

To do this, close off the PHP block at the bottom of the page with ?> and add the following HTML:

```
      echo $commrow['comment'];
      $i++;
   }
}
```

```
?>

<h3>Leave a comment</h3>

<form action="<?php echo $SCRIPT_NAME
 . "?id=" . $validentry; ?>" method="post">
<table>
<tr>
  <td>Your name</td>
  <td><input type="text" name="name"></td>
</tr>
<tr>
  <td>Comments</td>
  <td><textarea name="comment" rows="10" cols="50"></textarea></td>
</tr>
<tr>
  <td></td>
  <td><input type="submit" name="submit" value="Add comment"></td>
</tr>
</table>
</form>
```

This code creates a table that contains a number of form elements. In the <form> tag, action specifies the page that will process the data from this form. As shown here, you can use a special PHP variable called SCRIPT_NAME to reference the name of the current file (in this case, *viewentry.php*). This reference is useful if you later decide to change the filename of your script; you then don't need to change your code. The method attribute in the tag indicates whether you want to submit your variables as POST or GET variables.

Inside the action attribute, the validentry variable is added as a GET variable. When you process the data from the form, you need to indicate the ID of the blog entry to which you are posting the comment.

The HTML in the preceding form itself is pretty self-explanatory.

NOTE

GET Variables Versus Hidden Form Fields

Another technique of sharing a variable between the form and the script that processes it is to use the hidden form element:

```
<input type="hidden" name="example" value="21">
```

The value attribute of the form can then be accessed as a normal variable with _GET or _POST in your PHP code.

Processing forms on Web pages works in a rather backwards fashion. At the top of your page—before showing any HTML—you need to check to see if the Submit button has been clicked by checking for the _POST['submit'] variable. If this variable exists, the user has submitted a form. If the variable does not exist, you should assume that the user has not actually seen the form yet and, therefore, need to display it. It sounds crazy, but hang in there—it will all make sense momentarily.

Insert the following code after your validation code, before you include the *header.php* file:

```
else {
  $validentry = 0;
}

if($_POST['submit']) {
  $db = mysql_connect($dbhost, $dbuser, $dbpassword);
  mysql_select_db($dbdatabase, $db);

  $sql = "INSERT INTO comments(blog_id, dateposted,
 name, comment) VALUES(" .
    $validentry . ", NOW(), '" . $_POST['name']
 . "', '" . $_POST['comment'] . "');";
  mysql_query($sql);
  header("Location: http://" . $HTTP_HOST
 . $SCRIPT_NAME . "?id=" . $validentry);
}
else {
  // code will go here
}

require("header.php");
```

The first line checks if the submit POST variable exists. For explanation purposes, assume that the Submit button has been clicked and the variable exists. The code then connects to the database. (Remember, you have not included header.php yet, so no database connection is available.)

NOTE

Don't Blow Up Your Headers

When you use a header redirect, always ensure that *no* data is displayed on the page before the header is sent—this includes white space. As a simple example of how important this is, add a single space before the <?php instruction and reload the page. You should now get a lot of "headers been sent" errors. Whenever you see these errors, check that there are no erroneous letters or white space either in the page itself or within the files that are included (such as *config.php*).

The next line is the SQL query. This query inserts the data into the database with an INSERT statement. A typical INSERT statement looks like this:

```
INSERT INTO table(field1, field2)
    VALUES ('data for field 1', 'data for field 2');
```

When you construct the SQL statement in your sql variable, you concatenate the various variables from the form that are accessed with _POST. To demonstrate how this fits together, imagine that you are adding a comment to the blog entry with 2 as an ID, at 2:30 p.m. on August 10, 2005. Assume that the user types "Bob Smith" as the name and "I really like your blog. Cool stuff!" as the comment. Table 4-5 demonstrates how the query is built.

TABLE 4-5 The sql variable is built up into an INSERT statement

CONCATENATED ELEMENT	SQL STATEMENT
INSERT INTO comments(blog_id, dateposted, name, comment) VALUES(	**INSERT INTO comments(blog_id, dateposted, name, comment) VALUES(**
validentry	$INSERT INTO comments(blog_id, dateposted, name, comment) VALUES(**2**
, NOW(), '	INSERT INTO comments(blog_id, dateposted, name, comment) VALUES(2, **2005-08-10 14:30:00**, '
$_POST['name']	INSERT INTO comments(blog_id, dateposted, name, comment) VALUES(2, 2005-08-10, **'Bob Smith**
', '	INSERT INTO comments(blog_id, dateposted, name, comment) VALUES(2, 2005-08-10, 'Bob Smith','
$_POST['comment']	INSERT INTO comments(blog_id, dateposted, name, comment) VALUES(2, 2005-08-10, 'Bob Smith', **'I really like your blog. Cool stuff!**
');	INSERT INTO comments(blog_id, dateposted, name, comment) VALUES(2, 2005-08-10, 'Bob Smith', 'I really like your blog. Cool stuff!**');**

The left column lists each part of the code; the right column shows how the content of the page is built up in the query. As you read the table, remember that numbers don't need single quotes around them (such as the number in `validentry`) but strings (letters and sentences) do.

One part of the code that will be new to you is `NOW()`. This is a special MySQL function that provides the current date and time, and you will use `NOW()` to automatically fill the `dateposted` field.

NOTE

Built-In MySQL Functions

MySQL provides a range of these functions, and you can explore them from the comfort of phpMyAdmin. When you insert data, a Function drop-down box lists these different MySQL functions. Experiment with them to get a better idea of what they do.

The next line in the code—`mysql_query($sql);`—performs the actual query. You may have noticed that the line does not include a variable in which to store the result, such as `$result = mysql_query($sql)`. The reason is that the query is only sent; no results are returned. The final line uses the `header()` function to redirect to the current page.

Finally, the `if` block is closed, and the `else` begins (for cases when no Submit button has been clicked). At the bottom of the page, add the closing code:

```
</table>
</form>

<?php
}
require("footer.php");
?>
```

In effect, then, the entire page of HTML is shown if the user didn't reach *viewentry.php* via clicking the Submit button (on the form on that same page!).

BUILDING THE CATEGORY BROWSER

Within a site powered by Blogtastic, a large number of blog entries is going to build. With so much content available, it is important to have a means of easily browsing this content. In this section, you create a useful page for users to browse the different categories and see which blog entries have been posted in each category.

If you think about how this page should be designed, it seems logical to list the categories and let the user click on one to see any related blog entries (see Figure 4-7). This functionality is similar to a tree view in a file manager: The directories are listed, and then you click one to see the files and subdirectories.

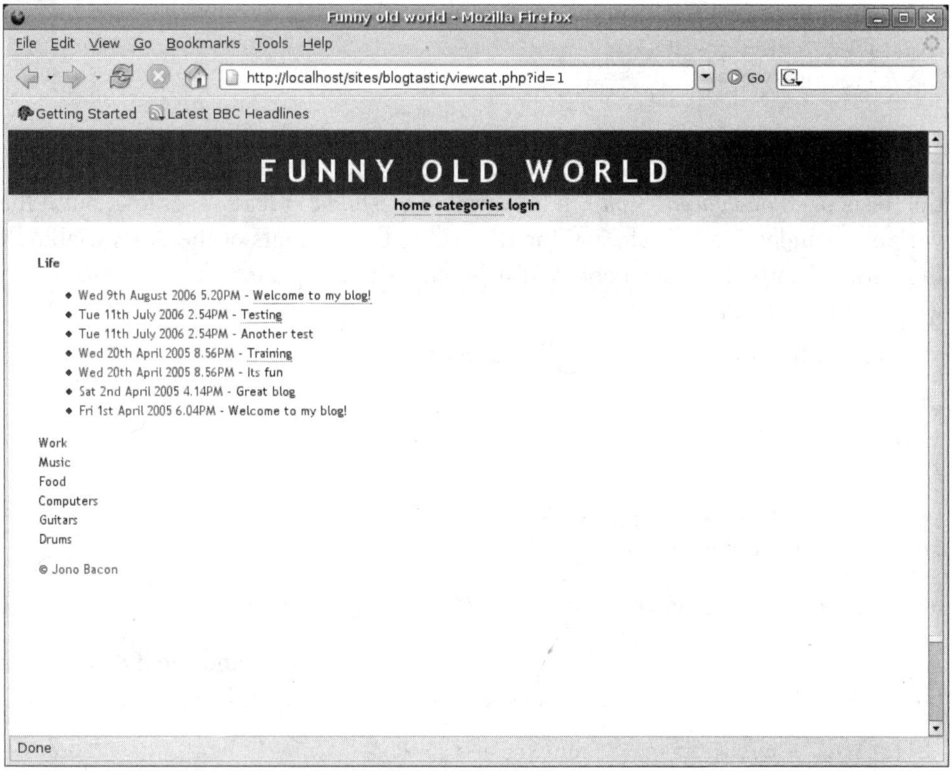

FIGURE 4-7 Click any category to view the entries in that category.

On *index.php* and *viewentry.php*, you made the category a link to a page called *viewcat.php*, and the ID of the category was passed as an `id` GET variable. To get started, create a new file called *viewcat.php* and add the following code:

```
require("config.php");

if(isset($_GET['id']) == TRUE) {
  if(is_numeric($id) == FALSE) {
    $error = 1;
  }
}
```

```
if($error == 1) {
  header("Location: " . $config_basedir . "/viewcat.php");
}
else {
  $validcat = $_GET['id'];
}
}
else {
  $validcat = 0;
}
```

This code should look familiar; it runs the id variable through the same valida-tion tests used on *viewentry.php*. If no variable exists, validcat is set to 0, but if the variable is indeed legitimate, validcat is set to the contents of the GET variable. If the variable fails the test to check if it is numeric, the page redirects to itself but without the id variable.

Select all of the records from the *categories* table:

```
else {
  $validcat = 0;
}

$sql = "SELECT * FROM categories";
$result = mysql_query($sql);

while($row = mysql_fetch_assoc($result)) {
```

Add the following code to check each row of the result set and see if $validcat is the same as the id variable. If it is, this means that the category is currently selected.

```
while($row = mysql_fetch_assoc($result)) {
  if($validcat == $row['id']) {
    echo "<strong>" . $row['cat'] . "</strong><br />";

    $entriessql = "SELECT * FROM entries WHERE cat_id = " . $validcat .
                  " ORDER BY dateposted DESC;";
    $entriesres = mysql_query($entriessql);
    $numrows_entries = mysql_num_rows($entriesres);

    echo "<ul>";
```

As the while loop iterates through each row, the first line checks if validcat is the same as the ID from the current row. If it is, the if block is executed. The first line inside the if outputs the name of the category in bold, instead of a link.

The query on the next line gets all blog entries in which cat_id is equal to validcat. These entries are requested in descending date order, so the most recent entry will display at the top of the list. The query is then run, and the returned rows are counted (to ensure that there are records to show). The final line starts the unordered list block that contains the results.

Check to see if any rows exist for the current category and display the relevant details:

```
echo "<ul>";
if($numrows_entries == 0) {
  echo "<li>No entries!</li>";
}
else {
  while($entriesrow = mysql_fetch_assoc($entriesres)) {
    echo "<li>" . date("D jS F Y g.iA", strtotime($entriesrow
['dateposted'])) .
        " - <a href='viewentry.php?id=" . $entriesrow['id'] . "'>" .
        $entriesrow['subject'] ."</a></li>";
  }
}
echo "</ul>";
}
```

If numrows_entries has zero rows, the browser displays a list item with the text No entries!. If there are rows, another while loop is opened to run through the results. Inside this while, a list item that displays the date of the entry and a link to *viewentry.php* (using the correct id value) is created. The subject of the post is the body of the link.

Finally, you can display the currently unselected categories:

```
echo "</ul>";
}
else {
  echo "<a href='viewcat.php?id=" . $row['id'] . "'>" . $row['cat'] .
"</a><br />";
}
}

require("footer.php");
```

You now have a complete archive of blog entries organized by category!

Don't Just Let Anyone Log In

Everything created so far in this project has been designed to be accessible by anyone who stumbles across the blog. As such, these pages have no built-in security—that is, the pages are not restricted to certain users. Because of the open nature and accessibility of the site, it is recommended that only information suitable for public consumption is present on these pages. You should avoid adding your credit card number, personal information, or those embarrassing photos of you at a fancy dress party. (That is how rumors get started.)

Allowing restricted access for the owner to add and remove content is an essential feature, however. Having to log into phpMyAdmin to add content is not an ideal solution, so the master plan is to create pages to provide a convenient means of adding content. You need to provide a way for someone to log in, and the login details the user enters should match the ones in the *logins* table. You will use PHP sessions (covered in Chapter 2) to track the user by sharing variables across different pages. If the user successfully logs in, you can set a session variable and then check to ensure that session variable exists on the restricted pages.

To begin, create a new file called *login.php* and add the login form:

```
<form action="<?php echo $SCRIPT_NAME ?>" method="post">

<table>
<tr>
  <td>Username</td>
  <td><input type="text" name="username"></td>
</tr>
<tr>
  <td>Password</td>
  <td><input type="password" name="password"></td>
</tr>
<tr>
  <td></td>
  <td><input type="submit" name="submit" value="Login!"></td>
</tr>
</table>
</form>
```

This form contains some familiar-looking text boxes (see Figure 4-8).

You may have noticed that the second <input> tag uses password as the type. When you use this type of form element, the contents are disguised as stars or dots to hide the password from nosey onlookers.

The next step is to process the form and check if the database contains the login details. Before you do this, however, add the usual introductory code at the start of the file (before any HTML):

```
<?php

session_start();

require("config.php");

$db = mysql_connect($dbhost, $dbuser, $dbpassword);
mysql_select_db($dbdatabase, $db);
```

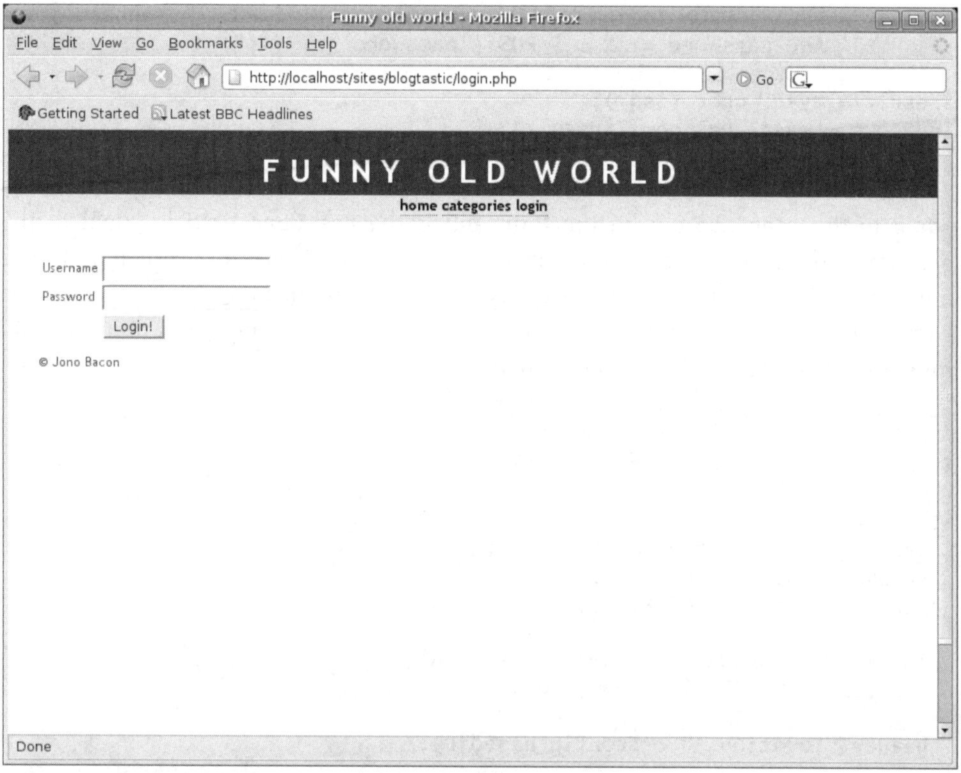

FIGURE 4-8 The login form looks like any other form.

NOTE

Forms Feel Insecure, Too

Although forms provide a means for people to securely identify themselves, the passwords transmitted to the server for processing are sent as plain text. This is a potential security risk inherent when using forms. The only solution to this risk is to encrypt form data with JavaScript when the form button is clicked, a technique beyond this project's scope.

Add the code that checks if the Submit button has been clicked (again, from the form you've already added):

```
mysql_select_db($dbdatabase, $db);

if($_POST['submit']) {
```

```
$sql = "SELECT * FROM logins WHERE username = '" . $_POST['username'] .
    "' AND password = '" . $_POST['password'] . "';";

$result = mysql_query($sql);
$numrows = mysql_num_rows($result);
```

The SQL statement is created to check if the username in the *logins* table is equal to the username box in the form and if the password field is equal to the password box in the form. The query is then run, and the rows are counted. The number of lines returned from the query indicates whether the details typed were correct. If the details are correct, a single row is returned—no more, no less. If no rows are returned, the details do not match.

Add the following code:

```
$numrows = mysql_num_rows($result);

if($numrows == 1) {
  $row = mysql_fetch_assoc($result);
  session_register("USERNAME");
  session_register("USERID");

  $_SESSION['USERNAME'] = $row['username'];
  $_SESSION['USERID'] = $row['id'];

  header("Location: " . $config_basedir);
}
else {
  header("Location: " . $config_basedir . "/login.php?error=1");
}
```

In the case where the login details are valid, a new session is created.

When using PHP sessions, you must register your session variables. The session_register() lines create two variables, called USERNAME and USERID.

NOTE

Be Consistant When Naming Variables

Naming session variables in uppercase is not mandatory, but it's useful because this helps them to stand out in your code as different types of variables.

The next two lines then use _SESSION (representing the user's session information) to use the variables and store information from the SQL query (the username and the id) in them. The final line performs a header redirect to *index.php*.

If the Submit button has not been clicked, a small chunk of code is run before the form displays:

```
        header("Location: " . $config_basedir . "/login.php?error=1");
    }
}
else {

    require("header.php");

    if($_GET['error']) {
      echo "Incorrect login, please try again!";
    }
?>
```

Include the *header.php* file and then check to see if there is a GET variable called error. If there is, the error message is displayed to indicate that the user typed an invalid username or password.

At the bottom of the page, after the HTML, add the final bits of code:

```
}
require("footer.php");
```

Signing Out the User

With the user now able to log in, you also need to give him the ability to log out—by destroying the session created on login. Create a new file called *logout.php* and add the following code:

```
<?php

session_start();
session_destroy();

require("config.php");

header("Location: " . $config_basedir);

?>
```

To log out the user, just use the `session_destroy()` function to delete all the registered session variables. The session is now destroyed, and the user is no longer logged in. You can then perform a header redirect to *index.php*.

NOTE

The Life and Death of a Session

When dealing with session-based code, you should always clear out any sessions when testing your code. Apart from creating the *logout.php* script, another option is to close the Web browser. Sessions will live only for the duration that the browser is open, and when you close the browser (not just the window), the session is lost.

When developing your code, closing your browser when you want to clear a session can be quite frustrating. To relieve the pain, use the Web Developers Toolbar extension that is available for Mozilla Firefox on all platforms. Download it from the Mozilla Extensions Web site at http://extension-room.mozdev.org.

Adding Session Support to the Application

With the new member login capability, you can supercharge your current pages to react differently when a member is logged in. The session variables created in the login page can be checked, and you can add extra options where appropriate.

Bolting On Options in the Header File

The first file to edit is *header.php*. In *login.php* and *logout.php*, you added `session_start()` at the beginning of the page. You will use `session_start()` in most of your pages, so add it to the top of *header.php*:

```
<?php

session_start();
```

This file already contains a list of links that are available to different parts of the site. When users are logged in, the Logout link should be visible; if they are not logged in, the Login link should be visible. Add the following code inside the PHP block under the *categories* link:

```
[<a href="viewcat.php">categories</a>]

<?php

if(isset($_SESSION['USERNAME']) == TRUE) {
```

```
    echo "[<a href='logout.php'>logout</a>]";
}
else {
  echo "[<a href='login.php'>login</a>]";
}
```

The isset() function is used to check if the USERNAME session variable is set. If it is, the Logout link is displayed; otherwise, the Login link is displayed.

Use the same method for adding additional links:

```
else {
  echo "[<a href='login.php'>login</a>]";
}

if(isset($_SESSION['USERNAME']) == TRUE) {
  echo " - ";
  echo "[<a href='addentry.php'>add entry</a>]";
  echo "[<a href='addcat.php'>add category</a>]";
}

?>
```

Adding Links to Update Blog Entries

When using Blogtastic, you will need to edit existing blog entries. Instead of just adding an Edit Blog Entry link to *header.php*, it is more intuitive to add an Edit link next to blog entry subjects. (Later in the project, you will create a file, called *updatentry.php*, to edit the blog entry.) Using a similar technique of checking if the session variable exists, add the following code in *index.php*, after the category and date line:

```
echo "<i>In <a href='viewcat.php?id=" . $row['cat_id'] ."'>" .
$row['cat'] ."</a> - Posted on " . date("D jS F Y g.iA",
strtotime($row['dateposted'])) ."</i>";

if(isset($_SESSION['USERNAME']) == TRUE) {
  echo " [<a href='updateentry.php?id=" . $row['id'] . "'>edit</a>]";
}
```

The *updateentry.php* file is passed an id variable that contains the ID of the blog entry to edit. Copy this same block of code to *viewentry.php*, after the same line where the date of the posting is listed. The links are displayed in Figure 4-9.

Welcome to my blog!

In Life - Posted on Wed 9th August 2006 5.20PM [edit]

Welcome to my brand new blog. This website will act as a place where I can talk about anything I like in as much detail as I like. So, prepare to get

FIGURE 4-9 Adding contextual links to administer the blog makes the application easier to use.

ROLLING YOUR OWN CATEGORIES

Adding blog categories is the next part of the game. This page is similar to the page used to add comments.

First, create the form in a new file called *addcat.php*:

```
<form action="<?php echo $SCRIPT_NAME ?>" method="post">

<table>
<tr>
  <td>Category</td>
  <td><input type="text" name="cat"></td>
</tr>
<tr>
  <td></td>
  <td><input type="submit" name="submit" value="Add Entry!"></td>
</tr>
</table>
</form>
```

Add the usual lines of code at the start of the file, before any HTML:

```
<?php

session_start();

require("config.php");

$db = mysql_connect($dbhost, $dbuser, $dbpassword);
mysql_select_db($dbdatabase, $db);
```

With this page available to restricted users only, you need to check if the user is logged in. Do this by checking if one of the session variables exists; if it doesn't, redirect to another page:

```
if(isset($_SESSION['USERNAME']) == FALSE) {
  header("Location: " . $config_basedir);
}
```

> **NOTE**
>
> **Never Assume**
>
> It might seem impossible to get to this page without clicking a link, and wouldn't that imply the user has already logged in? Although this sounds logical, someone could still type the URL directly. It's always better to explicitly check to ensure the user is logged in, rather than trust other pages to do that job for you.

Add the logic for when the user clicks the Submit button:

```
if(isset($_SESSION['USERNAME']) == FALSE) {
  header("Location: " . $config_basedir);
}

if($_POST['submit']) {
  $sql = "INSERT INTO categories(cat) VALUES('" . $_POST['cat'] . "');";
  mysql_query($sql);
  header("Location: " . $config_basedir . " viewcat.php");
}
else {
  require("header.php");

?>
```

Within this code, an INSERT query is created and sent to the database. After the query is run, the browser redirects to the *viewcat.php* page to view the newly created category.

Finally, close the else and include the *footer.php* file (all after the form):

```
<?php
}
require("footer.php");
?>
```

CREATING NEW BLOG ENTRIES

So far in Blogtastic, the capability to actually *add* a blog entry has been suspiciously missing. This essential feature requires almost all of the techniques you've seen so far, hence the delay. You are now ready, though, so it's time to knock out this page. The page behaves in a similar way to previous pages that added content, but this page also includes a drop-down combo box that is used to select the category under which the entry is filed.

Create a new file called *addentry.php* and start the form:

```
<h1>Add new entry</h1>
<form action="<?php echo $SCRIPT_NAME ?>" method="post">

<table>
```

Previously, you added the entire form first, but in this page, the very first form control will be the special drop-down box just discussed:

```
<tr>
  <td>Category</td>
  <td>
  <select name="cat">
  <?php
    $catsql = "SELECT * FROM categories;";
    $catres = mysql_query($catsql);
    while($catrow= mysql_fetch_assoc($catres)) {
      echo "<option value='" . $catrow['id']
  . "'>" . $catrow['cat'] . "</option>";
    }
  ?>
  </select>
  </td>
</tr>
```

The drop-down combo box presents a visual box with a series of options that the user can select. This involves two basic steps. First, create a `<select>` tag that contains the items within the box. Each item is housed within `<option>` tags. In these tags, add the text that you would like to appear in the box (in this case, the category name) and a `value` attribute. This contains the value that is passed when the user selects an item. Set this attribute to contain the ID of the category item.

In terms of making this work in code, the SQL query selects everything from the *categories* table. A loop iterates through the categories that are returned in the query. Within the `while` loop, the `<option>` tags are created, and the `id` from the query is added to the `value` attribute.

Complete the rest of the form:

```
  </select>
  </td>
</tr>

<tr>
  <td>Subject</td>
  <td><input type="text" name="subject"></td>
</tr>
<tr>
  <td>Body</td>
  <td><textarea name="body" rows="10" cols="50"></textarea></td>
</tr>
<tr>
  <td></td>
  <td><input type="submit" name="submit" value="Add Entry!"></td>
</tr>
</table>
</form>
```

The form is shown in Figure 4-10.

FIGURE 4-10 Adding new blog posts is simple.

Move to the beginning of the file and add the boilerplate introductory code:

```php
<?php

session_start();

require("config.php");

$db = mysql_connect($dbhost, $dbuser, $dbpassword);
mysql_select_db($dbdatabase, $db);

if(isset($_SESSION['USERNAME']) == FALSE) {
  header("Location: " . $config_basedir);
}
```

Add the logic that actually processes the form:

```
if(isset($_SESSION['USERNAME']) == FALSE) {
  header("Location: " . $config_basedir);
}

if($_POST['submit']) {
  $sql = "INSERT INTO entries(cat_id, dateposted, subject, body)
VALUES(" .
          $_POST['cat'] . ", NOW(), '" . $_POST['subject'] . "', '" .
          $_POST['body'] . "');";
  mysql_query($sql);
  header("Location: " . $config_basedir);
}
else {
  require("header.php");
?>
```

This code creates an INSERT query that is very similar to the ones on previous form-driven pages.

Finally, close the else block and add the *footer.php* code:

```
</tr>
</table>
</form>

<?php
}
require("footer.php");
?>
```

UPDATE A BLOG ENTRY

The final page is for updating blog entries. Earlier, when you added session support to Blogtastic, you went through some of the pages and added links to edit a particular blog entry. The link to edit blog entries was for a page called *updateentry.php*, which is passed an id variable. This ID indicates which record to update.

Instead of adding the form first, on this page you will work from the top to the bottom.

First, add the boilerplate code:

```
<?php

session_start();

require("config.php");
```

```php
if(isset($_SESSION['USERNAME']) == FALSE) {
  header("Location: " . $config_basedir);
}

$db = mysql_connect($dbhost, $dbuser, $dbpassword);
mysql_select_db($dbdatabase, $db);
```

The next block of code is identical to the validation code written earlier:

```php
if(isset($_GET['id']) == TRUE) {
  if(is_numeric($id) == FALSE) {
    $error = 1;
  }

  if($error == 1) {
    header("Location: " . $config_basedir);
  }
  else {
    $validentry = $_GET['id'];
  }
}
else {
  $validentry = 0;
}
```

Add the code to process the form:

```php
else {
  $validentry = 0;
}

if($_POST['submit']) {
  $sql = "UPDATE entries SET cat_id = "
. $_POST['cat'] . ", subject = '" .
        $_POST['subject'] ."', body = '"
. $_POST['body'] . "' WHERE id = " .
        $validentry . ";";
  mysql_query($sql);

  header("Location: " . $config_basedir . "/viewentry.php?id=" .
$validentry);
}
```

The SQL query implements an UPDATE command that will update each field in the database that has the id of validentry (the validated id variable). The UPDATE query indicates which table to update (UPDATE *entries*) and then provides a number of *database field = form element* sections. When the query is complete, another header redirect takes the user to the *viewentry.php* page with the correct id variable.

If the Submit button has not been clicked, the details of the entry are grabbed from MySQL so you can populate the form fields, starting with a query:

```
header("Location: " . $config_basedir
. "/viewentry.php?id=" . $validentry);
}
else {

    require("header.php");

    $fillsql = "SELECT * FROM entries WHERE id = " . $validentry . ";";
    $fillres = mysql_query($fillsql);
    $fillrow = mysql_fetch_assoc($fillres);

?>
```

Next, begin creating the form:

```
$fillrow = mysql_fetch_assoc($fillres);

?>

<h1>Update entry</h1>

<form action="<?php echo $SCRIPT_NAME . "?id="
. $validentry; ?>" method="post">

<table>
```

The first part of the form is the category field. You will need to have the chosen category automatically selected when the page is loaded. To do this, add selected at the end of the tag to be selected. An example of this in HTML is shown here (this is not actually in the project code, so don't add it):

```
<select name="example">
  <option value="1">Option 1</option>
  <option value="2" selected>Option 2</option>
  <option value="3">Option 3</option>
</select>
```

To accomplish this, add the following code to your form:

```
<form action="<?php echo $SCRIPT_NAME . "?id=" . $validentry; ?>"
method="post">

<table>

<tr>
  <td>Category</td>
  <td>
```

```
       <select name="cat">
       <?php
         $catsql = "SELECT * FROM categories;";
         $catres = mysql_query($catsql);
         while($catrow= mysql_fetch_assoc($catres)) {
           echo "<option value='" . $catrow['id'] . "'";

           if($catrow['id'] == $fillrow['cat_id']) {
             echo " selected";
           }

           echo ">" . $catrow['cat'] . "</option>";
         }
       ?>
       </select>
       </td>
</tr>
```

The query is run, and then the while loop iterates through each record. Inside the while loop, the <option value=<id from the record> is first printed and then a check is made to see if the category ID of the entry (fillrow['cat_id']) is the same as the current category row ID (catrow['id']). If the values match, " selected" (notice the space before the word) is added. After this, the rest of the line is created: >category</option>.

In the remaining parts of the form, small PHP blocks add the information from the query to the value attributes and between the <textarea> tags to populate the form:

```
     </select>
     </td>
</tr>

<tr>
  <td>Subject</td>
  <td><input type="text" name="subject"
 value="<?php echo $fillrow['subject']; ?>">
 </td>
</tr>
<tr>
  <td>Body</td>
  <td><textarea name="body" rows="10" cols="50">
    <?php echo $fillrow['body']; ?></textarea></td>
</tr>
<tr>
  <td></td>
  <td><input type="submit" name="submit" value="Update Entry!"></td>
</tr>
</table>
</form>
```

Finally, close `else` and insert the footer:

```php
<?php
}
require("footer.php");
?>
```

You can see the updated page in Figure 4-11.

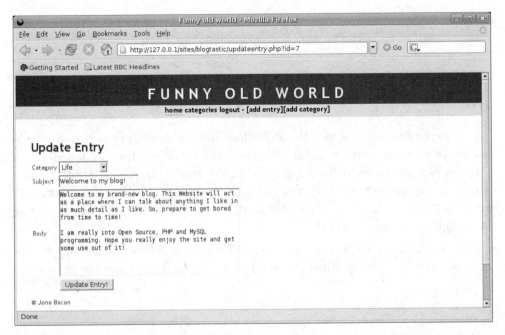

FIGURE 4-11 Updating blog entries uses a similar interface to adding new entries.

SUMMARY

In this project, you created your first full-featured, database-driven Web application. This application flexed your programming muscles, and covered an entire range of essential techniques. This included using database queries, adding data to the database, joining tables, updating records, performing validation, managing archived data, separating code across different pages, and ensuring interface usability.

Aside from providing a fun project to work on, this project also provided a base in which the rest of the projects in the book are based upon. You learned a number of skills that will be refined and built upon as you continue though the book. This is the start of an exciting journey, and reading this means that you have completed a large and important step. Stretch your fingers, dust off your keyboard, grab a cup of something hot, and get ready for the next project.

CHAPTER 5

Discussion Forums

Discussion forums have become a fundamental part of the Internet. Within these Web-based message boards, users discuss topics that are cogitated over by a close community of contributors. And within these discussion forums, Internet users can become part of a wider community. Discussion forums offer a compelling and interesting challenge to code. Features such as creating categories, forums, and topics; replying to messages; registering users; and more are common requirements.

After you've created a blog, writing the code behind a discussion board is a natural progression of your skills because it introduces the idea of two-way communication, as opposed to the relatively one-way perspective offered by a blog. As such, this chapter provides an important step in your programming experience—everyone should write some discussion forums at least once!

UNDER THE HOOD

Virtually all discussion forums have a very similar design that involves three primary entities: categories, forums, and topics. To explain this structure, take a look at Figure 5-1.

This figure shows a typical phpBB (http://www.phpbb.com/) installation. *phpBB* is a popular Open Source forums engine that adheres to these common usability methods. In the figure, you can see a list of categories (only one—LUGRadio), and the category has a number of forums (General Discussion, Ideas for the show, Mirrors, and LUGRadio Live). When you click a forum, the forum topics display, as shown in Figure 5-2.

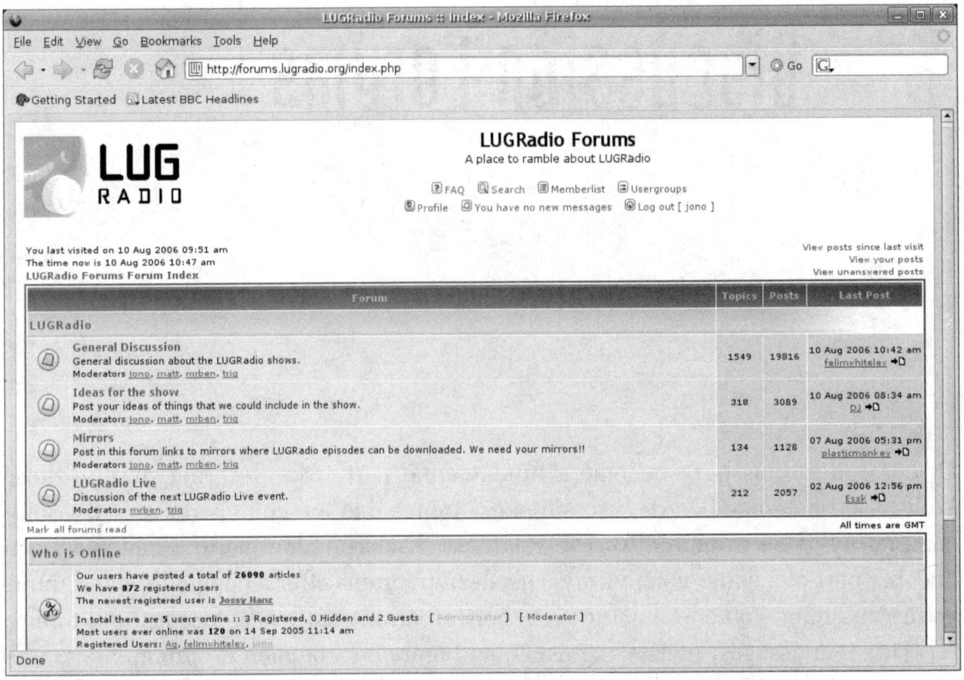

FIGURE 5-1 The front page of a phpBB forum

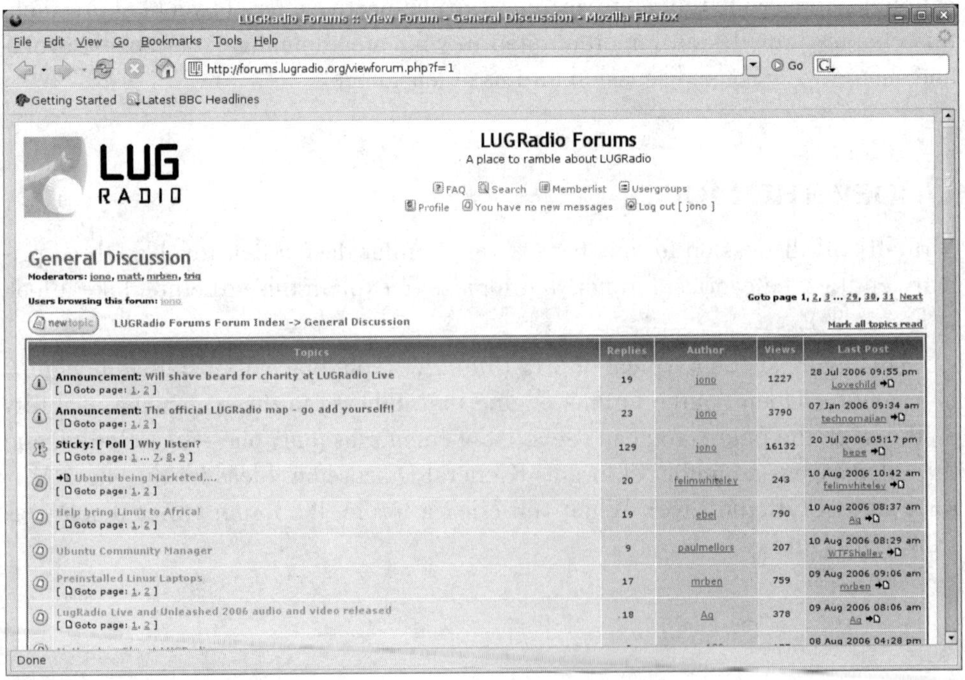

FIGURE 5-2 The topics list in the General Discussion forum

This figure displays a list of the *threads* in the forum. A thread is a discussion that starts with a specific topic. The originator of the thread posts a message, and the subject of the thread is listed in this screen. To view the messages in a thread, you click the thread. When you click a thread, a page similar to the one shown in Figure 5-3 displays.

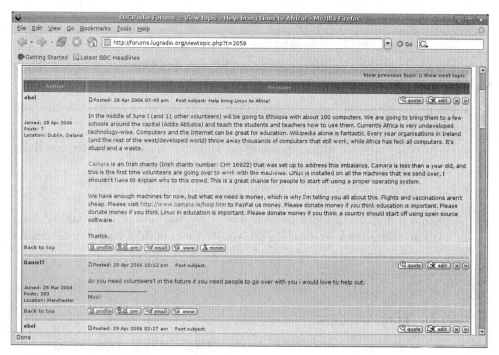

FIGURE 5-3 A discussion thread

Forum software has a distinctive set of parts, which combine to create a system that makes discussion easy. The challenge is to implement your own forum software. Figure 5-4 shows how these different parts relate to each other.

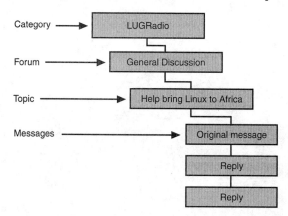

FIGURE 5-4

Discussion forums have a number of distinctive layers.

BUILDING YOUR OWN FORUMS

In this project, you will concentrate on the essential features that should go into discussion forum software, including the ability

- To display categories, forums, and topics.
- To log in as an administrator.
- For administrators to add categories and forums.
- For administrators to delete categories, forums, and topics.
- To log in as a user.
- For users to register. When a user fills in the registration form, a verification e-mail is sent.
- For users to view a category and forums, and then click a forum to view the topics. The user can also click a topic to view the thread.
- For users to post new threads or reply to existing ones.

Although hundreds of extra features could go into this project, adding them would take an entire book in itself. In this project, you build a core forums engine, but you can, of course, build additional features into it afterward.

BEFORE YOU BEGIN

This project uses some additional chunks of CSS. Copy *stylesheet.css* to the new project directory for this project and add the following lines to the end of *stylesheet.css*:

```
table {
    border: thin solid #cccccc;
    background: #ffffff;
}

th {
    letter-spacing: 2.5px;
    background: #eeeeeee;
    color: #000000;
    text-transform: uppercase;
    text-align: center;
    border-top: thick solid #eeeeee;
    border-bottom: thin solid #cccccc;
}

tr.head {
    letter-spacing: 1.5px;
```

```
   background: #dddddd;
   color: #000000;
   text-transform: uppercase;
   border-top: thick solid #eeeeee;
   border-bottom: thin solid #cccccc;
}

tr.body {
   background: #ffffff;
   color: #000000;
}

td {
   border: thin solid #cccccc;
   padding: 10px;
}
```

CREATING THE DATABASE

Within this project, a variety of tables relate to each other in different ways to store the different types of content discussed earlier. Figure 5-5 shows the database infrastructure you will create.

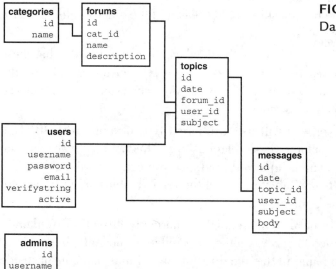

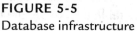
FIGURE 5-5
Database infrastructure

This project contains six important tables:

Table Name	What the Table Stores
categories	Three different categories.
forums	The different forums that are part of the categories.
topics	Details about the topics.
messages	The messages of the discussion thread.
admins	Login details for the site administrator.
users	Details about the users who can post to the forums.

There is an important relationship among the *categories, forums, topics,* and *messages* tables—each table stores the same id of the table to which it relates. For example, the *categories* and *forums* tables are related by storing the id of the relevant category in the cat_id field in the *forums* table.

Enforcing Relationships with InnoDB

When you create databases with MySQL, the MyISAM table type stores the data. This *non-transactional* table engine does not enforce relationships between tables. Imagine you have a table, called *orders*, that has a customer_id field that stores the same value as the id from the *customers* table. If you delete a record from the *customers* table, it would make sense to delete or update the respective entry in the *orders* table; otherwise, the relationship would break and the order would reference a customer who no longer exists.

With the default MyISAM table type, the database does not demand that these potential inaccuracies are resolved, and you *can* remove the customer and have the order refer to a non-existent customer. With MyISAM, the assumption is that you enforce these relationships in your code.

In this project, however, you will use a different type of table: InnoDB. This *transaction-safe* table can enforce these relationships. This not only gives you the peace of mind that your relationships work, but also you can perform a cascading delete, in which you delete one table and all of the related tables are also deleted. Feel the power, my friends.

Although it's a feature of MySQL, InnoDB is normally turned off by default (check with your distribution to verify whether it is in fact turned off). To enable it, load the *my.cnf* file (often found in the /etc directory on a Linux machine or inside the MySQL directory on a Windows machine) and look for skip-innodb. Comment out this option out by adding a # symbol:

```
#skip-innodb
```

Uncomment the other innodb lines so that the code looks something similar to the following:

```
innodb_data_home_dir = /opt/lampp/var/mysql/
innodb_data_file_path = ibdata1:10M:autoextend
innodb_log_group_home_dir = /opt/lampp/var/mysql/
innodb_log_arch_dir = /opt/lampp/var/mysql/
```

After you have switched on innodb support, restart MySQL for the changes to take effect.

WARNING!

When using transaction-safe tables such as InnoDB, be extremely careful with cascading deletes. If you mistakenly enforce a relationship, you could possibly lose data. This is typically quite rare because you need to deliberately enforce the relationship, but you are now cordially warned.

Building the Database

Fire up phpMyAdmin and create a new database called forum. Now add each of the tables below, complete with their fields:

The *admins* Table

- id. Set this to a TINYINT, make it a primary key, and enable auto_increment.
- username. Set this to VARCHAR with a length of 10 (a common length for usernames).
- password. Set this to VARCHAR with a length of 10.

The *categories* Table

- id. Set this to a TINYINT, make it a primary key, and enable auto_increment.
- name. Set this to VARCHAR with a length of 50.
- Set the table type to InnoDB.

NOTE

Setting the Table Type

Most of the tables need to have their table type set to InnoDB. In the table design screen where you configure the fields, a control at the bottom enables you to select the table type.

The *forums* Table

- id. Set this to a TINYINT, make it a primary key, and enable auto_increment.
- cat_id. Set this to TINYINT.
- name. Set this to VARCHAR with a length of 30.
- description. Set this to VARCHAR with a length of 255.
- Set the table type to InnoDB.

The *messages* Table

- id. Set this to a TINYINT, make it a primary key, and enable auto_increment.
- date. Set this to DATETIME.
- user_id. Set this to INT.
- topic_id. Set this to INT.
- subject. Set this to VARCHAR with a length of 100.
- body. Set this to TEXT.
- Set the table type to InnoDB.

The *topics* Table

- id. Set this to a TINYINT, make it a primary key, and enable auto_increment.
- date. Set this to DATETIME.
- user_id. Set this to INT.
- forum_id. Set this to TINYINT.
- subject. Set this to VARCHAR with a length of 100.
- Set the table type to InnoDB

The *users* Table

- id. Set this to a TINYINT, make it a primary key, and enable auto_increment.
- username. Set this to VARCHAR with a length of 10.
- password. Set this to VARCHAR with a length of 10.
- email. Set this to VARCHAR with a length of 100.
- verifystring. Set this to VARCHAR with a length of 20.
- active. Set this to TINYINT.
- Set the table type to InnoDB.

When you create the tables, be sure to set the correct table type where required. All of the tables, other than *admin*, need to be of the type InnoDB. If this is not set correctly, some of the features coded later will not work.

NOTE

Changing the Table Type After You Have Created It

If you want to change the table type for an existing table, click the Operations tab in phpMyAdmin and then use the box on that page to select a different table type.

At this point, the referential integrity between the tables has not been set, and no referential integrity is enforced. Later in the project, you will add some SQL to enforce it.

Adding Sample Data to the Database

When manually adding data to the database, you need to be careful that all the data relates correctly; otherwise, the forums will break. To get started, add a user and then add a few categories, forums, and topics.

NOTE

Don't Fill in the id Field

When you add data to any of these tables, remember to leave the id field blank; auto_increment will look after this for you.

The *users* Table

Add the details shown in Table 5-1 to the users table.

TABLE 5-1 A sample user

FIELD	VALUE
Username	Johnsmith
Password	Password
Email	john@foo.com
Verifystring	<leave blank>
Active	1

The *categories* Table

If you refer to Figure 5-4, the *categories* table is at the top of the tree of related tables. You need to first add data to this table and then work your way to the other tables. Add the two records in Table 5-2 to the table.

TABLE 5-2 Sample categories

FIELD	VALUE
Name	Movies
Name	Documentaties

The *forums* Table

With some categories defined, use the id from those categories when adding the forums. From the information in Table 5-3, create two forums in the *Movies* category (which has an id of 1); do not add any forums to the *Documentaries* category.

TABLE 5-3 Sample forums

FIELD	VALUE
Cat_id	1
name	Comedy
description	Films that make you laugh
Cat_id	1
name	Horror
description	Movies to hide behind the couch

Note here that you are referring to the *Comedy* category by putting its id into the cat_id field in this table.

The *topics* Table

The *topics* and *messages* tables are intrinsically linked as a topic and cannot exist without at least one message. The *topics* table contains only the subject of the topic to be discussed; you need to create at least one message in the *messages* table. Add the two topics from Table 5-4 to the *Comedy* category.

TABLE 5-4 Sample topics

FIELD	VALUE
Date	Select NOW from the Functions box
User_id	1
Forum_id	1
Subject	Classic comedy
Date	Select NOW from the Functions box
User_id	1
Forum_id	1
Subject	Fave comedy actor/actress

The *messages* Table

With the topics created, create the required messages from Table 5-5 for them.

TABLE 5-5 Sample messages

FIELD	VALUE
Date	Select NOW from the Function box
User_id	1
Topic_id	1
subject	Classic comedy
Body	Which black and white comedies do you like?
Date	Select NOW from the Function box
User_id	1
topic_id	2
Subject	Fave comedy actor/actress
Body	Who is your fave funny man/women?

CREATING THE SITE DESIGN

The first step in writing the code is to create the design. Create a new file called *config.php* and add the code shown in Example 5-1.

EXAMPLE 5-1 The configuration file stores settings about the site.

```php
<?php

$dbhost = "localhost";
$dbuser = "root";
$dbpassword = "";
$dbdatabase = "forum";

// Add the name of the forums below
$config_forumsname = "CineForums";

// Add your name below
$config_admin = "Jono Bacon";
$config_adminemail = "jono AT jonobacon DOT org";

// Add the location of your forums below
$config_basedir = "http://127.0.0.1/sites/forums/";

?>
```

Inside this file, you specify the variables used when connecting to the database as well as the variables used to configure the name and author of the site. In addition, $config_basedir contains the URL of forums; this will be used mainly when performing redirects.

Now, build the header file. Create a new file called *header.php* and add the following code:

```php
<?php

    session_start();

    require("config.php");

    $db = mysql_connect($dbhost, $dbuser, $dbpassword);
    mysql_select_db($dbdatabase, $db);

?>
```

You first add session support with session_start() and then include the configuration file. After this, you create the connection to the database.

Include the main HTML for the header:

```
?>

<!DOCTYPE HTML PUBLIC "-//W3C//DTD HTML 4.01 Transitional//EN"
"http://www.w3.org/TR/html4/loose.dtd">
<html>
<head>
    <title><?php echo $config_forumsname; ?></title>
    <link rel="stylesheet" href="stylesheet.css" type="text/css" />
</head>
<body>
<div id="header">
<h1><?php echo $config_forumsname; ?></h1>
[<a href="index.php">Home</a>]
```

The variables from *config.php* are used to set the title and name of the page.

Check the USERNAME session variable and display the relevant login/logout link:

```
<h1><?php echo $config_forumsname; ?></h1>
[<a href="index.php">Home</a>]

<?php

if(isset($_SESSION['USERNAME']) == TRUE) {
    echo "[<a href='logout.php'>Logout</a>]";
}
else {
    echo "[<a href='login.php'>Login</a>]";
    echo "[<a href='register.php'>Register</a>]";
}

?>
```

Add a final option so that users can post new topics:

```
}

?>

[<a href="newtopic.php">New Topic</a>]
</div>
<div id="main">
```

With the header file complete, create a new file called *footer.php* and add the footer code shown in Example 5-2.

EXAMPLE 5-2 The footer code is displayed at the bottom of the page.

```
</div>
<div id="footer">
&copy; 2005 <?php echo "<a href='mailto:"
 . $config_adminemail . "'>" .$config_admin . "</a>"; ?>

</div>
</body>
</html>
```

A link is added to the footer with the email address and author name from *config.php*.

DISPLAYING THE FORUMS

With the infrastructure complete, you can start to build the main forums code to present the categories, forums, and topics on different pages. If you refer back to the study of phpBB, you will see that the categories and forums are displayed on one page and the topics are displayed on another page that displays when you click a forum.

Creating the Front Page

The front page of the site displays the range of available forums. Create a file called *index.php* and start by including *header.php*:

```
<?php

require("header.php");
```

Run a query to get all of the categories:

```
require("header.php");

$catsql = "SELECT * FROM categories;";
$catresult = mysql_query($catsql);

echo "<table cellspacing=0>";

while($catrow = mysql_fetch_assoc($catresult)) {
    echo "<tr class='head'><td colspan=2>";
    echo "<strong>" . $catrow['name'] . "</strong></td>";
    echo "<tr>";
```

After each category has been displayed, check if the current category has any forums:

```
    echo "<tr>";

    $forumsql = "SELECT * FROM
forums WHERE cat_id = " . $catrow['id'] . ";";
    $forumresult = mysql_query($forumsql);
    $forumnumrows = mysql_num_rows($forumresult);
    if($forumnumrows == 0) {
        echo "<tr><td>No forums!</td></tr>";
    }
    else {
        while($forumrow = mysql_fetch_assoc($forumresult)) {
            echo "<tr>";
            echo "<td>";
```

After performing the query to check for forums with each category, the number of rows is counted and put it into $forumnumrows. The next line checks to see if this variable contains 0 (no rows), and if it does, No forums! is added to the table. If there *are* rows, the second while loop iterates through the list of forums to add each one to the table:

```
            echo "<td>";

            echo "<strong><a
href='viewforum.php?id="
. $forumrow['id'] . "'>" .
$forumrow['name'] . "</a></strong>";
            echo "<br/><i>" . $forumrow['description'] . "</i>";
            echo "</td>";
            echo "</tr>";
        }
    }
```

A link to viewforum.php is created with the id of the forum added as a GET variable. Below the link, the description is displayed.

Finally, end the first while, close the table, and include the footer file:

```
    }
    }
}

echo "</table>";

require("footer.php");

?>
```

The front page is now complete. This page provides a simple and familiar means of displaying the categories and forums (see Figure 5-6).

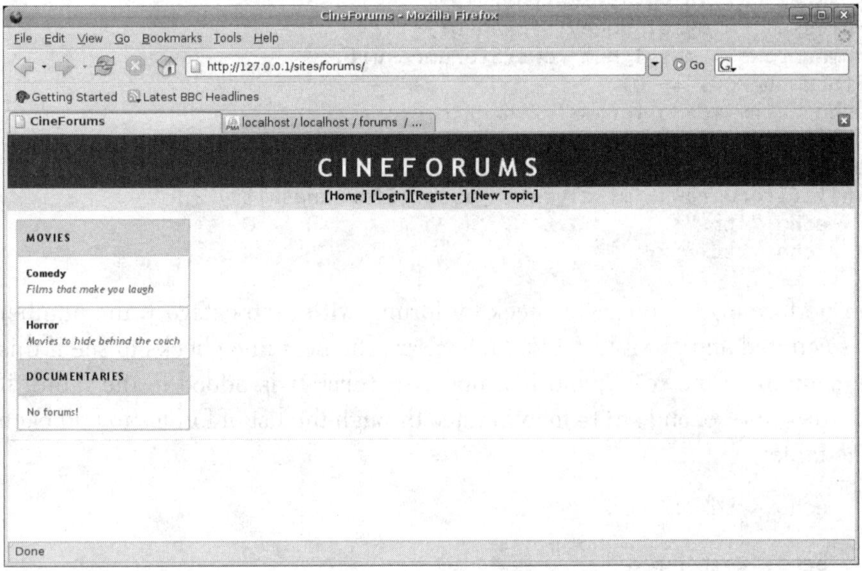

FIGURE 5-6 This is what the user sees when they visit the front page of the forums.

Next, you create the *viewforum.php* page to display the topics inside a chosen forum.

Viewing Forum Topics

This page has a simple purpose—to list the topics that are part of the forum, as well as the number of replies to the topic, the name of the author, and the date the topic was posted.

When this page is loaded, a GET variable called id has been passed to it. As with any GET variable, it is a wise idea to validate it. Create a new file called *viewforum.php* and add the following code:

```php
<?php

include("config.php");

if(isset($_GET['id']) == TRUE) {
   if(is_numeric($_GET['id']) == FALSE) {
      header("Location: " . $config_basedir);
   }
   $validforum = $_GET['id'];
```

```
}
else {
   header("Location: " . $config_basedir);
}
```

This code was used earlier perform the same kind of validation check.

Load the *header.php* file:

```
   header("Location: " . $config_basedir);
}
```

require("header.php");

Before you display the topics, display some general information on the page so that users know where they are in the site. This information includes the name of the current forum and a breadcrumb trail.

To add this information, perform a query to get the name of the forum that has the $validforum id and then display the name of the forum inside a second-level heading:

```
require("header.php");

$forumsql = "SELECT * FROM forums WHERE id = " . $validforum . ";";
$forumresult = mysql_query($forumsql);
$forumrow = mysql_fetch_assoc($forumresult);

echo "<h2>" . $forumrow['name'] . "</h2>";
```

The next step is to create the breadcrumb trail. A *breadcrumb trail* provides a series of links that shows the steps taken to get to the current page in the site. This concept is particularly useful with sites that have a number of sections.

> **NOTE**
>
> **Breadcrumb Trails: Useful or Not?**
>
> Within the Web development community are differing views about whether breadcrumb trails are actually useful. For some developers, a breadcrumb trail is seen as a poor excuse for a site that is difficult to navigate. Other developers, however, see the trail as a useful aid to navigation.
>
> When you are designing your Web applications, think about the navigation and whether a breadcrumb trail can help your users.

On this page, the breadcrumb trail is simple. Provide a link to return to the general forums page:

```
echo "<h2>" . $forumrow['name'] . "</h2>";
```

```
echo "<a href='index.php'>" . $config_forumsname
 . " forums</a><br /><br />";
```

Add a link that allows the user to add a new topic to this forum:

```
echo "<a href='index.php'>" . $config_forumsname
 . " forums</a><br /><br />";
```

```
echo "[<a href='newtopic.php?id=" . $validforum . "'>New Topic</a>]";
echo "<br /><br />";
```

Now you need to display the topics inside this forum. Although this may sound as simple as merely displaying all topics with the forum_id of $validforum, the query is actually more complex.

On this page, you need to display a range of information, much of it from different tables:

- The topic name lives in the *topics* table.
- The author name is in the users table that is linked by the user_id in the *topics* table.
- The date posted is in the *topics* table.

To make life more complicated, you also need to display the topic with the most recent post at the top of the list. Organizing these topics is quite tough—the actual posts are stored in the *messages* table and then joined to the *topics* table with topic_id. As such, you need to order the displayed topics with the newest topic as the message with the latest date from the *messages* table.

To solve this ordering problem, you will use a special function in MySQL called MAX(). This function selects the latest dates from the *messages* table. In addition, information from the *topics* and *users* table is selected. The *messages* and *topics* tables are then linked in the WHERE clause.

Now sit back, hold your breath, and run this epic query:

```
echo "<br /><br />";
```

```
$topicsql = "SELECT MAX( messages.date ) AS maxdate,
 topics.id AS topicid, topics.*, users.*
 FROM messages, topics, users WHERE messages.topic_id
 = topics.id AND topics.user_id = users.id  AND
 topics.forum_id = " . $validforum . " GROUP BY
 messages.topic_id ORDER BY maxdate DESC;";
$topicresult = mysql_query($topicsql);
$topicnumrows = mysql_num_rows($topicresult);
```

If $topicsnumrows contains 0, there are no topics:

```
$topicnumrows = mysql_num_rows($topicresult);

if($topicnumrows == 0) {
    echo "<table width='300px'><tr><td>No topics!</td></tr></table>";
}
```

This is cheating a little here. As you can see, you are creating a table to add a single record. But you want the No topics text to appear nicely formatted in the table. It is a slight cheat because you are not placing code further down the page inside the other table. This is for reasons of clarity. It is important to make sure you understand the code and not get wrapped up in table confusion.

If topics are present, you present them in a table. Create the table and table headings:

```
if($topicnumrows == 0) {
    echo "<table width='300px'><tr><td>No topics!</td></tr></table>";
}
else {

    echo "<table class='forum'>";

    echo "<tr>";
    echo "<th>Topic</th>";
    echo "<th>Replies</th>";
    echo "<th>Author</th>";
    echo "<th>Date Posted</th>";
    echo "</tr>";
```

Just before you display the rows, run another query to count the number of messages for the topic in the current row:

```
    echo "</tr>";

    while($topicrow = mysql_fetch_assoc($topicresult)) {
        $msgsql = "SELECT id FROM messages WHERE
topic_id = " . $topicrow['topicid'];
        $msgresult = mysql_query($msgsql);
        $msgnumrows = mysql_num_rows($msgresult);
```

Display the rows:

```
        $msgresult = mysql_query($msgsql);
        $msgnumrows = mysql_num_rows($msgresult);
```

```
        echo "<tr>";
        echo "<td>";
        echo "<strong>
<a href='viewmessages.php?id="
 . $topicrow['topicid'] . "'>"
 . $topicrow['subject'] . "</a></strong></td>";
        echo "<td>" . $msgnumrows . "</td>";
        echo "<td>" . $topicrow['username'] . "</td>";
        echo "<td>" . date("D jS F Y g.iA", strtotime($topicrow['date']))
 . "</td>";
        echo "<tr>";
    }
```

This code adds the subject of the topic and links it to *viewmessages.php* with the id of the topic as a GET variable. The number of messages in the thread, the user-name of the person who created the topic, and the topic date are also added.

Finally, close the table and add the footer:

```
        echo "<tr>";
    }

    echo "</table>";
}
require("footer.php");

?>
```

With this code up and running, you can see the completed forum view in Figure 5-7. The project is really starting to come together now.

Viewing a Thread

It probably comes as no surprise that the next page is the one that displays the discussion threads associated with a topic. When you created *viewforum.php*, you added a link to the topic subject to a page called *viewmessages.php*, which you will create now.

Create a new file called *viewmessages.php* and run the GET variable through some validation:

```
<?php

include("config.php");

if(isset($_GET['id']) == TRUE) {
    if(is_numeric($_GET['id']) == FALSE) {
        $error = 1;
    }
```

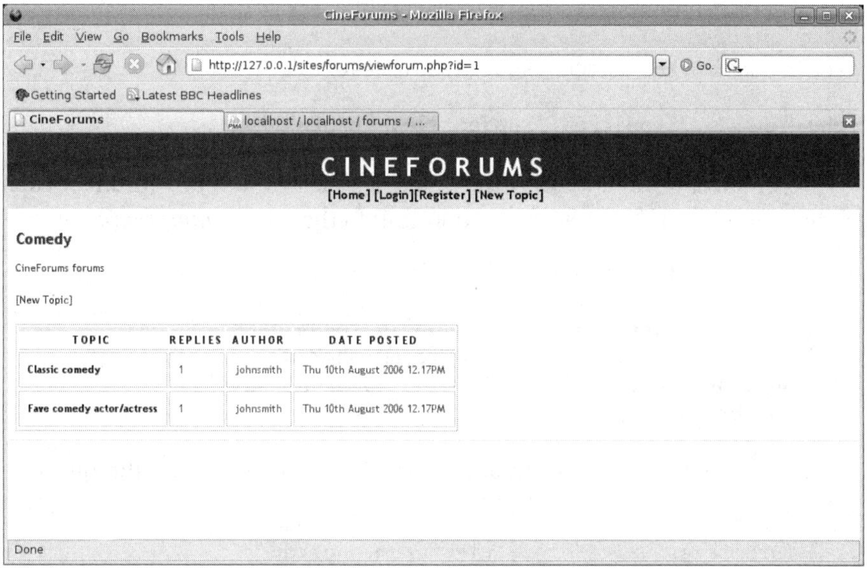

FIGURE 5-7 Viewing a forum

```
    if($error == 1) {
        header("Location: " . $config_basedir);
    }
    else {
        $validtopic = $_GET['id'];
    }
}
else {
    header("Location: " . $config_basedir);
}

require("header.php");
```

Add the name of the topic and the breadcrumb trail at the top of the page by first selecting the subject of the current topic, the forum name, and the id of the topic:

```
require("header.php");

$topicsql = "SELECT topics.subject,
 topics.forum_id, forums.name FROM topics,
 forums WHERE topics.forum_id = forums.id
 AND topics.id = " . $validtopic . ";";
$topicresult = mysql_query($topicsql);

$topicrow = mysql_fetch_assoc($topicresult);
```

Add the subject of the topic:

```
$topicrow = mysql_fetch_assoc($topicresult);

echo "<h2>" . $topicrow['subject'] . "</h2>";
```

To create the breadcrumb trail, add a link to the main forums. Then use the name of the forum from the query and link to the *viewforum.php* page:

```
echo "<h2>" . $topicrow['subject'] . "</h2>";

echo "<a href='index.php'>" . $config_forumsname
  . " forums</a> -> <a href='viewforum.php?id="
  . $topicrow['forum_id'] . "'>" . $topicrow['name']
  . "</a><br /><br />";
```

To display the messages that are part of the thread, create the query:

```
echo "<a href='index.php'>" . $config_forumsname
  . " forums</a> -> <a href='viewforum.php?id="
  . $topicrow['forum_id'] . "'>" . $topicrow['name']
  . "</a><br /><br />";

$threadsql = "SELECT messages.*, users.username
 FROM messages, users WHERE messages.user_id
 = users.id AND messages.topic_id = " . $validtopic
 . " ORDER BY messages.date;";
$threadresult = mysql_query($threadsql);
```

In this code, you select all fields from the messages table and the username from the *users* table and then join users.id and messages.user_id in which the topic_id is equal to $validtopic.

Present the messages by looping through the results:

```
$threadresult = mysql_query($threadsql);

echo "<table>";

while($threadrow = mysql_fetch_assoc($threadresult)) {
    echo "<tr><td><strong>Posted by <i>"
  . $threadrow['username'] . "</i> on "
  . date("D jS F Y g.iA", strtotime($threadrow['date']))
  . " - <i>" . $threadrow['subject']
  . "</i></strong></td></tr>";
    echo "<tr><td>" . $threadrow['body']. "</td></tr>";
    echo "<tr></tr>";
}

echo "<tr><td>[<a href='reply.php?id=" . $validtopic .
"'>reply</a>]</td></tr>";
echo "</table>";
```

Finally, add *footer.php*:

```
echo "</table>";

require("footer.php");

?>
```

When you run this script and view a thread, the output should look like Figure 5-8.

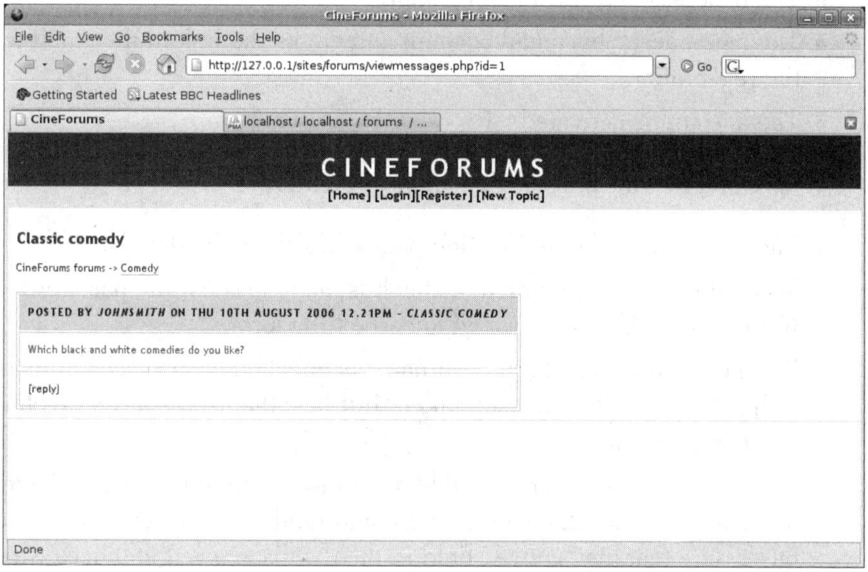

FIGURE 5-8 Viewing a thread

MANAGING USER LOGINS

Within the context of a forum, identity is important. Users want to post messages that come from them—not from a faceless anonymous user. In addition to normal users, you also need to support administrator logins. The administrator can perform tasks such as adding categories/forums and removing threads, forums, and categories. Luckily, PHP provides comprehensive support to make all of these requirements simple to add.

We are going to begin by building a User Registration system that will allow new users to automate the process of applying for membership. We will also build the requisite functionality to email the user a verification link they can click on to confirm their account.

User Registrations

Before you support user and administrator logins, you first must create support on the site for people to register a username. This page should authenticate users automatically.

When a user registers, this is the process:

- The user goes to the registration page and fills in a username, enters the password twice, and types an email address.
- The user is sent a verification email.
- The user checks his email account and clicks the link in the email to verify the registration.
- The account is activated.

Implementing this process in code is straightforward:

- The user goes to the registration page and fills in the details.
- When the form is submitted, a check is made to see if the passwords match. If they don't, the user is asked to correct the form.
- If the passwords match, the username is checked against the database to see if the name has already been taken. If it has, the user is asked to choose another username.
- If the username has not been taken, a random string is generated and the username, password, email address, and random string are added to the database. Note that the "active" field in the database is left at 0 because the account is currently inactive.
- An email is constructed with a URL that has GET variables containing the email address and random string. This email is then mailed to the address provided by the user.
- When the user clicks the link in the email, the page in the link checks the database to see if there is a record with the email address and random string provided. If there is, the active field is set to 1, and the account is activated.

To get started, create a new file called *register.php* and add the form:

```
<h2>Register</h2>
To register on the <?php echo
$config_forumsname; ?> forums, fill in the form below.
    <form action="<?php echo $SCRIPT_NAME ?>" method="POST">
    <table>
    <tr>
        <td>Username</td>
```

```
      <td><input type="text" name="username"></td>
   </tr>
   <tr>
      <td>Password</td>
      <td><input type="password" name="password1"></td>
   </tr>
   <tr>
      <td>Password (again)</td>
      <td><input type="password" name="password2"></td>
   </tr>
   <tr>
      <td>Email</td>
      <td><input type="text" name="email"></td>
   </tr>
   <tr>
      <td></td>
      <td><input type="submit"
 name="submit" value="Register!"></td>
   </tr>
   </table>
   </form>
```

Move to the top of the file and add the code to process the form:

```
<?php

session_start();

require("config.php");

$db = mysql_connect($dbhost, $dbuser, $dbpassword);
mysql_select_db($dbdatabase, $db);
```

After this introductory code, check if the Submit button has been clicked:

```
mysql_select_db($dbdatabase, $db);

if($_POST['submit']) {
   if($_POST['password1'] == $_POST['password2']) {
      $checksql = "SELECT * FROM users
 WHERE username = '" . $_POST['username'] . "';";
      $checkresult = mysql_query($checksql);
      $checknumrows = mysql_num_rows($checkresult);
```

This codes checks to see if the password1 box and the password2 box have the same password. If the passwords match, a query is made to see if the username field in the *users* table matches the username box from the form. After the query is executed, the number of rows is placed in a variable called $checknumrows.

NOTE

Quick Task: Remember to Check Those Variables!

In the preceding code snippet, you accessed the $_POST['username'] variable directly. To improve security, you should run that variable through the validation checks already discussed. Change this code to validate the variable.

See if there are any matches by checking the number of rows:

```
$checknumrows = mysql_num_rows($checkresult);

if($checknumrows == 1) {
    header("Location: " . $config_basedir .
"register.php?error=taken");
}
else {
```

If there is a match to the username—the username already exists—a header redirect is made to the same file, adding error=taken as a GET variable. This variable is checked later to display an error message on the form. If no match is made, the registration continues:

```
else {

    for($i = 0; $i < 16; $i++) {
        $randomstring .= chr(mt_rand(32,126));
    }
```

This code generates a random string. The for loop loops 16 times, and each time a random character is generated and added to a string that ultimately creates a 16-character string. The mt_rand() function generates a random number between 32 and 126, and then the chr() function converts this to a letter. The .= operator appends the new character to whatever is already in $randomstring.

Create the variables to use when sending the verification email:

```
for($i = 0; $i < 16; $i++) {
    $randomstring .= chr(mt_rand(32,126));
}

$verifyurl = "http://127.0.0.1/sites/forums/verify.php";
$verifystring = urlencode($randomstring);
```

```
$verifyemail = urlencode($_POST['email']);
$validusername = $_POST['username'];
```

These variables store different types of information, which is added to the verification URL. The first variable ($verifyurl) contains the location of the verification page, which you need to change to something relevant to your setup. The second variable ($verifystring) uses urlencode() to convert $randomstring into something that can be added to the address bar as a GET variable. The third variable uses urlencode() on the email address, and the final variable stores the username.

NOTE

Using urlencode()

The urlencode() function ensures that a string can be used as a GET variable on the URL. In addition to urlencode() is the urldecode() function, which converts the encoded string back into its original form.

Create a SQL query to insert the username, password, email address, and verifystring in the database while also setting the active field to 0 (inactive):

```
$validusername = $_POST['username'];

$sql = "INSERT INTO
users(username, password, email, verifystring,
active) VALUES('"
        . $_POST['username']
        . "', '" . $_POST['password1']
        . "', '" . $_POST['email']
        . "', '" . addslashes($randomstring)
        . "', 0);";
        mysql_query($sql);
```

Construct the email to send to the user for verification:

```
mysql_query($sql);

$mail_body=<<<_MAIL_

Hi $validusername,
```

```
Please click on the following link to verify your new account:

$verifyurl?email=$verifyemail&verify=$verifystring

_MAIL_;
```

You construct the mail message by using *heredoc* syntax. This special technique allows you to use <<< and an identifier (in this case, _MAIL_) to write a large chunk of text without requiring double quotes, single quotes, and new lines. The block ends when the identifier (_MAIL_) is added again. In the preceding snippet, the identifier is placed next to a variable declaration ($mail_body=) to add the heredoc text to the variable. This is a useful method of adding large chunks of text to a variable.

> ### NOTE
>
> **Don't Indent heredoc**
>
> When you use heredoc syntax, be sure to place the three angled brackets before the identifier (such as <<<IDENTIFIER) and place both identifiers at the start of a line (unless there is a variable before it, as in code in this example).

Send the email:

```
_MAIL_;

        mail($_POST['email'], $config_forumsname . " User
verification", $mail_body);
```

The mail() command sends the message. mail() has these three arguments:

- Email address
- Subject
- Body of the message

In this code, the email address from the form ($_POST_['email']) is used as the first argument, the forum name and User Verification are concatenated to make the subject, and finally the text from the heredoc syntax is added as the third argument.

Finally, display a message to indicate that the email has been sent:

```
        mail($_POST['email'],
$config_forumsname . " User verification",
$mail_body);
```

```
require("header.php");
echo "A link has been
emailed to the address you entered below.
Please follow the link in the email to validate
your account.";
    }
```

NOTE

Sending Email from PHP

When sending email with the mail() command, you need a working mail server running on your machine. If you are using Linux, a good mail server is Postfix (http://www.postfix.org/), which is fairly easy to install and run.

If you are using Windows, you can specify a separate SMTP server for sending mail. To do this, open php.ini and look for the SMTP option:

SMTP = your.mail.server

Although mail() is useful for sending simple emails, more complex tasks such as sending attachments are better handled by the PEAR Mail extension.

Earlier in the code, an if statement checked if the form passwords matched. Now, add the code that handles when they do not match:

```
        echo "A link has been emailed
to the address you entered below. Please follow the
link in the email to validate your account.";
        }
    }
    else {
        header("Location: " . $config_basedir .
"register.php?error=pass");
    }
```

A header redirect reloads the page and adds the error GET variable. (This variable is discussed later.) Earlier in the code, you checked if the Submit button was clicked. If it was, the code you just wrote is executed.

Add the else so that the form can be displayed if the submit POST variable was not detected:

```
    else {
        header("Location: " . $config_basedir .
"register.php?error=pass");
```

```
    }
}
else {
```

Just before you display the HTML form, include the header file and then process the error GET variable that is added when the page is redirected:

```
}
else {

    require("header.php");

    switch($_GET['error']) {
        case "pass":
            echo "Passwords do not match!";
        break;

        case "taken":
            echo "Username taken, please use another.";
        break;

        case "no":
            echo "Incorrect login details!";
        break;

    }
?>

<h2>Register</h2>
    To register on the <?php echo $config_forumsname; ?> forums, fill in
the form below.
    <form action="<?php echo $SCRIPT_NAME ?>" method="POST">
```

The variable is run through a switch statement to determine which error message is displayed; this depends on the value of the variable.

> **NOTE**
>
> **A Quick Task**
>
> We have deliberately not included any code here for validating the input in the registration form. Add some validation checks to make the script rock solid. This is a great time to practice adding validation to your code.

Below the form, close the else block and add the footer:

```
</table>
</form>
```

```php
<?php
}

require("footer.php");

?>
```

Figure 5-9 shows the completed registration form. Now we need to write the code that verifies the registration.

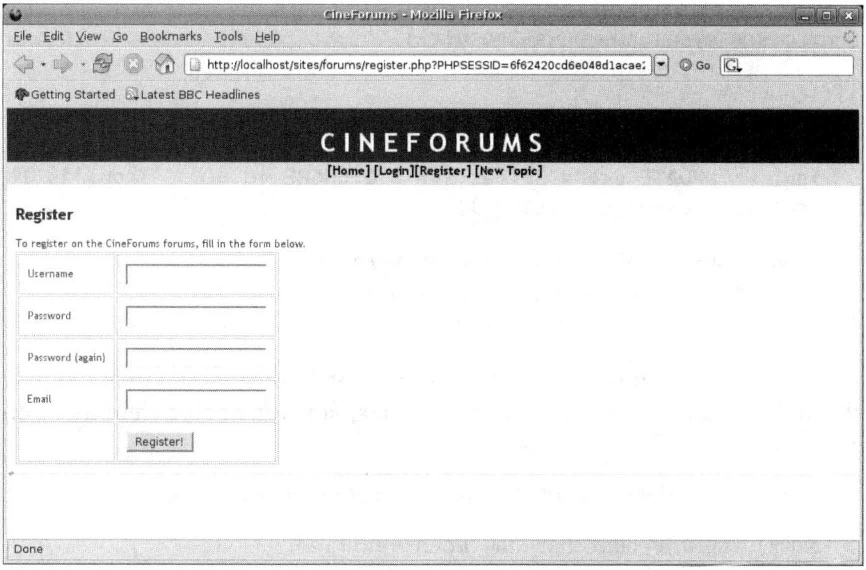

FIGURE 5-9 The registration form

Verifying the Account

With the verification email sent, you can create the page to which the link in the email points. This page simply decodes the GET variables (the urlencoded `email` and `verifystring` variables) and then checks if a row in the database matches. If there is a row, the account is activated by setting the `active` field in the *users* table to 1.

Create a new page called *verify.php* and add the initial code that decodes the variables:

```php
<?php

require("header.php");

$verifystring = urldecode($_GET['verify']);
$verifyemail = urldecode($_GET['email']);
```

Create the query that checks if the values exist in the database:

```php
$verifyemail = urldecode($_GET['email']);

$sql = "SELECT id FROM users WHERE verifystring
 = '" . $verifystring . "' AND email = '" .
 $verifyemail . "';";
$result = mysql_query($sql);
$numrows = mysql_num_rows($result);
```

Check if a row is returned:

```php
$numrows = mysql_num_rows($result);

if($numrows == 1) {
   $row = mysql_fetch_assoc($result);

   $sql = "UPDATE users SET active = 1 WHERE id = " . $row['id'];
   $result = mysql_query($sql);

   echo "Your account has now been verified.
 You can now <a href='login.php'>log in</a>";
}
```

If one row is returned, a match exists between the clicked link and the record in the table. When this occurs, an UPDATE query sets the active field to 1 with an id of $row['id'].

If the query does not return one row, display an error:

```php
   echo "Your account has now been verified.
 You can now <a href='login.php'>log in</a>";
}
else {
   echo "This account could not be verified.";
}
```

Finally, add the footer:

```php
   echo "This account could not be verified.";
}

require("footer.php");

?>
```

Logging In Users

The process for building the login page is similar to the one in other projects—the user types her details, the details are compared against the database, and then some sessions are set up.

Create a new file called *login.php* and add the form:

```
<form action="<?php echo pf_script_with_get($SCRIPT_NAME); ?>"
method="post">

<table>
<tr>
    <td>Username</td>
    <td><input type="text" name="username"></td>
</tr>
<tr>
    <td>Password</td>
    <td><input type="password" name="password"></td>
</tr>
<tr>
    <td></td>
    <td><input type="submit" name="submit" value="Login!"></td>
</tr>
</table>
</form>
Don't have an account? Go and <a href="register.php">Register</a>!
```

In the preceding code, you might have noticed something odd in the `action` attribute of the `<form>` tag. A function called `pf_script_with_get()` has been used to process the script name (`$SCRIPT_NAME`) to detect which GET variables are added to the current page and then bolt them on to the action of the form. You need to add the GET variable to the action if you want to access it in the code that processes the form. This is fine if you know the name of the GET variable, but if the variables could vary, you need to detect them and add them.

The reason you need this function is a result of the redirects. When a user clicks a link that requires her to be logged in (such as the New Topic link), the site should redirect to the login page. When the user has logged in, she should then be redirected to the original link. This would be simple enough if there was just a single GET variable (such as `redirect=page.php`), but if you are trying to add a topic to a specific forum and are passing the Add Topic page an id, there are two GET variables—the page and the id of the forum. Instead of trying to hard code this, it makes far more sense to detect which GET variables exist and add them automatically to the action part of the forum.

The `pf_script_with_get()` function is a custom function. Create a file called *functions.php* and add the following code:

```
<?php

function pf_script_with_get($script) {
    $page = $script;
    $page = $page . "?";

    foreach($_GET as $key => $val) {
```

```
    $page = $page . $key . "=" . $val . "&";
}

return substr($page, 0, strlen($page)-1);
}

?>
```

Within this function, you pass the function the page to get the GET variable from ($script). The first line sets $page to store the contents of $script, and the second line appends a question mark to the page (for example, page.php?).

The function then pulls out the GET variables by using the foreach() function to tear open the $_GET array and loop through it. In the foreach, you treat the key as $key and the value as $val and then glue them together in the format key=val&. Finally, you need to remove the final & from the link. To do this, use the substr() function to pass it $page, determine the length with strlen(), and then remove the last character (achieved with the -1 part).

With the function complete, process the form:

```php
<?php

session_start();

require("config.php");
require("functions.php");

$db = mysql_connect($dbhost, $dbuser, $dbpassword);
mysql_select_db($dbdatabase, $db);
$db = mysql_connect($dbhost, $dbuser, $dbpassword);
mysql_select_db($dbdatabase, $db);

if($_POST['submit']) {
$sql = "SELECT * FROM users WHERE username = '"
 . $_POST['username'] . "' AND password = '"
 . $_POST['password'] . "';";
   $result = mysql_query($sql);
   $numrows = mysql_num_rows($result);
   $result = mysql_query($sql);
   $numrows = mysql_num_rows($result);

   if($numrows == 1) {
      $row = mysql_fetch_assoc($result);
      if($row['active'] == 1) {
         session_register("USERNAME");
         session_register("USERID");
```

```
$_SESSION['USERNAME'] = $row['username'];
$_SESSION['USERID'] = $row['id'];
```

It's now time to perform any necessary redirection. Remember that pages requiring a user to be logged in redirect to the login page and then should be redirected to the original page. To handle this redirection, the page that redirects to *login.php* will also pass it the ref GET variable. This variable can have one of two possible values:

- newpost. The user has tried to make a new post. This should redirect to *newtopic.php*.

- reply. The user has tried to reply to a post. This should redirect to *reply.php*.

The next block reacts to these different options:

```
$_SESSION['USERNAME'] = $row['username'];
$_SESSION['USERID'] = $row['id'];

switch($_GET['ref']) {
    case "newpost":
        if(isset($_GET['id']) == FALSE) {
            header("Location: " . $config_basedir .
"/newtopic.php");
        }
        else {
            header("Location: " . $config_basedir .
"/newtopic.php?id=" . $_GET['id']);
        }
        break;

    case "reply":
        if(isset($_GET['id']) == FALSE) {
            header("Location: " . $config_basedir .
"/newtopic.php");
        }
        else {
            header("Location: " . $config_basedir .
"/newtopic.php?id=" . $_GET['id']);
        }
        break;

    default:
        header("Location: " . $config_basedir);
        break;
}
```

Finish the code to process the form:

```
default:
```

```
                    header("Location: " . $config_basedir);
                break;
            }
        }
        else {
            require("header.php");
            echo "This account is not verified yet. You were emailed a link
to verify the account. Please click on the link in the email to
continue.";
            }
            echo "This account is not verified yet. You were emailed a link
to verify the account. Please click on the link in the email to
continue.";
            }
        }
        else {
            header("Location: " . $config_basedir . "/login.php?error=1");
        }
    }
```

If a login error occurs, the page is redirected, and error=1 is added as a GET variable. This can be used to add an error message:

```
        else {
            header("Location: " . $config_basedir . "/login.php?error=1");
        }
    }
    else {

        require("header.php");

        if($_GET['error']) {
            echo "Incorrect login, please try again!";
        }

?>

<form action="<?php echo pf_script_with_get($SCRIPT_NAME); ?>"
method="post">
```

Finally, add the footer:

```
Don't have an account? Go and <a href="register.php">Register</a>!

<?php
}
require("footer.php");
?>
```

Logging In the Administrator

The login page for the administrator is fundamentally the same as the preceding page. Create a new file called *admin.php* and add the code shown in Example 5-3.

EXAMPLE 5-3 The administrator login page is virtually identical to the user login page.

```php
<?php

session_start();

require("config.php");
require("functions.php");

$db = mysql_connect($dbhost, $dbuser, $dbpassword);
mysql_select_db($dbdatabase, $db);

if($_POST['submit']) {
   $sql = "SELECT * FROM admins WHERE username = '" . $_POST['username']
. "' AND password = '" . $_POST['password'] . "';";

   $result = mysql_query($sql);
   $numrows = mysql_num_rows($result);

   if($numrows == 1) {
      $row = mysql_fetch_assoc($result);

      session_register("ADMIN");
      $_SESSION['ADMIN'] = $row['username'];

      switch($_GET['ref']) {
         case "add":
            header("Location: " . $config_basedir . "/addforum.php");
         break;

         case "cat":
            header("Location: " . $config_basedir . "/addcat.php");
         break;

         case "del":
            header("Location: " . $config_basedir);
         break;

         default:
            header("Location: " . $config_basedir);
         break;
```

continues

EXAMPLE 5-3 Continued

```php
        }
    }
    else {
        header("Location: " . $config_basedir . "/admin.php?error=1");
    }
}
else {

    require("header.php");

    echo "<h2>Admin login</h2>";

    if($_GET['error']) {
        echo "Incorrect login, please try again!";
    }

?>

<form action="<?php echo pf_script_with
_get($SCRIPT_NAME); ?>" method="post">

<table>
<tr>
    <td>Username</td>
    <td><input type="text" name="username"></td>
</tr>
<tr>
    <td>Password</td>
    <td><input type="password" name="password"></td>
</tr>
<tr>
    <td></td>
    <td><input type="submit" name="submit" value="Login!"></td>
</tr>
</table>
</form>

<?php
}
require("footer.php");
?>
```

The code here differs in only two ways:

- When the admin is successfully identified, the session variable registered is ADMIN, as opposed to USERNAME.

- The redirection trick (in which a user clicks a page that requires a login and it redirects to the page after the login page) is also used here. The difference is that the three options are add (redirects to *addforum.php*), cat (redirects to *addcat.php*), and del (redirects to *delete.php*).

With the ability for an administrator to log in, add the administrator links above the table on *index.php*:

```php
<?php

require("header.php");

if(isset($_SESSION['ADMIN']) == TRUE) {
    echo "[<a href='addcat.php'>Add new category</a>]";
    echo "[<a href='addforum.php'>Add new forum</a>]";
}

$catsql = "SELECT * FROM categories;";
$catresult = mysql_query($catsql);
```

Another piece of code to add are the Login and Logout links in *footer.php*. The same technique used in the header file for checking if the user is logged in and displaying the relevant link is used here, but on this page, you check the ADMIN session variable as opposed to the USERNAME variable:

```php
<?php
&copy; 2005 <?php echo "<a href='mailto:"
  . $config_adminemail . "'>" .$config_admin
  . "</a>"; ?>

if(isset($_SESSION['ADMIN']) == TRUE) {
    echo "[<a href='adminlogout.php'>Logout</a>]";
}
else {
    echo "[<a href='admin.php'>Login</a>]";
}

?>
```

Logging Out

With user and administration login pages complete, all that is left is to create the logout links. To do this, you use virtually the same code for both the user and administration logout pages, apart from the different ADMIN and USERNAME variables. To log out the user or admin, you simply use session_unregister() to unregister the relevant session variable.

For the user logout page, create a new file called *logout.php* and the following code:

```php
<?php

session_start();
session_unregister("USERNAME");
require("config.php");

header("Location: " . $config_basedir);

?>
```

To create the admin Logout link, create a new page called *adminlogout.php* and add the following code:

```php
<?php

session_start();
session_unregister("ADMIN");

require("config.php");

header("Location: " . $config_basedir);

?>
```

POSTS AND REPLIES

A fundamental feature in the forum software is the capability to post new content to a chosen forum or to reply to existing conversations. This process should be as simple and intuitive as possible, and it should be convenient to read a discussion and then post a reply.

The process of posting a new message and replying are fairly similar. To post a new message, a topic must first be created and then the id of the topic can be used when creating the message. It is important to remember that a new thread must include both a topic *and* a message. If you will create a reply, you simply need to know the id of the existing topic and then add a new entry to the messages table.

Posting a New Topic

To post a new topic, the page must essentially have two potential ways of working:

- The forum id is passed to the page as an id GET variable. This id can be used to determine to which forum the topic will be added.

- The user has clicked the main New Topic link in the *header.php* file, and as such, no forum id is passed to the page. The New Topic page should display a drop-down combo box on the form that contains a list of forums that the user can select to post the topic

The only part of the page that is different is that no id is passed to it to determine whether the combo box with the forums should be displayed.

Create a new file called *newtopic.php* and add the following code:

```php
<form action="<?php echo pf_script_with_get($SCRIPT_NAME); ?>"
method="post">
    <table>
    <?php

    if($validforum) == 0) {
        $forumssql = "SELECT * FROM forums ORDER BY name;";
        $forumsresult = mysql_query($forumssql);
    ?>
        <tr>
            <td>Forum</td>
            <td>
            <select name="forum">
            <?php
            while($forumsrow = mysql_fetch_assoc($forumsresult)) {
                echo "<option value='" . $forumsrow['id'] . "'>" .
$forumsrow['name'] . "</option>";
            }
            ?>
            </select>
            </td>
        </tr>
    <?php
    }
    ?>

    <tr>
        <td>Subject</td>
        <td><input type="text" name="subject"></td>
    </tr>
    <tr>
        <td>Body</td>
        <td><textarea name="body" rows="10" cols="50"></textarea></td>
    </tr>
    <tr>
        <td></td>
        <td><input type="submit" name="submit" value="Post!"></td>
    </tr>
    </table>
</form>
```

The usual suspects are present in this forum: the subject, body, and Submit button. At the top of the form, a check is made to see if $validforum is equal to 0. If it is, the combo box is created with the forums inside it. This $validforum variable is the result of the usual validation that exists at the top of the page.

Again, the pf_script_with_get() function is used on this page.

Add the code at the top of the page:

```php
<?php

session_start();

require("config.php");
require("functions.php");

$db = mysql_connect($dbhost, $dbuser, $dbpassword);
mysql_select_db($dbdatabase, $db);
```

After this initial code, run a quick query to check if any forums exist:

```php
mysql_select_db($dbdatabase, $db);

$forchecksql = "SELECT * FROM forums;";
$forcheckresult = mysql_query($forchecksql);
$forchecknumrows = mysql_num_rows($forcheckresult);

if($forchecknumrows == 0) {
    header("Location: " . $config_basedir);
}
```

The if check redirects the page if there are no rows.

Validate the GET variable:

```php
if($forchecknumrows == 0) {
    header("Location: " . $config_basedir);
}

if(isset($_GET['id']) == TRUE) {
    if(is_numeric($_GET['id']) == FALSE) {
        $error = 1;
    }

    if($error == 1) {
        header("Location: " . $config_basedir);
    }
    else {
```

```
         $validforum = $_GET['id'];
    }
}
else {
    $validforum = 0;
}
```

Check if the user is logged in, and if not, deny access:

```
else {
    $validforum = 0;
}

if(isset($_SESSION['USERNAME']) == FALSE) {
    header("Location: " . $config_basedir . "/login.php?ref=newpost&id="
. $validforum);
```

Now you can process the form. You need to first check which SQL statement you build:

- If the page was passed an id GET variable, use $validforum in the INSERT statement.

- If the page was not passed the variable, use the id from the drop-down combo box that was added to the form.

Here is the code:

```
if(isset($_SESSION['USERNAME']) == FALSE) {
    header("Location: " . $config_basedir . "/login.php?ref=newpost&id="
. $validforum);
}

if($_POST['submit']) {
    if($validforum == 0) {
        $topicsql = "INSERT INTO topics(date, user_id, forum_id, subject)
VALUES(NOW()
          , " . $_SESSION['USERID']
          . ", " . $_POST['forum']
          . ", '" . $_POST['subject']
          . "');";
    }
    else {
        $topicsql = "INSERT INTO
 topics(date, user_id, forum_id, subject) VALUES(NOW()
          , " . $_SESSION['USERID']
          . ", " . $validforum
          . ", '" . $_POST['subject']
          . "');";

    }
```

In this code, the `if` checks to see if `$validforum` is equal to 0 (no variable passed to the page), and if it is, one SQL statement is defined; otherwise, the SQL statement in the `else` is defined.

Run the query:

```
        $topicsql = "INSERT INTO
topics(date, user_id, lastpostuser_id, forum_id,
subject) VALUES(NOW()
        , " . $_SESSION['USERID']
        . ", " . $_SESSION['USERID']
        . ", " . $validforum
        . ", '" . $_POST['subject']
        . "');";

    }

    mysql_query($topicsql);
    $topicid = mysql_insert_id();
```

This example uses a new function called `mysql_insert_id()`. This function returns the generated `id` (the `auto_increment` id) from the last `INSERT` statement.

Build and execute the SQL for the *messages* table:

```
    $topicid = mysql_insert_id();

    $messagesql = "INSERT INTO messages(date,
user_id, topic_id, subject, body) VALUES(NOW()
        , " . $_SESSION['USERID']
        . ", " . mysql_insert_id()
        . ", '" . $_POST['subject']
        . "', '" . $_POST['body']
        . "');";
    mysql_query($messagesql);
    header("Location: " . $config_basedir . "/viewmessages.php?id=" .
$topicid);
}
```

In this code, the page redirects to the *viewmessages.php* page and the `id` from `mysql_insert_id()` is passed as a `GET` variable to it to display the new message.

Build the `else` part of the code that is executed when the submit `POST` variable has not been detected:

```
   header("Location: " . $config_basedir . "/viewmessages.php?id=" .
$topicid);
}
else {
   require("header.php");

   if($validforum != 0) {
      $namesql = "SELECT name FROM forums ORDER BY name;";
      $nameresult = mysql_query($namesql);
      $namerow = mysql_fetch_assoc($nameresult);

      echo "<h2>Post new message to the " . $namerow['name'] . "
forum</h2>";
   }
   else {
      echo "<h2>Post a new message</h2>";
   }

?>

   <form action="<?php echo
 pf_script_with_get($SCRIPT_NAME); ?>" method="post">
   <table>
```

Here you check if the $validforum variable is not equal (!=) to 0 (a valid forum
id was passed to the page). This id is used to get the name of the forum and add the
heading Post new message to the <forum> forum. If $validforum is equal to 0 (no
valid id GET variable was posted to the page), the generic Post a new message
heading is added.

Finally, add the closing code:

```
   </table>
   </form>

<?php
}

require("footer.php");

?>
```

Your completed page for posting a new message can be seen in Figure 5-10.

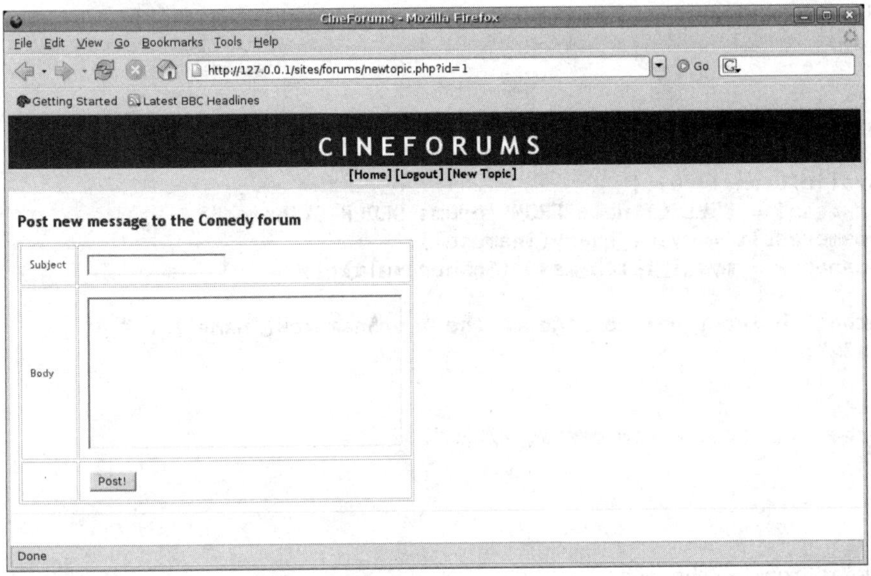

FIGURE 5-10 Posting a new message

Replying to Threads

Writing a page to reply to threads is fairly simple. The page is passed the topic id as an `id` GET variable, and this is used to take the content from the form and insert it into the *messages* table.

Create a file called *reply.php* and add the form:

```
<form action="<?php echo
pf_script_with_get($SCRIPT_NAME); ?>" method="post">
  <table>
  <tr>
    <td>Subject</td>
    <td><input type="text" name="subject"></td>
  </tr>
  <tr>
    <td>Body</td>
    <td><textarea name="body" rows="10" cols="50"></textarea></td>
  </tr>
  <tr>
    <td></td>
    <td><input type="submit" name="submit" value="Post!"></td>
  </tr>
  </table>
  </form>
```

Move to the start of the file and add the introductory code:

```php
<?php

session_start();

require("config.php");
require("functions.php");
```

Run the id GET variable through the usual validation code:

```php
require("config.php");
require("functions.php");

$db = mysql_connect($dbhost, $dbuser, $dbpassword);
mysql_select_db($dbdatabase, $db);

if(isset($_GET['id']) == TRUE) {
    if(is_numeric($_GET['id']) == FALSE) {
        $error = 1;
    }

    if($error == 1) {
        header("Location: " . $config_basedir);
    }
    else {
        $validtopic = $_GET['id'];
    }
}
else {
    header("Location: " . $config_basedir);
}
```

Check that the user is logged in:

```php
else {
    header("Location: " . $config_basedir);
}

if(isset($_SESSION['USERNAME']) == FALSE) {
    header("Location: " . $config_basedir . "/login.php?ref=reply&id=" .
$validtopic);
}
```

To process the form, run the INSERT query:

```php
if(isset($_SESSION['USERNAME']) == FALSE) {
    header("Location: " . $config_basedir . "/login.php?ref=reply&id=" .
$validtopic);
}
```

```php
if($_POST['submit']) {
   $messagesql = "INSERT INTO messages(date,
 user_id, topic_id, subject, body) VALUES(NOW()
      , " . $_SESSION['USERID']
      . ", " . $validtopic
      . ", '" . $_POST['subject']
      . "', '" . $_POST['body']
      . "');";

   mysql_query($messagesql);
   header("Location: " . $config_basedir . "/viewmessages.php?id=" .
$validtopic);
}
```

If the Submit button is not clicked, include the header file and display the form:

```php
   header("Location: " . $config_basedir . "/viewmessages.php?id=" .
$validtopic);
}
else {
   require("header.php");

?>

   <form action="<?php echo pf_script_with_get($SCRIPT_NAME); ?>"
method="post">
   <table>
```

Finally, add the footer:

```php
   </table>
   </form>

<?php
}

require("footer.php");

?>
```

CREATING ADMINISTRATOR-SPECIFIC PAGES

With the user-accessible pages complete, you can now create the administrator-specific pages. These pages deal with the management of the forums and allow you to add and remove categories, forums, and threads.

Incorporating these administrative features into the forums involves two steps. First, for the addition of content, specific pages are created (*addcat.php* and *addforum.php*). Next, for the deletion of content, *X* links are added next to categories, forums, and threads when the administrator is logged in. Clicking the link deletes the content.

Adding Categories

This page is a simple form and inserts a query script. First, create a file called *addcat.php* and add the form:

```
<h2>Add a new category</h2>

<form action="<?php echo
pf_script_with_get($SCRIPT_NAME); ?>" method="post">
<table>
<tr>
   <td>Category</td>
   <td><input type="text" name="cat"></td>
</tr>
<tr>
   <td></td>
   <td><input type="submit"
name="submit" value="Add Category!"></td>
</tr>
</table>
</form>
```

Move to the top of the file and begin to add the code:

```
<?php

session_start();

require("config.php");
require("functions.php");
```

Determine if the user is logged in and can access this page:

```
require("functions.php");

if(isset($_SESSION['ADMIN']) == FALSE) {
   header("Location: " . $config_basedir . "/admin.php?ref=cat");
}
```

Process the form:

```
if(isset($_SESSION['ADMIN']) == FALSE) {
   header("Location: " . $config_basedir . "/admin.php?ref=cat");
```

```
}

if($_POST['submit']) {
    $db = mysql_connect($dbhost, $dbuser, $dbpassword);
    mysql_select_db($dbdatabase, $db);

    $catsql = "INSERT INTO categories(name) VALUES('" . $_POST['cat'] .
"');";
    mysql_query($catsql);

    header("Location: " . $config_basedir);
}
```

In this code, the database connection details are added and an INSERT query is made to the *categories* table in which the data from the form is added. The query is executed, and the page redirects.

Add the `else` that contains the form:

```
    header("Location: " . $config_basedir);
}
else {
    require("header.php");

?>

    <h2>Add a new category</h2>

    <form action="<?php echo
pf_script_with_get($SCRIPT_NAME); ?>" method="post">
```

Finally, after the form, add the closing code:

```
    </table>
    </form>

<?php
}

require("footer.php");

?>
```

Adding Forums

This page adds forums to a particular category. The logic behind this script is simple: You present the user with a form in which she can select a category from a drop-down box. The data is then added to the forums table.

Create a new file called *addforum.php* and add the following code:

```
<h2>Add a new forum</h2>

<form action="<?php echo pf_script_with_get($SCRIPT_NAME); ?>"
method="post">
<table>
<?php

if($validforum == 0) {
    $forumssql = "SELECT * FROM categories ORDER BY name;";
    $forumsresult = mysql_query($forumssql);
?>
    <tr>
        <td>Forum</td>
        <td>
        <select name="cat">
        <?php
        while($forumsrow = mysql_fetch_assoc($forumsresult)) {
            echo "<option value='"
. $forumsrow['id'] . "'>" . $forumsrow['name']
. "</option>";
        }
        ?>
        </select>
        </td>
    </tr>
<?php
}
?>

    <tr>
        <td>Name</td>
        <td><input type="text" name="name"></td>
    </tr>
    <tr>
        <td>Description</td>
        <td><textarea name="description"
rows="10" cols="50"></textarea></td>
    </tr>
    <tr>
        <td></td>
        <td><input type="submit" name="submit"
value="Add Forum!"></td>
    </tr>
</table>
</form>
```

Add the usual code at the start of the file:

```
<?php
```

```
session_start();

require("config.php");
require("functions.php");

$db = mysql_connect($dbhost, $dbuser, $dbpassword);
mysql_select_db($dbdatabase, $db);
$db = mysql_connect($dbhost, $dbuser, $dbpassword);
mysql_select_db($dbdatabase, $db);

if(isset($_SESSION['ADMIN']) == FALSE) {
    header("Location: " . $config_basedir . "/admin.php?ref=add");
}
```

To process the form, simply insert the data from the form into the database with an INSERT statement:

```
if(isset($_SESSION['ADMIN']) == FALSE) {
    header("Location: " . $config_basedir . "/admin.php?ref=add");
}

if($_POST['submit']) {
    $topicsql = "INSERT INTO forums(cat_id, name, description) VALUES("
        . $_POST['cat']
        . ", '" . $_POST['name']
        . "', '" . $_POST['description']
        . "');";

    mysql_query($topicsql);

    header("Location: " . $config_basedir);
}
```

If the Submit button has not been clicked, the `else` is executed and the form code occurs after the next block:

```
    header("Location: " . $config_basedir);
}
else {
    require("header.php");
?>

    <h2>Add a new forum</h2>

    <form action="<?php echo pf_script_with_get($SCRIPT_NAME); ?>"
method="post">
```

Finally, place the closing code below the form:

```
    </table>
    </form>
```

```php
<?php
}

require("footer.php");

?>
```

Figure 5-11 shows the completed page for adding a forum.

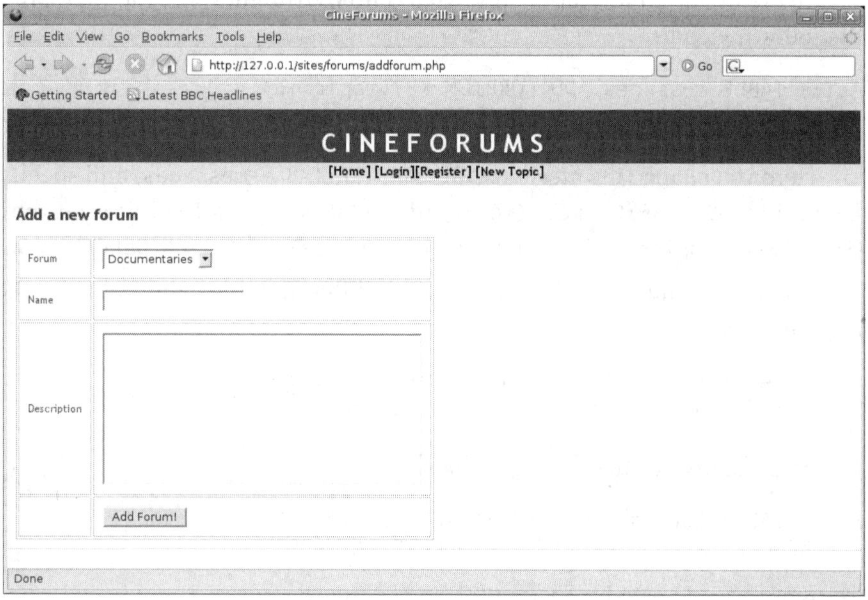

FIGURE 5-11 Adding a forum

Deleting

Deleting content from tables that are related can often be quite a challenge if the relationships are not enforced by the database. When you delete a category, you really want all dependent content, such as the forums and messages, to be deleted also. When referential integrity is not enforced, a series of SQL statements are needed to delete all dependent content.

At the start of the project, you used the InnoDB table type when creating your tables. With this type of table, you can enforce referential integrity, but it is not currently switched on.

To turn on referential integrity, specify the relationships between the tables in SQL. In this project, the intention is to allow all dependent records in other tables to be deleted. This is called a *cascading delete*. Before writing the SQL to do this, take a moment to understand how these relationships are defined:

- The topic_id field in the *messages* table stores the same value as the id field in the topics table.

- The forum_id field in the *topics* table stores the same value as the id field in the *forums* table.

- The cat_id field in the *forums* table stores the same value as the id field in the *categories* table.

To create the first relationship, go to phpMyAdmin, click the SQL tab, and add the following code:

```
ALTER TABLE messages ADD FOREIGN KEY(topic_id)
REFERENCES topics (id) ON DELETE CASCADE;
```

Here you change the *messages* table (ALTER TABLE messages) and specify that the topic_id (ADD FOREIGN KEY (topic_id)) relates to the id field in the topics table (REFERENCES topics (id)) with cascading deletes enabled (ON DELETE CASCADE).

Run a very similar statement, but with different tables and fields for the second relationship:

```
ALTER TABLE topics ADD FOREIGN KEY(forum_id)
REFERENCES forums (id) ON DELETE CASCADE;
```

And, finally, for the third relationship:

```
ALTER TABLE forums ADD FOREIGN KEY(cat_id)
REFERENCES categories (id) ON DELETE CASCADE;
```

Before you write the SQL code to actually delete the records, you need to add some controls for the administrator to select what to delete. To do this, you will put a small *X* next to an item, and if the administrators clicks it, it will be deleted.

First, add a delete button just before the category is added. Fire up *index.php* and look for the line in which the category is outputted. Just before the line, add the following code:

```
while($catrow = mysql_fetch_assoc($catresult)) {
    echo "<tr><td colspan=2>";

        if($_SESSION['ADMIN']) {
            echo
"[<a href='delete.php?func=cat&id="
. $forumrow['id'] . "'>X</a>] - ";
        }

    echo "<strong>" . $catrow['name'] . "</strong></td>";
```

This code links to a page that has two GET variables: func and id. The func variable is passed either cat, forum, or thread as a value, and these options determine what is deleted. The second variable, id, provides the id of the resource to be deleted.

Move further down where the forum is outputted and add the following code:

```
while($forumrow = mysql_fetch_assoc($forumresult)) {
    echo "<tr>";
    echo "<td>";

    if($_SESSION['ADMIN']) {
        echo
 "[<a href='delete.php?func=forum&id="
 . $forumrow['id'] . "'>X</a>] - ";
    }

        echo "<strong><a href='viewforum.php?id=" . $forumrow['id'] .
"'>" . $forumrow['name'] . "</a></strong>";
```

Finally, load *viewforum.php* and add the following code next to the thread:

```
echo "<tr>";
echo "<td>";

if($_SESSION['ADMIN']) {
    echo "[<a href='delete.php?func=thread&id=" .
$topicrow['topicid'] . "?forum=" . $validforum . "'>X</a>] - ";
}

    echo "<strong><a href='viewmessages.php?id=" .
$topicrow['topicid'] . "'>" . $topicrow['subject'] .
"</a></td></strong>";
```

Create a new file called *delete.php* and add the following code:

```php
<?php

include("config.php");

$db = mysql_connect($dbhost, $dbuser, $dbpassword);
mysql_select_db($dbdatabase, $db);
```

Validate the id GET variable as usual:

```
$db = mysql_connect($dbhost, $dbuser, $dbpassword);
mysql_select_db($dbdatabase, $db);

if(isset($_GET['id']) == TRUE) {
   if(is_numeric($_GET['id']) == FALSE) {
      $error = 1;
```

```
   }

   if($error == 1) {
      header("Location: " . $config_basedir);
   }
   else {
      $validid = $_GET['id'];
   }
}
else {
   header("Location: " . $config_basedir);
}
```

To perform the delete, run the func GET variable through a switch statement to determine what it is and then issue the relevant delete:

```
else {
   header("Location: " . $config_basedir);
}

switch($_GET['func']) {
   case "cat":
      $delsql = "DELETE FROM categories
 WHERE id = " . $validid . ";";
      mysql_query($delsql);
      header("Location: " . $config_basedir);
   break;

   case "forum":
      $delsql = "DELETE FROM forums WHERE id = " . $validid . ";";
      mysql_query($delsql);
      header("Location: " . $config_basedir);
   break;

   case "thread":
      $delsql = "DELETE FROM topics WHERE id = " . $validid . ";";
      mysql_query($delsql);
      header("Location: "
 . $config_basedir . "/viewforum.php?id="
 . $_GET['forum']);
   break;

   default:
      header("Location: " . $config_basedir);
   break;

}
?>
```

The delete SQL syntax is fairly simple: DELETE FROM <*table*> WHERE id = <*the id of the thing you want to delete*>. After the delete is made, the page redirects to the next level up in the page hierarchy. As an example, when you delete a topic, the forum topics page will be deleted. See Figure 5-12.

TOPIC	REPLIES	AUTHOR	DATE POSTED
[X] - **Classic comedy**	1	johnsmith	Thu 10th August 2006 12.17PM
[X] - **Fave comedy actor/actress**	1	johnsmith	Thu 10th August 2006 12.17PM

FIGURE 5-12
Deleting content is simple.

TIP

In *delete.php*, when deleting a thread, you use $_GET['forum'] to redirect to the forum page after the thread has been deleted. Don't worry too much about validating this variable; it does not reference data going into the database and is merely used for displaying a page. If you are still concerned, however, and to be doubly safe against SQL injection attacks, validate the variable.

Summary

With another project completed, many essential topics have been worked on and refined when building your forums. Every project you work on will provide a range of specific challenges that will further your knowledge and experience with PHP and MySQL, and the projects in this book have been chosen to explore these skills.

In addition to learning new topics, the repetition of existing skills furthers your understanding of these skills. As an example, each time you issue a SQL query, you are cementing your knowledge of this element of PHP more and more. Before you know it, you will no longer need to refer to the book or existing code to connect to MySQL—you will be able to do it automatically.

Without further ado, it's time for the next project.

CHAPTER 6

Creating a Shopping Cart

For many developers, the humble shopping cart holds a special place in their hearts. Although PHP and MySQL are the fodder for a range of Web applications, many developers learned their trade with the ambition to write the ubiquitous shopping cart. If there is a Zen to Web development, it is likely to be experienced while writing a shopping cart.

Although a common sight on the Web, shopping carts do come in a variety of different flavors. The various incarnations typically differ in ways that are specific to the type of business using the software. For example, the sale of items such as books, CDs, and DVDs differs from the sale of cables, food, building materials, and janitorial products. The core difference is quantity; you generally buy only a single book or DVD at time, but it is not uncommon for a restaurant to buy 10 packs of dinner rolls.

PROJECT OVERVIEW

In this project, you create the core features of a shopping cart. To get a clear idea of how the project works, take a look at the following use case:

> John needs to buy some teabags for his mobile café. He goes to a popular online shop that was created by an owner of this very book. John does not have a user account on the Web site but starts shopping anyway. He clicks the Beverages category and sees the list of teabags. He clicks the Buy link and is taken to another page, where he can choose the quantity. He selects 10 boxes of teabags and adds them to his shopping cart. The page now refreshes, and he sees the contents of his shopping cart. John then buys coffee, and his cart is updated again. John realizes he does not need the coffee after all, so he clicks the X link to delete the coffee from his cart. John finishes choosing items and clicks the Go to the Checkout link. He is prompted for his address, which he fills in, and is taken to the payment screen. John can choose to pay with PayPal or by check. John clicks the PayPal button and taken to the PayPal payment screen at paypal.com, where he pays for the order.
>
> Pauline needs some teabags, too. Pauline already has an account on the site, so she logs in. She adds the items she needs to her cart and clicks the Go to the Checkout link. At the address page, she can choose between a new address and the address stored with her user account. She chooses the account address and is taken to the payment screen. Pauline chooses to pay by check and is given instructions about where to send the check and to whom to make it payable.
>
> Ken runs the Web site and wants to see all current orders. He logs in with his administrator username and password and is provided with a list of orders. Ken looks at each item, packages the order, and writes the address on the parcel. To confirm the completion of the order, Ken clicks the Confirm Payment link. The order is now complete.

The shopping cart you build in this chapter satisfies all of the features discussed in the preceding use case, but there is still a huge scope for development. Shopping carts can become huge and complex systems, and an entire book would do the subject of building shopping carts justice. This project will provide a solid foundation in which you can continue to build in extra features.

BUILDING THE DATABASE

The database you will create is shown in Figure 6-1.

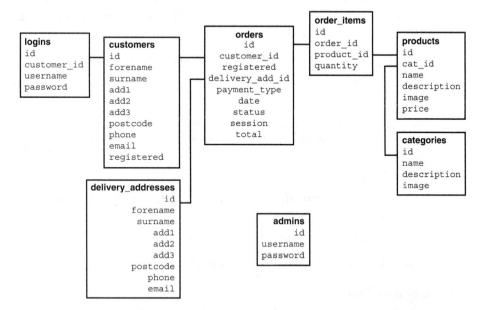

FIGURE 6-1 The database schema revolves around the main *orders* table.

This entire project fundamentally hinges on orders stored in the *orders* table. This table relates to the *customers* (contains registered customer address details) and *delivery_addresses* (contains unregistered and alternative addresses) tables. Each product (stored in the *products* table) in the order is stored in the *order_items* table. Other tables include *logins* (stores the registered user's login details), *categories* (contains the categories that the products are part of), and *admins* (stores administrator login details).

Implementing the Database

Start phpMyAdmin, create a new database called *shoppingcart*, and add the following tables:

NOTE

Always Know Your Status

In the *orders* table is a field called *status*. The purpose of this field is to indicate at what point in the shopping cart the user has progressed. This field has four possible values:

0   The user is still adding items to her shopping cart.

1   The user has entered her address.

2   The user has paid for the item.

10   The administrator has confirmed the transaction and sent the item.

The *admins* Table

- id. Make this a TINYINT (lots of users are possible) and turn on auto_increment. Set this field as a primary key.
- username. Make this a VARCHAR with a length of 10.
- password. Make this a VARCHAR with a length of 10.

The *categories* Table

- id. Make this a TINYINT (there will be few categories) and turn on auto_increment in the Extras column. Make this field a primary key.
- name. Make this a VARCHAR and set the size to 20. (It is unlikely a category title will be longer than 20 letters.)

The *customers* Table

- id. Make this an INT (lots of users are possible) and turn on auto_increment. Set this field as a primary key.
- forename. Make this a VARCHAR with a length of 50.
- surname. Make this a VARCHAR with a length of 50.
- add1. Make this a VARCHAR with a length of 50.
- add2. Make this a VARCHAR with a length of 50.
- add3. Make this a VARCHAR with a length of 50.
- postcode. Make this a VARCHAR with a length of 10.
- phone. Make this a VARCHAR with a length of 20.
- email. Make this a VARCHAR with a length of 100.
- registered. Make this a TINYINT.

The *delivery_addresses* Table

- id. Make this an INT (lots of users are possible) and turn on auto_increment. Set this field as a primary key.
- forename. Make this a VARCHAR with a length of 50.
- surname. Make this a VARCHAR with a length of 50.
- add1. Make this a VARCHAR with a length of 50.
- add2. Make this a VARCHAR with a length of 50.
- add3. Make this a VARCHAR with a length of 50.
- postcode. Make this a VARCHAR with a length of 10.
- phone. Make this a VARCHAR with a length of 20.
- email. Make this a VARCHAR with a length of 100.

The *logins Table*

- id. Make this an INT (lots of users are possible) and turn on auto_increment. Set this field as a primary key.
- customer_id. Make this an INT.
- username. Make this a VARCHAR with a length of 10.
- password. Make this a VARCHAR with a length of 10.

The *orderitems* Table

- id. Make this an INT (lots of items are possible) and turn on auto_increment. Set this field as a primary key.
- order_id. Make this an INT.
- product_id. Make this an INT.
- quantity. Make this an INT.

The *orders Table*

- id. Make this an INT (lots of orders are possible) and turn on auto_increment. Set this field as a primary key.
- customer_id. Make this an INT.
- registered. Make this an INT.
- delivery_add_id. Make this an INT.
- payment_type. Make this an INT.

- date. Make this a DATETIME.
- status. Make this a TINYINT.
- session. Make this a VARCHAR and set the size to 50.
- total. Make this a FLOAT.

The *products* Table

- id. Make this an INT (lots of images are possible) and turn on auto_increment. Set this field as a primary key.
- cat_id. Make this a TINYINT.
- name. Make this a VARCHAR with a length of 100. It is likely there will be long product names.
- description. Make this a TEXT.
- image. Make this a VARCHAR and set the size to 30.
- price. Make this a FLOAT.

Insert Sample Data

With a solid set of tables ready to go, add some sample data to get started. Remember, do not fill in a number in the id column; this is handled by auto_increment. Feel free to add your own sample data, or use the suggested information.

Sample Data for the *admins* Table

Create a username and password for the administrator. This example uses jono as the username and bacon as the password.

Sample Data for the *categories* Table

Add two categories: beverages and cakes.

Sample Data for the *customers* Table

Add the following customers, as shown in Table 6-1.

TABLE 6-1 The customers and logins tables store details about registered users.

FORENAME	SURNAME	ADD1	ADD2	ADD3	POSTAL CODE	PHONE	EMAIL	REGISTERED
Craig	Tucker	19, The Grove	Ziggy Road	Smalltown	T3 TR4	01234 567890	craig@ hissite.com	1
Lee	Jordan	19, Oak Street	Booth Road	Thistown	T1 FG3	01234 098765	lee@lee-tastic.com	1

Sample Data for the *logins* Table

Add the login details from Table 6-2 for each customer.

TABLE 6-2 Make sure you match the customer_id field to the id field in the customers table.

CUSTOMER_ID	USERNAME	PASSWORD
1	Craig	Tucker
2	Lee	Jordan

Sample Data for the *delivery_addresses* Table

Leave this table empty.

Sample Data for the *products* Table

Add the products shown in Table 6-3 to the *products* table.

TABLE 6-3 The image field contains the name of an image if it exists.

CAT_ID	NAME	DESCRIPTION	IMAGE	PRICE
1	Best Bags	A quality pack of tea bags. 200 bags in each box.	<empty>	2.99
1	Best Orange Juice	One gallon of quality squeezed orange juice.	bestorange-juice.jpg	0.90

Sample Data for the *orders* Table

Leave this table empty.

Sample Data for the *orderitems* Table

Leave this table empty.

STARTING TO CODE

One of the challenges in creating a shopping cart is dealing with both registered and unregistered users. For registered users, there is no problem because, when adding information to the tables, you can use their IDs to track them. The challenge arises with unregistered users. How do you track them?

The solution is to use session IDs. When the user loads the first page with the session_start() function, a special session ID is generated. This ID is unique to that specific user and tracks which session variables are assigned to which user visiting the site. Although you have not referred to the session ID before, in this project you will use the session ID extensively.

Every time a user visits the shopping cart and adds his first item, an order is added to the *orders* table. For registered users, the user's id is added to the customer_id field in the table. For unregistered users, the unique session id is added to the session field. When this order has been added to the table, a session variable called SESS_ORDERNUM is created with the id of the order. SESS_ORDERNUM can now be used to track the order's progress throughout the site.

To get started, build the usual configuration file that stores generic information about the site. Create a new directory called *shoppingcart* and add the code shown in Example 6-1 to *config.php*.

EXAMPLE 6-1 The configuration file is similar to the other projects in the book.

```php
<?php

$dbhost = "localhost";
$dbuser = "root";
$dbpassword = "";
$dbdatabase = "shoppingcart";

$config_basedir = "http://localhost/sites/shoppingcart/";

$config_sitename = "BidTastic Aucions";

?>
```

To make life easier when dealing with redirects, create a file called *db.php* that contains just the database connection details, as shown in Example 6-2.

EXAMPLE 6-2 The db.php file will be included when you need a database connection but don't want to include header.php because of a redirect.

```php
<?php

    require("config.php");

    $db = mysql_connect($dbhost, $dbuser, $dbpassword);
    mysql_select_db($dbdatabase, $db);
?>
```

Create *header.php* as shown in Example 6-3.

EXAMPLE 6-3 The header file adds the menu options, includes the sidebar, and adds some login/logout links.

```php
<?php

    session_start();
    if(isset($_SESSION['SESS_CHANGEID']) == TRUE)
    {
        session_unset();
        session_regenerate_id();
    }
    require("config.php");

    $db = mysql_connect($dbhost, $dbuser, $dbpassword);
    mysql_select_db($dbdatabase, $db);

?>
<!DOCTYPE HTML PUBLIC "-//W3C//DTD HTML 4.01 Transitional//EN"
"http://www.w3.org/TR/html4/loose.dtd">
<head>
    <title><?php echo $config_sitename; ?></title>
    <link href="../stylesheet.css" rel="stylesheet">
</head>
<body>
    <div id="header">
    <h1><?php echo $config_sitename; ?></h1>
    </div>
    <div id="menu">
        <a href="<?php echo $config_basedir; ?>">Home</a> -
        <a href="<?php echo $config_basedir;
 ?>showcart.php">View Basket/Checkout</a>
    </div>
    <div id="container">
        <div id="bar">
            <?php

            require("bar.php");
            echo "<hr>";

            if(isset($_SESSION['SESS_LOGGEDIN']) == TRUE)
            {
                echo "Logged in as <strong>" . $_SESSION['SESS_USERNAME']
. "</strong>
 [<a href='" . $config_basedir
 . "logout.php'>logout</a>]";
            }
            else
            {
```

continues

EXAMPLE 6-3 Continued

```
            echo "<a href='"
. $config_basedir . "login.php'>Login</a>";
        }
    ?>

</div>

<div id="main">
```

Take a moment to review the following interesting points about *header.php*:

- At the top of the file, a check is made for a session variable called SESS_CHANGEID. If it exists, the session is unset (deleted) and the session id is regenerated. Later, when the order is complete, SESS_CHANGEID is created when the session system should be reset.

- A check is made to see if the SESS_LOGGEDIN variable exists. If it does, it indicates the user is currently logged in, and his username and a Logout link are displayed. The username is stored in SESS_USERNAME; this variable is created in *login.php*, which is covered later.

- The same *stylesheet.css* file from the previous projects in the book is used here.

A file called *bar.php* is also included in the header file. This file contains the list of categories shown in Example 6-4.

EXAMPLE 6-4 Although the code in bar.php could have been added to header.php, you can use this file to cleanly add other content if needed.

```
<h1>Product Categories</h1>
<ul>
<?php

    $catsql = "SELECT * FROM categories;";
    $catres = mysql_query($catsql);

    while($catrow = mysql_fetch_assoc($catres))
    {
        echo "<li><a href='" . $config_basedir
. "/products.php?id=" . $catrow['id'] . "'>"
. $catrow['name'] . "</a></li>";
    }
?>
</ul>
```

The code in *bar.php* performs a SELECT query to gather all the categories and display them in an unordered list. Each category links to products.php, which is created later.

Create *footer.php* and add the code shown in Example 6-5.

EXAMPLE 6-5 The footer file adds admin links when the administrator is logged in.

```php
<?php
    echo "<p><i>All content on this site is &copy; "
 . $config_sitename . "</i></p>";

    if($_SESSION['SESS_ADMINLOGGEDIN'] == 1)
    {
        echo "[<a href='" . $config_basedir . "adminorders.php'>admin</a>]
[<a href='"
 . $config_basedir
 . "adminlogout.php'>admin logout</a>]";
    }
?>

</div>
    </div>
</body>
</html>
```

Create the main *index.php* for site, using the code shown in Example 6-6.

EXAMPLE 6-6 It may come as a surprise to see such a minimal index.php file. This file is really intended for generic information about the store.

```php
<?php
    require("header.php");
?>
    <h1>Welcome!!</h1>
    Welcome to the <strong>
<?php echo $config_sitename; ?></strong> website.
 Click on one of the pages to explore the site.
 We have a wide range of different products
 available.

<?php

  require("footer.php");
?>
```

With the main design complete, your browser should display something similar to Figure 6-2.

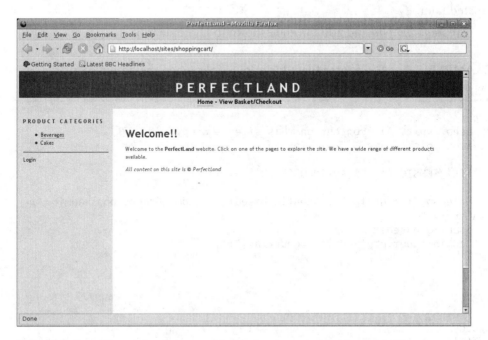

FIGURE 6-2 The main page provides a simple and clean interface for the shopping cart.

MANAGING USER LOGINS

Users are a critical element in a shopping cart, and tracking both registered and unregistered users is important. Many of the different scripts that form the site have two strands of functionality: one if the user is logged in and one if not.

The login page is similar to the others in the book. Create a file called *login.php* and add the form:

```
<form action="<?php echo $SCRIPT_NAME; ?>" method="POST">
<table>
    <tr>
        <td>Username</td>
        <td><input type="textbox" name="userBox"></td>
    </tr>
    <tr>
        <td>Password</td>
        <td><input type="password" name="passBox"></td>
    </tr>
    <tr>
        <td></td>
        <td><input type="submit" name="submit" value="Log in">
```

```
    </tr>
  </table>
  </form>
```

Move to the start of the file and begin adding the code:

```php
<?php
  session_start();
  require("db.php");

  if(isset($_SESSION['SESS_LOGGEDIN']) == TRUE) {
     header("Location: " . $config_basedir);
  }
```

A check is made to see if the user is already logged in. If so, there is no point in loading the login page, so the page redirects to the base URL of the site.

Process the form:

```php
  if(isset($_SESSION['SESS_LOGGEDIN']) == TRUE) {
     header("Location: " . $config_basedir);
  }

  if($_POST['submit'])
  {
     $loginsql = "SELECT * FROM logins
WHERE username = '" . $_POST['userBox']
. "' AND password = '" . $_POST['passBox']
. "'";
     $loginres = mysql_query($loginsql);
     $numrows = mysql_num_rows($loginres);

     if($numrows == 1)
     {
        $loginrow = mysql_fetch_assoc($loginres);

        session_register("SESS_LOGGEDIN");
        session_register("SESS_USERNAME");
        session_register("SESS_USERID");

        $_SESSION['SESS_LOGGEDIN'] = 1;
        $_SESSION['SESS_USERNAME'] = $loginrow['username'];
        $_SESSION['SESS_USERID'] = $loginrow['id'];

        $ordersql = "SELECT id FROM orders
WHERE customer_id = " . $_SESSION['SESS_USERID']
. " AND status < 2";
        $orderres = mysql_query($ordersql);
        $orderrow = mysql_fetch_assoc($orderres);

        session_register("SESS_ORDERNUM");
        $_SESSION['SESS_ORDERNUM'] = $orderrow['id'];
```

```
        header("Location: " . $config_basedir);
    }
    else
    {
        header("Location: http://" . $HTTP_HOST
. $SCRIPT_NAME . "?error=1");
    }
}
```

This code uses the same technique shown earlier for logging in a user. When a successful login occurs, three session variables are created:

- SESS_LOGGEDIN. Set to 1 to indicate the user is currently logged in.
- SESS_USERNAME. Contains the username of the user.
- SESS_USERID. Contains the id of the user.

In addition to these variables, a SELECT statement pulls the id from the *orders* table, in which the customer_id field matches the id of the current user. Another session variable called SESS_ORDERNUM is then set to the id returned from this query. This process can have one of two outcomes:

- No order exists. If no order exists in the *orders* table, SESS_ORDERNUM is not set to anything.
- An order exists. If an id is returned from the query, SESS_ORDERNUM is set to this id. This is useful if the user was selecting items for the shopping cart and then logged out. When the user logs in again, the shopping cart contains the same items from the previous visit and the user can continue to select items. This functionality provides some important continuity.

When the form is successfully submitted and the session variables are set, the page redirects to the base URL of the site. The page will display the text *Logged in as <foo>* in the sidebar.

Add the rest of the code:

```
        header("Location: http://" . $HTTP_HOST
. $SCRIPT_NAME . "?error=1");
    }
}

else
{
    require("header.php");
?>
    <h1>Customer Login</h1>
    Please enter your username and password to
log into the websites. If you do not
```

```
have an account, you can get one for free by <a
href="register.php">registering</a>.
<p>

<?php
   if($_GET['error']) {
       echo "<strong>Incorrect username/password</strong>";
   }
?>

<form action="<?php echo $SCRIPT_NAME; ?>" method="POST">
<table>
```

Finally, add the code after the form:

```
</table>
</form>

<?php
   }

   require("footer.php");
?>
```

The completed results should look similar to the page shown in Figure 6-3.

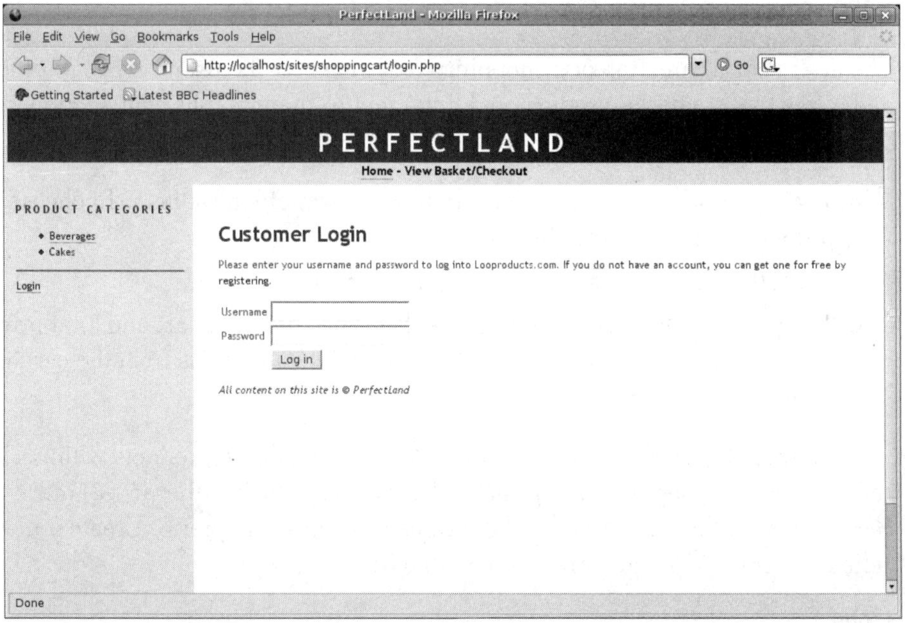

FIGURE 6-3 The completed login screen

Logging Out Users

The process of logging out a user is a little different from some of the earlier projects in the book. Instead of destroying the entire session with session_destroy(), you instead un-register the user's session variables. You can't run session_destroy() because it destroys the administrator's login session when the administrator is logged in as both a normal user and an admin.

Create *logout.php* and add the code:

```php
<?php

    session_start();

    require("config.php");

    session_unregister("SESS_LOGGEDIN");
    session_unregister("SESS_USERNAME");
    session_unregister("SESS_USERID");

    header("Location: " . $config_basedir);
?>
```

DISPLAYING AND SELECTING PRODUCTS

The most central function of a shopping cart is to show the user a range of products and allow her to choose products, adding them to the metaphorical shopping cart. This involves a few different processes:

- The user clicks a product category to view available products. To choose a product, she clicks the Buy link.
- Next, the user selects the quantity of items.
- The page displays the current contents of the shopping cart and total price. The user can also click the *X* symbols to delete any items from the cart and recalculate the total.

The first step in this process is to display the available products within a category. Before you begin creating the code, you need to use the pf_validate_number() function that you wrote in the forums project in Chapter 5. Create a new file called *functions.php* and copy the code into it:

```php
<?php
function pf_validate_number($value, $function, $redirect) {
    if(isset($value) == TRUE) {
        if(is_numeric($value) == FALSE) {
```

```
            $error = 1;
        }

        if($error == 1) {
            header("Location: " . $redirect);
        }
        else {
            $final = $value;
        }
    }
    else {
        if($function == 'redirect') {
            header("Location: " . $redirect);
        }

        if($function == "value") {
            $final = 0;
        }
    }

    return $final;
}
?>
```

For this project, you should also create some product images, such as those shown in Figure 6-4, for use with your shopping cart. You need to create at least one image, called *dummy.jpg*, that can be loaded when no image exists for a product. If you used the sample data earlier in this chapter, the image for the Best Orange Juice product is called *bestorangejuice.jpg*.

FIGURE 6-4
Each image should be 150×150 in size and saved as a JPG.

Create a new file called *products.php* and start to add the code:

```
<?php
    require("db.php");
    require("functions.php");

    $validid = pf_validate_number($_GET['id'],
  "redirect", $config_basedir);
```

The `pf_validate_number()` function validates the category `id` GET variable that is passed to the page. If no `id` GET variable exists, the function redirects to the site's base URL.

Select the products from the database:

```
$validid = pf_validate_number($_GET['id'],
"redirect", $config_basedir);

require("header.php");

$prodcatsql = "SELECT * FROM products WHERE
cat_id = " . $_GET['id'] . ";";
$prodcatres = mysql_query($prodcatsql);
$numrows = mysql_num_rows($prodcatres);

if($numrows == 0)
{
    echo "<h1>No products</h1>";
    echo "There are no products in this category.";
}
```

If a category has no products, the text *No products* is displayed on the page. (To determine whether a category has projects, check if the number of rows returned is 0.) If a category contains products, a `while()` loop iterates through each row:

```
    echo "There are no products in this category.";
}

else
{

    echo "<table cellpadding='10'>";

    while($prodrow = mysql_fetch_assoc($prodcatres))
    {
        echo "<tr>";
            if(empty($prodrow['image'])) {
                echo "<td><img
src='./productimages/dummy.jpg' alt='"
. $prodrow['name'] . "'></td>";
            }
            else {
                echo "<td><img src='./productimages/" . $prodrow['image']
. "' alt='"
. $prodrow['name'] . "'></td>";
            }

            echo "<td>";
                echo "<h2>" . $prodrow['name'] . "</h2>";
                echo "<p>" . $prodrow['description'];
```

```
            echo "<p><strong>OUR PRICE: &pound;"
  . sprintf('%.2f', $prodrow['price']) . "</strong>";
            echo "<p>[<a href='addtobasket.php?id="
  . $prodrow['id'] . "'>buy</a>]";
         echo "</td>";
       echo "</tr>";
    }

    echo "</table>";
```

The information about each product is displayed, and a Buy link is linked to *addtobasket.php*. The link also passes the id of the product as a GET variable.

Finally, add the closing code:

```
    echo "</table>";

  }
  require("footer.php");
?>
```

Adding the Item to the Cart

The purpose of *addtobasket.php* is to add the selected item to the *orderitems* table and then redirect to a page that summarizes the items in the shopping cart.

The *addtobasket.php* page is quite a large script with lots of nested if statements. This makes it fairly difficult to break down and discuss piece by piece, as has been done with most other scripts. To make this easier to understand, add the entire code to the file. You'll run through it step by step at the end.

Create *addtobasket.php* and add the code:

```
<?php
  session_start();

  require("db.php");
  require("functions.php");

  $validid = pf_validate_number($_GET['id'],
 "redirect", $config_basedir);

  $prodsql = "SELECT * FROM products WHERE id = " . $_GET['id'] . ";";
  $prodres = mysql_query($prodsql);
  $numrows = mysql_num_rows($prodres);
  $prodrow = mysql_fetch_assoc($prodres);

  if($numrows == 0)
  {
```

```
    header("Location: " . $config_basedir);
}
else
{
    if($_POST['submit'])
    {
        if($_SESSION['SESS_ORDERNUM'])
        {
            $itemsql = "INSERT INTO orderitems(order_id,
product_id, quantity) VALUES("
                . $_SESSION['SESS_ORDERNUM'] . ", "
. $_GET['id'] . ", "
                . $_POST['amountBox'] . ")";
            mysql_query($itemsql);
        }
        else
        {
            if($_SESSION['SESS_LOGGEDIN'])
            {
            $sql = "INSERT INTO orders(customer_id,
registered, date) VALUES("
                    . $_SESSION['SESS_USERID'] . ", 1, NOW())";
            mysql_query($sql);
            session_register("SESS_ORDERNUM");
            $_SESSION['SESS_ORDERNUM'] = mysql_insert_id();

            $itemsql = "INSERT INTO
orderitems(order_id, product_id, quantity) VALUES("
                    . $_SESSION['SESS_ORDERNUM']
. ", " . $_GET['id'] . ", "
                    . $_POST['amountBox'] . ")";

            mysql_query($itemsql);
            }
            else
            {
            $sql = "INSERT INTO orders(registered,
date, session) VALUES("
                    . "0, NOW(), '" . session_id() . "')";
            mysql_query($sql);
            session_register("SESS_ORDERNUM");
            $_SESSION['SESS_ORDERNUM'] = mysql_insert_id();

            $itemsql = "INSERT INTO
orderitems(order_id, product_id, quantity) VALUES("
                . $_SESSION['SESS_ORDERNUM'] . ", " . $_GET['id'] . ", "
                . $_POST['amountBox'] . ")";
```

```
            mysql_query($itemsql);
        }
    }


        $totalprice = $prodrow['price'] * $_POST['amountBox'] ;

        $updsql = "UPDATE orders SET total = total + "
. $totalprice . " WHERE id = "
. $_SESSION['SESS_ORDERNUM'] . ";";
        mysql_query($updres);

        header("Location: " . $config_basedir . "showcart.php");
    }
    else
    {
        require("header.php");

        echo "<form action='addtobasket.php?id="
. $_GET['id'] . "' method='POST'>";
        echo "<table cellpadding='10'>";


        echo "<tr>";
            if(empty($prodrow['image'])) {
                echo "<td><img
src='./productimages/dummy.jpg' width='50' alt='"
. $prodrow['name'] . "'></td>";
            }
            else {
                echo "<td>
<img src='./productimages/" . $prodrow['image']
. "' width='50' alt='" . $prodrow['name']
. "'></td>";
            }

        echo "<td>" . $prodrow['name'] . "</td>";
        echo "<td>Select Quantity <select name='amountBox'>";

        for($i=1;$i<=100;$i++)
        {
            echo "<option>" . $i . "</option>";
        }

        echo "</select></td>";
        echo "<td><strong>&pound;"
. sprintf('%.2f', $prodrow['price'])
```

```
        . "</strong></td>";
                echo "<td><input type='submit'
name='submit' value='Add to basket'></td>";
            echo "</tr>";

            echo "</table>";
            echo "</form>";
        }
    }

    require("footer.php");
?>
```

To best explain this code, review the following bulleted points to see what happens. As you read each bullet, reference the code you typed into your editor. All set? Here goes...

- At the top of the page, a query returns the product with the id GET variable. If no rows are returned, the page redirects to the site's base URL.

- The form is displayed and includes a drop-down select box that uses a for loop to provide options from 1 to 100. In addition to the form, some product information is displayed.

- When the user submits the form, the page is reloaded and a check is made to see if a SESS_ORDERNUM variable exists. If it does, this means an order is already open and an INSERT statement adds the product id and quantity to the *orderitems* table, in which the order_id is SESS_ORDERNUM.

- If no SESS_ORDERNUM exists, an order must be created in the *orders* table before you can add the item to the *orderitems* table. A check is then made to see if the SESS_LOGGEDIN session variable exists. If it does, the user is already logged in and an order is created before the item is added to the *orderitems* table. If SESS_LOGGEDIN does not exist, the user is not currently logged in (they possibly don't have a user account). As such, an order is created in the *orders* table (using session_id() to get the unique session id) and then the item is added to the *orderitems* table.

- The total field in the *orders* table is updated. This is performed by calculating the price multiplied by the quantity (the result is stored in $totalprice).

- Finally, the page redirects to the cart summary page on *showcart.php*.

Before you click the Submit button, make sure your page looks similar to the one shown in Figure 6-5.

FIGURE 6-5 The completed Add To Basket script

Displaying the Basket Summary

When the *addtobasket.php* script has finished processing, the page redirects to *showcart.php*. This page provides a summary of the items added to the shopping cart.

Occasionally, you might need to display a summary of the items. To prevent duplication of code, a function called `showcart()` has been created to display the summary. Before you look at the function, create a new file called *showcart.php* and add the following code, which uses the `showcart()`function:

```php
<?php
    session_start();

    require("header.php");
    require("functions.php");

    echo "<h1>Your shopping cart</h1>";
    showcart();

    if(isset($_SESSION['SESS_ORDERNUM']) == TRUE) {
        $sql = "SELECT * FROM orderitems WHERE
 order_id = " . $_SESSION['SESS_ORDERNUM'] . ";";
        $result = mysql_query($sql);
        $numrows = mysql_num_rows($result);

        if($numrows >= 1) {
            echo "<h2><a href='checkout-address.php'>
 Go to the checkout</a></h2>";
        }
    }

    require("footer.php");
?>
```

The showcart() function does not include a link to the checkout, because not every page needs one. The block of code after the function call checks if an order number is available and if so, a check is made to see if the cart contains any items. If the cart contains one or more items, the checkout link is displayed.

Add the showcart() code to *functions.php*:

```
function showcart()
{

   if($_SESSION['SESS_ORDERNUM'])
   {
      if($_SESSION['SESS_LOGGEDIN'])
      {
         $custsql = "SELECT id, status from
orders WHERE customer_id = "
. $_SESSION['SESS_USERID']
. " AND status < 2;";
         $custres = mysql_query($custsql);
         $custrow = mysql_fetch_assoc($custres);
```

The outer if check in the function determines if an order number exists. If it does, a second if checks if the user is logged in. If this is the case, the query selects the row from the *orders* table that has the user id for the user and in which the status is 0 or 1. The query should return a single row only.

The main query to grab the item details is now ready to run:

```
         $custrow = mysql_fetch_assoc($custres);

         $itemssql = "SELECT products.*, orderitems.*, orderitems.id AS
itemid FROM products, orderitems WHERE orderitems.product_id =
products.id AND order_id = " . $custrow['id'];
         $itemsres = mysql_query($itemssql);
         $itemnumrows = mysql_num_rows($itemsres);
      }
```

If no user is logged in, a similar SELECT query is made to get the order number, but the match is made on the current session id. After this query, the list of items is returned:

```
         $itemnumrows = mysql_num_rows($itemsres);
      }


      else
      {
         $custsql = "SELECT id, status from orders
WHERE session = '" . session_id()
```

```
            . "' AND status < 2;";
        $custres = mysql_query($custsql);
        $custrow = mysql_fetch_assoc($custres);

        $itemssql = "SELECT products.*,
orderitems.*, orderitems.id AS itemid
FROM products, orderitems WHERE
orderitems.product_id = products.id AND
order_id = " . $custrow['id'];
        $itemsres = mysql_query($itemssql);
        $itemnumrows = mysql_num_rows($itemsres);
```

If no SESS_ORDERNUM variable is available, the $itemnumrows variable is set to 0:

```
        $itemnumrows = mysql_num_rows($itemsres);

    }
}
else
{
    $itemnumrows = 0;
}
```

This code checks $itemnumrows to see what value it contains. If the value is 0, a message displays to indicate the cart is empty:

```
        $itemnumrows = 0;
}

if($itemnumrows == 0)
{
    echo "You have not added anything to your shopping cart yet.";
}
```

If $itemnumrows has a value, the items are displayed:

```
    echo "You have not added anything to your shopping cart yet.";
}

else
{
    echo "<table cellpadding='10'>";
    echo "<tr>";
        echo "<td></td>";
        echo "<td><strong>Item</strong></td>";
        echo "<td><strong>Quantity</strong></td>";
        echo "<td><strong>Unit Price</strong></td>";
        echo "<td><strong>Total Price</strong></td>";
        echo "<td></td>";
    echo "</tr>";
```

```php
    while($itemsrow = mysql_fetch_assoc($itemsres))
    {
        $quantitytotal =
$itemsrow['price'] * $itemsrow['quantity'];
    echo "<tr>";

        if(empty($itemsrow['image'])) {
            echo "<td><img
src='./productimages/dummy.jpg' width='50' alt='"
. $itemsrow['name'] . "'></td>";
        }
        else {
            echo "<td><img src='./productimages/" .
$itemsrow['image'] . "' width='50' alt='"
. $itemsrow['name'] . "'></td>";
        }

        echo "<td>" . $itemsrow['name'] . "</td>";
        echo "<td>" . $itemsrow['quantity'] . "</td>";
        echo "<td><strong>&pound;"
. sprintf('%.2f', $itemsrow['price'])
. "</strong></td>";
        echo "<td><strong>&pound;"
. sprintf('%.2f', $quantitytotal) . "</strong></td>";
        echo "<td>[<a href='"
. $config_basedir . "delete.php?id="
. $itemsrow['itemid'] . "'>X</a>]</td>";
        echo "</tr>";

    $total = $total + $quantitytotal;
    $totalsql = "UPDATE orders SET total = "
. $total . " WHERE id = "
. $_SESSION['SESS_ORDERNUM'];
        $totalres = mysql_query($totalsql);
    }

    echo "<tr>";
        echo "<td></td>";
        echo "<td></td>";
        echo "<td></td>";
        echo "<td>TOTAL</td>";
        echo "<td><strong>&pound;"
. sprintf('%.2f', $total) . "</strong></td>";
        echo "<td></td>";
    echo "</tr>";

    echo "</table>";

    echo "<p><a href='checkout-address.php'>Go to the checkout</a></p>";


    }
}
```

Deleting Items

The showcart() function contains a link to *delete.php*, in which you can remove an item from the shopping cart. By clicking the link, the item is removed from the *orderitems* table, and the total price in the *orders* table is updated.

Create *delete.php* and begin adding the code:

```php
<?php

    require("config.php");
    require("db.php");
    require("functions.php");

    $validid = pf_validate_number($_GET['id'],
 "redirect", $config_basedir . "showcart.php");

    $itemsql = "SELECT * FROM orderitems WHERE id = "
 . $_GET['id'] . ";";
    $itemres = mysql_query($itemsql);
    $numrows = mysql_num_rows($itemres);

    if($numrows == 0) {
        header("Location: " . $config_basedir . "showcart.php");
    }

    $itemrow = mysql_fetch_assoc($itemres);
```

In this code, the query pulls the item from the *orderitems* table, and the number of rows returned is checked. This check prevents someone modifying the URL and adding delete.php?id=73 if there is no item with an id of 73. If no rows are returned, a header redirect jumps to *showcart.php*. If a row is returned, the script continues:

```php
    $itemrow = mysql_fetch_assoc($itemres);

    $prodsql = "SELECT price FROM products
 WHERE id = " . $itemrow['product_id'] . ";";
    $prodres = mysql_query($prodsql);
    $prodrow = mysql_fetch_assoc($prodres);

    $sql = "DELETE FROM orderitems WHERE id = " . $_GET['id'];
    mysql_query($sql);
```

In this block, the price of the product is selected first and then a separate query removes the item from *orderitems*.

Update the *orders* table with the new total price:

```
mysql_query($sql);

$totalprice = $prodrow['price'] * $itemrow['quantity'] ;

$updsql = "UPDATE orders SET total = total - "
. $totalprice . " WHERE id = "
. $_SESSION['SESS_ORDERNUM'] . ";";
mysql_query($updres);

header("Location: " . $config_basedir . "/showcart.php");

?>
```

With the cart summary function and pages complete, your browser should show something similar to the page shown in Figure 6-6.

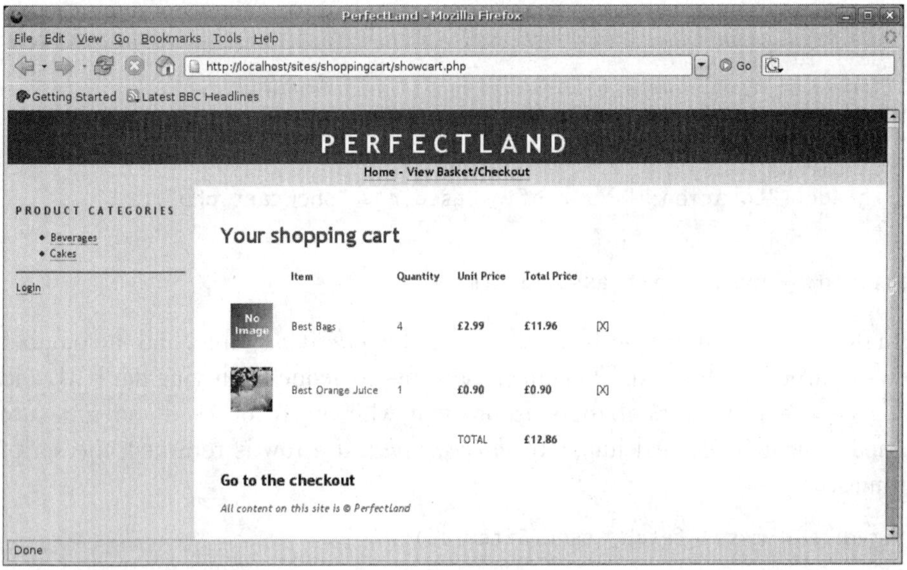

FIGURE 6-6 The shopping cart summary displays a current list of items and the ability to remove them.

CHECKING IT OUT

After the user has finished adding items to his shopping cart, the checkout process can begin. This process involves two steps:

- Prompt the user for a delivery address. If the user is already logged in, he should be asked if he wants to use the address he registered or use a different address. All addresses should be validated.

- Prompt the user to choose a payment method, either PayPal or a check.

Create *checkout-address.php* and add the form:

```
require("header.php");
echo "<h1>Add a delivery address</h1>";

if(isset($_GET['error']) == TRUE) {
    echo "<strong>Please fill in the missing
information from the form</strong>";
}

echo "<form action='" . $SCRIPT_NAME . "' method='POST'>";

if($_SESSION['SESS_LOGGEDIN'])
{
?>
<input type="radio" name="addselecBox"
value="1" checked>Use the address from my
account</input><br>
<input type="radio" name="addselecBox"
value="2">Use the address below:</input>

<?php
}

?>
    <table>
    <tr>
       <td>Forename</td>
       <td><input type="text" name="forenameBox"></td>
    </tr>
    <tr>
       <td>Surname</td>
       <td><input type="text" name="surnameBox"></td>
    </tr>
    <tr>
       <td>House Number, Street</td>
       <td><input type="text" name="add1Box"></td>
    </tr>
    <tr>
       <td>Town/City</td>
       <td><input type="text" name="add2Box"></td>
    </tr>
    <tr>
       <td>County</td>
       <td><input type="text" name="add3Box"></td>
    </tr>
    <tr>
       <td>Postcode</td>
       <td><input type="text" name="postcodeBox"></td>
    </tr>
    <tr>
       <td>Phone</td>
       <td><input type="text" name="phoneBox"></td>
```

```
      </tr>
      <tr>
         <td>Email</td>
         <td><input type="text" name="emailBox"></td>
      </tr>
      <tr>
         <td></td>
         <td><input type="submit" name="submit"
 value="Add Address (press only once)"></td>
      </tr>
      </table>
   </form>
```

Before the form is displayed, an if checks if an error GET variable exists. If it does, an error message is displayed. The script then checks if the user is logged in, and if so, two radio buttons are added so that the user can choose between the address he registered and a different address.

Move to the start of the file and add the following code:

```
<?php
   session_start();
   require("db.php");

   $statussql = "SELECT status FROM orders WHERE id = " .
$_SESSION['SESS_ORDERNUM'];
   $statusres = mysql_query($statussql);
   $statusrow = mysql_fetch_assoc($statusres);
   $status = $statusrow['status'];
```

The first step is to determine the current status of the order. If the user has already been through the address stage of the checkout process, redirect the page to the payment screen. Obtain the status by searching for a record in the *orders* table that matches SESS_ORDERNUM. Then, set the $status variable to the correct status.

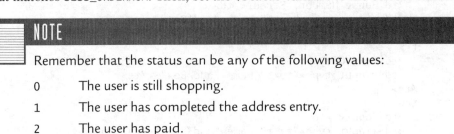

NOTE

Remember that the status can be any of the following values:

0	The user is still shopping.
1	The user has completed the address entry.
2	The user has paid.
10	The administrator has confirmed the order.

If the status is set to 1, the user has already entered an address and the page redirects to the payment screen. If the status is 2 or higher, the order has been completed. Redirect the page to the base URL of the site:

```
$status = $statusrow['status'];

    if($status == 1) {
        header("Location: " . $config_basedir . "checkout-pay.php");
    }

    if($status >= 2) {
        header("Location: " . $config_basedir);
    }
```

Begin processing the form:

```
    if($status >= 2) {
        header("Location: " . $config_basedir);
    }

if($_POST['submit'])
{
    if($_SESSION['SESS_LOGGEDIN'])
    {
        if($_POST['addselecBox'] == 2)
        {
            if(empty($_POST['forenameBox']) ||
                empty($_POST['surnameBox']) ||
                empty($_POST['add1Box']) ||
                empty($_POST['add2Box']) ||
                empty($_POST['add3Box']) ||
                empty($_POST['postcodeBox']) ||
                empty($_POST['phoneBox']) ||
                empty($_POST['emailBox']))
            {
                header("Location: " . $basedir . "checkout-
address.php?error=1");
                exit;
            }
```

The first nested if checks if the user is logged in. A check is then made to see if the user selected the second radio button (Use the address below). If so, the form fields are checked to see if they are empty. If they are, the page is reloaded with the error GET variable so that the error message can be displayed.

If the form is not empty, add the address to the *delivery_addresses* table and update the *orders* table:

```
                exit;
        }

        $addsql = "INSERT INTO
delivery_addresses(forename, surname, add1,
add2, add3, postcode, phone, email)
```

```
                          VALUES('"
                    . strip_tags(addslashes(
$_POST['forenameBox'])) . "', '"
                    . strip_tags(addslashes(
$_POST['surnameBox'])) . "', '"
                    . strip_tags(addslashes(
$_POST['add1Box'])) . "', '"
                    . strip_tags(addslashes(
$_POST['add2Box'])) . "', '"
                    . strip_tags(addslashes(
$_POST['add3Box'])) . "', '"
                    . strip_tags(addslashes(
$_POST['postcodeBox'])) . "', '"
                    . strip_tags(addslashes(
$_POST['phoneBox'])) . "', '"
                    . strip_tags(addslashes(
$_POST['emailBox'])) . "')";

            mysql_query($addsql);

            $setaddsql = "UPDATE orders SET
delivery_add_id = " . mysql_insert_id() . ",
status = 1 WHERE id = "
. $_SESSION['SESS_ORDERNUM'];
            mysql_query($setaddsql);

            header("Location: "
. $config_basedir . "checkout-pay.php");
        }
```

The *delivery_addresses* table contains a list of addresses for unregistered users and registered users who select a different address. When the information is added to the table, the strip_tags() function removes any HTML tags that may have been added, and the addslashes() function escapes any quotes. Finally, the *orders* table is updated with the id of the record from *delivery_addresses*, and the status is changed to 1. When this is complete, the page redirects to *checkout-pay.php*.

If the user is logged in but selects the address on file, the *orders* table is updated also:

```
            header("Location: "
. $config_basedir . "checkout-pay.php");
        }

        else
        {
            $custsql = "UPDATE orders SET
delivery_add_id = 0, status = 1 WHERE id = " .
$_SESSION['SESS_ORDERNUM'];
            mysql_query($custsql);
```

```
            header("Location: " . $config_basedir
 . "checkout-pay.php");
        }
    }
```

If no user is logged in, the form is validated and the address is added to the database:

```
            header("Location: " . $config_basedir
 . "checkout-pay.php");
        }
    }

    else
    {
        if(empty($_POST['forenameBox']) ||
            empty($_POST['surnameBox']) ||
            empty($_POST['add1Box']) ||
            empty($_POST['add2Box']) ||
            empty($_POST['add3Box']) ||
            empty($_POST['postcodeBox']) ||
            empty($_POST['phoneBox']) ||
            empty($_POST['emailBox']))
        {
            header("Location: " . "checkout-address.php?error=1");
            exit;
        }

        $addsql = "INSERT INTO
delivery_addresses(forename, surname, add1,
add2, add3, postcode, phone, email)
                VALUES('"
                . $_POST['forenameBox'] . "', '"
                . $_POST['surnameBox'] . "', '"
                . $_POST['add1Box'] . "', '"
                . $_POST['add2Box'] . "', '"
                . $_POST['add3Box'] . "', '"
                . $_POST['postcodeBox'] . "', '"
                . $_POST['phoneBox'] . "', '"
                . $_POST['emailBox'] . "')";

        mysql_query($addsql);

        $setaddsql = "UPDATE orders
SET delivery_add_id = " . mysql_insert_id()
. ", status = 1 WHERE session = '"
. session_id() . "'";
        mysql_query($setaddsql);

        header("Location: " . $config_basedir . "checkout-pay.php");
    }
}
```

In this block of code, the address is added to the *delivery_addresses* table, and the *orders* table is updated with the *delivery_addresses* id and the status is set to 1.

Begin the form block:

```
        header("Location: " . $config_basedir . "checkout-pay.php");
    }
}

else
{

require("header.php");
echo "<h1>Add a delivery address</h1>";
```

Finally, add the code after the form:

```
    </table>
</form>

<?php
    }
    require("footer.php");
?>
```

With the address code complete, your browser should display a page similar to Figure 6-7—when a user is logged in.

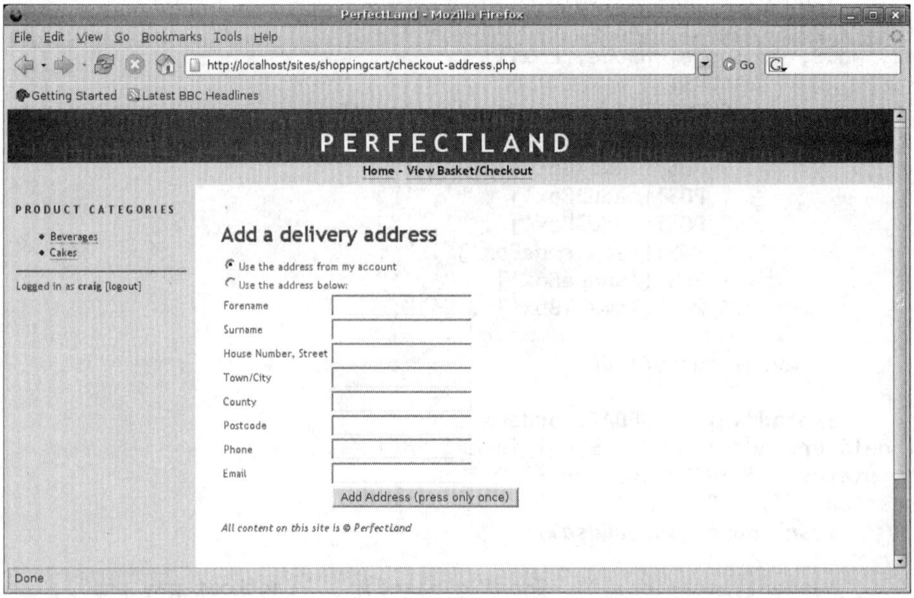

FIGURE 6-7 When the user is logged in, the radio buttons prompt users which address to use.

Paying

The final part of the checkout process is to take payment. Dealing with payments on a Web site can take a variety of different routes: PayPal, NOCHEX, Worldpay, and more. This project offers two payment methods: PayPal and checks. These two methods demonstrate how to deal with automatic (PayPal) and manual (check) purchases.

Create a new file called *checkout-pay.php* and add the form:

```
<h2>Select a payment method</h2>
<form action='checkout-pay.php' method='POST'>
<table cellspacing=10>
<tr>
    <td><h3>PayPal</h3></td>
    <td>
    This site uses PayPal to accept
Switch/Visa/Mastercard cards. No PayPal account
is required - you simply fill in your credit
card details
    and the correct payment will be taken from your account.
    </td>
    <td><input type="submit"
name="paypalsubmit" value="Pay with PayPal"></td>
    </tr>
    <tr>
    <td><h3>Cheque</h3></td>
    <td>
    If you would like to pay by cheque, you
can post the cheque for the final
    amount to the office.
    </td>
    <td><input type="submit"
name="chequesubmit" value="Pay by cheque"></td>
    </tr>
    </table>
    </form>
```

This simple form provides two Submit buttons only—one to pay by PayPal and the other to pay by check. Processing the form involves two main sections—one for PayPal and one for the check.

At the top of the file, begin adding the code:

```
<?php
    session_start();

    require("db.php");
    require("functions.php");
```

If the user clicks the PayPal button, process the order:

```
    require("functions.php");
```

```
if($_POST['paypalsubmit'])
{
    $upsql = "UPDATE orders SET status = 2, payment
_type = 1 WHERE id = " . $_SESSION['SESS_ORDERNUM'];
    $upres = mysql_query($upsql);

    $itemssql = "SELECT total FROM orders WHERE
id = " . $_SESSION['SESS_ORDERNUM'];
    $itemsres = mysql_query($itemssql);
    $row = mysql_fetch_assoc($itemsres);
```

The *orders* table is updated to reflect the completion of the order. The status field is changed to 2 and the payment_type field is set to 1 (PayPal). A query then gets the total price from the order so that the PayPal link can be constructed later.

Reset the order session:

```
$row = mysql_fetch_assoc($itemsres);

if($_SESSION['SESS_LOGGEDIN'])
{
    unset($_SESSION['SESS_ORDERNUM']);
}
else
{
    session_register("SESS_CHANGEID");
    $_SESSION['SESS_CHANGEID'] = 1;
}
```

If the user is logged in, the SESS_ORDERNUM session variable is removed with unset(). If not, a new session variable called SESS_CHANGEID is created. The next time *header.php* is loaded, the code at the top of *header.php* will regenerate the new session and id.

Redirect to www.paypal.com with the payment details:

```
    $_SESSION['SESS_CHANGEID'] = 1;
}

header("Location: https://www.paypal.com/
cgi-bin/webscr?cmd=_xclick&business=
you%40youraddress.com&item_name="
 . urlencode($config_sitename)
 . "+Order&item_number=PROD" . $row['id']
 ."&amount=" . urlencode(sprintf('%.2f',
 $row['total'])) . "&no_note=1&currency_code=GBP&lc=GB&
submit.x=41&submit.y=15");

}
```

On this line, a series of GET variables pass data to the PayPal Web site. These GET variables are reserved words that PayPal can use to process the order. Table 6-4 explains the purpose of each variable.

TABLE 6-4 PayPal variables, explained

PayPal Variable	Setting	Description
business	"you%40youraddress.com&"	The name of the business running the site.
item_name	urlencode($config_site-name) . "+Order"	A small name for the order—in this case, '<sitename> Order'.
item_number	"PROD" . $row['id']	A product code. Here you concatenate 'PROD' and the order number (PROD12, for example).
amount	urlencode(sprintf('%.2f', $row['total']))	The amount of the order.
no_note	1	The no_note variable specifies whether the customer should specify a note with the payment. Setting this to 1 indicates that no note is required.
currency_code	GBP	The currency type for the transaction.
lc	GB	The locale of the transaction.

It is important to remember that any textual information transmitted as a GET variable should be run through urlencode() to escape nonstandard characters.

Start writing the code to process a check payment. The code is similar to the PayPal code.

```
header("Location: https://www.paypal.com/
cgi-bin/webscr?cmd=_xclick&business=you%40
youraddress.com&item_name="
. urlencode($config_sitename)
. "+Order&item_number=PROD" . $row['id']
."&amount=" . urlencode(sprintf('%.2f',
$row['total'])) . "&no_note=1&currency
_code=GBP&lc=GB&submit.x=41&submit.y=15");
```

```
    }
    else if($_POST['chequesubmit'])
    {
        $upsql = "UPDATE orders SET status = 2,
payment_type = 2 WHERE id = "
. $_SESSION['SESS_ORDERNUM'];
        $upres = mysql_query($upsql);
```

Here you again update the orders table, but this time the payment_type is 2 instead of 1.

Reset the order as you did previously:

```
    $upres = mysql_query($upsql);

    if($_SESSION['SESS_LOGGEDIN'])
    {
        unset($_SESSION['SESS_ORDERNUM']);
    }
    else
    {
        session_register("SESS_CHANGEID");
        $_SESSION['SESS_CHANGEID'] = 1;
    }
```

Finally, display the details of where the user should send the check:

```
    $_SESSION['SESS_CHANGEID'] = 1;
    }

    require("header.php");
?>
    <h1>Paying by cheque</h1>
    Please make your cheque payable to
<strong><?php echo $config_sitename; ?></strong>.
    <p>
    Send the cheque to:
    <p>
    <?php echo $config_sitename; ?><br>
    22, This Place,<br>
    This town,<br>
    This county,<br>
    FG43 F3D.<br>
<?php
    }
```

The processing is now complete

Open the block to display the form. Before you reach the form, however, add the showcart() function to summarize the current cart:

```php
<?php
    }

    else
    {
        require("header.php");
        echo "<h1>Payment</h1>";
        showcart();
?>

        <h2>Select a payment method</h2>
        <form action='checkout-pay.php' method='POST'>
```

Finally, add the closing code:

```
        </table>
        </form>
```

```php
<?php
    }

    require("footer.php");
?>
```

Your brand-new, home-grown payment screen should now resemble Figure 6-8.

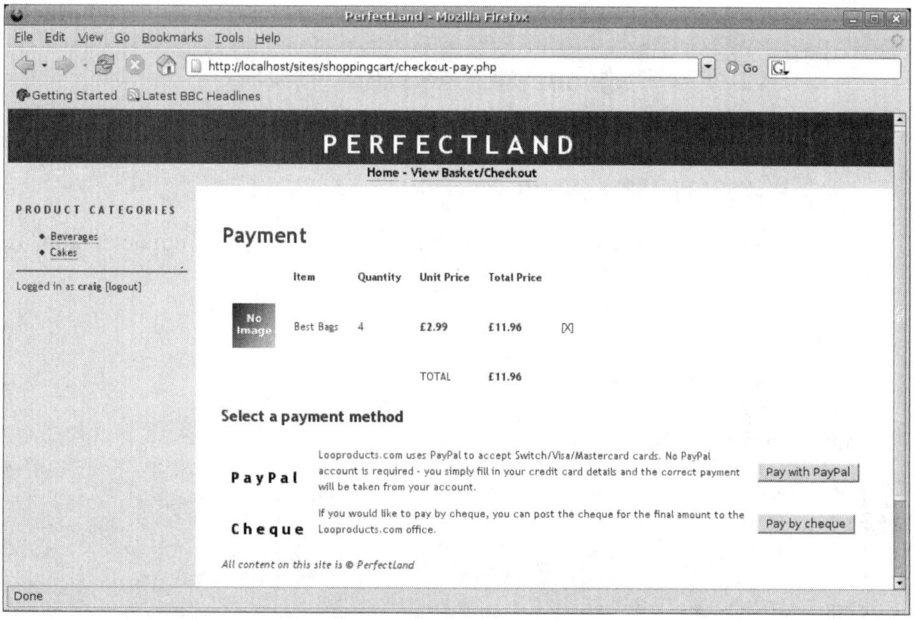

FIGURE 6-8 The finished payment screen

ADMINISTRATOR PAGES

The administration side of the shopping cart is very simple. The primary function for the admin is to view and confirm completed orders. When an order has been confirmed, the administrator has successfully sent out the product.

The first step is to provide an administrator login. Create a new file called *adminlogin.php* and add the following code:

```php
<?php
    session_start();

    require("db.php");

    if(isset($_SESSION['SESS_ADMINLOGGEDIN']) == TRUE) {
        header("Location: " . $config_basedir);
    }

    if($_POST['submit'])
    {
        $loginsql = "SELECT * FROM admins WHERE
username = '" . $_POST['userBox'] . "' AND
password = '" . $_POST['passBox'] . "'";
        $loginres = mysql_query($loginsql);
        $numrows = mysql_num_rows($loginres);

        if($numrows == 1)
        {
            $loginrow = mysql_fetch_assoc($loginres);

            session_register("SESS_ADMINLOGGEDIN");

            $_SESSION['SESS_ADMINLOGGEDIN'] = 1;

            header("Location: " . $config_basedir . "adminorders.php");

        }
        else
        {
            header("Location: "
. $config_basedir
. "adminlogin.php?error=1");
        }
    }
    else
    {

    require("header.php");

    echo "<h1>Admin Login</h1>";
```

```
    if($_GET['error'] == 1) {
       echo "<strong>Incorrect username/password!</strong>";
    }
?>
    <p>
    <form action="<?php echo $SCRIPT_NAME; ?>" method="POST">
    <table>
       <tr>
          <td>Username</td>
          <td><input type="textbox" name="userBox">
       </tr>
       <tr>
          <td>Password</td>
          <td><input type="password" name="passBox">
       </tr>
       <tr>
          <td></td>
          <td><input type="submit" name="submit" value="Log in">
       </tr>
    </table>
    </form>

<?php
    }

    require("footer.php");
?>
```

Much of this code should look familiar to you. When the admin has successfully logged in, the SESS_ADMINLOGGEDIN variable is created.

Logging Out the Administrator

To log out the administrator, create a file called *adminlogout.php* and add the following code:

```
<?php

    session_start();

    require("config.php");

    session_unregister("SESS_ADMINLOGGEDIN");

    header("Location: " . $config_basedir);
?>
```

As with the normal user logout, you unregister the variable—as opposed to destroying the entire session. This prevents against the administrator being logged out completely when logged in as both an admin and a user.

Managing Completed Orders

The main administrator page shows the list of completed orders. The purpose of this page is to enable an admin to see which orders need products mailed. The admin can then create the package and confirm the order after it has been mailed.

This page is fairly straightforward; it simply outputs data from some tables. The script has two primary states: either displaying orders or confirming them. The default page displays the orders. If you pass the page func=conf GET variable and the order number, the order will be confirmed.

Create a new file called *adminorders.php* and begin adding the code:

```php
<?php
    session_start();

    require("config.php");
    require("db.php");
    require("functions.php");

    if(isset($_SESSION['SESS_ADMINLOGGEDIN']) == FALSE) {
        header("Location: " . $config_basedir);
    }
```

After the usual introductory code, make a check to see if the func GET variable exists:

```php
    if(isset($_GET['func']) == TRUE) {

        if($_GET['func'] != "conf") {
            header("Location: " . $config_basedir);
        }

        $validid = pf_validate_number($_GET['id'],
    "redirect", $config_basedir);

        $funcsql = "UPDATE orders SET
    status = 10 WHERE id = " . $_GET['id'];
        mysql_query($funcsql);

        header("Location: " . $config_basedir . "adminorders.php");
    }
```

If the func GET variable exists, the page redirects when the variable is set to anything other than conf; this prevents against a SQL injection attack. Next, the id GET variable is validated. The order is finally confirmed by updating the *orders* table and setting the status field to 10. The page then redirects to the orders summary.

If no func GET variable exists, set the page to display completed orders:

```
else {
     require("header.php");
     echo "<h1>Outstanding orders</h1>";
     $orderssql = "SELECT * FROM orders WHERE status = 2";
     $ordersres = mysql_query($orderssql);
     $numrows = mysql_num_rows($ordersres);

     if($numrows == 0)
     {
        echo "<strong>No orders</strong>";
     }
     else
     {
        echo "<table cellspacing=10>";

        while($row = mysql_fetch_assoc($ordersres))
        {
           echo "<tr>";
              echo "<td>[<a
href='adminorderdetails.php?id=" . $row['id']
. "'>View</a>]</td>";
              echo "<td>"
. date("D jS F Y g.iA", strtotime($row['date']))
. "</td>";
              echo "<td>";

              if($row['registered'] == 1)
              {
                 echo "Registered Customer";
              }
              else
              {
                 echo "Non-Registered Customer";
              }

              echo "</td>";

              echo "<td>&pound;" . sprintf('%.2f',
$row['total']) . "</td>";

              echo "<td>";

              if($row['payment_type'] == 1)
              {
```

```
                  echo "PayPal";
              }
              else
              {
                  echo "Cheque";
              }

              echo "</td>";

              echo "<td><a
href='adminorders.php?func=conf&id=" . $row['id']
. "'>Confirm Payment</a></td>";
          echo "</tr>";
        }

        echo "</table>";
    }
}

require("footer.php");
?>
```

If all went well, the completed orders summary should look similar to the page shown Figure 6-9.

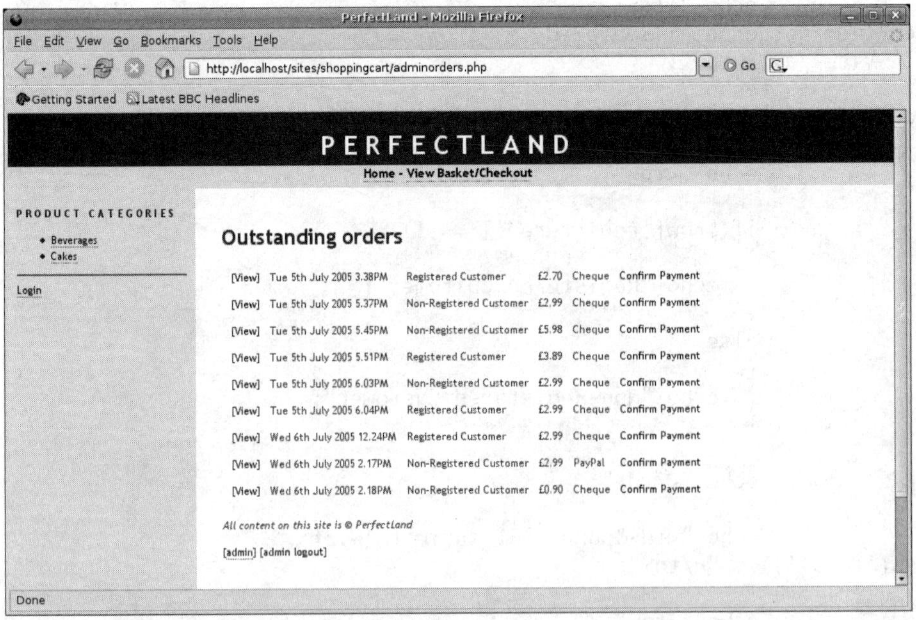

FIGURE 6-9 The outstanding orders page provides a simple means of viewing orders that need products sent out.

Viewing a Specific Order

For the administrator to get the postal address for a particular order, she needs to view the specific details for the order. This next page lists the order information (order number, address, products purchased, payment method, and so on).

Create a new file called *adminorderdetails.php* and add the following code:

```php
<?php

    session_start();

    require("config.php");
    require("functions.php");

    if(isset($_SESSION['SESS_ADMINLOGGEDIN']) == FALSE) {
        header("Location: " . $basedir);
    }

    $validid = pf_validate_number($_GET['id'],
  "redirect", $config_basedir . "adminorders.php");

    require("header.php");

    echo "<h1>Order Details</h1>";
    echo "<a href='adminorders.php'><- go back
 to the main orders screen</a>";

    $ordsql = "SELECT * from orders WHERE id = " . $validid;
    $ordres = mysql_query($ordsql);
    $ordrow = mysql_fetch_assoc($ordres);

    echo "<table cellpadding=10>";
    echo "<tr><td><strong>Order Number</strong>
</td><td>" . $ordrow['id'] . "</td>";
    echo "<tr><td><strong>Date of order</strong>
</td><td>" . date('D jS F Y g.iA',
 strtotime($ordrow['date'])) . "</td>";
    echo "<tr><td><strong>Payment Type</strong></td><td>";
    if($ordrow['payment_type'] == 1)
    {
        echo "PayPal";
    }
    else
    {
        echo "Cheque";
    }
    echo "</td>";
    echo "</table>";
```

```php
    if($ordrow['delivery_add_id'] == 0)
    {
        $addsql = "SELECT * FROM customers
WHERE id = " . $ordrow['customer_id'];
        $addres = mysql_query($addsql);
    }
    else
    {
        $addsql = "SELECT * FROM delivery_addresses
WHERE id = " . $ordrow['delivery_add_id'];
        $addres = mysql_query($addsql);
    }

    $addrow = mysql_fetch_assoc($addres);

    echo "<table cellpadding=10>";
    echo "<tr>";
    echo "<td><strong>Address</strong></td>";
    echo "<td>" . $addrow['forename'] . " "
. $addrow['surname'] . "<br>";
    echo $addrow['add1'] . "<br>";
    echo $addrow['add2'] . "<br>";
    echo $addrow['add3'] . "<br>";
    echo $addrow['postcode'] . "<br>";

    echo "<br>";

    if($ordrow['delivery_add_id'] == 0)
    {
        echo "<i>Address from member account</i>";
    }
    else
    {
        echo "<i>Different delivery address</i>";
    }

    echo "</td></tr>";
    echo "<tr><td><strong>Phone</strong></td><td>"
. $addrow['phone'] . "</td></tr>";
    echo "<tr><td><strong>Email</strong></td>
<td><a href='mailto:" . $addrow['email'] . "'>"
. $addrow['email'] . "</a></td></tr>";
    echo "</table>";


    $itemssql = "SELECT products.*, orderitems.*,
orderitems.id AS itemid FROM products, orderitems
WHERE orderitems.product_id = products.id AND order
_id = " . $validid;
    $itemsres = mysql_query($itemssql);
    $itemnumrows = mysql_num_rows($itemsres);
```

```php
    echo "<h1>Products Purchased</h1>";

    echo "<table cellpadding=10>";
    echo "<th></th>";
    echo "<th>Product</th>";
    echo "<th>Quantity</th>";
    echo "<th>Price</th>";
    echo "<th>Total</th>";

        while($itemsrow = mysql_fetch_assoc($itemsres))
        {
            $quantitytotal = $itemsrow['price']
* $itemsrow['quantity'];
        echo "<tr>";

            if(empty($itemsrow['image'])) {
                echo "<td><img
src='./productimages/dummy.jpg' width='50' alt='"
. $itemsrow['name'] . "'></td>";
            }
            else {
                echo "<td><img src='./productimages/"
. $itemsrow['image'] . "' width='50' alt='"
. $itemsrow['name'] . "'></td>";
            }

            echo "<td>" . $itemsrow['name'] . "</td>";
            echo "<td>" . $itemsrow['quantity'] . " x </td>";
            echo "<td><strong>&pound;" . sprintf('%.2f',
$itemsrow['price']) . "</strong></td>";
            echo "<td><strong>&pound;" . sprintf('%.2f',
$quantitytotal) . "</strong></td>";

            echo "</tr>";

        }

    echo "<tr>";
        echo "<td></td>";
        echo "<td></td>";
        echo "<td></td>";
        echo "<td>TOTAL</td>";
        echo "<td><strong>&pound;" . sprintf('%.2f', $total)
. "</strong></td>";
    echo "</tr>";

    echo "</table>";

    require("footer.php");
?>
```

This code should look familiar you to you; it simply displays details from the *orders*, *orderitems*, and *delivery_addresses* tables.

The completed page should look like the one shown in Figure 6-10.

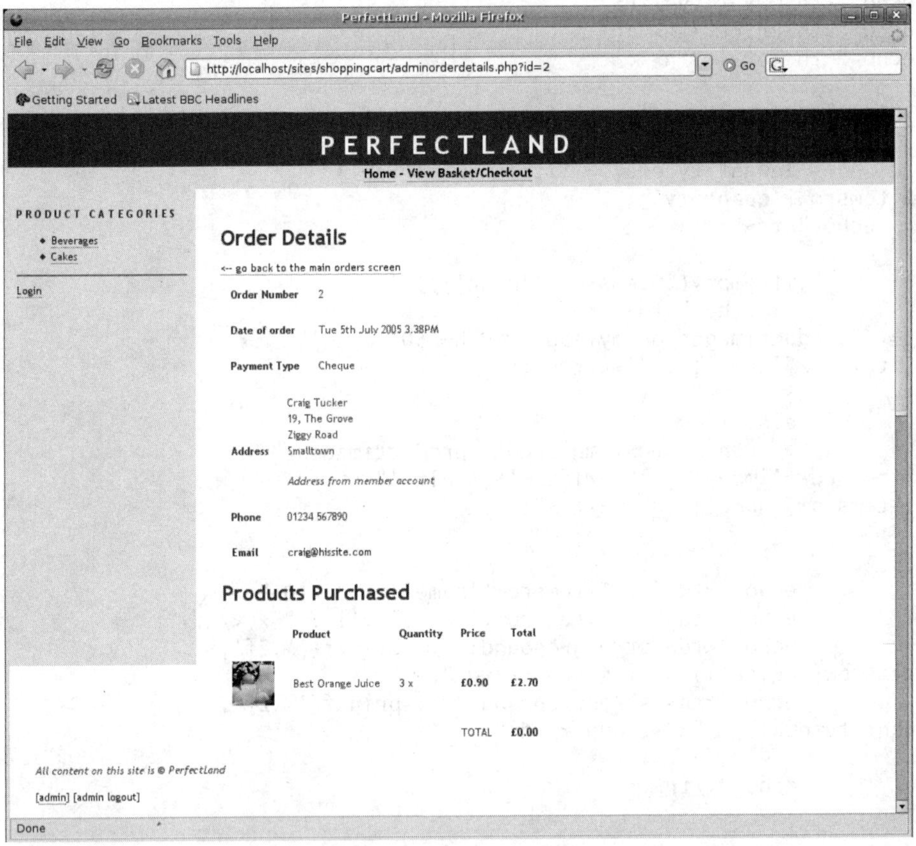

FIGURE 6-10 The order summary in the admin interface

SUMMARY

Within this project, a number of different skills are tied together to create a consistent product. Although you scratched only the surface of the possible features you could add to a shopping cart system, you developed the core functionality. You could make a huge range of possible additions, including the following:

- Send confirmation emails to the user and the admin when an order is complete.
- Provide a random product box on the front page. This could be used to display an image of a product to attract users.

- Create a ratings system in which users can review a product.
- Create a comments and reviews system so that users can leave their thoughts on how effective a product is.
- Create sales reports.

You can develop each of these possible additions by using the skills already covered in this book. Just sit back, sketch an initial idea of how to code the feature, and then hack it in.

CHAPTER 7

Building an Online Auction Site

If you wander around the Internet, you will likely find only a handful of people who have never visited or used eBay. This popular auction site has become part and parcel of Internet life for many users, and an afternoon can be easily whiled away browsing for all sorts of items.

In this chapter, you will create your own auction site. Rather than creating a successor to eBay, the aim of this project is to teach you many of the concepts involved in coding an auction site. And many of these concepts come in handy when working with other projects. An example of this is the core feature of dealing with bids. You can apply the same logic used to deal with bidding to online voting sites, polls, quizzes, and more. As such, the benefit of this chapter is not so much the product you have at the end, but the journey you traveled to create it.

PROJECT OVERVIEW

This project implements the following core features of an auction site:

- The page displays a series of different categories for different types of items.
- On the front page, a list of items will be available for all categories. The user can click a category name to view items within it. Only items before the bid deadline are displayed.
- The user can register and log in to the site.
- The user can view an item—complete with pictures—and place a bid.
- The users can add items—complete with pictures—to the site.
- When an auction is complete, the owner of the item and the winning bidder receive email messages that include the details of the closing auction.

From the outset, an auction site seems quite straightforward to build. In reality, there are a few interesting challenges that can test the scope of your PHP and SQL knowledge. As such, this project will add some useful new skills to your toolbox.

BUILDING THE DATABASE

The database you use in this project is relatively straightforward and includes five tables. These tables are shown in Figure 7-1.

FIGURE 7-1 The entire database schema revolves around the *items* table.

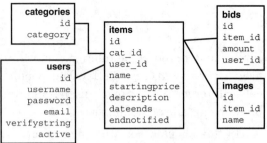

Each table in the database is related to the *items* table, which provides information about an item on the site. Within the *items* table, you also reference the *categories* table (to determine the category to which the item belongs), the *users* table (to specify which user added the item), the *bids* table (to store each bid made for particular item), and the *images* table (to store images added to the items).

Implementing the Database

Fire up phpMyAdmin. Create a new database called *auction* and add the following tables:

The *categories* Table
- id. Make this a TINYINT (there will not be many categories) and turn on auto_increment in the Extras column. Make this field a primary key.
- cat. Make this a VARCHAR and set the size to 20. It is unlikely a category title will be longer than 20 letters.

The *users* Table
- id. Make this an INT (several users are possible) and turn on auto_increment. Set this field as a primary key.
- username. Make this a VARCHAR with a length of 10.

- password. Make this a VARCHAR with a length of 10.
- email. Make this a VARCHAR with a length of 100. You would be surprised by the length of some governmental email addresses!
- verifystring. Make this a VARCHAR with a length of 20.
- active. Make this a TINYINT.

The *items* Table

- id. Make this an INT (several items are possible) and turn on auto_increment. Make this field a primary key.
- user_id. Make this an INT.
- cat_id. Make this a TINYINT.
- name. Make this a VARCHAR with a length of 100. It is common for item titles to be quite long.
- startingprice. Make this a FLOAT. You use this type for store prices that have a decimal point (such as $22.90); FLOAT supports the decimal point.
- description. Make this a TEXT.
- dateends. Make this a DATETIME.
- endnotified. Make this a TINYINT.

The *bids* Table

- id. Make this an INT (several bids are possible). Turn on auto_increment. Make this field a primary key.
- item_id. Make this an INT.
- amount. Make this a FLOAT for store prices that have a decimal point.
- user_id. Make this an INT.

The *images* Table

- id. Make this an INT (several images are possible). Turn on auto_increment. Make this field a primary key.
- item_id. Make this an INT.
- name. Make this a VARCHAR with a length of 100. Long image filenames are likely.

Insert Sample Data

With the tables created, it is useful to fill some initial data into some tables for testing the code as you write. Remember that when you are adding data to any of these tables not to fill in a number in the id column; this is handled by auto_increment.

Sample Data for the *categories* Table

Add the following categories in this order: Computing, Musical Instruments.

Sample Data for the *items* Table

Add the information shown in Table 7-1 to the items table.

TABLE 7-1 Data for the *items* table

USER_ID	CAT_ID	NAME	STARTINGPRICE	DESCRIPTION	DATEENDS	ENDNOTIFIED
1	1	Web Develop-ment Laptop	200.00	A quality Web devel-opment laptop.	Add a date in the future.	0
1	1	56k Modem	39.99	Brand-new 56k modem.	Add a date in the future	0

In this example, you are referencing the first entry from the *categories* table (Computing) in the cat_id and a reference to a user in the *users* table (with the user_id field). This creates the relationship between the tables.

Sample Data for the *users* Table

Add the information shown in Table 7-2 to the users table.

TABLE 7-2 Two users are added to the *users* table.

USERNAME	PASSWORD	EMAIL	VERIFYSTRING	ACTIVE
johnsmith	password	john@smith.com		1
bob	password	foo@bar.com		1

Sample Data for the *bids* and *images* Tables

Leave these tables empty.

STARTING TO CODE

First, create the usual configuration file to store generic information about the site (as seen in Example 7-1). Create it in a new directory and call it *config.php*.

EXAMPLE 7-1 This configuration file stores general information about the site.

```php
<?php

$dbhost = "localhost";
$dbuser = "root";
$dbpassword = "";
$dbdatabase = "auction";

// Add your name below
$config_admin = "Jono Bacon";
$config_adminemail = "jono AT jonobacon DOT org";

// Add the location of your forums below
$config_basedir = "http://localhost/sites/auction/";

// The currency used on the auction
$config_currency = "$";
?>
```

Most of these settings will be familiar to you now. The only addition to the file is the $config_currency variable, which stores the currency type that the site uses (such as dollars, pounds, euros, and so on). You can use this variable to easily switch to a different currency if your lucrative auction empire grows.

Build another simple structure in which to wrap your pages. Create a file called *header.php* and add the code shown in Example 7-2.

EXAMPLE 7-2 The header code presents the top portion of the site design.

```php
<?php

    session_start();

    require("config.php");

    $db = mysql_connect($dbhost, $dbuser, $dbpassword);
    mysql_select_db($dbdatabase, $db);

?>
```

continues

EXAMPLE 7-2 Continued.

```html
<!DOCTYPE HTML PUBLIC "-//W3C//DTD HTML 4.01
 Transitional//EN" "http://www.w3.org/TR/html4/loose.dtd">
<html>
<head>
    <title><?php echo $config_forumsname; ?></title>
    <link rel="stylesheet" href="stylesheet.css" type="text/css" />
</head>
<body>
<div id="header">
<h1>BidTastic Auctions</h1>
 <div id="menu">
<a href="index.php">Home</a>
<?php

if(isset($_SESSION['USERNAME']) == TRUE) {
    echo "<a href='logout.php'>Logout</a>";
}
else {
    echo "<a href='login.php'>Login</a>";
}

?>

<a href="newitem.php">New Item</a>
</div>
<div id="container">

<div id="bar">
    <?php require("bar.php"); ?>
</div>

<div id="main">
```

This header file is virtually identical to the ones you created in previous projects.

Create *footer.php*, as shown in Example 7-3.

EXAMPLE 7-3 The footer code for the site

```php
<p>&copy; <?php echo "<a href='mailto:"
 . $config_adminemail . "'>" .$config_admin
 . "</a>"; ?></p>
</div>
</div>
</body>
</html>
```

The final file to create before beginning the code for the auction is *functions.php*. In this project, you use the pf_script_with_get() function that you used in the forums project, but you will also create another snazzy function called pf_validate_number(). Copy *functions.php* from the forums project and add the code shown in Example 7-4 after the pf_script_with_get() function.

EXAMPLE 7-4 The *pf_validate_number()* function validates a number and either returns 0 or redirects.

```
    return substr($page, 0, strlen($page)-1);
}

function pf_validate_number($value, $function, $redirect) {
    if(isset($value) == TRUE) {
        if(is_numeric($value) == FALSE) {
            $error = 1;
        }

        if($error == 1) {
            header("Location: " . $redirect);
        }
        else {
            $final = $value;
        }
    }
    else {
        if($function == 'redirect') {
            header("Location: " . $redirect);
        }

        if($function == "value") {
            $final = 0;
        }
    }

    return $final;
}

?>
```

This function takes the number validation code that you wrote in previous pages and wraps it inside a function. This makes the files less cluttered because any reproduced code can be stored away in a function you can call.

The function takes three options. The first option passes the value that you want validated to the function. You set the second option to either redirect or value.

If you pass redirect, the third option is used as the page to redirect to when the value to validate fails. If you pass the function value, zero (0) is returned from the function if the variable to validate is invalid.

DISPLAYING AUCTION ITEMS

The first challenge is to create a list of auction categories and a list of auction items. These lists will look similar to the ones shown in Figure 7-2.

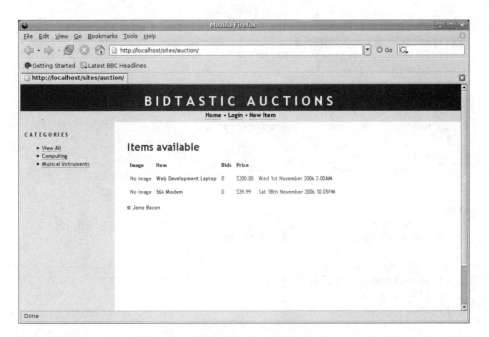

FIGURE 7-2 The sidebar is an ideal area to include a categories list.

This process involves creating a drill-down so that when the user clicks an item, he can view more information about it on a separate page.

The items table is where most of the action happens. Inside this table, the typical details such as item name, description, and starting price are stored. (Each auction needs a starting price, even if that starting price is 0.) The dateends field is particularly important and indicates the date when the auction finishes; this is used extensively later. The final field (endnotified) is irrelevant for creating the item listing page. This field is used later when you send emails summarizing the final price and bidder for the item. You can ignore this field for the moment.

NOTE

The Rights and Wrongs of Drill-Downs

The primary aim of a drill-down is to provide a summarized list of items, each of which can be clicked to provide more information. This technique is a useful means of organizing information effectively throughout a site.

When using drill-downs, you need to think about what information to summarize in the list. In many cases this is fairly obvious, but in some cases you may need to do a little research to get a clear idea of the information that people primarily look for on a Web site.

Displaying the Categories

To make the categories appear on the left sidebar as a bullet point list, add the following code to *bar.php*:

```
require("header.php");

$catsql = "SELECT * FROM categories ORDER BY category ASC;";
$catresult = mysql_query($catsql);

echo "<h1>Categories</h1>";
echo "<ul>";
    echo "<li><a href='index.php'>View All</a></li>";
while($catrow = mysql_fetch_assoc($catresult)) {
    echo "<li><a href='index.php?id="
 . $catrow['id'] . "'>" . $catrow['category']
 . "</a></li>";
}

echo "</ul>";
```

The query selects everything from the categories table in alphabetical order. An unordered list houses the categories, and the first entry (View All) is added; this entry links to *index.php* with no id GET variable. With the pf_validate_number() function added earlier, if no id GET variable exists, $validid is set to 0; this is what happens when the user clicks View All. Next, the while loop iterates through the categories and creates a link to *index.php*, in which the category id is passed as a GET variable (again, called id). The categories list is now complete.

Viewing the Items in a Category

The front page of the Web site displays the list of available items. The vast majority of people who visit an auctions site want to instantly find the range of items offered, so it makes sense to put this information on the front page.

Create a file called *index.php* and add the following code:

```php
<?php

require("config.php");
require("functions.php");
```

One of the planned features for *index.php* is to list a range of categories that users can click to see the items in that category. To create this functionality, the categories are listed as a series of links, and each link is passed the category id as a GET variable (called id). Use the pf_validate_number() function to validate this variable:

```php
require("functions.php");

$validid = pf_validate_number($_GET['id'], "value", $config_basedir);
```

To begin displaying information on the page, add the *header.php* code:

```php
$validid = pf_validate_number($_GET['id'], "value", $config_basedir);

require("header.php");
```

When displaying auction items on the main page, you need a different query depending on whether the id GET variable is present. If it is not, the user clicked View All, and no category is selected, so the page should display all of the items. If the id GET variable *is* present, only the items within that category should be displayed. When you used the pf_validate_number() function, you used the value option as the second argument so that the function returns 0 if no id GET variable exists.

Check what $validid is set to so that you can determine which SQL query is used:

```php
require("header.php");

if($validid == 0) {
   $sql = "SELECT items.* FROM items WHERE dateends > NOW()";
}
else {
   $sql = "SELECT * FROM items WHERE dateends > NOW()
 AND cat_id = " . $validid . ";";
}
$result = mysql_query($sql);
$numrows = mysql_num_rows($result);
```

If $validid is equal to 0, those items from the *items* table where dateends is greater than (newer than) the current date and time (NOW()) are selected. If $validid is set to a value, the items from the *items* table that are newer than the current date and where cat_id matches the value of $validid is selected.

Create a new <div> and add a table to list the items:

```
$result = mysql_query($sql);
$numrows = mysql_num_rows($result);

echo "<h1>Items available</h1>";
echo "<table cellpadding='5'>";
echo "<tr>";
   echo "<th>Image</th>";
   echo "<th>Item</th>";
   echo "<th>Bids</th>";
   echo "<th>Price</th>";
echo "</tr>";
```

Determine if any items are available by checking the value of $numrows:

```
   echo "<th>Bids</th>";
   echo "<th>Price</th>";
echo "</tr>";

if($numrows == 0) {
   echo "<tr><td colspan=4>No items!</td></tr>";
}
```

If $numrows is equal to 0 (no rows were returned), the text No items! is displayed in the table.

If items were returned and $numrows is greater than 0, you can iterate through each item and display them in the table:

```
if($numrows == 0) {
   echo "<tr><td colspan=4>No items!</td></tr>";
}
else {
   while($row = mysql_fetch_assoc($result)) {

      $imagesql = "SELECT * FROM images WHERE
 item_id = " . $row['id'] . " LIMIT 1";
      $imageresult = mysql_query($imagesql);
      $imagenumrows = mysql_num_rows($imageresult);

      echo "<tr>";
         if($imagenumrows == 0) {
            echo "<td>No image</td>";
         }
         else {
            $imagerow = mysql_fetch_assoc($imageresult);
            echo "<td><img src='./images/"
 . $imagerow['name'] . "' width='100'></td>";
         }
```

The `while` loop to iterates through the results. Inside the loop, a query selects a single record from the *images* table in which `item_id` matches the `id` from the current row. The table row is then opened, and a check is made to see if `$imagenumrows` is equal to 0. If it is, the text `No image` is displayed in the table. If `$imagenumrows` is not equal to 0, a row is extracted from the result of the image query and an image tag is constructed. When the image tag is created, `./images/` and then the name of the image from the table is added to the `src` attribute. This appends the `images` directory to the current directory. Much of this code will make more sense later when you write the functionality to upload images.

Add the next column, which contains the item name, to the table:

```php
            echo "<td><img src='./images/"
. $imagerow['name'] . "' width='100'></td>";
        }

        echo "<td>";
        echo "<a href='itemdetails.php?id="
. $row['id'] . "'>" . $row['name'] . "</a>";
        if($_SESSION['USERID'] == $row['user_id']) {
            echo " - [<a href='edititem.php?id="
. $row['id'] . "'>edit</a>]";
        }
        echo "</td>";
```

This code adds the name of the item from the first query. You make the item a link to *itemdetails.php* (which provides more details about the item), appending the `id` of the item as an `id` GET variable. The `if` statement also checks to see if a session variable called USERID is equal to `user_id` from the row. If it is, the current user logged in is the user who added the item, and an `edit` link is added. The `edit` link links to a page called *edititem.php* that, predictably, edits the current item.

Add another column to display the number of bids and the highest bid:

```php
        echo "</td>";

        $bidsql = "SELECT item_id, MAX(amount) AS
highestbid, COUNT(id) AS numberofbids FROM bids
WHERE item_id=" . $row['id'] . " GROUP BY item_id;";
        $bidresult = mysql_query($bidsql);
        $bidrow = mysql_fetch_assoc($bidresult);
        $bidnumrows = mysql_num_rows($bidresult);


        echo "<td>";
        if($bidnumrows == 0) {
            echo "0";
        }
        else {
```

```
        echo $bidrow['numberofbids'] . "</td>";
    }

    echo "<td>" . $config_currency;

    if($bidnumrows == 0) {
        echo sprintf('%.2f', $row['startingprice']);
    }
    else {
        echo sprintf('%.2f', $bidrow['highestbid']);
    }
    echo "</td>";
```

This query uses a few MySQL functions to determine the highest bid and the number of bids. To better explain this, read the SQL from left to right:

> Select (SELECT) the item_id (item_id), use the MySQL MAX() function to find the highest value within the amount field and alias the field as highest bid (MAX(amount) AS highestbid). Use the MySQL COUNT() function to count the number of records and alias the field as numberofbids (COUNT(id) AS numberofbids) from the *bids* table (FROM *bids*), in which the item_id is equal to $row['id'] (WHERE item_id = $row['id']), and group the records by item_id (GROUP BY item_id;).

If no rows are returned from the query, 0 is added to the table; otherwise, the value of numberofbids is added. $bidnumrows does not return 0 when no rows exist because if there are no bids, there are no entries in the *bids* table to count with the COUNT() function. As such, nothing is returned. Always remember in programming that 0 is a value, and it is often different to the concept of nothing.

The next column is the latest price. Before a value is displayed, the currency is added from the $config_currency field.

NOTE

Dealing with Currencies

When dealing with monetary units such as prices, quotes, figures, and other numbers, never include the currency sign in the database. Currency is really just an additional piece of information that gives the number a context. If you want the currency symbol in the database, store the number and symbol as a VARCHAR.

Storing the price as a number and without the symbol allows you to do things such as taxes, addition expenses, currency conversion, and other calculations.

If `$bidnumrows` has no rows, the `startingprice` field from the first query is displayed (if there are no bids, the starting price should be displayed). If there are bids, the highest bid is displayed (`$bidrow['highestbid']`) from the last query. Both prices are formatted.

NOTE

Formatting Prices

When you use a `FLOAT` to store a price in the database, the trailing zeros are removed by default. To reformat the price with zeros, use the PHP function `sprintf()`. The function takes two arguments: the formatting string and the value to format. The formatting string takes a value such as `%.2f`, which asks for two decimal places (`.2`) on a floating point number (`f`).

Finally, display and format the `dateends` field:

```
        }
            echo "</td>";

            echo "<td>" . date("D jS F Y g.iA",
    strtotime($row['dateends'])) . "</td>";
            echo "</tr>";
        }
}

echo "</table>";
require("footer.php");

?>
```

Viewing Item Details and Placing Bids

The next page is linked from the name of the item on the page you just created. This script has two primary purposes:

- To display information about the item, including images of it.
- To allow a user to bid on the item.

To place a bid, you need to check if the user is logged in, and if so, display a form into which she can type a bid amount. The page then checks that the amount is legitimate and adds the bid to the *bids* table.

Create a new file called *itemdetails.php* and add the usual introductory code:

```php
<?php

session_start();

include("config.php");
include("functions.php");

$db = mysql_connect($dbhost, $dbuser, $dbpassword);
mysql_select_db($dbdatabase, $db);

$validid = pf_validate_number($_GET['id'], "redirect", $config_basedir);
```

Create a query to grab the item information:

```php
$validid = pf_validate_number($_GET['id'], "redirect",
 $config_basedir);

require("header.php");

$itemsql = "SELECT UNIX_TIMESTAMP(dateends) AS dateepoch,
 items.* FROM items WHERE id = " . $validid . ";";
$itemresult = mysql_query($itemsql);

$itemrow = mysql_fetch_assoc($itemresult);
```

In *index.php*, only items that were newer than the date and time were returned by the MySQL NOW() function. For completeness, the page checks this with PHP rather than MySQL.

Inside the query, the UNIX_TIMESTAMP() command converts the dateends field into the number of seconds since the epoch. The query is then executed, and a row is stored in the $itemrow array.

Check to see if the current item has ended:

```php
$itemrow = mysql_fetch_assoc($itemresult);

$nowepoch = mktime();
$rowepoch = $itemrow['dateepoch'];

if($rowepoch > $nowepoch) {
    $VALIDAUCTION = 1;
}
```

The mktime() function stores the seconds since the epoch for the current time in the $nowepoch variable. The $rowepoch variable then stores the epoch returned from the row. A check is made to see if $rowepoch is greater than $nowepoch and if so, a variable called $VALIDAUCTION is set to 1 (the capitalization of the variable is used only to make it stand out in the code). $VALIDAUCTION is checked later to determine if the auction is valid (still available to bid on).

Add the name of the item in a second-level heading tag:

```
if($rowepoch > $nowepoch) {
    $VALIDAUCTION = 1;
}

echo "<h2>" . $itemrow['name'] . "</h2>";
```

Now run a query to get any images that are associated with an item:

```
echo "<h2>" . $itemrow['name'] . "</h2>";

$imagesql = "SELECT * FROM images WHERE item_id = " . $validid . ";";
$imageresult = mysql_query($imagesql);
$imagenumrows = mysql_num_rows($imageresult);
```

The next query returns the highest bid and the number of bids for the item:

```
$imagenumrows = mysql_num_rows($imageresult);

$bidsql = "SELECT item_id, MAX(amount) AS highestbid,
 COUNT(id) AS number_of_bids FROM bids WHERE item_id="
 . $validid . " GROUP BY item_id;";
$bidresult = mysql_query($bidsql);
$bidnumrows = mysql_num_rows($bidresult);
```

The preceding query is similar to the one used on *index.php* to get the same information.

Display the information from the queries:

```
$bidnumrows = mysql_num_rows($bidresult);

echo "<p>";

if($bidnumrows == 0) {
    echo "<strong>This item has had no bids</strong>
 - <strong>Starting Price</strong>: " . $config_currency
 . sprintf('%.2f', $itemrow['startingprice']);
}
else {
    $bidrow = mysql_fetch_assoc($bidresult);
```

```
    echo "<strong>Number Of Bids</strong>: "
  . $bidrow['number_of_bids'] . "
  - <strong>Current Price</strong>: " . $config_currency
  . sprintf('%.2f', $bidrow['highestbid']);
}
```

If no rows are counted in $bidnumrows, the page displays not only with text that indicate no bids were placed but also with the starting price. When rows *are* present, the page displays both the number of bids and the highest bid price.

Display the date when the auction ends:

```
    echo "<strong>Number Of Bids</strong>: "
  . $bidrow['number_of_bids'] . "
  - <strong>Current Price</strong>: " . $config_currency
  . sprintf('%.2f', $bidrow['highestbid']);
}
```

```
echo " - <strong>Auction ends</strong>: "
  . date("D jS F Y g.iA", $rowepoch);
```

Display any images of the item:

```
echo " - <strong>Auction ends</strong>: "
  . date("D jS F Y g.iA", $rowepoch);
```

```
echo "</p>";
```

```
if($imagenumrows == 0) {
    echo "No images.";
}
else {
    while($imagerow = mysql_fetch_assoc($imageresult)) {
        echo "<img src='./images/" . $imagerow['name'] ."' width='200'>";
    }
}
```

The $imagenumrows variable is checked to see if any rows were returned. If not, the text No images displays. If rows were returned, the while loop displays each image.

Add the item description. Use the nl2br() function to ensure that any white-space lines are added:

```
    }
}
```

```
echo "<p>" . nl2br($itemrow['description']) . "</p>";
```

You can now start work on adding the bid entry box. This functionality should be available only if the user is logged in. First, display a heading to indicate the bidding area:

```
echo "<p>" . nl2br($itemrow['description']) . "</p>";

echo "<a name='bidbox'>";
echo "<h2>Bid for this item</h2>";
```

The anchor in this code is used when the user is not logged in, clicks the link to log in, and is then redirected to the bidding area.

To see if the user is logged in, check the USERNAME session variable:

```
echo "<h3>Bid for this item</h3>";

if(isset($_SESSION['USERNAME']) == FALSE) {
    echo "To bid, you need to log in. Login
 <a href='login.php?id=" . $validid . "&ref=addbid'>here</a>.";
}
```

If the user is not logged in and the isset() functions returns FALSE, the user can click the link to log in. The login link adds the id of the item and a variable called ref as GET variables. This is the same technique used in the forums project.

Run the code if the user is logged in:

```
    echo "To bid, you need to log in. Login
 <a href='login.php?id=" . $validid . "&ref=addbid'>here</a>.";
}
else {
    if($VALIDAUCTION == 1) {
        echo "Enter the bid amount into the box below.";
        echo "<p>";

        switch($_GET['error']) {
            case "lowprice":
                echo "The bid entered is too low.
 Please enter another price.";
            break;

            case "letter":
                echo "The value entered is not a number.";
            break;
        }
    }

?>
```

If $VALIDAUCTION is equal to 1, a switch statement checks the value of the error GET variable, and the page displays the relevant error.

Add the form:

```
      break;
   }

?>
```

```
      <form action="<?php echo pf_script_with_get($SCRIPT_NAME);
?>" method="post">
      <table>
      <tr>
         <td><input type="text" name="bid"></td>
         <td><input type="submit" name="submit" value="Bid!"></td>
      </tr>
      </table>
      </form>
```

If $VALIDAUCTION is not set to 1, inform the user that the auction has ended:

```
      </table>
      </form>
```

```
<?php
   }
   else {
      echo "This auction has now ended.";
   }
```

After the bid box, it is helpful to list a history of bids and the users who placed them:

```
      echo "This auction has now ended.";
   }

   $historysql = "SELECT bids.amount, users.username FROM bids,
users WHERE bids.user_id = users.id AND item_id = "
. $validid . " ORDER BY amount DESC";
   $historyresult = mysql_query($historysql);
   $historynumrows = mysql_num_rows($historyresult);

   if($historynumrows >= 1) {
      echo "<h2>Bid History</h2>";
      echo "<ul>";

      while($historyrow = mysql_fetch_assoc($historyresult)) {
         echo "<li>" . $historyrow['username'] . " - " .
$config_currency . sprintf('%.2f', $historyrow['amount']) . "</li>";
      }

      echo "</ul>";
   }
```

The preceding code creates a query to return the bid amount and username in descending order. Then a check is made to see if the number of rows is equal to or greater than (>=) 1. If it is, the bid history is displayed.

Finally, add the footer:

```
    echo "</ul>";
  }
}
require("footer.php");

?>
```

With the main page complete, add the code that processes the bids. Add this code at the start of *itemdetails.php*:

```
$validid = pf_validate_number($_GET['id'], "redirect", $config_basedir);

if($_POST['submit']) {
   if(is_numeric($_POST['bid']) == FALSE) {
      header("Location: " . $config_basedir
 . "itemdetails.php?id=" . $validid . "&error=letter");
   }
```

A check is made to see if the bid is numerical. If it isn't, the page redirects.

Add the following queries to get some information before the bid is accepted:

```
      header("Location: " . $config_basedir
 . "/itemdetails.php?id=" . $validid . "&error=letter");
   }

   $theitemsql = "SELECT * FROM items WHERE id = " . $validid . ";";
   $theitemresult = mysql_query($theitemsql);
   $theitemrow = mysql_fetch_assoc($theitemresult);

   $checkbidsql = "SELECT item_id, max(amount) AS
highestbid, count(id) AS number_of_bids FROM
bids WHERE item_id=" . $validid . " GROUP BY item_id;";
   $checkbidresult = mysql_query($checkbidsql);
   $checkbidnumrows = mysql_num_rows($checkbidresult);
```

Check to see if any bids are returned:

```
   $checkbidresult = mysql_query($checkbidsql);
   $checkbidnumrows = mysql_num_rows($checkbidresult);

   if($checkbidnumrows == 0) {
      if($theitemrow['startingprice'] > $_POST['bid']) {
         header("Location: " . $config_basedir
 . "itemdetails.php?id=" . $validid . "&error=lowprice#bidbox");
      }
   }
```

If no rows were returned, it means the entered bid is the first bid entered (no others bids have been previously entered). Next, a check is made to see if the starting price is greater than the entered bid. If it is, a header redirect is made to the same page, but the error GET variable is added with a value of lowprice.

When previous bids exist, ensure the current highest bid is not higher than the entered bid:

```
    }
  }
  else {
    $checkbidrow = mysql_fetch_assoc($checkbidresult);

    if($checkbidrow['highestbid'] > $_POST['bid']) {
      header("Location: " . $config_basedir . "itemdetails.php?id=" .
$validid . "&error=lowprice#bidbox");
    }
  }
```

If highestbid is higher than the bid entered, a header redirect is made.

With the checks out of the way, run the INSERT query to actually add the bid to the bids table:

```
        header("Location: " . $config_basedir
  . "/itemdetails.php?id=" . $validid
  . "&error=lowprice#bidbox");
      }

    $inssql = "INSERT INTO bids(item_id, amount, user_id) VALUES("
      . $validid
      . ", " . $_POST['bid']
      . ", " . $_SESSION['USERID']
      . ");";
    mysql_query($inssql);
```

Close the block and prepare to add the rest of the code:

```
      . ");";
    mysql_query($inssql);

    header("Location: " . $config_basedir
  . "itemdetails.php?id=" . $validid);
}
else {
```

Finally, at the bottom of the file, add a curly bracket to close the else block:

```
      echo "</ul>";
    }
  }
}

require("footer.php");
```

The completed page should resemble something similar to Figure 7-3.

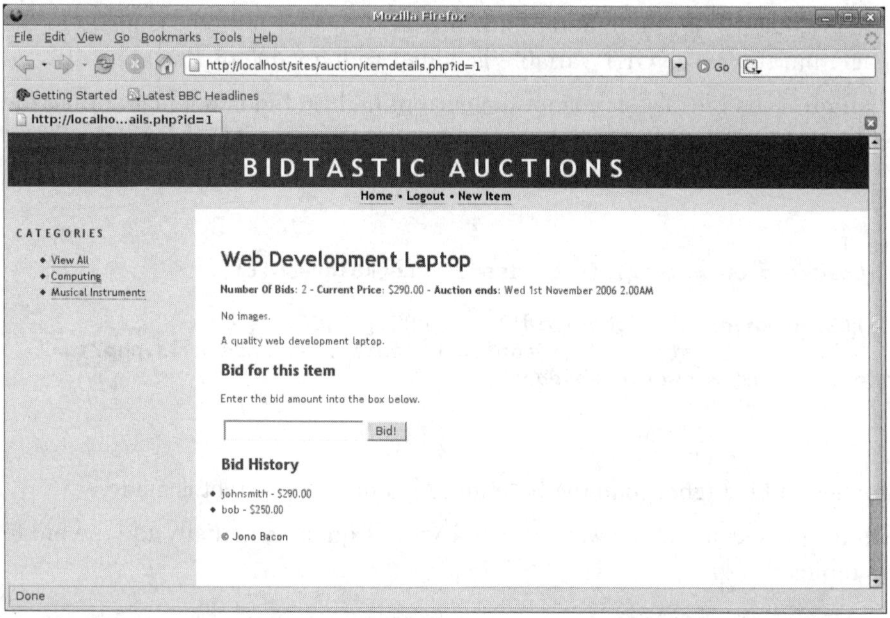

FIGURE 7-3 When the user is logged in, the bid box and bid history are shown.

DEALING WITH USERS

Like many of the other projects in this book, you need to add functionality so that users can log in to access various portions of the site. The process of logging in users is virtually identical to the *login.php* script from the forums project. The only differences are the referrer types for dealing with the ref GET variable. See Example 7-5.

EXAMPLE 7-5 The user login page

```php
<?php

session_start();

require("config.php");
require("functions.php");

$db = mysql_connect($dbhost, $dbuser, $dbpassword);
mysql_select_db($dbdatabase, $db);

if($_POST['submit']) {
```

```php
    $sql = "SELECT * FROM users WHERE username = '"
. $_POST['username'] . "' AND password = '"
. $_POST['password'] . "';";

    $result = mysql_query($sql);
    $numrows = mysql_num_rows($result);

    if($numrows == 1) {
        $row = mysql_fetch_assoc($result);

        if($row['active'] == 1) {
            session_register("USERNAME");
            session_register("USERID");

            $_SESSION['USERNAME'] = $row['username'];
            $_SESSION['USERID'] = $row['id'];

            switch($_GET['ref']) {
                case "addbid":
                    header("Location: " . $config_basedir
. "/itemdetails.php?id=" . $_GET['id'] . "#bidbox");
                break;

                case "newitem":
                    header("Location: " . $config_basedir . "/newitem.php");
                break;

                case "images":
                    header("Location: " . $config_basedir
. "/addimages.php?id=" . $_GET['id']);
                break;

                default:
                    header("Location: " . $config_basedir);
                break;
            }
        }
        else {
            require("header.php");
            echo "This account is not verified yet. You were
emailed a link to verify the account. Please click on the
link in the email to continue.";
        }
    }
    else {
        header("Location: " . $config_basedir . "/login.php?error=1");
    }
}
else {

    require("header.php");

    echo "<h1>Login</h1>";
```

continues

EXAMPLE 7-5 Continued.

```php
    if($_GET['error']) {
        echo "Incorrect login, please try again!";
    }

?>
<form action="<?php echo
 pf_script_with_get($SCRIPT_NAME); ?>" method="post">

<table>
<tr>
    <td>Username</td>
    <td><input type="text" name="username"></td>
</tr>
<tr>
    <td>Password</td>
    <td><input type="password" name="password"></td>
</tr>
<tr>
    <td></td>
    <td><input type="submit" name="submit" value="Login!"></td>
</tr>
</table>
</form>
Don't have an account? Go and <a href="register.php">Register</a>!
<?php
}
require("footer.php");
?>
```

The completed login page should look similar to the one shown in Figure 7-4.

Logging Out

The logout page, *logout.php*, is also the same. See Example 7-6.

EXAMPLE 7-6 Logging users out

```php
<?php

session_start();
session_unregister("USERNAME");
require("config.php");

header("Location: " . $config_basedir);

?>
```

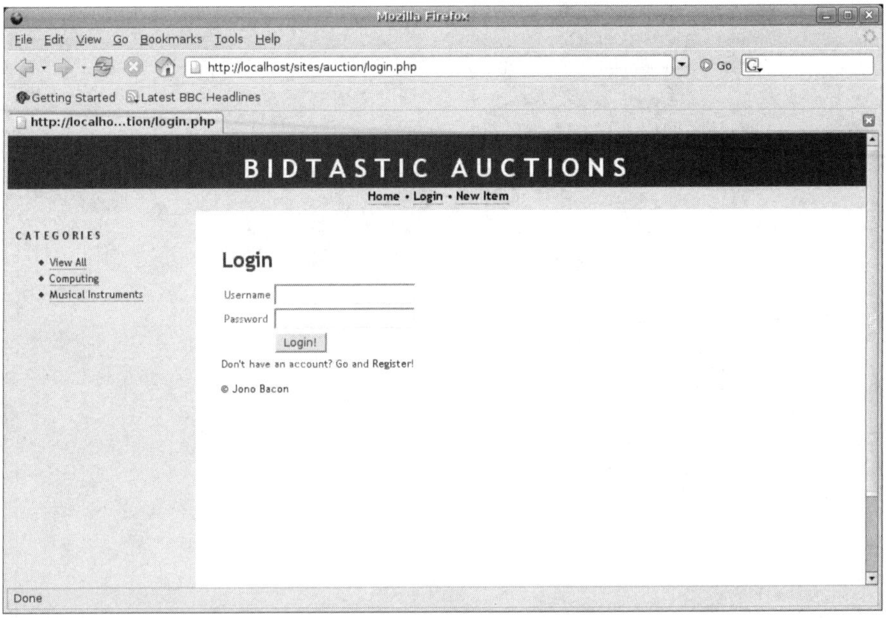

FIGURE 7-4 The login beast looks similar to most others.

User Registration

The user registration code is also the same as in the forums project. Copy the *register.php* and *validate.php* files to the current project and change the relevant parts.

ADDING AN ITEM

Adding an item to the auction site is a fairly simple two-step process. The first step is to present the user with a form that adds the item information to the database (see Figure 7-5). When this is complete, the second step is to allow the user to upload images that can be displayed with the item.

The form prompts the user for the following information:

- Category in which the item is included. This will be in the form of a drop-down combo box, with the categories listed.
- Name of the item.
- Item description.
- Ending date of the auction. This will be presented as a number of combo boxes for the different parts of the date. This will include one for the day, month and year, as well as hour and minutes.
- Starting price.

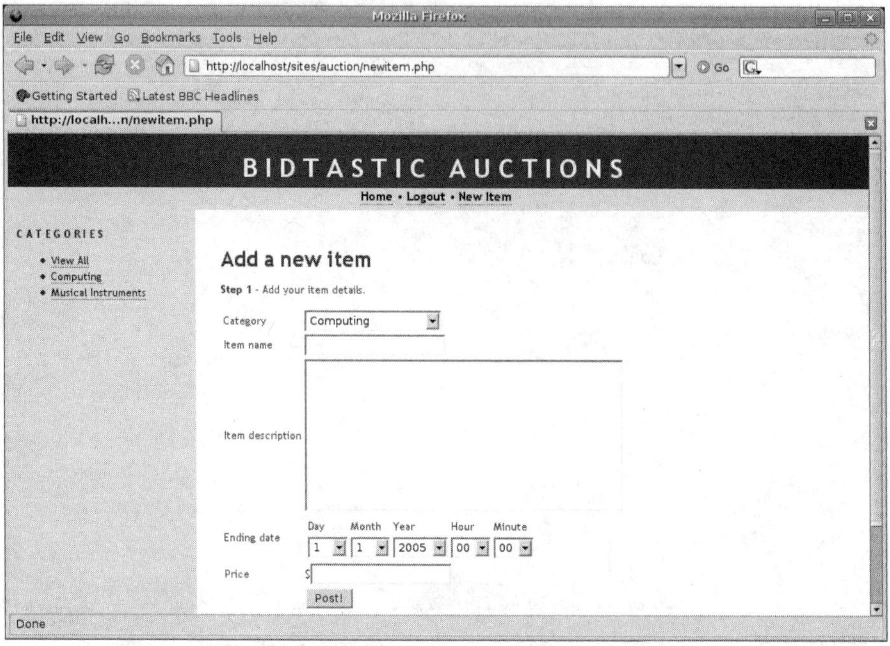

FIGURE 7-5 The first step of adding an item involves filling in the item details.

Create a new file called *newitem.php* and add the form:

```
<h1>Add a new item</h1>
<strong>Step 1</strong> - Add your item details.
<p>
<?php
    switch($_GET['error']) {
        case "date":
            echo "<strong>Invalid date - please
choose another!</strong>";
        break;
    }
?>
</p>
<form action="<?php echo
pf_script_with_get($SCRIPT_NAME); ?>" method="post">
<table>
<?php
    $catsql = "SELECT * FROM categories ORDER BY category;";
    $catresult = mysql_query($catsql);
?>
    <tr>
        <td>Category</td>
        <td>
        <select name="cat">
```

```
        <?php
        while($catrow = mysql_fetch_assoc($catresult)) {
            echo "<option value='"
. $catrow['id'] . "'>" . $catrow['category']
. "</option>";
        }
        ?>
        </select>
        </td>
    </tr>
  <tr>
    <td>Item name</td>
    <td><input type="text" name="name"></td>
  </tr>
  <tr>
    <td>Item description</td>
    <td><textarea name="description" rows="10"
cols="50"></textarea></td>
  </tr>
  <tr>
    <td>Ending date</td>
    <td>
    <table>
        <tr>
            <td>Day</td>
            <td>Month</td>
            <td>Year</td>
            <td>Hour</td>
            <td>Minute</td>
        </tr>
        <tr>
            <td>
            <select name="day">
            <?php
                for($i=1;$i<=31;$i++) {
                    echo "<option>" . $i . "</option>";
                }
            ?>
            </select>
            </td>
            <td>
            <select name="month">
            <?php
                for($i=1;$i<=12;$i++) {
                    echo "<option>" . $i . "</option>";
                }
            ?>
            </select>
            </td>
            <td>
            <select name="year">
            <?php
```

```
                        for($i=2005;$i<=2008;$i++) {
                            echo "<option>" . $i . "</option>";
                        }
                    ?>
                    </select>
                    </td>
                    <td>
                    <select name="hour">
                    <?php
                        for($i=0;$i<=23;$i++) {
                            echo "<option>" . sprintf("%02d",$i) . "</option>";
                        }
                    ?>
                    </select>
                    </td>
                    <td>
                    <select name="minute">
                    <?php
                        for($i=0;$i<=60;$i++) {
                            echo "<option>" . sprintf("%02d",$i) . "</option>";
                        }
                    ?>
                    </select>
                    </td>
                </tr>
            </table>
            </td>
        </tr>
        <tr>
            <td>Price</td>
            <td><?php echo $config_currency; ?><input type="text"
    name="price"></td>
        </tr>
        <tr>
            <td></td>
            <td><input type="submit" name="submit" value="Post!"></td>
        </tr>
        </table>
        </form>
```

The majority of this form should look straightforward by now. The only new feature is the date ending boxes. Inside these select boxes, a series of `for` loops loop from the minimum to maximum values (such as 1 to 31 for the day).

Start adding the code to process the form. Add the following code before the form:

```php
<?php

session_start();

require("config.php");
require("functions.php");
```

```
$db = mysql_connect($dbhost, $dbuser, $dbpassword);
mysql_select_db($dbdatabase, $db);
```

After this initial code, protect the page from people who are not logged in. Use the usual trick of checking to see if a USERNAME session variable exists:

```
$db = mysql_connect($dbhost, $dbuser, $dbpassword);
mysql_select_db($dbdatabase, $db);

if(isset($_SESSION['USERNAME']) == FALSE) {
   header("Location: " . $config_basedir . "/login.php?ref=newitem");
}
```

Begin processing the form:

```
if(isset($_SESSION['USERNAME']) == FALSE) {
   header("Location: " . $config_basedir . "/login.php?ref=newitem");
}

if($_POST['submit']) {
   $validdate = checkdate($_POST['month'], $_POST['day'],
 $_POST['year']);
```

After you check to see if the Submit button has been clicked, you use a special function called checkdate(). This PHP function is passed a month, day, and year in numbers and determines whether the combination of values is a valid date. This function is useful for determining invalid dates such as February 31, 2005. In this new line of code, the variables from the form are passed to the function. If the date is valid, the function returns TRUE; if not, the function returns FALSE.

Next, you check the result of the function and act accordingly. First, check to see if the date is valid:

```
if($_POST['submit']) {
   $validdate = checkdate($_POST['month'], $_POST['day'],
 $_POST['year']);

   if($validdate == TRUE) {
     $concatdate = $_POST['year']
       . "-" . sprintf("%02d", $_POST['day'])
       . "-" . sprintf("%02d", $_POST['month'])
       . " " . $_POST['hour']
       . ":" . $_POST['minute']
       . ":00";
```

If the date is valid, the numbers are concatenated to form a valid MySQL date. MySQL dates come in the form 0000-00-00 00:00 (year, month, day, hour, minute). Imagine that the user selected 10 as the day, 12 as the month, 2005 as the year, 11 as the hour, and 30 as the minute. With these numbers, the valid date would be 2005-12-10 11:30. The sprintf() function (which you used earlier to pad prices with zeros) was used again, this time to ensure that single digits have a leading zero (so 1 would become 01 and so on). This is important for the date to be a valid MySQL date.

Construct the query to insert the data:

```php
$concatdate = $_POST['year']
    . "-" . sprintf("%02d", $_POST['day'])
    . "-" . sprintf("%02d", $_POST['month'])
    . " " . $_POST['hour']
    . ":" . $_POST['minute']
    . ":00";

$itemsql = "INSERT INTO items(user_id, cat_id, name,
startingprice, description, dateends) VALUES("
    . $_SESSION['USERID']
    . ", " . $_POST['cat']
    . ", '" . addslashes($_POST['name'])
    . "', " . $_POST['price']
    . ", '" . addslashes($_POST['description'])
    . "', '" . $concatdate
    . "');";

mysql_query($itemsql);
$itemid = mysql_insert_id();

header("Location: " . $config_basedir
    . "/addimages.php?id=" . $itemid);
}
```

Within the query, a new function called addslashes() was wrapped around the boxes that accept input in the form of letters. This helps to prevent input errors.

Finally, a header redirect jumps to the *addimages.php* page and passes it a GET variable, called id, with the insert id.

Earlier in the code, you made a check to see if the date was valid. If the date was invalid, reload the page and pass the error flag:

```php
header("Location: " . $config_basedir . "/addimages.php?id=" .
$itemid);
}
else {
    header("Location: " . $config_basedir .
"/newitem.php?error=date");
}
}
```

NOTE

The Risks with Input

When you accept any kind of input from a user, there is a risk that the input could break the query. The most common breakage occurs when a user types a single quotation mark, because the quotation mark ends the input and anything after the second quotation mark is ignored. Imagine that the user types 'Tim O'Chin'. The query would be as follows:

INSERT INTO users(name) VALUES('Tim O'Chin');

In this query, the second quotation mark (in O'Chin) ends the input and causes a SQL error.

In your projects, it is unlikely that you have encountered this error. This is because a feature called magic_quotes is likely to be turned on in your *php.ini* file. With this feature, any quotation marks accepted from a form are automatically escaped. The act of escaping a quotation mark happens when you use a forward slash to make the quotation mark legitimate. As such, a properly escaped query would be:

INSERT INTO users(name) VALUES('Tim O\'Chin');

You can run this project with magic_quotes turned off if you wrap your data withaddslashes(); this function escapes the quotation marks.

After closing the main `if` block, begin the `else` that displays the form:

```
    }
}
else {
    require("header.php");
?>

    <h1>Add a new item</h1>
    <strong>Step 1</strong> - Add your item details.
```

After the form, add the closing curly bracket and footer code:

```
    </table>
    </form>

<?php
}

require("footer.php");

?>
```

Adding the Images

Being able to upload images is a common and useful skill used when developing Web sites. The basic technique is as follows:

1. Provide a form the user can use to select an image.

2. When the user clicks the Submit button, transfer the image to a temporary location on the server. Inside this location, give the file a random, temporary filename.

3. Check that the image is valid and copy it to a specific directory on the Web server.

4. Add the name of the image and the id of the item it is associated with to the *images* table.

With this process complete, you can iterate through the *images* table for items with the same id and then add the filename to the image HTML tag from the table.

Create a new file called *addimages.php* and add the following form:

```
<form enctype="multipart/form-data" action="<?php
 pf_script_with_get($SCRIPT_NAME); ?>" method="POST">
<input type="hidden" name="MAX_FILE_SIZE" value="3000000">

<table>
<tr>
    <td>Image to upload</td>
    <td><input name="userfile" type="file"></td>
</tr>
<tr>
    <td colspan="2"><input type="submit" name="submit"
 value="Upload File"></td>
</tr>
</table>
</form>
When you have finished adding photos, go and
 <a href="<?php echo "itemdetails.php?id="
 . $validid; ?>">see your item</a>!
```

Within the form tag, you created a new attribute, called enctype, that ensures the form submits the image data in an understandable format. The first <input> tag creates a special hidden form element that can be used to store hidden information and variables in the form. In this example, the hidden element stores the maximum size of the image. The second input element is a userfile type and adds a browse button that the user can click to select the image to upload. The preceding code also adds a Submit button.

Jump to the beginning of the page (before the form) and start adding the code to process the form:

```php
<?php

session_start();

include("config.php");
include("functions.php");

$db = mysql_connect($dbhost, $dbuser, $dbpassword);
mysql_select_db($dbdatabase, $db);
$validid = pf_validate_number($_GET['id'], "redirect", "index.php");
```

After the usual introductory code, protect the page from users who are not logged in:

```php
$validid = pf_validate_number($_GET['id'], "redirect", "index.php");

if(isset($_SESSION['USERNAME']) == FALSE) {
    header("Location: " . $HOST_NAME
. "login.php?ref=images&id=" . $validid);
}
```

Select the user_id from the *items* table for the current item. This is required so you can check that the owner of the item—not a random user—is accessing the page.

```php
if(isset($_SESSION['USERNAME']) == FALSE) {
    header("Location: " . $HOST_NAME
. "login.php?ref=images&id=" . $validid);
}

$theitemsql = "SELECT user_id FROM items WHERE id = " . $validid . ";";
$theitemresult = mysql_query($theitemsql);
$theitemrow = mysql_fetch_assoc($theitemresult);
```

Check if the current user owns the item by checking if the data from the query matches the USERID session variable. If not, redirect the user:

```php
$theitemresult = mysql_query($theitemsql);
$theitemrow = mysql_fetch_assoc($theitemresult);

if($theitemrow['user_id'] != $_SESSION['USERID']) {
    header("Location: " . $config_basedir);
}
```

To process the form, you use a new PHP superglobal called $_FILES, which you can used to access uploaded files. When a file is uploaded, it contains a number of different attributes, such as the file name, size, type, and so on.

NOTE

Poking at $_FILES

If you want to see what is in the $_FILES array, or any other variable or array for that matter, use print_r():

```
print_r($_FILES);
```

To access specific information from a specific array, use the following format:

```
$_FILES['array']['item']
```

For example, you could refer to the filename of the file in the userfile box that you added by using:

```
$_FILES['userfile']['name']
```

Before the file is authorized, you will run the file through a series of validation checks to ensure that a file was actually uploaded, that it is a legitimate photo, and that the size is not too large. First, check that a file was uploaded:

```
if($theitemrow['user_id'] != $_SESSION['USERID']) {
    header("Location: " . $config_basedir);
}

if($_POST['submit']) {
    if($_FILES['userfile']['name'] == '') {
        header("Location: " . $HOST_NAME . $SCRIPT_NAME
. "?error=nophoto");
    }
```

This code checks to see if the name information in the $_FILES array has a value. If it does not, the page reloads with an appended error variable.

Now you can run a further set of tests. First, check to see if the size is legitimate (not zero):

```
    header("Location: " . $HOST_NAME . $SCRIPT_NAME
. "?error=nophoto");
    }
    elseif($_FILES['userfile']['size'] == 0) {
        header("Location: " . $HOST_NAME . $SCRIPT_NAME
. "?error=photoprob");
    }
```

Check that the size is not greater than the maximum file size set in the hidden field:

```
    header("Location: " . $HOST_NAME . $SCRIPT_NAME
. "?error=photoprob");
    }
    elseif($_FILES['userfile']['size'] > $MAX_FILE_SIZE) {
    header("Location: " . $HOST_NAME . $SCRIPT_NAME
. "?error=large");
    }
```

Run the PHP `getimagesize()` function to determine how the image size. If this returns FALSE, the image is invalid. Remember that the exclamation mark in the `elseif` means *NOT*:

```
    header("Location: " . $HOST_NAME . $SCRIPT_NAME
. "?error=large");
    }
    elseif(!getimagesize($_FILES['userfile']['tmp_name'])) {
    header("Location: " . $HOST_NAME . $SCRIPT_NAME
. "?error=invalid");
    }
```

If this battery of tests does not cause the page to reload with an error, the image is legitimate and the file can be copied to a safe directory.

First, specify the safe directory for images:

```
    header("Location: " . $HOST_NAME . $SCRIPT_NAME
. "?error=invalid");
    }
    else {
    $uploaddir = "/opt/lampp/htdocs/sites/auction/images/";
    $uploadfile = $uploaddir . $_FILES['userfile']['name'];
```

NOTE

Temporary Means Temporary

When you upload the image with the form, the file is stored in a temporary directory. This directory really is temporary and is likely to be cleaned out regularly or on reboot.

Configure this directory inside *php.ini* by setting the `upload_tmp_dir` option in *php.ini*.

You create a variable called $uploaddir, which should point to a legitimate location inside the main project directory. Create a new directory called *images* with read and write access permissions and change $uploaddir to your directory. The second line concatenates this directory and adds the file name. The $uploaddir variable needs a trailing forward slash (/) to ensure that the image name is concatenated correctly.

Copy the file and add the name to the database:

```
$uploaddir = "/opt/lampp/htdocs/sites/auction/images/";
$uploadfile = $uploaddir . $_FILES['userfile']['name'];

if(move_uploaded_file($_FILES['userfile']['tmp_name'],
$uploadfile)) {

    $inssql = "INSERT INTO images(item_id, name)
VALUES(" . $validid . ", '" . $_FILES['userfile']['name']
. "')";
    mysql_query($inssql);

    header("Location: " . $HOST_NAME . $SCRIPT_NAME
. "?id=" . $validid);
    }
```

The move_uploaded_file() function moves the file by passing it the name of the temporary file ($_FILES['userfile']['tmp_name']), the destination, and the name it will be saved as ($uploadfile). You then insert the filename and item_id into the *images* table and reload the page.

If for some reason move_uploaded_file() fails (such as incorrect file permissions), display an error message:

```
    header("Location: " . $HOST_NAME . $SCRIPT_NAME
. "?id=" . $validid);
    }
    else {
        echo 'There was a problem uploading your file.<br />';
    }
    }
}
```

With the processing complete, you can now display the existing images before the form. You can also display any error messages that resulted from the earlier tests.

Select all of the records from the *images* table with the current item id (stored in $validid):

```
    }
    }
}
```

```
else {
  require("header.php");

  $imagessql = "SELECT * FROM images WHERE item_id = " . $validid
. ";";
  $imagesresult = mysql_query($imagessql);
  $imagesnumrows = mysql_num_rows($imagesresult);
```

Display the images:

```
  $imagesresult = mysql_query($imagessql);
  $imagesnumrows = mysql_num_rows($imagesresult);

  echo "<h1>Current images</h1>";

  if($imagesnumrows == 0) {
    echo "No images.";
  }
  else {
    echo "<table>";
    while($imagesrow = mysql_fetch_assoc($imagesresult)) {
      echo "<tr>";
      echo "<td><img src='" . $config_basedir . "/images/"
. $imagesrow['name'] . "' width='100'></td>";
      echo "<td>[<a href='deleteimage.php?image_id="
. $imagesrow['id'] . "&item_id=" . $validid
. "'>delete</a>]</td>";
      echo "</tr>";
    }
    echo "</table>";
```

If no rows are returned, the text No images is displayed; otherwise, a table is created and a while loop iterates through the images. In addition to displaying the image, a link is made to a page called *delete.php*, and the id of both the image and item are added to the link as GET variables.

After the images are displayed, the form is displayed. Just before the form code, add a switch statement to display the errors:

```
    }
    echo "</table>";
  }
  switch($_GET['error']) {
    case "empty":
      echo 'You did not select anything.';
    break;

    case "nophoto":
      echo 'You did not select a photo to upload.';
    break;
```

```
    case "photoprob":
        echo 'There appears to be a problem with the
photo you are uploading';
    break;

    case "large":
        echo 'The photo you selected is too large';
    break;

    case "invalid":
        echo 'The photo you selected is not a valid image file';
    break;
    }

?>
```

Finally, add the closing curly bracket after the form and add the footer file:

```
When you have finished adding photos, go and
 <a href="<?php echo "itemdetails.php?id="
 . $validid; ?>">see your item</a>!

<?php
}

require("footer.php");
?>
```

The completed page is shown in Figure 7-6.

Deleting an Image

In this section, you create the Delete page that was created in the previous script.

When the user clicks the Delete link, the *delete.php* page prompts you to verify that you want to delete the image. With this message, there will be two Submit buttons, with either Yes and No written on them. You can then check which Submit button has been clicked and respond accordingly:

- If the user clicks the Yes button, the image is deleted, the record is removed from the *images* table, and the page redirects to *addimages.php*.
- If the user clicks the No button, the page redirects to *addimages.php*.

The first step is to add the form. Create a new page called deleteimage.php and the following code:

```
    <h2>Delete image?</h2>
    <form action="<?php echo
pf_script_with_get($SCRIPT_NAME); ?>" method="post">
```

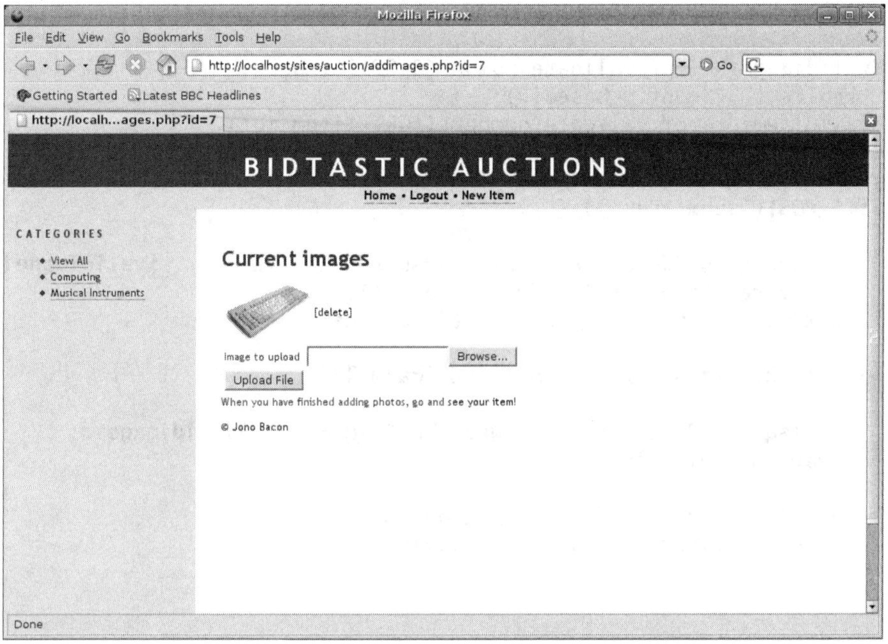

FIGURE 7-6 An item can have a number of images attached to it.

```
Are you sure you want to delete this image?
<p>
<input type="submit" name="submityes"
value="Yes"> <input type="submit" name="submitno" value="No">
</p>
</form>
```

An important point to note about that the form is that the two submit buttons in the preceding code have different names: submityes and submitno.

Move to the top of the page and add the initial code to process the form:

```
<?php

require("config.php");
require("functions.php");

$db = mysql_connect($dbhost, $dbuser, $dbpassword);
mysql_select_db($dbdatabase, $db);

$validimageid = pf_validate_number($_GET['image_id'], "redirect",
$config_basedir);
$validitemid = pf_validate_number($_GET['item_id'], "redirect",
$config_basedir);
```

Check to see if the Yes button was clicked (submityes):

```php
$validimageid = pf_validate_number($_GET['image_id'],
 "redirect", $config_basedir);
$validitemid = pf_validate_number($_GET['item_id'],
 "redirect", $config_basedir);

if($_POST['submityes']) {

    $imagesql = "SELECT name FROM images WHERE id = " . $validimageid;
    $imageresult = mysql_query($imagesql);
    $imagerow = mysql_fetch_assoc($imageresult);

    unlink("./images/" . $imagerow['name']);

    $delsql = "DELETE FROM images WHERE id = " . $validimageid;
    mysql_query($delsql);

    header("Location: " . $config_basedir
 . "addimages.php?id=" . $validitemid);

}
```

If the Yes button *is* clicked, the query selects the name of the image from the *images* table with the id of $validimageid. After the query is run, the unlink() command physically deletes the file. Finally, the DELETE query removes the record, and the page is redirected.

If the No button is clicked, the page redirects to *addimages.php*:

```php
    header("Location: " . $config_basedir . "addimages.php?id="
 . $validitemid);

}
elseif($_POST['submitno']) {
    header("Location: " . $config_basedir . "addimages.php?id="
 . $validitemid);
}
```

Display the form:

```php
else {
    require("header.php");
?>

    <h2>Delete image?</h2>
    <form action="<?php
 echo pf_script_with_get($SCRIPT_NAME); ?>" method="post">
```

Finally, at the bottom of the file, add the closing code:

```
    </p>
    </form>
```

```php
<?php
}
require("footer.php");
?>
```

PROCESSING AUCTIONS

With most auction sites, when an auction ends, email messages are sent to the owner of the item and the winning bidder (if there is one) to indicate the result of the auction. This message typically includes the name of the item and the details of the owner/winner, depending on which email is sent. The challenge with this feature is in sending the emails when the auction has finished. PHP and MySQL do not include features to specify a particular time at which a piece of code should be executed. So how do you do it?

The solution is to first create a page that determines which auctions have ended and sent the emails. To ensure processing is kept to a minimum, the endnotified field in the *items* table is set to 1 when an item has been processed. As such, you can search for items with an enddate older than NOW() in which endnotifed is 0. This page can be used to process all auctions by simply running it.

To solve the problem of processing the auctions when they have finished, you can use a scheduled tasks tool such as cron (Linux) or Windows Scheduler (Windows) to schedule that the page is accessed approximately every five minutes. You can use the wget command-line tool to do this.

Create a page called *processauctions.php* and run a query to select all the items:

```php
<?php

require("config.php");
require("header.php");

$itemssql = "SELECT users.username, users.email, items.id,
 items.name FROM items, users WHERE dateends < NOW() AND
 items.user_id = users.id AND endnotified = 0;";
$itemsresult = mysql_query($itemssql);
```

This query selects the username, email, item id, and name for all records in which dateends is in the past and in which endnotified is set to 0. Each record returned is an ended auction.

Iterate through the records:

```
$itemssql = "SELECT users.username, users.email, items.id,
 items.name FROM items, users WHERE dateends < NOW() AND
 items.user_id = users.id AND endnotified = 0;";
$itemsresult = mysql_query($itemssql);

while($itemsrow = mysql_fetch_assoc($itemsresult)) {
    $bidssql = "SELECT bids.amount, users.username,
 users.email FROM bids, users WHERE bids.user_id = users.id
 AND item_id = " . $itemsrow['id'] . " ORDER BY amount
 DESC LIMIT 1;";
    $bidsresult = mysql_query($bidssql);
    $bidsnumrows = mysql_num_rows($bidsresult);
```

For each ended auction, a check is made to see if any bids were placed, and the highest amount and username and email address of the highest bidder is returned. The query works by asking for the username, email, and bid amount for a record in which item_id is equal to $itemsrow['id']. Each record is ordered in descending order by amount and returns only a single row (LIMIT 1). Ordering in descending order and only returning one row returns the latest entry in the table. This is a nice alternative to using the MAX() function to determine the highest price.

With the data gathered, now you can construct and send the emails. To generate the mails, use the *heredoc* syntax that was discussed in Chapter 5. When using this syntax, you cannot use arrays inside it. Instead, extract data into normal variables:

```
$bidsresult = mysql_query($bidssql);
$bidsnumrows = mysql_num_rows($bidsresult);

$own_owner = $itemsrow['username'];
$own_email = $itemsrow['email'];
$own_name = $itemsrow['name'];
```

There are three possible scenarios in which emails need to be sent. You would send them to

- The owner of the auction to indicate that no bids were made on the item.
- The owner to indicate the highest bidder and the bidder's contact details.
- The winning bidder to indicate the owner of the auction.

First, create the one that is sent to the owner indicating that no bids were made. To see if there were any bids, check if the $bidsnumrows has a value. If not, create the following email message:

```
$own_email = $itemsrow['email'];
$own_name = $itemsrow['name'];
```

```
    if($bidsnumrows == 0) {
$owner_body=<<<_OWNER_

Hi $own_owner,

Sorry, but your item '$own_name', did not have any bids placed with it.

_OWNER_;

        mail($own_email, "Your item '" . $own_name
. "' did not sell", $owner_body);
    }
```

If there were rows in the *bids* table, construct the other two types of email message:

```
        mail($own_email, "Your item '" . $own_name
. "' did not sell", $owner_body);
    }
    else {
    echo "item with bids" . $itemsrow['id'];
        $bidsrow = mysql_fetch_assoc($bidsresult);

        $own_highestbid = $bidsrow['amount'];

        $win_winner = $bidsrow['username'];
        $win_email = $bidsrow['email'];

$owner_body=<<<_OWNER_

Hi $own_owner,

Congratulations! The auction for your item '$own_name',
 has completed with a winning bid
of $config_currency$own_highestbid bidded by $win_winner!

Bid details:

Item: $own_name
Amount: $config_currency$own_highestbid
Winning bidder: $win_winner ($win_email)

It is recommended that you contact the winning bidder within 3 days.

_OWNER_;

        $winner_body=<<<_WINNER_

Hi $win_winner,

Congratulations! Your bid of $config_currency$own_highestbid for
the item '$own_name' was the highest bid!
```

```
Bid details:

Item: $own_name
Amount: $config_currency$own_highestbid
Owner: $own_owner ($own_email)

It is recommended that you contact the owner of the item within 3 days.

_WINNER_;

        mail($own_email, "Your item '" . $own_name
    . "' has sold", $owner_body);
        mail($win_email, "You won item '" . $own_name
    . "'!", $winner_body);
```

Update the *items* table and set endnotified to 1 to indicate that the auction has been processed:

```
        mail($own_email, "Your item '" . $own_name
    . "' has sold", $owner_body);
        mail($win_email, "You won item '" . $own_name
    . "'!", $winner_body);
    }

    $updsql = "UPDATE items SET endnotified = 1 WHERE id = " .
$itemsrow['id'];
    echo $updsql;
    mysql_query($updsql);
}
```

Finally, add the footer code:

```
    mysql_query($updsql);
}

require("footer.php");

?>
```

SCHEDULING THE PAGE TO BE RUN

To schedule the page to be run at regular intervals, use the wget download utility to perform the visit. The wget utility is mainly used for downloading files, so on Linux you will need to send any output to /dev/null:

```
foo@bar:~$ wget --delete-after
http://localhost/auction/processauctions.php
```

To schedule this to occur at regular intervals, add the following line to a cron job. First, load the crontab with the following:

```
foo@bar:~$ crontab -e
```

To run the command every five minutes, add the following line to the crontab:

```
*/5 * * * * wget —delete-after
http://localhost/auction/processauctions.php
```

You can set this in Windows by using the Schedule Tasks option in the Control Panel. Inside this dialog box, select the program to run and specify the time.

Be sure to change the URL to one that is relevant to your computer.

SUMMARY

In this project, you explored a number of different challenges and problems faced with writing an auction site. This project has been useful for practicing skills for checking dates, dealing with prices, and running queries to summarize data from the database.

Many more possibilities exist for adding more functionality, and as you learn more and more features in PHP, you can return to this project to enhance different parts of the code. An example of this is the form handling. In this project, you deliberately processed the forms manually to learn how to use addslashes() to handle user input. In a later project, you will use HTML_QuickForm to manage the forms.

TIP

Another possibility is to add an administration section with tools to manage the auction site in the same way we have developed administration sections in previous projects. Each project in this book is not intended to be a complete, finished application, and there is plenty of scope to add additional features and improve the projects in different ways. Simply use your imagination and fill in the gaps where needed. This is part of the fun of software development—when you know the technology, the sky is the limit. Good luck!

CHAPTER 8

Creating a Web-Based Calendar

For most of us, life is increasingly busy. Unless you made a few million in the stock market and now live aboard a gold-plated yacht, keeping your meetings, social events, dentist appointments, and basket weaving club meetings straight is a daily struggle.

In this project, you will create a Web-based calendar to help with these struggles. The project implements everything you need to manage your life—the ability to view months at a time, display event information, and add new events. Although simple in concept, calendars offer a number of interesting challenges for developers. To make the project even more interesting, you explore Ajax, a technology set that provides for highly dynamic Web sites that function much like desktop applications. Plug yourself in, stretch those fingers, and get ready!

PROJECT OVERVIEW

To get a clear idea of how the project will work, take a look at the following use case:

> Susan has a terrible memory. Although she is extremely popular among her friends and co-workers, Susan often accepts invitations to parties and events and then promptly forgets about them. After one too many missed dinner appointments, she decides to use a Web-based calendar, one she can access from any Web browser, anywhere in the world.
>
> Susan goes to her calendar and enters her login details. After she successfully logs in, she can see the current month, as well as each of the events she booked for that month—all located on the correct day. The calendar's sidebar

also includes a list of the events occurring in the near future. To view information about a specific event, Susan clicks the event name, and the details appear (also in the calendar sidebar).

Susan realizes that she added an event for the coming Saturday, which she needs to cancel. To delete it, she clicks the X button next to event. The calendar is updated, and the event disappears.

Susan now needs to add a new event (her dachshund's training class) to the calendar. She clicks on the day that the class is scheduled, and the sidebar is redrawn with a form that she can fill in. She adds the name of the event, the start and end times, and a short description. She then clicks the Add Event button, and the calendar refreshes, displaying the new event.

BUILDING THE DATABASE

The database you will create is shown in Figure 8-1.

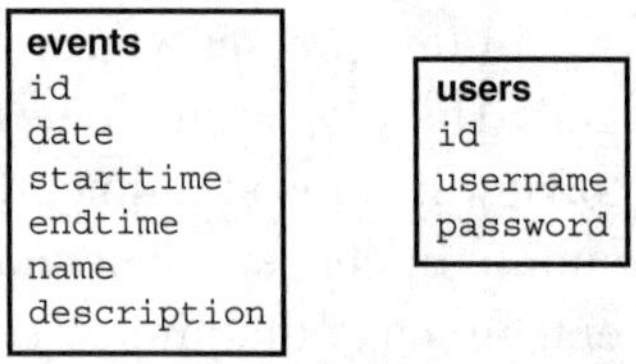

FIGURE 8-1
To say that the database in this project is simple is quite an understatement!

```
events
id
date
starttime
endtime
name
description
```

```
users
id
username
password
```

With only two tables in the project (neither of which are related), this is an incredibly simple database to set up. The events table contains a list of the events in the calendar, and the users table contains the user logins.

Implementing the Database

Start phpMyAdmin. Create a new database called simplecal and add the following tables.

The *events* Table

- id. Make this an INT (several events are possible) and turn on auto_increment. Set this field as a primary key.
- date. Make this a DATE.
- starttime. Make this a TIME.
- endtime. Make this a TIME.
- name. Make this a VARCHAR with a length of 50.
- description. Make this a TEXT.

The *logins* Table

- id. Make this a TINYINT and turn on auto_increment. Set this field as a primary key.
- username. Make this a VARCHAR with a length of 10.
- password. Make this a VARCHAR with a length of 10.

Insert Sample Data

In this section, you add some sample data to get started. Remember, do not fill in a number in the id column; auto_increment takes care of this for you. Feel free to add your own sample data or use the data shown in Table 8-1.

Sample Data for the *events* Table

Add the sample events from Table 8-1.

TABLE 8-1   Sample events make it easier to check if the calendar works.

DATE	STARTTIME	ENDTIME	NAME	DESCRIPTION
2007-10-14	12:00:00	14:00:00	Meeting with Emily	Important meeting to discuss future projects.
2007-10-14	18:00:00	19:30:00	Meal with Lee	Meal with Lee to celebrate working together.
2007-11-20	08:30:00	09:30:00	Working breakfast	Meeting with Cliff to talk shop.

Sample Data for the *logins* Table

Add a username and password for the *logins* table (and keep the password handy!).

STARTING TO CODE

First, you need to take care of the site template, style, and some utility functions. Then you can move into login screens and the actual calendar pages and scripts.

Site Layout and Style

As you've done in previous chapters, the first step is to create the configuration, header, and footer files. Create a new directory called *simplecal*. Now copy the db.php file from previous projects to the *simplecal* directory. Next, create a new file called *config.php*, the contents of which are shown in Example 8-1.

EXAMPLE 8-1   A simple configuration file

```php
<?php

$dbhost = "localhost";
$dbuser = "root";
$dbpassword = "";
$dbdatabase = "simplecal";

$config_name = "James Hillchin's Calendar";

$config_basedir = "http://localhost/sites/simplecal/";

?>
```

Just as *config.php* was used in previous projects, the same stylesheet from previous projects is used here. You will need to make a few additions at the bottom, however. Create a new file called *stylesheet.css* and add the code shown in Example 8-2.

EXAMPLE 8-2   The additional elements in the stylesheet are used to customize the calendar view.

```css
body {
    font-family: "trebuchet ms", verdana, sans-serif;
    font-size: 12px;
    line-height: 1.5em;
    color: #333;
    background: #ffffff;
    margin: 0;
    padding: 0;
    text-align: center;
    width: 100%;
}

p {
    margin-top: 10px;
}

h3 {
```

```
    font: bold 140% trebuchet ms, sans-serif;
    letter-spacing: 5px;
    margin-bottom: 0;
    color: #000000;
}

hr {
    color: #eee;
    background-color: #000;
    height: 2px;
}

a:link {
    text-decoration: none;
    color: #000;
}

a:visited {
    text-decoration: none;
    color: #000;
}

a:hover, a:active {
    text-decoration: none;
    color: #000;
}


img {
    border: 0;
}

#container {
    position: absolute;
    top: 85px;
    left: 0px;
    background: #ffffff;
    margin: 0 auto 0 auto;
    border-bottom: 1px solid #eee;
    text-align: left;
    width: 100%;
    height: 100%;
}

#menu {
    font-family: "trebuchet ms", verdana, sans-serif;
    font-size: 14px;
    font-weight: bold;
    position: absolute;
    height: 27px;
    top: 60px;
```

continues

EXAMPLE 8-2   Continued.

```css
    left: 0px;
    width: 100%;
    padding: 0px;
    color: #000000;
    background-color: #eee
}

#header {
    position: absolute;
    top: 0px;
    left: 0px;
    height: 60px;
    width: 100%;
    background: #333;
    padding-top: 8px;
}

#header h1 {
    font-size: 30px;
    text-transform: uppercase;
    letter-spacing: 0.3em;
    color: #fff;
}

#main {
    margin: 5px 5px 5px 5px;
    padding: 5px 5px 5px 5px;
    background: #FFFFFF;
}


#bar {
    float: left;
    width: 200px;
    background: #eee;
    z-index: 1;
    padding: 10px;
    margin-right: 30px;
    height: 100%;
}

#bar h1 {
    font-size: 12px;
    text-transform: uppercase;
    letter-spacing: 0.3em;
}

/* ---- calendar specific styles ---- */
```

```
a.cal_date:link {
text-decoration:none;color:white;
display:block;width:100%;height:100%;
}

a.cal_date:visited {
text-decoration:none;color:white;display:block;width:100%;
height:100%;
}

a.cal_date:hover {
text-decoration:none;color:white;display:block;width:100%;
height:100%;
}

a.cal_date:active {
text-decoration:none;color:white;display:block;width:100%;
height:100%;
}

a.cal:link {
text-decoration:none;color:red;display:block;
height:100%;background:white;padding:3px;
}

a.cal:visited {
text-decoration:none;color:red;
display:block;width:100%;height:100%;background:white;
padding:3px;
}

a.cal:hover {
text-decoration:none;color:white;
display:block;width:100%;height:100%;background:#dddddd;
border: thin solid black;padding:0px;
}

a.cal:active {
text-decoration:none;color:red;
display:block;width:100%;height:100%;background:white;
padding:3px;
}

a.event:link {
text-decoration:none;color:blue;width:100%;
background:lightblue;padding:3px;}

a.event:visited {
text-decoration:none;color:blue;width:100%;
background:lightblue;padding:3px;
}
```

continues

EXAMPLE 8-2 Continued.

```css
a.deleteevent:link {
text-decoration:none;color:blue;background:red;
padding:3px;border:thin solid black;
}

a.deleteevent:visited {
text-decoration:none;color:blue;background:red;
padding:3px;border:thin solid black;
}


table.cal {
   border: thin solid black;
}

th.cal {
  background: #000000;
  color: #ffffff;
}

td.cal_date {
  background: #333333;
  color: #ffffff;
}

td.cal {
}

span.datepicker {
   font-family: "trebuchet ms", verdana, sans-serif;
   font-size: 18px;
   font-weight: bold;
   text-align: center;
}

#login {
   font-family: "trebuchet ms", verdana, sans-serif;
   font-size: 12px;
   border: thin solid black;
   width: 300px;
   margin: 20px auto 0 auto;
   background: #eeeeee;
   padding: 10px;
}
```

Create *header.php* and add the header code shown in Example 8-3.

EXAMPLE 8-3   With the exception of a few additions, the header file is very similar to those used in previous projects.

```php
<?php

session_start();

require("config.php");

$db = mysql_connect($dbhost, $dbuser, $dbpassword);
mysql_select_db($dbdatabase, $db);

?>
<!DOCTYPE HTML PUBLIC "-//W3C//DTD HTML 4.01
 Transitional//EN" "http://www.w3.org/TR/html4/loose.dtd">
<html>
<head>
   <title><?php echo $config_name; ?></title>
   <script language="javascript" type="text/javascript"
        src="./internal_request.js">
   </script>
   <link href="stylesheet.css" rel="stylesheet">
</head>
<body>
<div id="header">
<h1><?php echo $config_name; ?></h1>
</div>
   <div id="menu">
      &bull;
      <a href="<?php echo $config_basedir; ?>">This month</a>
      &bull;
      <a href="<?php echo $config_basedir; ?>/logout.php">Logout</a>
      &bull;
   </div>
<div id="container">
   <div id="bar">
      <?php require("bar.php"); ?>
   </div>
```

In this code, there is one distinctive addition:

```
<script language="javascript" type="text/javascript"
        src="./internal_request.js">
</script>
```

This snippet of code includes a special JavaScript file, which contains functions that you'll use in several portions of the calendar site. Like in other projects, *bar.php* is included in the header file. This file is covered in depth later in the chapter.

Add the small but perfectly formed footer code to *footer.php*, as shown in Example 8-4.

EXAMPLE 8-4 The footer file closes off the main content <div> and the body and html tags.

```
</div>
</body>
</html>
```

The final file to create—at least in this startup phase—is *functions.php*. Add the pf_validate_function() code from a previous project to the file, as shown in Example 8-5.

EXAMPLE 8-5 The *pf_validate_number()* function is used again to validate GET variables.

```php
<?php

function pf_validate_number($value, $function, $redirect) {
   if(isset($value) == TRUE) {
      if(is_numeric($value) == FALSE) {
         $error = 1;
      }

      if($error == 1) {
         header("Location: " . $redirect);
      }
      else {
         $final = $value;
      }
   }
   else {
      if($function == 'redirect') {
         header("Location: " . $redirect);
      }

      if($function == "value") {
         $final = 0;
      }
   }

   return $final;
}

?>
```

Building the Login Screen

For the purposes of this project, the calendar is intended to be a private Web application for use by a single person. To ensure that other people do not snoop around the calendar, you'll protect it with a login page. This login page takes a username and password, and then redirects you to the main calendar page after a successful login.

This page is no different from the code used in previous login pages. The only difference is the name of the session variable: LOGGEDIN. Create a new file called *index.php* and add the code from Example 8-6.

EXAMPLE 8-6 The login page is virtually identical to the login code from previous projects.

```php
<?php
    session_start();

    require("db.php");

    if(isset($_SESSION['LOGGEDIN']) == TRUE) {
        header("Location: " . $config_basedir . "view.php");
    }

    if($_POST['submit'])
    {
        $loginsql = "SELECT * FROM logins WHERE username = '"
. $_POST['userBox'] . "' AND password = '"
. $_POST['passBox'] . "'";
        $loginres = mysql_query($loginsql);
        $numrows = mysql_num_rows($loginres);

        if($numrows == 1)
        {
            $loginrow = mysql_fetch_assoc($loginres);

            session_register("LOGGEDIN");

            $_SESSION['LOGGEDIN'] = 1;

            header("Location: " . $config_basedir . "view.php");
        }
        else
        {
            header("Location: http://" . $HTTP_HOST
. $SCRIPT_NAME . "?error=1");
        }
    }
```

continues

EXAMPLE 8-6 Continued

```
   else
   {
?>
<!DOCTYPE HTML PUBLIC "-//W3C//DTD HTML 4.01
 Transitional//EN" "http://www.w3.org/TR/html4/loose.dtd">
<html>
<head>
   <title></title>
   <link href="stylesheet.css" rel="stylesheet">
</head>
<body>
   <div id="login">

   <h1>Calendar Login</h1>
   Please enter your username and password to log on.
   <p>

   <?php
      if($_GET['error']) {
         echo "<strong>Incorrect username/password</strong>";
      }
   ?>

   <form action="<?php echo $SCRIPT_NAME; ?>" method="POST">
   <table>
      <tr>
         <td>Username</td>
         <td><input type="text" name="userBox">
      </tr>
      <tr>
         <td>Password</td>
         <td><input type="password" name="passBox">
      </tr>
      <tr>
         <td></td>
         <td><input type="submit" name="submit" value="Log in">
      </tr>
   </table>
   </form>
</div>
<?php
   }

?>
```

Some HTML is included in the file because the page does not include the header and footer template files. This results in the login page looking quite a bit different from the rest of the site; however, this is an intentional difference, rather than an accidental one. Having the login page look substantially different from the rest of an application makes users aware that they should pay special attention to the unique-looking page. The completed login page should resemble something similar to the page shown in Figure 8-2.

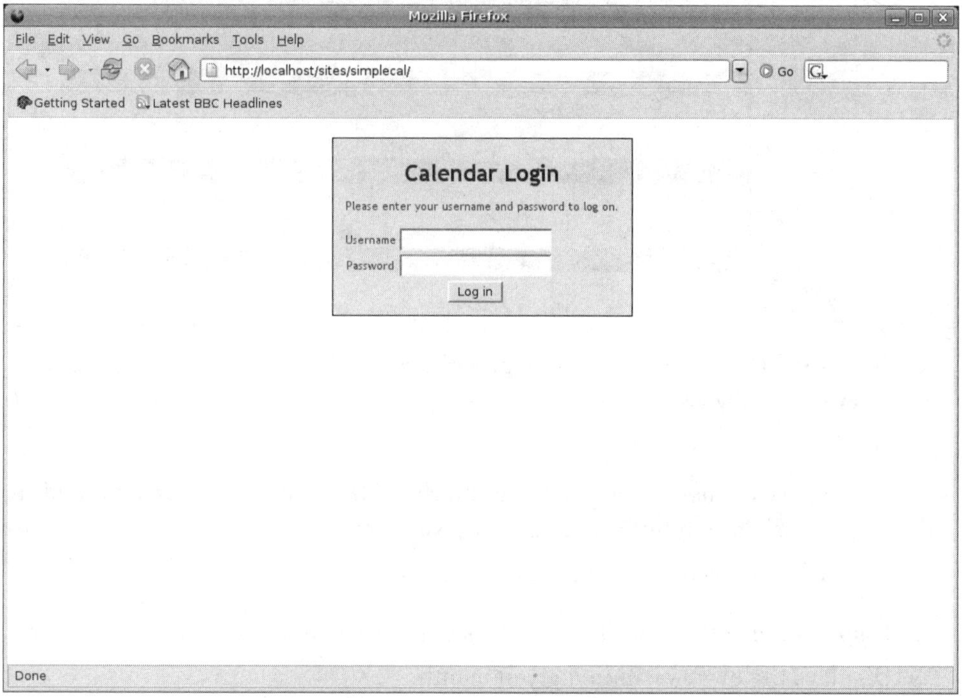

FIGURE 8-2   Because you don't want just anyone looking at your events, a login screen—with its own unique look and feel—protects the calendar.

VIEWING EVENTS

The vast majority of calendars have a very similar interface. This interface typically includes a view of the entire month, with each day shown with its date. Usually, the days are represented as squares, and events on those days are positioned inside the squares. And, for usability, each day's events are normally listed in chronological order. Because this design has worked for so long, we'll stick with it here. Figure 8-3 shows the user interface for the calendar.

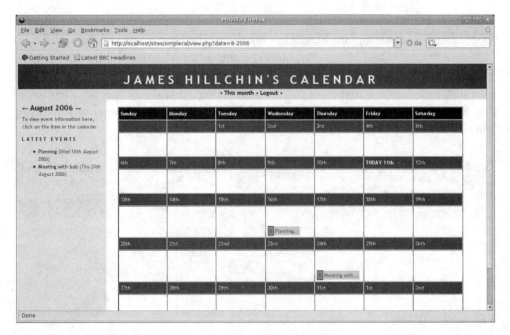

FIGURE 8-3 The calendar interface provides a simple means of viewing and deleting events in any given month.

Two primary elements comprise the interface: the main calendar view and the sidebar. Each of these interface areas has several key functions.

The key functions of the main calendar are as follows:

- Displays a month, as well as the days of the week and the dates for each day.
- Displays the events within a given month.
- Allows the user to click an event and view information about that event.
- Allows the user to add events by clicking any open space for a given day.

The key functions of the sidebar are as follows:

- Displays the current month's name and year. The user can use the arrows to choose previous or future months.
- Allows the user to click an event in the main calendar to display the event information in the sidebar.
- Allows the user to add a new event and displays the new event form in the sidebar.
- Displays a list of upcoming events.

In previous projects, you accessed each piece of project functionality by loading different pages. For example, the New Topic page was used to add a new post to the forums project. In this project, however, the Web interface doesn't need to change much, even when accessing different features. A calendar will always be visible, and the sidebar will always display different types of information. Therefore, there's no need to create multiple pages. This further simplifies the application, which is never a bad thing.

To make the calendar even more dynamic, you will use an exciting technology called Ajax to prevent the need for refreshing the entire page when you want to access new functionality.

All About Ajax

Ajax, which is sometimes referred to as Asynchronous JavaScript and XML, is an exciting technology that has been taking the Web development world by storm. Ajax has been largely spurred on by some innovative uses of the technology by Google with Gmail (http://mail.google.com) and Google Maps (http://maps.google.com).

The idea behind Ajax is that you can send requests to a server, as you normally do; but instead of refreshing the entire page, you use JavaScript to update only a portion of the page. As a result, Web applications aren't constantly forcing users to wait for entirely new pages to be loaded in their browsers; the application feels more like a desktop program.

A good example of this is Google's Gmail application. To compose a new message, you type the first few letters of the email address into a form. After you type the first few letters, a new window prompts you to select from a list of email addresses of people you have already emailed. In the background, Gmail is using Ajax to grab the list of email addresses from the server and present this list—without sending a new HTML page to the browser. Ajax offers you a fantastic way of providing a more dynamic experience for your users.

Ajax is not a singular new technology, but instead a combination of a range of technologies. These include the following:

- HTML
- CSS
- Document Object Model (or DOM)
- JavaScript
- XML HTTP Requests

In this project, you use Ajax to refresh a specific part of the calendar sidebar—preventing the need to refresh the entire screen. This makes the application feel smoother and allows you to flex your Ajax muscles.

How Ajax Works

Before discussing how to actually implement an Ajax application, it's helpful to take a minute to understand how Ajax works at a conceptual level. This is best explained with a diagram, as shown in Figure 8-4.

FIGURE 8-4
Ajax takes a number of different steps between a user clicking a link and the page being updated.

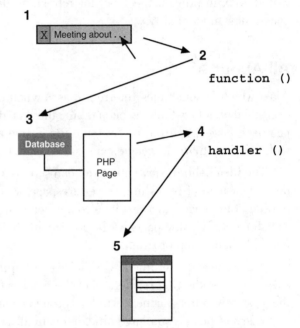

Five distinct steps typically occur in Ajax requests. To demonstrate this, the following list describes how Ajax is applied when the user clicks an event in the calendar:

1. The user clicks an event in which he is interested. Instead of the link connecting to another HTML or PHP page, it triggers a JavaScript function.

2. The JavaScript function connects to a script that can handle the request. The function also requests that it be notified as soon as that request is answered (it does this by *registering a handler* to the response).

3. The PHP script that handles the request processes it and connects to the database to get the required information about the specified event.

4. When the script has gathered the event information, it responds to the JavaScript handler registered in Step 2. This handler—which now contains

the event information—replaces the area in the sidebar with the event data from Step 3.

Easy enough, right? Time to put these steps into action.

Creating the Sidebar

The sidebar contains three main areas, each of which is then added to *bar.php* (which was loaded in *header.php*; refer to Example 8-3).

Dealing with Dates

The first area of the sidebar displays the name and year of the month being viewed, and also provides arrows to allow the user to select the previous or next month. These arrows link to *view.php* and pass it a date GET variable with the month in the format <month>-<year>, such as view.php?date=10-2005 (for October 2005).

The left arrow (go to the previous month) simply subtracts 1 from the current month, and the right arrow adds 1 to the month (to go to the next month). You also need to provide some code to deal with January and December. If the user is looking at 1-2005 (January 2005), the left arrow should link to 12-2004 (December 2004). Likewise, the right arrow for 12-2005 should link to 1-2006.

With all this in mind, create *bar.php* and add the following code:

```php
<?php

    if(isset($_GET['date']) == TRUE) {
       $exploddeddate = explode("-", $_GET['date']);
       $month = $exploddeddate[0];
       $year = $exploddeddate[1];
       $numdays = date("t", mktime(0, 0, 0, $month, 1, $year));
    }
    else {
       $month = date("n", mktime());
       $numdays = date("t", mktime());
       $year = date("Y", mktime());
    }
```

If a date GET variable exists, you can view the relevant month. If the variable does not exist, the script uses the current month (this latter case occurs the first time the application is opened in a session).

If a date is present, the code uses explode() to tear open the date and put the month in $month and the year in $year. The number of days is calculated by feeding $month and $year into the mktime() function. This function takes a number of arguments:

```
mktime(0,     0,    0,    $month,    1,    $year);
         |      |     |       |       |       |
       hour  minute second  month    day    year
```

The result of the function is run through `date()`, and the number of days is returned.

Use the same technique to create the date label (such as July 2006) that is displayed in the sidebar:

```
    $numdays = date("t", mktime());
    $year = date("Y", mktime());
}

$displaydate = date("F Y", mktime(0, 0, 0, $month, 1, $year));
```

Calculate the previous date (for when the user clicks on the left arrow):

```
<?php

...

$displaydate = date("F Y", mktime(0, 0, 0, $month, 1, $year));

if($month == 1) {
    $prevdate = "12-" . ($year-1);
}
else {
    $prevdate = ($month-1) . "-" . $year;
}
```

If the month is January, the date is set to December in the previous year. Otherwise, 1 is subtracted from the month.

Repeat for the "next month" arrow, by adding 1 to the month and then dealing with the December special case:

```
$displaydate = date("F Y", mktime(0, 0, 0, $month, 1, $year));

if($month == 1) {
    $prevdate = "12-" . ($year-1);
}
else {
    $prevdate = ($month-1) . "-" . $year;
}

if($month == 12) {
    $nextdate = "1-" . ($year+1);
}
else {
```

```
        $nextdate = ($month+1) . "-" . $year;
    }
```

Display the date:

```
echo "<span class='datepicker'>";
echo "<a href='$SCRIPT_NAME?date=" . $prevdate . "'>&larr;</a> ";
echo $displaydate;
echo " <a href='$SCRIPT_NAME?date=" . $nextdate . "'>&rarr;</a> ";
echo "</span>";

echo "<br />";
?>
```

In this code, the date GET variable is constructed for the current page. The links are applied to two arrows, which are shown using the ← and → HTML entities.

> **NOTE**
>
> ### Use HTML Entities Where Possible
>
> A wide range of special symbols is available as HTML entities. These symbols can be used by referencing the entity code in your HTML, as you just did with the arrows. For a complete list of available entities, see http://www.htmlhelp.com/reference/html40/entities/.
>
> You should always use HTML entities whenever possible, because entities can prevent the need for unnecessary graphics. Entities also improve the accessibility and performance of the Web application.

Preparing for Ajax

With the date picker complete, add the second component of the sidebar:

```
<div id="eventcage">
<p>To view event information here, click on the item in the
calendar.</p>
</div>
```

This creates a <div> called an *event cage*. This is the area of the sidebar that is replaced later by the Ajax requests.

Displaying Upcoming Events

Add the third component for the sidebar:

```
<?php

    echo "<h1>Latest Events</h1>";
```

```
  echo "<ul>";
  $nearsql = "SELECT * FROM events WHERE date >= NOW()
ORDER BY starttime;";
  $nearres = mysql_query($nearsql);
  $nearnumrows = mysql_num_rows($nearres);

  if($nearnumrows == 0) {
     echo "No events!";
  }
  else {
     while($nearrow = mysql_fetch_assoc($nearres)) {
        echo "<li><a href='#' onclick='getEvent("
. $nearrow['id'] . ")'>" . $nearrow['name'] . "</a> (<i>"
. $nearrow['date'] . "</i>)</li>";
     }
  }

  echo "</ul>";

?>
```

Here, a fairly simple SELECT query is issued to return all events that are from the current day onward. A check is made to see if no rows are returned. If this is the case, the text No events! is displayed. Otherwise, a link is added to runs the getEvent() JavaScript function (which you'll review in detail shortly).

Example 8-7 shows the completed sidebar code.

EXAMPLE 8-7 The sidebar handles months, event details, and upcoming events.

```
<?php

  if(isset($_GET['date']) == TRUE) {
     $explodeddate = explode("-", $_GET['date']);
     $month = $explodeddate[0];
     $year = $explodeddate[1];
     $numdays = date("t", mktime(0, 0, 0, $month, 1, $year));
  }
  else {
     $month = date("n", mktime());
     $numdays = date("t", mktime());
     $year = date("Y", mktime());
  }

  $displaydate = date("F Y", mktime(0, 0, 0, $month, 1, $year));

  if($month == 1) {
```

```php
        $prevdate = "12-" .  ($year-1);
    }
    else {
        $prevdate = ($month-1) . "-" . $year;
    }

    if($month == 12) {
        $nextdate = "1-" .  ($year+1);
    }
    else {
        $nextdate = ($month+1) . "-" . $year;
    }

    echo "<span class='datepicker'>";
    echo "<a href='$SCRIPT_NAME?date=" . $prevdate . "'>&larr;</a> ";
    echo $displaydate;
    echo " <a href='$SCRIPT_NAME?date=" . $nextdate . "'>&rarr;</a> ";
    echo "</span>";

    echo "<br />";
?>

<div id="eventcage">
<p>To view event information here, click on the item in
 the calendar.</p>
</div>

<?php

    echo "<h1>Latest Events</h1>";

    echo "<ul>";
    $nearsql = "SELECT * FROM events WHERE date >= NOW()
 ORDER BY starttime;";
    $nearres = mysql_query($nearsql);
    $nearnumrows = mysql_num_rows($nearres);

    if($nearnumrows == 0) {
        echo "No events!";
    }
    else {
        while($nearrow = mysql_fetch_assoc($nearres)) {
            echo "<li><a href='#' onclick='getEvent(" . $nearrow['id']
 . ")'>" . $nearrow['name'] . "</a> (<i>" . $nearrow['date'] .
"</i>)</li>";
        }
    }

    echo "</ul>";

?>
```

The Calendar View

The main calendar view displays a calendar month and lists any events for that month on the appropriate day.

Constructing a calendar month involves creating a number of rows, as shown in Figure 8-5.

To build something like this, you first need to create a table and then add each row, one by one. The weekdays are table headings, and then you gradually build up each row of individual days.

> **NOTE**
>
> **Fair Warning**
>
> Building a calendar view is a surprisingly tricky piece of code to write. If you lose track of the logic, you will spend hours trying to understand why you are getting slightly different results than you expected. The trick is to build up the calendar step by step.

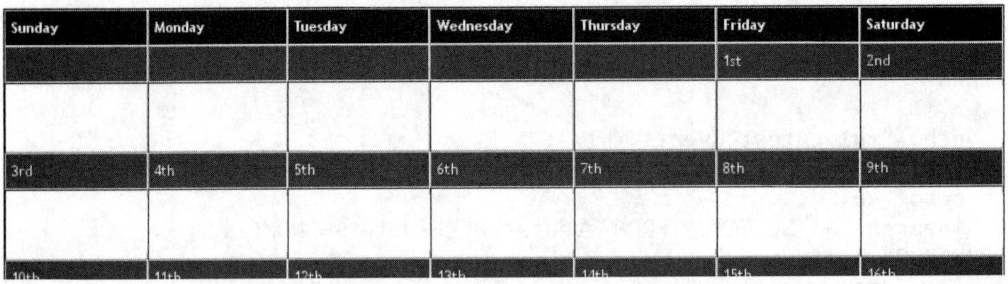

Sunday	Monday	Tuesday	Wednesday	Thursday	Friday	Saturday
					1st	2nd
3rd	4th	5th	6th	7th	8th	9th
10th	11th	12th	13th	14th	15th	16th

FIGURE 8-5 The calendar view contains a number of rows, including the weekdays, the dates, and an area in which events are located.

Create a new file called *view.php* and add this code:

```php
<?php

session_start();

require("config.php");

if(isset($_SESSION['LOGGEDIN']) == FALSE) {
    header("Location: " . $config_basedir);
}
```

After you have protected the page from any users not logged in, create a small function:

```php
<?php

session_start();

require("config.php");

if(isset($_SESSION['LOGGEDIN']) == FALSE) {
    header("Location: " . $config_basedir);
}

function short_event($name) {
    $final = "";
    $final = (substr($name, 0, 12) . "...");

    return $final;
}
```

This function shortens the name of the event that is added to a calendar day. With your Working Breakfast event, the name is shorted to Working Brea… on the calendar. This will keep the event to a single line. To do this, the function uses substr() to cut out the first 12 letters and then append … to the end of the string.

Continue adding code:

```php
    return $final;
}

require("header.php");

if($_GET['error']) {
    echo "<script>newEvent('" . $_GET['eventdate'] . "', 1)</script>";
}
```

This code if checks to see if an error GET variable exists. If so, a <script> tag is added. This block is intended for when the user has entered a new event into the form later. If the form contains errors, the page is reloaded and the <script> tag runs the newEvent() JavaScript function. This function is passed two arguments: the date and an error code. (newEvent()is discussed in detail later in this chapter.)

Create the variables and add the table headings:

```php
if($_GET['error']) {
    echo "<script>newEvent('" . $_GET['eventdate'] . "', 1)</script>";
}

$cols = 7;
$weekday = date("w", mktime(0, 0, 0, $month, 1, $year));
```

```
$numrows = ceil(($numdays + $weekday) / $cols);

echo "<br />";
echo "<table class='cal' cellspacing=0 cellpadding=5 border=1>";
echo "<tr>";
echo "<th class='cal'>Sunday</th>";
echo "<th class='cal'>Monday</th>";
echo "<th class='cal'>Tuesday</th>";
echo "<th class='cal'>Wednesday</th>";
echo "<th class='cal'>Thursday</th>";
echo "<th class='cal'>Friday</th>";
echo "<th class='cal'>Saturday</th>";
echo "</tr>";

$counter = 1;
$newcounter = 1;
```

The first three lines set up some essential variables. You first specify the number of columns in the $cols variable—you are using 7, one for each day. Next, the $weekday variable returns the number of the day in the week for the first of the month. For example, if the day is Friday, it is the sixth day and the function returns 5.

NOTE

Counting from Zero

Many functions in PHP begin counting at zero. When you code and get results that are just slightly different (such as 8 cells appearing instead of 7), it could be because you have assumed that a function begins counting at 1. Although this can be the case, most functions begin at 0.

The $numrows variable takes the $numdays variable from *bar.php*, adds the $weekday, and divides by the number of columns (7). The reason you add $weekday to $numdays is to pad out the days remaining from the previous month. Referring to Figure 8-5, you can see that the month begins on Friday, but the Sunday to Thursday days do not contain any dates. By adding $weekday, you set the amount of days that are padded. In this example, Friday returns 5, and if you count from left to right (starting with 0), you get Friday.

After setting these variables, the table headings are added and, finally, two variables are set to 1. These variables will be used as counters later in the code.

Now you can add the first row of cells that add the date for a given day. Before you begin adding the actual dates, pad out the days before the first of the month:

```
$counter = 1;
$newcounter = 1;

echo "<tr>";

$daysleft = 6 - $weekday-;

for($f=0;$f<=$weekday;$f++) {
    echo "<td class='cal_date' width='110' height='10'>";
    echo "</td>";
}
```

Here, you calculate the days left by removing $weekday- ($weekday minus 1) from 6 (the number of days in a week—remember, this function starts at 0). The reason $weekday minus 1 is taken into account is that the weekday is counted from 0 instead of 1.

Add the remaining days for the first row:

```
    echo "</td>";
}

for($f=0;$f<=$daysleft;$f++) {
    echo "<td class='cal_date' width='100' height='10'>";

    $display = date("jS", mktime(0, 0, 0, $month, $counter, $year));

    $todayday = date("d");
    $todaymonth = date("n");
    $todayyear = date("Y");

    if($counter == $todayday AND $month == $todaymonth AND
 $year == $todayyear) {
        echo "<strong>TODAY " . $display . "</strong>";
    }
    else {
        echo $display;
    }


    echo "</td>";
    $counter++;
}

echo "</tr>";
```

Inside the loop, the $display variable is created by using date() to store the formatted date. The $todayday, $todaymonth, and $todayyear variables are then filled with the relevant parts of today's date. Next, a check is made to see if today's details match the respective $counter, $month, and $year variables created earlier.

If so, TODAY is added to the cell to indicate the current day. Otherwise, only the date is displayed.

Before you add the cells that contain the events, pad out the days before the first of the month:

```
}

echo "</tr>";

echo "<tr>";
for($f=0;$f<=$weekday;$f++) {
    echo "<td class='cal' width='110' height='10'>";
    if($newcounter <= $numdays) {
    }

    echo "</td>";
}
```

For the remaining cells on the first row, grab the events from the database and display them:

```
    echo "</td>";
}

for($f=0;$f<=$daysleft;$f++) {
    echo "<td class='cal' width='110' height='40'>";

        $date = $year . "-" . $month . "-" . $newcounter;
        echo "<a class='cal' href='#' onclick=\"newEvent('"
. $date . "')\"></a>";

        $eventsql = "SELECT * FROM events WHERE date = '"
. $date . "';";
        $eventres = mysql_query($eventsql);

        while($eventrow = mysql_fetch_assoc($eventres)) {
            echo "<a class='deleteevent' href='delete.php?id="
. $eventrow['id'] . "' onclick=\"return confirm('Are you
sure you want to delete `" . $eventrow['name'] ."`?');\">X</a>";
            echo "<a class='event' href='#'
onclick='getEvent(" . $eventrow['id'] . ")'>"
. short_event($eventrow['name']) . "</a><br />";
        }
    echo "</td>";
    $newcounter++;
}

echo "</tr>";
```

This code creates a variable called $date that stores the date for the current cell in the format YYYY-MM-DD (the same format in which MySQL stores dates). Next, a link is added that loads the Javascript newEvent() function when the link is clicked. This link does not contain anything; the stylesheet formats it to take up the space of the cell and gives it a gray background.

Next, the query grabs the events for the current day (passing it $date), and the while loop adds two links. The first links to *delete.php*, but the link also uses the Javascript confirm() function in the onclick handler to prompt the user to delete the current event. If the user clicks the OK button, the link continues. If the user clicks Cancel, the link is cancelled.

The second link displays the event and uses the short_event() function, created earlier, to show the first 12 letters of the event in the cell. This link runs the Javascript getEvent() function when clicked. After the links are added, the $newcounter variable is incremented to reflect the next date.

To fill in the rest of the rows, an outer for loop loops through each row. Inside the for, repeat the same code:

```
    $newcounter++;
}

echo "</tr>";

for($i=1;$i<=($numrows-1);$i++) {

   echo "<tr>";

   for($a=0;$a<=($cols-1);$a++) {

        echo "<td class='cal_date' width='110' height='10'>";

        $display = date("jS", mktime(0, 0, 0, $month, $counter,
$year));

        $todayday = date("d");
        $todaymonth = date("n");
        $todayyear = date("Y");

        if($counter == $todayday AND $month == $todaymonth AND
$year == $todayyear) {
            echo "<strong>TODAY " . $display . "</strong>";
        }
        else {
            echo $display;
        }

        echo "</td>";
```

```
                $counter++;
        }

    echo "</tr>";

    echo "<tr>";

    for($aa=1;$aa<=$cols;$aa++) {
        echo "<td class='cal' width='110' height='40'>";
        if($newcounter <= $numdays) {
            $date = $year . "-" . $month . "-" . $newcounter;
            echo "<a class='cal' href='#' onclick=\"newEvent('" . $date
. "')\"></a>";

            $eventsql = "SELECT * FROM events WHERE date = '" . $date
. "';";
            $eventres = mysql_query($eventsql);

            while($eventrow = mysql_fetch_assoc($eventres)) {
                echo "<a class='deleteevent' href='delete.php?id="
. $eventrow['id'] . "' onclick=\"return confirm('Are you sure
you want to delete `" . $eventrow['name'] ."`?');\">X</a>";
                echo "<a class='event' href='#' onclick='getEvent("
. $eventrow['id'] . ")'>" . short_event($eventrow['name'])
. "</a><br />";
            }

        }
        echo "</td>";
        $newcounter++;
    }

    echo "</tr>";
}
```

Finally, close the table and add the footer:

```
    }

    echo "</tr>";
}

echo "</table>";

require("footer.php");

?>
```

With the page complete, you can use the arrows in the sidebar to jump to different months, and the events that you added to the *events* table are visible. The next challenge is to make the links in the calendar actually do something.

Fill In the Ajax Functionality

When you added the links for new and existing events to the main calendar view, they loaded the newEvent() and getEvent() JavaScript functions. You will create them now.

Way back when you created the *header.php* file, you included the following chunk of code at the top:

```
<script language="javascript" type="text/javascript"
    src="./internal_request.js">
</script>
```

This code includes the *internal_request.js* file, which contains some JavaScript code. By including this file at the top of the header file, the code inside the file is accessible from any script that includes *header.php* (similar in concept to including files in PHP). This file will contain the newEvent() and getEvent() functions.

Before you can perform any Ajax requests, you need to create an XML HTTP request object that transports your requests around. This object is used to transport data from the client (the browser) to the server using XML. With it, you tunnel data through between the client and server and then update the page dynamically.

Unfortunately, the Microsoft and Netscape/Mozilla browsers have different objects. To determine which object is loaded, you can detect the browser and create the relevant object.

Create a new file called *internal_request.js* and add the function shown in Example 8-8. Remember that this file contains JavaScript, not PHP.

EXAMPLE 8-8 This function loads the right XML HTTP request object for the browser.

```
function createRequestObject(){
   var request_o;
   var browser = navigator.appName;
   if(browser == "Microsoft Internet Explorer"){
      request_o = new ActiveXObject("Microsoft.XMLHTTP");
   } else{
      request_o = new XMLHttpRequest();
   }
   return request_o;
}
```

The first line creates a new variable called request_o. The next line detects the name of the Web browser and stores it in the browser variable. An if then checks if the browser is Microsoft Internet Explorer and sets `request_o` to the relevant ActiveX object. Otherwise, `request_o` is set to the Netscape/Mozilla object.

Run the function to instantiate the object:

```
var http = createRequestObject();
```

At this point, you now have a working XML HTTP request object available. You can begin adding the functions that were called earlier in the main calendar view.

Viewing Event Information

If the user clicks an event, the details should appear in the sidebar. The event link calls the `getEvent()` function (shown in Example 8-9), so add it to *internal_request.js*.

EXAMPLE 8-9 This function loads the page to request the event details from the database.

```
function getEvent(eventid){
    http.open('get', 'internal_request.php?action=getevent&id='
 + eventid);
    http.onreadystatechange = handleEvent;
    http.send(null);
}
```

The first line uses the `open()` method from the XML HTTP request object to open the page to deal with the request. This method takes two arguments. The first is the mechanics of how the request is submitted (GET or POST). Second, you specify the script to deal with the request. In this line, you access internal_request.php (not to be confused with internal_request.js) and pass it a GET variable called `id`. This variable is set to the number that is passed to the function.

When the request has been made, you indicate which method should deal with the response; the second line specifies `handleEvent` as this method. Finally, the third line actually sends the data. Null is passed to the `send()` method, because you are using GET (if you used POST, you would use a value other than null).

Add the `handletEvent()` method to deal with the result of the request:

```
function handleEvent(){
    if(http.readyState == 4){
        var response = http.responseText;
        document.getElementById('eventcage').innerHTML = response;
    }
}
```

On the first line, you check the status of the request. The readyState method can return one of five possible status codes. These codes are shown in Table 8-2.

TABLE 8-2   Use *readyState* to check which status code the request currently has.

CODE	MEANING
0	Uninitialized
1	Loading
2	Loaded
3	Interactive
4	Finished

If the returned code is 4 (Finished), the returned text from the query (referred to with responseText) is stored in a variable called response. You now use the getElementById method to refer to the eventcage <div> in the sidebar and use the innerHTML method to change the contents of the <div> to the contents of the response variable.

As shown in Example 8-10, create the *internal_request.php* page that you referred to earlier in the getEvent() function.

EXAMPLE 8-10   This code simply requests the record that matches the id GET variable.

```php
<?php

session_start();

require("db.php");
require("config.php");

if(isset($_SESSION['LOGGEDIN']) == FALSE) {
    header("Location: " . $config_basedir);
}

if($_GET['action'] == 'getevent'){
    $sql = "SELECT * FROM events WHERE id = " . $_GET['id'] . ";";
    $result = mysql_query($sql);
    $row = mysql_fetch_assoc($result);

    echo "<h1>Event Details</h1>";
```

continues

EXAMPLE 8-10   Continued.

```
    echo $row['name'];
    echo "<p>" . $row['description'] . "</p>";
    echo "<p><strong>Date:</strong> " . date("D jS F Y",
strtotime($row['date'])) . "<br />";
    echo "<strong>Time:</strong> " . $row['starttime']
. " - " . $row['endtime'] . "</p>";
}


?>
```

Within this script, you check to see if the `action` GET variable is equal to `getevent`. The `action` variable is used to distinguish among different features on page. You could create another block of code for a different action.

Within the `if`, the record from the *events* table with the same id as the `id` GET variable is returned and displayed. When this functionality is complete, the event information is displayed in the sidebar when the user clicks an item, as shown in Figure 8-6.

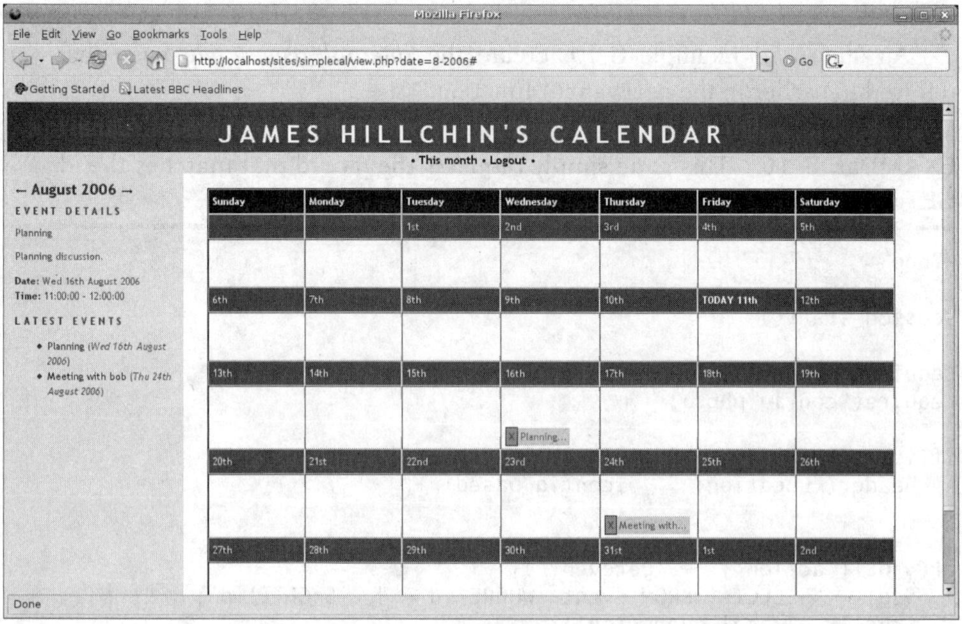

FIGURE 8-6   The dynamic nature of Ajax is not given justice by a static screen-shot, but rest assured, it makes the application feel much sleeker.

Adding a New Event

The mechanics of adding a new event to the calendar is handled in a very similar way to viewing event information—a function is loaded, the request is made, and the eventcage <div> from *bar.php* is updated.

Figure 8-7 shows the interface for this feature.

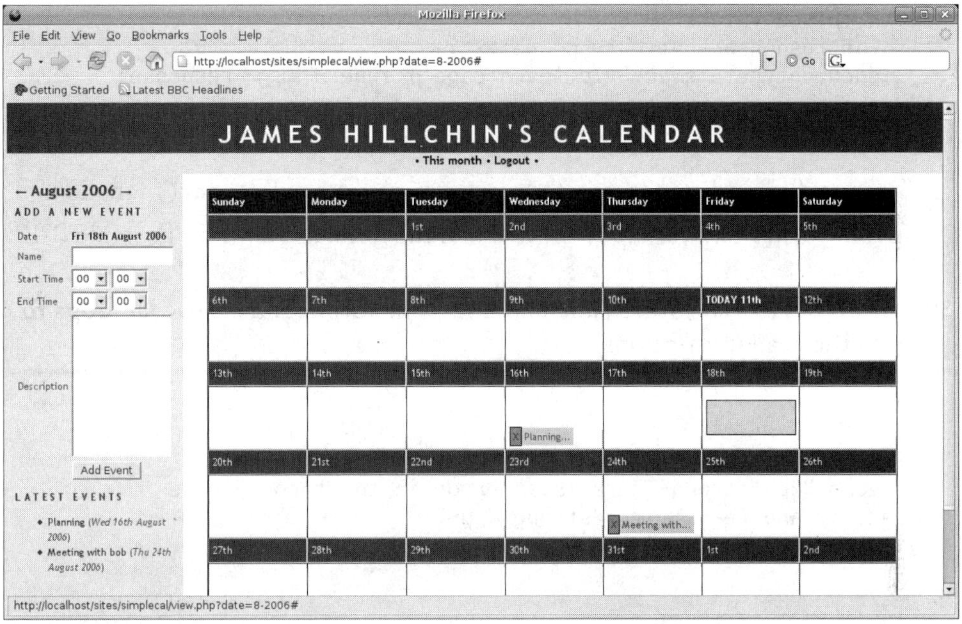

FIGURE 8-7 When the user hovers over some empty space in a cell, the background appears gray; the user can then click to access the New Event form.

The first step is to implement the function that is called in the link that you added to the main calendar view in *view.php*. Load *internal_request.js* and add the function shown in Example 8-11.

EXAMPLE 8-11 This function uses *open()* to load the script that displays the form.

```
function newEvent(eventdate, error){
   http.open('get', 'neweventform.php?date=' + eventdate + "&error=" +
error);
   http.onreadystatechange = handleNewEvent;
   http.send(null);
}
```

This function works in a virtually identical fashion to getEvent(), which was covered earlier. The request, however, loads the form (stored in *neweventform.php*). The function also passes an error code to the page. The handler for this request is handleNewEvent.

Add the handler below the newEvent() function to *internal_request.js*:

```
function handleNewEvent(){
    if(http.readyState == 4){
        var response = http.responseText;
        document.getElementById('eventcage').innerHTML = response;
    }
}
```

This handler works in exactly the same way as the handleEvent() function.

Create the *neweventform.php* file and add the form, as shown in Example 8-12.

EXAMPLE 8-12 The Start Time and End Time form controls use *for* loops to generate the available options.

```
<?php

    if($_GET['error'] == 1) {
        echo "<p><strong>There is an error in the form. Please
 correct it and re-submit.</strong></p>";
    }


?>
<h1>Add a new event</h1>
<form action="processnewevent.php?date=<?php echo $_GET['date']; ?>"
method="POST">
<table>
<tr>
    <td>Date</td>
    <td>
    <?php echo "<strong>" . date("D jS F Y",
 strtotime($_GET['date'])) . "</strong>"; ?>
    <input type="hidden" name="date" value="
<?php echo $_GET['date']; ?>">
    </td>
</tr>
<tr>
    <td>Name</td>
    <td><input type="text" name="name" size="15"></td>
</tr>
<tr>
    <td>Start Time</td>
    <td>
    <select name="starthour">
    <?php
```

```
        for($i=0;$i<=23;$i++) {
            echo "<option value=" . sprintf("%02d", $i) . ">"
  . sprintf("%02d", $i) . "</option>";
        }
    ?>
    </select>

    <select name="startminute">
    <?php
        for($i=0;$i<=60;$i++) {
            echo "<option value=" . sprintf("%02d", $i) . ">"
  . sprintf("%02d", $i) . "</option>";
        }
    ?>
    </select>

    </td>
</tr>
<tr>
    <td>End Time</td>
    <td>
    <select name="endhour">
    <?php
        for($i=0;$i<=23;$i++) {
            echo "<option value=" . sprintf("%02d", $i) . ">"
  . sprintf("%02d", $i) . "</option>";
        }
    ?>
    </select>

    <select name="endminute">
    <?php
        for($i=0;$i<=60;$i++) {
            echo "<option value=" . sprintf("%02d", $i) . ">"
  . sprintf("%02d", $i) . "</option>";
        }
    ?>
    </select>

    </td>
</tr>
<tr>
    <td>Description</td>
    <td><textarea cols="15" rows="10" name="description"></textarea></td>
</tr>
<tr>
    <td></td>
    <td><input type="submit" name="submit" value="Add Event"></td>
</tr>
</table>
</form>
```

At the top of the form, a check is made to see if the error GET variable is available. If it is, an error message is displayed.

The script to process the form is *processnewevent.php*. Create this file and begin adding the following code:

```php
<?php
    require("db.php");

    if(empty($_POST['name'])) {
        $error = 1;
    }

    if(empty($_POST['description'])) {
        $error = 1;
    }

    if($_POST['starthour'] > $_POST['endhour']) {
        $error = 1;
    }

    if($_POST['starthour'] == $_POST['endhour']) {
        $error = 1;
    }

    if($error == 1) {
        header("Location: " . $config_basedir
 . "view.php?error=1&eventdate=" . $_GET['date']);
        exit;
    }
```

This batch of if statements perform some validation checks. These checks work similarly to previous validation examples—if a check fails, the $error variable is created and the page redirects. The checks are made to ensure that the end time is not earlier than the start time and that the start and end time are not the same. A check is also made to ensure that the text boxes are not empty.

Prepare the variables:

```php
    if($error == 1) {
        header("Location: " . $config_basedir .
"view.php?error=1&eventdate=" . $_GET['date']);
        exit;
    }
```

```
$elements = explode("-", $_POST['date']);
$redirectdate = $elements[1] . "-" . $elements[0];

$finalstart = $_POST['starthour'] . ":" . $_POST['startminute']
. ":00";
$finalend = $_POST['endhour'] . ":" . $_POST['endminute'] . ":00";
```

The first line in this block uses explode() to fill the $elements array with the
different parts of the date. The second line constructs a variable with just the month
and year elements (these elements are used when browsing the months, such as
with the arrows in the sidebar).

The second two lines format the times in a format that can work in the TIME
database field. This field requires the 00:00:00 format, so each line concatenates
the form elements into this format.

Insert the data and use $redirectdate to redirect to the month to which the
date was added:

```
$finalstart = $_POST['starthour'] . ":" . $_POST['startminute']
. ":00";
$finalend = $_POST['endhour'] . ":" . $_POST['endminute'] . ":00";

$inssql = "INSERT INTO events(date, starttime, endtime, name,
description) VALUES("
. "'" . $_POST['date']
. "', '" . $finalstart
. "', '" . $finalend
. "', '" . addslashes($_POST['name'])
. "', '" . addslashes($_POST['description'])
. "');";

mysql_query($inssql);

header("Location: " . $config_basedir . "view.php?date="
. $redirectdate);

?>
```

The feature is now complete.

Deleting Events

Deleting an event happens when the user clicks the red *X* block next to an event.
Create a new file called *delete.php* and add the code shown in Example 8-13.

EXAMPLE 8-13   To delete an event, remove the record from the database.

```php
<?php

    require("db.php");

    $sql = "DELETE FROM events WHERE id = " . $_GET['id'];
    mysql_query($sql);

    echo "<script>javascript: history.go(-1)</script>";

?>
```

The usual code for deleting an event from the database is shown here. Then you use a different type of redirect, this time using JavaScript. You could use one of the other types of redirect; this one was used to show you another option.

SUMMARY

In this project, you created a different type of Web application. Unlike the publicly hosted and accessible applications elsewhere in the book, this project involved creating something used by a single person. This application was also more like a traditional application than some of the other projects, largely due to the Ajax functionality.

Ajax has become a key Web development technology, and the skills you explored here will help you to create more dynamic and flexible Web applications.

CHAPTER 9

FAQ Content Management System

If you attend any reasonably large IT conference, one of the buzzwords you are likely to hear tossed around the shop floor is *content management*. The buzzword and its vehicle of choice, the *Content Management System* (CMS), refer to Web applications that provide a simple and effective means of managing content.

Building a CMS is not a walk in the park. The major challenge that you face is in presenting all of the necessary tools needed to manage the content in a way that is simple but comprehensive. Many CMSs also deal with different types of users (admins, normal users, moderators, and so on), so you also need to provide a secure and consistent permissions system.

In this chapter, you carefully step over the fear and doubt, and take the challenge head on. Prepare yourselves to build a fully buzzword-compliant CMS.

> ## NOTE
>
> **Learn by Doing It Wrong**
>
> The project in this chapter was one that I developed some years ago as an independent CMS. Although I released the code on the Internet in an alpha state, the project was largely unfinished and still needed additional work to complete the application.
>
> While preparing for this chapter, I took the original code, corrected it, and completed it. This process involved fixing all of the nasty nested tables and other bad programming habits that I picked up while learning PHP. Although fixing the code involved practically rewriting it, the process was a satisfying example of the progress I made since the project was originally written.
>
> I recommend you regularly revisit your old projects and give them a spring-cleaning. If nothing else, it will provide a satisfying reminder of the progress you are making in your development.

PROJECT OVERVIEW

In this chapter, you will create a CMS for Frequently Asked Questions (FAQ) lists. The questions are typically displayed as links, which in turn display the answer to the question.

To get a better feel for the project, you first explore a number of use cases that better explain the different types of functionality:

> Bill goes to the FAQ Web site and wants to find out more about PHP. When the site loads, he can see a list of subjects in the sidebar. One of the subjects is PHP, so Bill clicks the link and the page displays a list of topics that are part of the PHP subject. Bill then clicks one of the topics, *Variables*, and a list of related questions is displayed, with a short summary of the answers. Bill chooses one of the questions; the page now displays the question, the answer, and some related comments. As he reads the question, Bill decides he would like to post a comment. He logs into the site with his username and password and then returns to the question. A form is now displayed under the comments, so Bill enters his thoughts into the form and submits it. The comment now appears on the page.

This use case demonstrates how a typical user can come to the site, browse the content, and add comments to a question. The sidebar acts as a mechanism to navigate between the subjects and topics, and the main content (the questions) is displayed on the body of the page.

To make the site as community-oriented as possible, users should be able to own a subject and manage how content is added to that subject:

> Ade takes a look at the PHP subject information page on the Web site. The page displays who owns the subject, but he notes that it currently has no owner. Because Ade is currently logged in, a link appears that allows him to propose himself as a new owner for the subject. He clicks the link and is taken to a page where he can enter the reasons he should be chosen as the owner.

> Later, the administrator logs in and reviews the list of submitted ownership requests. She views Ade's request and decides that Ade is a suitable owner. She accepts Ade's request, and an email indicating his successful application is sent to him automatically.

Another key use case describes how to add and remove content from the project:

Now that Ade is the new owner of the PHP subject, he can add topics and questions. When Ade logs in, the new subject appears in his Control Panel (a page with information about his account). Ade can now use the Add Topic and Add Questions page to add content to the subject.

While Bill is browsing the PHP subject, he can also add questions by clicking the Add Question link on the subject information page. When Bill submits a question, it is held for moderation so that either Ade or the administrator can allow it.

Ade logs into the site and looks at the questions held for moderation. Inside the page, he can view the question details, and accept or deny it. He clicks the Accept link to make the question live.

These use cases have identified the core feature requirements for the application. When you build, you might find it useful to reread these use cases to get a better idea of how the application should work.

BUILDING THE DATABASE

The database you will create is shown in Figure 9-1.

The four core tables are *subject, topics, questions*, and *comments*. These related tables also hook up with the *users* table, which stores user accounts. The *mod_sub-owner* table stores ownership requests.

Implementing the Database

Start phpMyAdmin. Create a new database called *faq* and add the following tables:

The *admins* Table
- id. Make this an TINYINT (few admins are necessary) and turn on auto_increment. Set this field as a primary key.
- username. Make this a VARCHAR with a length of 10.
- password. Make this a VARCHAR with a length of 10.

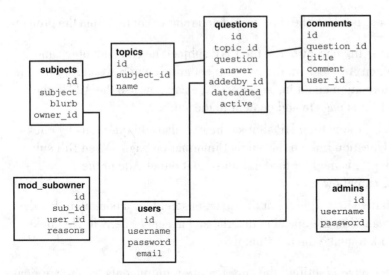

FIGURE 9-1 The relationship of content over four tables (subjects, topics, questions, comments) is similar to the forums project.

NOTE

Active and Inactive Questions

The active field lives inside the *questions* table. This field identifies whether the question is live. If the field contains 0, the question is currently being held for moderation. If the field is set to 1, the question is live.

When a user who does not own the subject submits a question, active is set to 0 (requires moderation). When the owner adds a question, active is set to 1. When a question to be moderated is accepted, active is changed from 0 to 1.

The *comments* Table

- id. Make this a BIGINT (several comments are possible) and turn on auto_increment in the Extras column. Set this field as a primary key.
- question_id. Make this an INT.
- title_id. Make this a VARCHAR and set the size to 20.
- comment. Make this a TEXT.
- user_id. Make this an INT.
- For this table, select the InnoDB table type.

The *mod_subowner* Table

- id. Make this an INT (several requests are possible) and turn on auto_increment. Set this field as a primary key.
- sub_id. Make this an INT.
- user_id. Make this an INT.
- reasons . Make this a TEXT.

The *questions* Table

- id. Make this an INT (several questions are possible) and turn on auto_increment. Set this field as a primary key.
- topic_id. Make this an INT.
- question. Make this a VARCHAR with a length of 50.
- answer. Make this a TEXT.
- addedby_id. Make this an INT.
- dateadded. Make this a DATETIME.
- active. Make this a TINYINT.
- For this table, select the InnoDB table type.

The *subjects* Table

- id. Make this an INT (several subjects are possible) and turn on auto_increment. Set this field as a primary key.
- subject. Make this a VARCHAR with a length of 20.
- blurb. Make this a TEXT.
- owner_id. Make this an INT.
- For this table, select the InnoDB table type.

The *topics* Table

- id. Make this an INT (several topics are possible) and turn on auto_increment. Set this field as a primary key.
- subject_id. Make this an INT.
- name. Make this a VARCHAR with a length of 20.
- For this table, select the InnoDB table type.

The *users* Table

- id. Make this an INT (several orders are possible) and turn on auto_increment. Set this field as a primary key.
- username. Make this a VARCHAR and set the size to 10.
- password. Make this a VARCHAR and set the size to 10.
- email. Make this a VARCHAR and set the size to 50.

Creating the Table Relationships

With so many different types of content and sub-content (subjects -> topics -> questions -> comments), you need to support cascading deletes. Cascading deletes were first covered in the forums project in Chapter 5.

In phpMyAdmin, click the SQL tab and add the following three queries separately:

```
ALTER TABLE comments ADD FOREIGN KEY(question_id)
REFERENCES questions (id) ON DELETE CASCADE;

ALTER TABLE questions ADD FOREIGN KEY(topic_id)
REFERENCES topics (id) ON DELETE CASCADE;

ALTER TABLE topics ADD FOREIGN KEY(subject_id)
REFERENCES subjects (id) ON DELETE CASCADE;
```

When you now delete data, all dependent information from other tables is removed also.

Inserting Sample Data

With a solid set of tables ready to go, you're ready to add some sample data. Remember, do not fill in a number in the id column; auto_increment takes care of this for you. Feel free to add your own sample data or the data used in this example.

Sample Data for the *admins* Table

Create a username and password for the administrator. This example uses admin as the username and password as the password.

Sample Data for the *users* Table

Create usernames, passwords, and email addresses for the users. This project uses bill and password for one user, and ade and password for another. Add email addresses that actually work for each sample user; you use the email address to send ownership accept or deny emails to the user.

Sample Data for the *subjects, topics, questions,* and *comments* Tables

When adding sample data to these tables, you need to ensure that the relationships among them are correct; otherwise, the database logic in the project will break.

First, add a few subjects to the *subjects* table, as shown in Table 9-1.

TABLE 9-1   The *subjects* table contains the major subject areas.

SUBJECT	BLURB	OWNER_ID
PHP	<add your own blurb>	0
MySQL	<add your own blurb>	2

In the preceding table, you gave the PHP subject an owner_id of 0, which means that the subject has no owner and is therefore available for ownership. The second user owns the second subject.

Add the content to the *topics* table, as shown in Table 9-2.

TABLE 9-2   The *topics* table stores subcategories inside the subject.

SUBJECT_ID	NAME
1	Variables
1	Functions

In this case, you added two topics, both of which are in the first subject (PHP).

Add the questions to the *questions* table, as shown in Table 9-3.

TABLE 9-3   The active field indicates whether a question is live.

TOPIC_ID	QUESTION	ANSWER	ADDEDBY_ID	DATEADDED	ACTIVE
1	How do you define variables?	<add your own answer>	1	NOW()	1
1	Why are PHP variables not given a type?	<add your own answer>	1	NOW()	1

When adding these questions, select NOW from the Functions combo box in the dateadded field. The active field indicates whether the question is live. If this field is set to another value (typically 0), the question is awaiting moderation from the owner of the subject.

Finally, add a comment for the first question in the *comments* table, as shown in Table 9-4.

TABLE 9-4 Comments are a useful way to provide additional information for a question.

QUESTION_ID	TITLE	COMMENT	USER_ID
1	Book recommendation	If you want to learn about variables in more detail, refer to Variable Foo Machine by Foo Bar.	2

Sample Data for the *mod_subowner* Table

Leave this table empty.

STARTING TO CODE

To get started, create a new project directory and create the config/header/footer and main index files. First, copy *db.php* from a previous project to the current directory and then create a new file called *config.php* and add the code shown in Example 9-1.

EXAMPLE 9-1 The configuration file is virtually the same as in previous projects.

```php
<?php

    $dbhost = "localhost";
    $dbuser ="root";
    $dbpassword = "";
    $dbdatabase = "faq";

    $config_basedir = "http://localhost/sites/faq/";

    $config_sitename = "You ask the questions";
?>
```

Create *header.php* and add the code shown in Example 9-2.

EXAMPLE 9-2   The header file lays out the usual array of <div> elements.

```php
<?php

        require("config.php");

        $db = mysql_connect($dbhost, $dbuser, $dbpassword);
        mysql_select_db($dbdatabase, $db);


?>
<!DOCTYPE HTML PUBLIC "-//W3C//DTD HTML 4.01
 Transitional//EN" "http://www.w3.org/TR/html4/loose.dtd">
<html>
<head>
  <title><?php echo $config_sitename; ?></title>
  <link href="stylesheet.css" rel="stylesheet">
</head>
<body>
<div id="header">
        <?php echo "<h1>" . $config_sitename . "</h1>"; ?>
</div>

<div id="menu">
    &bull;
    <a href="index.php">Home</a>
    &bull;
    <?php
    if($_SESSION['SESS_USERNAME']) {
        echo "<a href='userlogout.php'>Logout</a>";
    }
    else {
        echo "<a href='login.php'>Login</a>";
    }
    ?>
    &bull;
</div>
<div id="container">
<div id="bar">
<?php
require("bar.php");
?>
</div>

<div id="main">
```

Create *footer.php* and add the remaining code, as shown in Example 9-3.

EXAMPLE 9-3 The footer file

```
        </div>
    </div>
    </body>
    </html>
```

A More Involved Sidebar

The sidebar contains a number of different elements for different parts of the site. This file is built up step by step as you work through the project and cover the different sections. The first task is to present the Subject and Topic lists, as discussed in the use cases.

The subjects are presented in a list. When the user clicks a subject, *index.php* is reloaded with a subject GET variable that contains the id of the subject. Later in the code, you check to see if this variable exists and if so display the list of topics. The first time the page is loaded (no subject variable), only the subjects are displayed, but when the user has clicked the subject (subject variable is now available), the topics are displayed.

Create *bar.php* and begin adding the code:

```php
<?php

    $subsql = "SELECT * FROM subjects";
    $subres = mysql_query($subsql);

    echo "<h1>Subjects</h1>";

    echo "<table>";

    while($subrow = mysql_fetch_assoc($subres)) {
        echo "<tr>";
        echo "<td width='5%'>";

        if($subrow['id'] == $_GET['subject']) {
            echo "&bull;";
        }

        echo "</td>";
        echo "<td><a href='index.php?subject=" . $subrow['id'] .
"'>" . $subrow['subject'] . "</a></td>";
```

This code selects the subjects and then creates a table in which to display them. Using a table instead of an unordered list enables you to display a dot next to the currently selected subject. Inside the while loop, a check is made in the first cell to see if the id from the current row is the same as the subject GET variable. If it is, a dot is displayed (with the • HTML entity). In the next table cell, the link is created.

A check is now made to see if an admin is logged in and if so, a delete link (X) is added:

```
echo "</td>";
echo "<td><a href='index.php?subject=" . $subrow['id']
. "'>" . $subrow['subject'] . "</a></td>";

if($_SESSION['SESS_ADMINUSER']) {
    echo "<td>[<a href='deletesubject.php?subject=" .
$subrow['id'] . "'>X</a>]</td>";
}
```

Finally, close the row, while loop, and table:

```
        echo "<td>[<a href='deletesubject.php?subject="
. $subrow['id'] . "'>X</a>]</td>";
    }

    echo "</tr>";
}

echo "</table>";
```

With the subjects list complete, add the topics:

```
echo "</table>";

if(isset($_GET['subject'])) {
    $topsql = "SELECT * FROM topics WHERE subject_id = "
. $_GET['subject'] . ";";
    $topres = mysql_query($topsql);

    echo "<h1>Topics</h1>";

    if(mysql_num_rows($topres) == 0) {
        echo "No topics!";
    }

    echo "<table width='100%'>";

    while($toprow = mysql_fetch_assoc($topres)) {
        echo "<tr>";
        echo "<td width='5%'>";

        if($toprow['id'] == $_GET['topic']) {
            echo "&bull;";
        }
```

```
                  echo "</td>";

                  echo "<td><a href='questions.php?subject="
. $subject . "&amp;topic=" . $toprow['id'] . "'>"
. $toprow['name'] . "</a></td>";

                  if($_SESSION['SESS_ADMINUSER']) {
                        echo "<td>[<a href='deletetopic.php?subject="
. $toprow['subject_id'] . "&amp;topic=" . $toprow['id']
. "'>X</a>]</td>";
                  }

                  echo "</tr>";
            }

      echo "</table>";
      }
?>
```

A check is made to see if the subject GET variable is present. If it exists, the same mechanism is used to display the list of topics, and each topic links to *questions.php*, in which the subject and topic are passed.

Creating the Functions

In this project, you use two functions that you create yourself:

- pf_fix_slashes(). This function provides a more intelligent method of ensuring that quotes are properly escaped when adding information to the database.

- pf_check_number(). This funtion is a variant of the pf_validate_number() function used in previous projects. This version checks if the variable is valid but does not perform any redirection.

Create a new file called *functions.php* and add the first function:

```
<?php

function pf_fix_slashes($string) {
      if (get_magic_quotes_gpc() == 1) {
            return($string);
      }
      else {
            return(addslashes($string));
      }
}
```

In previous projects, you used addslashes() to escape quotes in user input destined for the database. Although this works fine, the function makes the assumption that the magic_quotes_gpc option in *php.ini* is turned off. If the option is turned on and you use addslashes(), additional slashes are added in front of the slashes that were added by magic_quotes_gpc. The result is a visible slash added to your data.

To solve this problem, the new function uses the get_magic_quotes_gpc() to check if the feature is turned on or off. If the function returns 1 or TRUE, magic quotes is turned on and the normal string is returned. If magic quotes are turned off, the string is run through addslashes() and then returned. This new function ensures that your application can work with magic quotes turned on or off and requires no modification. Sweet, no?

The next function to roll in is pf_check_number():

```
function pf_check_number($value) {
     if(isset($value) == FALSE) {
          $error = 1;
     }

     if(is_numeric($value) == FALSE) {
          $error = 1;
     }

     if($error == 1) {
          return FALSE;
     }
     else {
          return TRUE;
     }
}

?>
```

This function is virtually identical to the pf_validate_number() function used in previous projects, but the if check on $error returns FALSE if there is an error and TRUE if there is not.

NOTE

Why Use This Slightly Different Function?

Some of the pages in this project have two personalities: one that is triggered with a GET variable and one without. If you used pf_validate_number() in these pages, the personality that does not need the GET variable would fail (pf_validate_number() checks if the variable is present) and redirect to another page.

The pf_check_number() function does not include the redirect functionality. As such, the function can be used to validate a GET variable if it is present.

Building the Main Page

The next page to create is *index.php*. This script has two main functions:

- If the page is not passed a subject GET variable, the page displays the last 10 questions.
- If the page does have a subject GET variable, information about that specific subject is displayed. This information includes both the name and description of the subject, as well as some statistical information about the number of topics and questions.

Create the file and begin adding the code:

```php
<?php

session_start();

require("config.php");
require("functions.php");

if($_GET['subject']) {
        if(pf_check_number($_GET['subject']) == TRUE) {
                $validsub = $_GET['subject'];
        }
        else {
                header("Location: " . $config_basedir);
        }
}

require("header.php");
```

You checked if the subject GET variable is present and if so, it is run through pf_check_number(). If it passes the validation (and returns TRUE), $validsub is set to the number. Otherwise, the page re-directs.

Now check if the subject GET variable is present and if so, display the information about the subject:

```php
require("header.php");

if($_GET['subject']) {

    $subsql = "SELECT users.username, subjects.* FROM subjects
 LEFT JOIN users ON subjects.owner_id = users.id
 WHERE subjects.id = " . $validsub . ";";
    $subresult = mysql_query($subsql);
    $subrow = mysql_fetch_assoc($subresult);

    echo "<h1>" . $subrow['subject'] . " Summary</h1>";
```

A query is created to gather the subject information and the username that maps to the subjects.owner_id field. In previous projects the join was made using the WHERE clause in the SQL, but here you are using the LEFT JOIN syntax. The following paragraph describes how the syntax works:

> Select the username and subject information (SELECT users.username, subjects.*) from the *subjects* table (FROM subjects) and then join the *subjects* and *users* tables (LEFT JOIN users) with the relevant condition (ON subjects.owner_id = users.id) in which the subject id is the same as $validsub (WHERE subjects.id = $validsub).

When writing joins, you can use a variety of different types of join (INNER, OUTER, LEFT, and RIGHT), with INNER and LEFT as the most common variants. An INNER join connects tables with the conditions that you specify. A LEFT join performs the same process but also fills in any mismatched fields with NULL values.

Check the data returned to see if the subject has an owner. If 0 is returned, no owner exists:

```
echo "<h1>" . $subrow['subject'] . " Summary</h1>";

if($subrow['owner_id'] == 0) {
    echo "This subject has no owner.";
```

NOTE

Using the LEFT Join on this Page

The reason for using the LEFT join on this page is important. If the subjects table has an owner_id set to something other than 0, an INNER or LEFT join can relate the owner_id to the user id in the *users* table. If, however, the subject has no owner and the owner_id is set to 0, an INNER join fails because no user with the id 0 exists in the *users* table. When you use a LEFT join, this mismatch still returns the data, but the mismatched information is set to NULL.

In this project, you use a combination of joins that use the JOIN and WHERE syntax. This ensures that you are exposed to both methods of creating joins.

If the subject has no owner, check to see if a user is logged in and display a link to the subject ownership page:

```
if($subrow['owner_id'] == 0) {
    echo "This subject has no owner.";
```

```
        if($_SESSION['SESS_USERNAME']) {
            echo " If you would like to apply to own this subject,
click <a href='applysubowner.php?subject=" . $subject
. "'>here</a>.";
        }
    }
```

If the query returns an owner, display the username:

```
            echo " If you would like to apply to own this subject,
click <a href='applysubowner.php?subject=" . $subject
. "'>here</a>.";
        }
    }

    else {
        echo "This subject is owned by <strong>" .
$subrow['username'] . "</strong>.";
    }
```

Display the blurb for the subject in *italic* tags:

```
            echo "This subject is owned by <strong>" .
$subrow['username'] . "</strong>.";
    }

    echo "<p><i>" . $subrow['blurb'] . "</i></p>";
```

The next step is to gather some statistical information about the subject. Count the number of topics and questions included within the subject:

```
    echo "<p><i>" . $subrow['blurb'] . "</i></p>";

    $topsql = "SELECT count(distinct(topics.id)) AS numtopics,
count(questions.id) AS numquestions FROM subjects LEFT JOIN
topics ON subjects.id = topics.subject_id LEFT JOIN questions
ON topics.id = questions.topic_id WHERE subjects.id = "
. $validsub . " AND active = 1;";
    $topresult = mysql_query($topsql);
    $toprow = mysql_fetch_assoc($topresult);
```

To gather this information, you performed a single large query. The following paragraph describes how the query works:

Select (SELECT) the number of distinctive topic ids (count(distinct (topics.id)) AS numtopics) and the number of question ids (count (questions.id) AS numquestions) from the *subjects* table (FROM subjects). Join the table with *topics* (LEFT JOIN topics), in which the subject id is the same as the subject_id field in the *topics* table (ON subjects.id = topics.subject_id), and then join this to the *questions* table (LEFT JOIN questions), in which the topic id is equal to the topic_id field in the *questions* table (ON topics.id = questions.topic_id) where the whole query has the subject id of $validsub (WHERE subjects.id = $validsub) and the question is active (AND active = 1).

Display the results of the query in a table:

```
$toprow = mysql_fetch_assoc($topresult);

echo "<table class='visible' cellspacing=0 cellpadding=5>";
echo "<tr><th class='visible' colspan=2>Statistics</th></tr>";
echo "<tr>";
echo "<td>Total Topics</td><td>" . $toprow['numtopics']
. "</td>";
echo "</tr>";
echo "<tr>";
echo "<td>Total Questions</td><td>" . $toprow['numquestions']
. "</td>";
echo "</tr>";
echo "</table>";
}
```

This section should look like Figure 9-2 when it's finished.

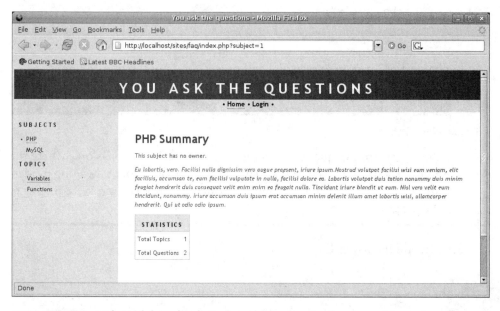

FIGURE 9-2   The sidebar displays the relevant topics for the subject.

If no subject GET variable exists, display the latest 10 questions:

```
        echo "</table>";
}
else
{
        $latqsql = "SELECT questions.id, question, subject
FROM subjects, questions, topics WHERE questions.topic_id =
topics.id AND topics.subject_id = subjects.id AND active = 1
ORDER BY questions.dateadded DESC;";
        $latqresult = mysql_query($latqsql);
        $latqnumrows = mysql_num_rows($latqresult);

        echo "<h1>Latest Questions</h1>";

        if($latqnumrows == 0) {
                echo "No questions!";
        }
        else {
                echo "<ul>";

                while($latqrow = mysql_fetch_assoc($latqresult)) {
                        echo "<li><a href='answer.php?id=" . $latqrow['id'] .
"'>" . $latqrow['question'] . "</a> (<i>" . $latqrow['subject'] .
"</i>)</li>";
                }

                echo "</ul>";
        }
}
```

Each question links to *answer.php* and passes the id of the question to it.

 NOTE

Remember...

When performing queries, remember to only return records only where the active field is set to 1. If this field is set to 0, the question is awaiting moderation. You will learn more about the question moderation system later in the project.

Finally, add the footer file:

```
                echo "</ul>";
        }
}

require("footer.php");

?>
```

This functionality should look similar to the page shown in Figure 9-3.

FIGURE 9-3   The interface provides a simple way to begin using the application.

DISPLAYING QUESTIONS

Questions and answers are the lifeblood of a FAQ site, and in this section, you create the code to display them. The functionality is spread across two pages. The first page (*questions.php*) displays a summary of the questions inside the topic, and the second page (*answer.php*) displays the answer and comments for that specific question.

Displaying Question Summary

Create a file called *questions.php* and start adding the code:

```php
<?php
session_start();
require("functions.php");

if(pf_check_number($_GET['topic']) == TRUE) {
      $validtopic = $_GET['topic'];
}
else {
      header("Location: " . $config_basedir);
}
```

```
if(pf_check_number($_GET['subject']) == TRUE) {
    $validsubject = $_GET['subject'];
}
else {
    header("Location: " . $config_basedir);
}
```

In this block, you first validate the topic and submit GET variables. If the validation fails, the page redirects to the site's base page.

Each question on this page includes a short summary of the answer, as shown in Figure 9-4.

How do you define variables?	Ut duis molestie nostrud vel, eros, sit dolor feugait esse aliquip amet, wisi co...

FIGURE 9-4 The question summary provides a nice way to show the first line of the question.

To create this short summary, you create a small function called question_summary():

```
    header("Location: " . $config_basedir);
}

function question_summary($question) {
    $final = "";
    $final = (substr($question, 0, 80) . "...");

    return $final;
}
```

The question_summary() function is similar to the short_event() function that was created in the calendar project in the preceding chapter. The function uses substr() to cut out the first 80 letters, and then appends ....

Perform the query:

```
    return $final;
}

require("header.php");

echo "<h1>Questions</h1>";

$qsql = "SELECT * FROM questions WHERE topic_id = "
 . $validtopic . " AND active = 1;";
$qresult = mysql_query($qsql);
$numrows = mysql_num_rows($qresult);
```

If no records were returned, display No Questions:

```
$numrows = mysql_num_rows($qresult);

if($numrows == 0) {
      echo "No Questions";
}
```

Display the questions in the table:

```
      echo "No Questions";
}
else {
      echo "<table cellspacing=0 cellpadding=5>";

      while($qrow = mysql_fetch_assoc($qresult)) {
            echo "<tr>";

            echo "<td><a href='answer.php?id=" . $qrow['id']
. "'>" . $qrow['question'] . "</a></td>";
            echo "<td><i>" . question_summary($qrow['answer'])
. "</i></td>";

            if($_SESSION['SESS_ADMINUSER'] AND $numrows >= 1) {
                  echo "<td><a href='deletequestion.php?topic="
. $validtopic . "&subject=" . $validsubject . "&questionid="
. $qrow['id'] . "'>Delete Question</a></td>";
            }

            echo "</tr>";
      }

      echo "</table>";
}
```

A while loop iterates through each question returned and then displays the question and summary. If the administrator is logged in, a Delete Question link is added also.

Finally, if the user is logged in, add a link to add a new question:

```
      echo "</table>";
}

if($_SESSION['SESS_USERNAME'])
{
      echo "<h2>Options</h2>";
      echo "<a href='addquestion.php?subject=$subject&topic=$topic'>
Add a question</a>";
}

require("footer.php");

?>
```

The current page should look similar to the one shown in Figure 9-5.

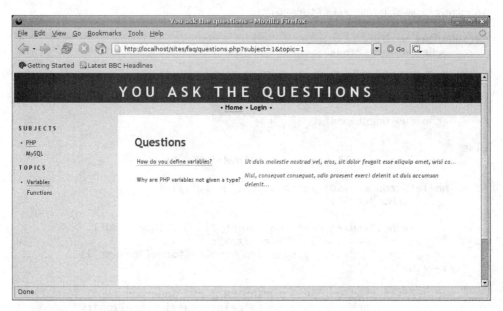

FIGURE 9-5 Displaying the questions

Showing a Specific Question

It is now time to create the page to display the answer for a specific question. This page not only displays the question and the answer, but also displays comments that users have contributed to the question. If the user is logged in, you display the comment addition form; otherwise, you display only the comments themselves.

The following list describes the four major sections of code you'll add on this page:

1. The first section of code checks if the Submit button was clicked (if the form was displayed) and adds the comment to the database. This code is useful only if the user logs in and adds a comment; otherwise, the code is ignored.

2. The second section displays the question and answer.

3. The third section displays the comments under the question.

4. Finally, a check is made to see if the user is logged in and if so, the form is displayed.

The final interface, when the user is not logged in, looks like the page shown in Figure 9-6.

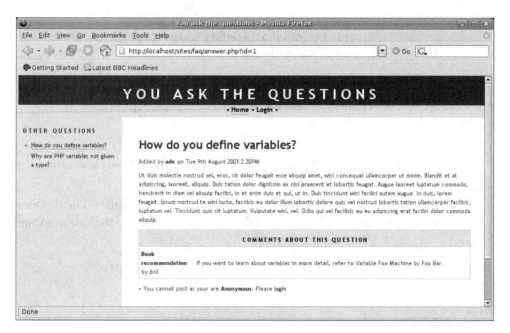

FIGURE 9-6 The interface used to view the question is simple and clear.

Create a file called *answer.php* and begin by adding the code to perform valida-tion on the `id` GET variable:

```php
<?php

session_start();

require("db.php");
require("functions.php");

if(pf_check_number($_GET['id']) == TRUE) {
     $validid = $_GET['id'];
}
else {
     header("Location: " . $config_basedir);
}
```

Begin writing the first chunk of code (processing the form):

```php
     header("Location: " . $config_basedir);
}

if($_POST['submit']) {
     $qsql = "INSERT INTO comments(question_id, title, comment,
  user_id) VALUES('"
            . $validid
```

```
                . "','" . pf_fix_slashes($_POST['titleBox'])
                . "','" . pf_fix_slashes($_POST['commentBox'])
                . "', '" . $SESS_USERID
                . "')";

        mysql_query($qsql);
        header("Location: " . $config_basedir . "answer.php?id="
 . $validid);
}
```

The preceding query uses the `pf_fix_slashes()` function from *functions.php* to safely add the information from the form to the database.

If no Submit button is clicked (either the form was not displayed or the form was displayed but the user had not used it), begin to display the question and answer:

```
        header("Location: " . $config_basedir . "answer.php?id="
 . $validid);
}
else {
        require("header.php");

        $qsql = "SELECT questions.question, questions.dateadded,
 questions.answer, users.username  FROM questions, users WHERE
 addedby_id = users.id AND questions.id = " . $_GET['id']
 . " AND active = 1;";
        $qresult = mysql_query($qsql);
        $qrow = mysql_fetch_assoc($qresult);
```

In the preceding query, you used a join to gather the question details. The join returns the username from the *users* table, in which `questions.addedby_id` and `users.id` are the same.

If no results are returned, tell the user:

```
        $qrow = mysql_fetch_assoc($qresult);

        if(mysql_num_rows($qresult) == 0) {
                echo "No Questions";
        }
```

Otherwise, display the question and answer details:

```
                echo "No Questions";
        }
        else {
                echo "<h1>" . $qrow['question'] . "</h1>";
```

```
        echo "Added by <strong>" . $qrow['username']
. "</strong> on " . date("D jS F Y g.iA",
strtotime($qrow['dateadded']));

        echo "<p>";
        echo $qrow['answer'];
        echo "</p>";
```

Add the code to display the comments for the question:

```
        echo "</p>";

        $csql = "SELECT comments.title, comments.comment,
users.username FROM comments, users WHERE comments.user_id =
users.id AND question_id = " . $validid . ";";
        $cresult = mysql_query($csql);
```

In this code, you created a query to gather the comment details and the username of the contributor.

Loop through the comments:

```
        $cresult = mysql_query($csql);

        echo "<table class='visible' width='100%' cellspacing=0
cellpadding=5>";
        echo "<tr><th class='visible' colspan=2>Comments about
this question</th></tr>";

        if(mysql_num_rows($cresult) == 0) {
                echo "<tr><td colspan=2><strong>No
comments!</strong></td></tr>";
        }
        else {
                while($crow = mysql_fetch_assoc($cresult))
                {
                        echo "<tr>";
                        echo "<td width='15%'><strong>"
. $crow['title'] . "</strong> by <i>" . $crow['username']
. "</i></td>";
                        echo "<td>" . $crow['comment'] . "</td>";
                        echo "</tr>";
                }
        }

        echo "</table>";
```

The comments are displayed in a table with two columns.

Check to see if the user is logged in. If so, display the form:

```
echo "</table>";

if($_SESSION['SESS_USERNAME']) {
        echo "<h2>Add a comment</h2>";
        echo "<form action='answer.php?id=" . $_GET['id']
. "' method='POST'>";
        echo "<table width='100%'>";
        echo "<tr>";
        echo "<td>Title</td>";
        echo "<td><input type='text' name='titleBox'></td>";
        echo "</tr>";
        echo "<tr>";
        echo "<td>Comment</td>";
        echo "<td><textarea rows=10 cols=50
name='commentBox'></textarea></td>";
        echo "</tr>";
        echo "<tr>";
        echo "<td></td>";
        echo "<td><input type='submit'
name='submit'value='Post Comment'></td>";
        echo "</tr>";
        echo "</table>";
        echo "</form>";
    }
```

If the user is not logged in, display a message:

```
        echo "</form>";
    }

    else {
        echo "<p>&bull; You cannot post as you are
<strong>Anonymous</strong>. Please <a href='login.php'>login</a>
</p>";
    }
```

Finally, add the closing code:

```
        echo "<p>&bull; You cannot post as you are
<strong>Anonymous</strong>. Please <a href='login.php'>login</a>
</p>";
    }

    }
}

require("footer.php");
?>
```

With the four major sections added, the page is now complete. If you have the time, run through this section again to familiarize yourself with how the different sections fit together.

> ### NOTE
>
> **By the Way...**
>
> In this project, many of the pages have sections that are not laid out in a linear (top-to-bottom) fashion. To fully understand how these different parts fit together, re-read the preceding section and refer to the code on the screen.

Updating the Sidebar

Eagle-eyed readers who were looking over Figure 9-6 at the start of this section will have noticed that the sidebar displays other questions in the same topic. This feature was added to ease navigation between different questions in the same topic. It is likely that readers of a topic will want to read most, or even all, of the questions in the current topic.

Load *bar.php* and move to the beginning of the file to add the code:

```php
<?php

if(basename($SCRIPT_NAME) == "answer.php") {
    echo "<h1>Other questions</h1>";
    $subsql = "SELECT topic_id FROM questions WHERE id = "
. $_GET['id'] . ";";
    $subresult = mysql_query($subsql);
    $subrow = mysql_fetch_assoc($subresult);

    $othersql = "SELECT id, question FROM questions WHERE
topic_id = " . $subrow['topic_id'] . " AND active = 1;";
    $otherresult = mysql_query($othersql);
```

The first query returns the topic that the current question is a part of, and the second query returns the questions inside that topic.

Display the questions:

```php
    $otherresult = mysql_query($othersql);

    echo "<table width='100%'>";

    while($otherrow = mysql_fetch_assoc($otherresult)) {
        echo "<tr>";
```

```
        echo "<td width='5%'>";

        if($otherrow['id'] == $_GET['id']) {
            echo "&bull;";
        }

        echo "<td><a href='answer.php?id=" . $otherrow['id'] . "'>"
. $otherrow['question']  . "</a></td>";
        echo "</tr>";
    }

    echo "</table>";
}
else {

    $subsql = "SELECT * FROM subjects";
    $subres = mysql_query($subsql);
}
```

DEALING WITH LOGINS

In any CMS, users need to be properly managed. Different systems have different user requirements, ranging from simple user logins to multi-user, layered permissions systems. Having a properly designed plan of how users will be managed, who can access what, and what kind of restrictions are in place is essential.

The user management system in this project is fairly simple. The system has two types of users: *normal users* and *administrators*. Normal users and administrators are different primarily in the capabilities that they offer (administrators can naturally manage many more parts of the system).

Normal User Logins

The vast majority of users on the system are normal users. A normal user can perform the following actions:

- Browse subjects, topics, and questions
- Leave a comment for a particular question
- Submit a question to be included in a topic

When a user submits a question for inclusion in a topic, the subject's owner or administrators can moderate the question. Any user can own a subject; she can apply to own an orphaned subject, and the administrator will accept or deny the request. This method of applying for subject ownership will be developed later.

> ### NOTE
>
> **Hiding the Administrator Login screen**
>
> Those of you with a penchant for small detail may have noticed that figures in this chapter have no link to an Administrator login page. This is a deliberate and enforced decision to improve the security of the site.
>
> If you are providing the opportunity for an administrator to log into the site, don't provide a link to the login page. If a link is available, the vermin of the Internet may descend on it and try to fake a login. By hiding the link, the aforementioned vermin need to find the login page before they can try to crack it. This may be frustrating enough for many of them to give up.
>
> This technique should by no means be your only security solution, but every little bit helps.
>
> Always remember that security is about a number of small steps and not just one large step. A number of different measures, large and small, can help improve your site's security.

First, build the login page. Create a new file called *login.php* and add the code shown in Example 9-4.

EXAMPLE 9-4   This code is virtually the same as previous login pages.

```php
<?php

session_start();

require("config.php");

if($_SESSION['SESS_USERNAME']) {
    header("Location: " . $config_basedir . "userhome.php");
}

$db = mysql_connect($dbhost, $dbuser, $dbpassword);
mysql_select_db($dbdatabase, $db);

if($_POST['submit']) {
    $sql = "SELECT * FROM users WHERE username = '"
. $_POST['username'] . "' AND password = '"
. $_POST['password'] . "';";

    $result = mysql_query($sql);
    $numrows = mysql_num_rows($result);

        if($numrows == 1) {
```

continues

EXAMPLE 9-4 Continued.

```php
                    $row = mysql_fetch_assoc($result);

                    session_register("SESS_USERNAME");
                    session_register("SESS_USERID");

                    $SESS_USERNAME = $_POST['username'];
                    $SESS_USERID = $row['id'];

                    header("Location: " . $config_basedir
    . "userhome.php");
            }
            else {
                    header("Location: " . $config_basedir
    . "/login.php?error=1");
            }
}
else {
        require("header.php");

        if($_GET['error']) {
        echo "Incorrect login, please try again!";
        }

?>
        <h1>Login</h1>

        <form action="<?php echo $SCRIPT_NAME ?>" method="post">

        <table>
        <tr>
        <td>Username</td>
        <td><input type="text" name="username"></td>
        </tr>
        <tr>
        <td>Password</td>
        <td><input type="password" name="password"></td>
        </tr>
        <tr>
        <td></td>
        <td><input type="submit" name="submit" value="Login!"></td>
        </tr>
        </table>
        </form>

<?php

}

require("footer.php");

?>
```

When the user has successfully logged in, two session variables are created: SESS_USERNAME and SESS_USERID. These variables are used throughout the code to check if a user is logged in and refer to the user's username and id. Before you can actually log in, though, you need to create the user's control panel.

Displaying the Control Panel

When the user has successfully logged into the system, the page redirects to a control panel that shows a number of options available to that specific user. This page looks like the one shown in Figure 9-7.

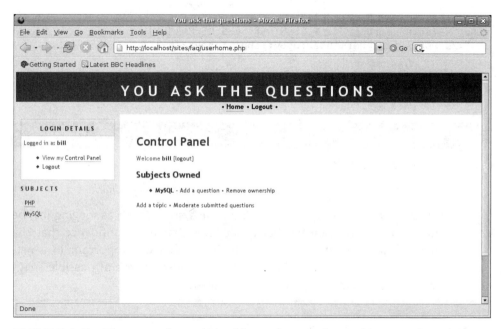

FIGURE 9-7   The control panel provides a place to show relevant options for specific users.

This page provides links to a number of different features related to an owned subject. These features include the ability to add questions, remove ownership, and moderate submitted questions. This functionality is spread over a number of pages, which are discussed later.

Create a new file called *userhome.php* and add the following code:

```php
<?php

session_start();

require("config.php");
```

```
if(!$_SESSION['SESS_USERNAME']) {
      header("Location: " . $config_basedir . "login.php");
}
```

```
require("header.php");
```

You first protect the page from users who are not logged in. If the SESS_USER-NAME variable does not exist, the page redirects.

Specify which user is logged in:

```
require("header.php");
```

```
echo "<h1>Control Panel</h1>";
echo "Welcome <strong>" . $_SESSION['SESS_USERNAME']
 . "</strong> [<a href='userlogout.php'>logout</a>]";
```

Adding a message, such as "Welcome Bob," so that the user knows he logged in correctly can improve a user's confidence with the site.

NOTE

Say It with Usability

One of the most critical concepts in good usability is *feedback*.

Whenever a user completes a task on the system (such as logging in), be sure to always provide feedback that gives that user confidence that she successfully completed the task. This is particularly important in a networked environment, such as the Web, because of several possible snags between your computer and the Web server.

Perform a query to gather the subjects that the user owns:

```
echo "Welcome <strong>" . $_SESSION['SESS_USERNAME']
 . "</strong> [<a href='userlogout.php'>logout</a>]";
```

```
echo "<h2>Subjects Owned</h2>";
```

```
$ownsql = "SELECT * FROM subjects WHERE owner_id ="
 . $_SESSION['SESS_USERID'] . ";";
$ownres = mysql_query($ownsql);
```

In this query, you used the SESS_USERID session variable to refer to the current user's user id. Setting a session variable with this information is a useful method of accessing the value without having to add another SQL query. As long as the user is logged in, this number never changes, so it makes sense to store the value in a session variable.

Check to see if any rows were returned and if so, display the subjects:

```php
$ownres = mysql_query($ownsql);

if(mysql_num_rows($ownres) >= 1)
{
      echo "<ul>";

      while($ownrow = mysql_fetch_assoc($ownres)) {
            echo "<li><strong><a href='index.php?subject="
 . $ownrow['id'] . "'>" . $ownrow['subject'] . "</a></strong>
 - <a href='addquestion.php?subject=" . $ownrow['id'] . "'>
Add a question</a> &bull; <a href='removesubown.php?subject="
 . $ownrow['id'] . "'>Remove ownership</a></li>";
      }

      echo "</ul>";

      echo "<a href='addtopic.php'>Add a topic</a>";
      echo " &bull; ";
      echo "<a href='adminmodquestions.php?func=main'>
Moderate submitted questions</a>";
}
else
{
      echo "No subjects are owned";
}
```

Each subject that is outputted includes a link to remove the ownership and, as such, orphans the subject. At the bottom of the list of owner subjects, a link is added to moderate questions that appear within the listed subjects.

Finally, add the footer file:

```php
      echo "No subjects are owned";
}

require("footer.php");

?>
```

Logging Out

Create a file called *userlogout.php* and add the code to log the user out, as shown in Example 9-5.

EXAMPLE 9-5 The logout code unregisters the user's session variables.

```php
<?php

    session_start();
    require("config.php");

        session_unregister('SESS_USERNAME');
        session_unregister('SESS_USERID');

    header("Location: " . $config_basedir . "index.php");
?>
```

To prevent logging out both the user and admin out when both are logged in, this code does not destroy the session. The script simply unregisters the session variables, and they become inactive, logging out the user.

Adding Feedback in the Sidebar

When a user logs into a Web site, it is always useful to clearly indicate in the login status. The natural place to indicate this is in the sidebar. Fire up *bar.php* and add the following code at the start of the file:

```php
<?php

if($_SESSION['SESS_USERNAME']) {
      echo "<table class='visible' width='100%'cellspacing=0
 cellpadding=5>";
      echo "<tr><th class='visible'>Login details</th></tr>";
      echo "<tr><td>";
      echo "Logged in as <strong>" . $_SESSION['SESS_USERNAME']
. "</strong>";
      echo "<ul>";
      echo "<li>View my <a href='userhome.php'>Control Panel</a></li>";
      echo "<li><a href='userlogout.php'>Logout</a></li>";
      echo "</ul>";
      echo "</td></tr>";
      echo "</table>";
}

if(basename($SCRIPT_NAME) == "answer.php") {
      echo "<h1>Other questions</h1>";
```

In this code, you indicate the name of the user that is logged in and provide a link to the control panel. This provides a handy method of identifying that the user is logged in as well as accessing the control panel at any time.

Administrator Logins

Aside from the different session variables, administrator logins are very similar to user logins. In an eerily familiar fashion (OK, not that eerie), you will create the login page first.

Add the code shown in Example 9-6 to *adminlogin.php*.

EXAMPLE 9-6   The admin login page is virtually identical to the normal user login page.

```php
<?php

session_start();

require("db.php");

if($_SESSION['SESS_ADMINUSER']) {
    header("Location: " . $config_basedir . "adminhome.php");
}

if($_POST['submit']) {

    $sql = "SELECT * FROM admins WHERE username = '"
. $_POST['username'] . "' AND password = '" .
$_POST['password'] . "';";
    $result = mysql_query($sql);
    $numrows = mysql_num_rows($result);

    if($numrows == 1) {
        $row = mysql_fetch_assoc($result);

        session_register("SESS_ADMIN");
        session_register("SESS_ADMINUSER");
        session_register("SESS_ADMINID");

        $SESS_ADMINUSER = $_POST['username'];
        $SESS_ADMINID = $qow['id'];

        header("Location: " . $config_basedir . "adminhome.php");
    }
    else {
        header("Location: " . $config_basedir
. "/adminlogin.php?error=1");
    }
}
else {
```

continues

EXAMPLE 9-6 Continued.

```php
        require("header.php");

        echo "<h1>Admin Login</h1>";

        if($_GET['error']) {
        echo "<p>Incorrect login, please try again!</p>";
        }
?>
        <form action="<?php echo $SCRIPT_NAME ?>" method="post">

        <table>
        <tr>
        <td>Username</td>
        <td><input type="text" name="username"></td>
        </tr>
        <tr>
        <td>Password</td>
        <td><input type="password" name="password"></td>
        </tr>
        <tr>
        <td></td>
        <td><input type="submit" name="submit" value="Login!"></td>
        </tr>
        </table>
        </form>

<?php
}

require("footer.php");

?>
```

In this file, you use the SESS_ADMINUSER and SESS_ADMINID session variables to identify that the administrator is logged in.

Logout

Create *adminlogout.php* and add the logout code shown in Example 9-7.

Again, you unregister the relevant session variables.

EXAMPLE 9-7   Guess what? This code is quite similar to the normal user logout code.

```php
<?php

session_start();

require("config.php");

session_unregister('SESS_ADMINUSER');
session_unregister('SESS_ADMINID');

header("Location: " . $config_basedir);

?>
```

Becoming an Admin and Playing With More Toys

Although the *adminlogin.php* and *adminlogout.php* pages are very similar to their normal user counterparts, the administrator gets a lot more toys in his control center. The administrator is able to perform the following tasks, which the normal user cannot:

- Add subjects
- Add topics
- Moderate submitted questions
- Moderate subject ownership requests

Create a new file called *adminhome.php* and add the code shown in Example 9-8.

EXAMPLE 9-8   The admin home includes special admin-only options, such as adding subjects and moderating ownership requests.

```php
<?php

session_start();

if(isset($_SESSION['SESS_ADMINUSER']) == FALSE) {
    header("Location: " . $config_basedir . "adminlogin.php");
}

require("header.php");
    echo "<h1>Admin Panel</h1>";
    echo "Welcome <strong>" . $_SESSION['SESS_ADMINUSER']
 . "</strong> [<a href='adminlogout.php'>logout</a>]";
```

continues

EXAMPLE 9-8 Continued.

```
?>
<table border="0" cellspacing="5" cellpadding="5">
  <tr>
    <td><a href="addsubject.php">Add a subject</a></td>
    <td>Add a new subject</td>
  </tr>
  <tr>
    <td><a href="addtopic.php">Add a topic</a></td>
    <td>Add a new topic</td>
  </tr>
  <tr>
    <td><a href="adminmodquestions.php?func=main">
Moderated Questions</a></td>
    <td>Authorize or Reject submitted questions</td>
  </tr>
  <tr>
    <td><a href="adminmodsubown.php?func=main">
Subject Ownership Requests</a></td>
    <td>Authorize or Reject submitted questions</td>
  </tr>
</table>

<?php
      require("footer.php");
?>
```

To keep the project simple, administrator functionality has been limited to these core areas. Of course, you could implement many other features, such as the ability to do the following:

- View site statistics
- Configure site-wide options
- Manage the site content

Adding More Feedback to That Sidebar

The same technique that you used to display a box in the sidebar when the user is logged in will be used to show when the administrator is logged in. Add the following code to *bar.php*:

```
        echo "</td></tr>";
        echo "</table>";
}

if($_SESSION['SESS_ADMINUSER']) {
```

```
    echo "<table class='visible' width='100%'cellspacing=0
cellpadding=5>";
    echo "<tr><th class='visible'>Login details</th></tr>";
    echo "<tr><td>";
    echo "Logged in as <strong>" . $_SESSION['SESS_ADMINUSER']
. "</strong>";
    echo "<ul>";
    echo "<li>View my <a href='adminhome.php'>Admin Panel</a></li>";
    echo "<li><a href='adminlogout.php'>Logout</a></li>";
    echo "</ul>";
    echo "</td></tr>";
    echo "</table>";
}
```

The completed administrator page should look something similar to the page shown in Figure 9-8.

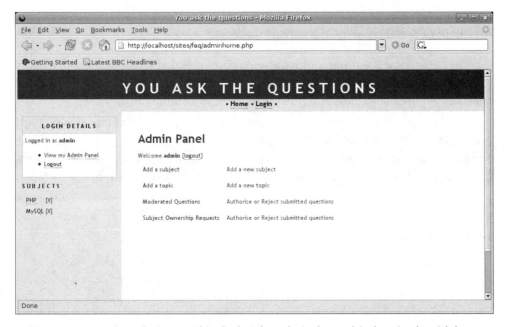

FIGURE 9-8   The admin panel includes the admin-logged-in box in the sidebar.

ADDING AND MODERATING QUESTIONS

One of the most difficult challenges to overcome when installing and using a CMS is generating new content. Imagine the following situation:

> Bob Scratchings installs a CMS with the aim of providing lots of interesting content. For a few weeks, Bob spends each night religiously updating the site, but as the weeks roll into months, he spends less and less time on it.

Before long, the site never gets updated and becomes another dusty, old, unmaintained husk on the Internet.

To solve this problem, you need to encourage site users to become involved and contribute content themselves. With this in mind, you will add functionality to allow any user to submit questions. The owner of the subject (another contributor) can moderate the wheat from the chaff. This will encourage some community spirit.

Adding Questions

When adding questions to a topic, the script needs to take into account two possible modes of operation:

- If the user is the subject owner, the question should be added instantly to the range of available questions for the subject.
- If the user is not the owner of the subject, the submitted question should be held for moderation by the subject owner.

The logistics of handling which questions are intended for moderation is simply a case of adjusting the `active` field in the *questions* table. If this field is set to 0, the question requires moderation; if it is set to 1, the question is live.

In addition to handling these questions differently, this script can also be used in two possible places. When browsing the topics, the topic view contains a link to add a question. In this case, the script is passed the id of the topic to which the question is added. The selected topic is displayed on the form, as shown in Figure 9-9.

FIGURE 9-9
If known, the name of the topic is added to the form.

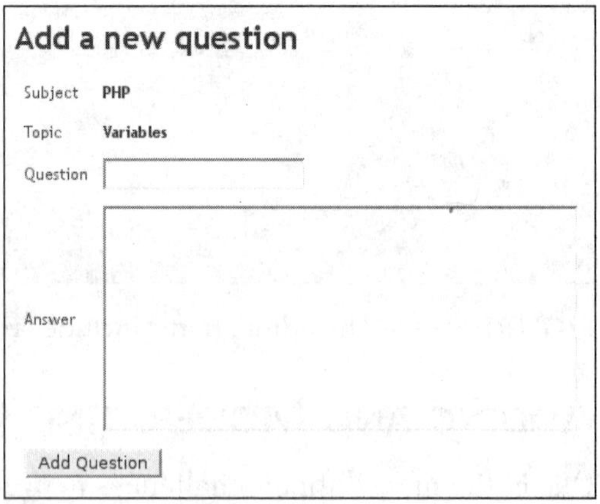

The user's control panel also provides a link to add a question to a subject. In this case, the topic is not known, and the script provides a list of topics from the subject, as shown in Figure 9-10.

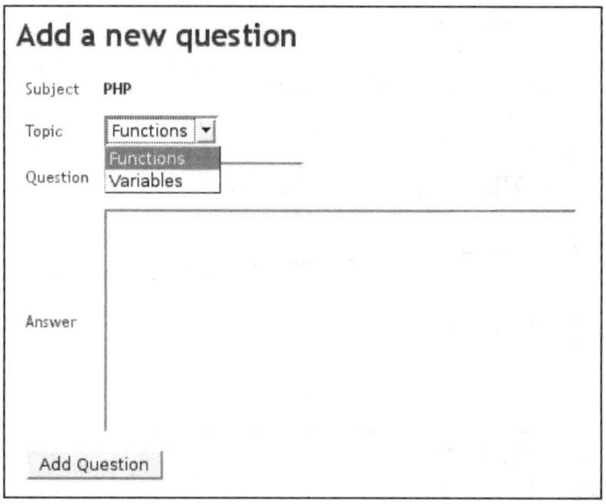

Add a new question

Subject **PHP**

Topic Functions ▾
Functions
Question Variables

Answer

Add Question

FIGURE 9-10
If the topic is not known, the user can select it from the combo box.

NOTE

What About No Topics?

If no topics are available in the subject, and the subject owner tries to add a question, the script should prompt the owner to first add a topic. This fail-safe technique is used in the code for this project.

Create a new file called *addquestion.php* and add the following code:

```php
<?php

session_start();

require("db.php");
require("functions.php");
```

Only logged-in users should use this page, so check if a user is logged in and then redirect any users who are trying to post questions but have not logged in:

```php
require("functions.php");

if(!$_SESSION['SESS_USERNAME']) {
    header("Location: " . $config_basedir . "login.php");
}
```

Validate the GET variables:

```
    header("Location: " . $config_basedir . "login.php");
}

if(pf_check_number($_GET['subject']) == TRUE) {
    $validsubject = $_GET['subject'];
}
else {
    header("Location: " . $config_basedir);
}

if(isset($_GET['topic']) == TRUE) {
    if(is_numeric($_GET['topic']) == TRUE) {
        $validtopic = $_GET['topic'];
    }
    else {
        header("Location: " . $config_basedir);
    }
}
```

The `subject` and `topic` GET variables are validated. If they fail, the page redirects.

Begin adding the code for the form displayed to the user. First, add the queries to pull in the subject and topic information displayed in the form:

```
        header("Location: " . $config_basedir);
    }
}

    require("header.php");

    $subsql = "SELECT * FROM subjects WHERE id = "
. $validsubject . ";";
    $subq = mysql_query($subsql);
    $subrow = mysql_fetch_assoc($subq);

    $toplistsql = "SELECT * FROM topics WHERE subject_id = "
. $validsubject . " ORDER BY name ASC;";
    $toplistresult = mysql_query($toplistsql);
    $toplistnumrows = mysql_num_rows($toplistresult);
```

Check if any topics are available:

```
    $toplistnumrows = mysql_num_rows($toplistresult);

    echo "<h1>Add a new question</h1>";

    if($_SESSION['SESS_USERID'] == $subrow['owner_id']) {
        if($toplistnumrows == 0) {
            $notopics = TRUE;
```

```
        }
    }
```

This code checks if the current user is the owner of the subject and then checks if the number of topics returned was 0. If the number is indeed 0, the $notopics variable is set to TRUE. The only time you display the list of topics is when the user is the owner of the subject, so you check the number of topics returned.

If no topics exist, a subject has been added (but there are no topics inside it). Instruct the user to create some topics:

```
                $notopics = TRUE;
        }
    }

    if($notopics == TRUE) {
        echo "No topics have been created. Click
<a href='addtopic.php'>here</a> to create one!";
    }
```

Start a table and begin creating the interface:

```
                echo "No topics have been created. Click <a
href='addtopic.php'>here</a> to create one!";
        }
        else {
            echo "<p>";
            echo "<form action='addquestion.php?subject="
. $validsubject . "' method='POST'>";
            echo "<table cellpadding=5>";
            echo "<tr>";
            echo "<td>Subject</td>";
            echo "<td><strong>" . $subrow['subject']
. "</strong></td>";
            echo "</tr>";
            echo "<tr>";
            echo "<td>Topic</td>";
            echo "<td>";
```

In this block, you create the form in a table and then add the name of the subject from the query to a row in the table.

The next row in the table should display the topic if it is known (if a topic GET variable exists) or display a drop-down box with the topics in the subject if only the subject is known. You achieve this by checking that the $validtopic variable is present:

```
            echo "<td>Topic</td>";
            echo "<td>";

            if(!$validtopic) {
                echo "<select name='topic'>";
```

```
                        while($toplistrow =
mysql_fetch_assoc($toplistresult)) {
                            echo "<option value='"
 . $toplistrow['id'] . "'>" . $toplistrow['name']
 . "</option>";
                        }

                        echo "</select>";
            }
```

If the variable is unavailable, the combo box is added and the `while` loop adds each topic. If the variable *is* available, display the topic:

```
                echo "</select>";
            }
            else {
                $topsql = "SELECT * FROM topics WHERE id = "
 . $validtopic . ";";
                $topq = mysql_query($topsql);
                $toprow = mysql_fetch_assoc($topq);

                echo "<strong>" . $toprow['name'] . "</strong>";
                echo "<input type='hidden' name='topic' value='"
 . $toprow['id'] . "'>";
            }
```

A query first grabs the name of the topic and then displays the name in the cell. In addition, a hidden form element is added to the page so that you can refer to the id of the selected topic with `$_POST['topic']` regardless of whether the combo box or topic name were displayed.

NOTE

Using Hidden Form Elements

Hidden form elements are particularly useful in situations where you need to refer to a value but the page could behave in different ways. By using the hidden form element, you can place a value in the form and then later refer to it with the normal $_GET or $_POST array.

Add the form input elements:

```
                echo "<input type='hidden' name='topic' value='"
 . $toprow['id'] . "'>";
            }

        echo "</td>";
```

```
            echo "</tr>";
            echo "<tr>";
            echo "<td>Question</td>";
            echo "<td><input type='text' name='question'></td>";
            echo "</tr>";
            echo "<tr>";
            echo "<td>Answer</td>";
            echo "<td><textarea name='answer' rows=10
cols=50></textarea></td>";
            echo "</tr>";
            echo "<tr>";
            echo "<td colspan=2><input type='submit' name='submit'
value='Add Question'></td>";
            echo "</tr>";
            echo "</table>";
            echo "</form>";
    }
```

With the form complete, you can add the code to process it. This involves the usual step of checking if the Submit button was clicked and processing the form accordingly. Seasoned veterans who have completed previous projects in the book will expect the form display code to be encased in an else block, which is exactly what happens.

At the beginning of the file, adding the processing code after the validation code:

```
            header("Location: " . $config_basedir);
    }
}

if($_POST['submit']) {
    $authsql = "SELECT * FROM subjects WHERE id = " . $validsubject
. " AND owner_id = " . $_SESSION['SESS_USERID'] . ";";
    $authresult = mysql_query($authsql);
    $authnumrows = mysql_num_rows($authresult);
```

When processing the code, check if the current user is the owner of the subject—this affects whether the question needs to be moderated. This block of code sends a query to the database to determine the status of the user.

Check if any results were returned:

```
    $authnumrows = mysql_num_rows($authresult);

    if($authnumrows == 1) {
        $qsql = "INSERT INTO questions(topic_id, question, answer,
addedby_id, dateadded, active) VALUES("
            . $_POST['topic']
            . ", '" . pf_fix_slashes($_POST['question'])
        . "', '" . pf_fix_slashes($_POST['answer'])
```

```
            . "', " . $_SESSION['SESS_USERID']
        . ", NOW()"
        . ", 1);";
        $qresult = mysql_query($qsql);

        header("Location: " . $config_basedir . "answer.php?id="
    . mysql_insert_id());
    }
```

If a row was returned, the current user is the owner of the subject. An INSERT query is created to add the data to the *questions* table, and active is set to 1 (the question is live).

Add the code that is run when the current user is not the subject owner:

```
        header("Location: " . $config_basedir . "answer.php?id=" .
    mysql_insert_id());
    }
    else {
        $qsql = "INSERT INTO questions(topic_id, question, answer,
    addedby_id, dateadded, active) VALUES("
        . $_POST['topic']
        . ", '" . pf_fix_slashes($_POST['question'])
        . "', '" . pf_fix_slashes($_POST['answer'])
            . "', " . $_SESSION['SESS_USERID']
        . ", NOW()"
        . ", 0);";

        $qresult = mysql_query($qsql);

        require("header.php");

        echo "<h1>Awaiting moderation</h1>";
        echo "Your question requires moderator approval before it is
    posted.";
    }
}
```

In this block, the same query is performed, but active is set to 0 so that the question can be moderated. A message informs the user of this moderation process.

Open the main else that encases the form display code:

```
        echo "Your question requires moderator approval before it
    is posted.";
    }
}
else {
```

Finally, after the form display code, add the closing footer:

```
}
```

```php
require("footer.php");

?>
```

Affirm Some Power and Moderate Some Questions

Question moderation is open to both the site administrator and the owner of the subject to which the question was added. To make this process as simple as possible, the added questions are listed as shown in Figure 9-11.

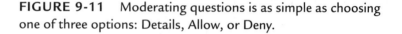

Questions submitted for moderation

Subject	Topic	Question	Submitted By			
PHP	Functions	How do I create a function?	ade	Details	Allow	Deny
PHP	Functions	Why would I use a function?	ade	Details	Allow	Deny

FIGURE 9-11   Moderating questions is as simple as choosing one of three options: Details, Allow, or Deny.

Each question has three possible options: to view the details, or to allow or deny the question.

This script has a number of different personalities. To access the different pieces of functionality, the page is passed a `func` GET variable, which is then run through a `switch` statement that has five possible outcomes:

- `main`. This section displays the summary of the questions, as seen in Figure 9-11.
- `details`. When the user clicks the Details link, this section is loaded and displays the details about the question.
- `allow`. If the user clicks the Allow link, this section sets the question status to live.
- `deny`. If the user rejects the question and clicks the Deny link, this section prompts the user—with Yes and No options—to be sure he wants to deny the question.
- `denyconf`. If the Yes option is clicked, the question is deleted.

Create a new file called *adminmodquestions.php* and add the following code:

```php
<?php

session_start();

require("db.php");
require("functions.php");

function set_validid() {
    if(pf_check_number($_GET['id']) == TRUE) {
        return $_GET['id'];
    }
    else {
        header("Location: " . $config_basedir);
    }
}

switch($_GET['func'])
{
```

You created a function called set_validid(), which validates the id GET variable. This function is created because not every block of the switch (such as the main block) needs an id variable.

The *main* Block

Create each of the blocks inside the switch, starting with main:

```php
switch($_GET['func'])
{

    case "main":
        require("header.php");
```

To gather the questions required for moderation, the query is different for the administrator and for a normal user. For the administrator, you simply need to view all questions that require moderation:

```php
    case "main":
        require("header.php");

        if($_SESSION['SESS_ADMINUSER']) {
            $modqsql = "SELECT questions.*, users.username FROM users
INNER JOIN questions on questions.addedby_id=users.id INNER JOIN
topics on questions.topic_id=topics.id INNER JOIN subjects on
topics.subject_id=subjects.id WHERE questions.active = 0;";
        }
```

An inner join is used to get the username of the person who submitted the question. All questions in which active is set to 0 are returned.

For a normal user, only the questions within the subject(s) that he owns should be returned:

```
    $modqsql = "SELECT questions.*, users.username FROM users
INNER JOIN questions on questions.addedby_id=users.id INNER JOIN
topics on questions.topic_id=topics.id INNER JOIN subjects on
topics.subject_id=subjects.id WHERE questions.active = 0;";
    }
    else {
        $modqsql = "SELECT questions.*, users.username FROM users
inner join questions on questions.addedby_id=users.id inner join
topics on questions.topic_id=topics.id inner join subjects on
topics.subject_id=subjects.id WHERE questions.active = 0 AND
subjects.owner_id = " . $_SESSION['SESS_USERID'] . ";";
    }
```

Run the relevant query:

```
    $modqsql = "SELECT questions.*, users.username FROM users
inner join questions on questions.addedby_id=users.id inner join
topics on questions.topic_id=topics.id inner join subjects on
topics.subject_id=subjects.id WHERE questions.active = 0 AND
subjects.owner_id = " . $_SESSION['SESS_USERID'] . ";";
    }

    $modresult = mysql_query($modqsql);
```

Create a table and add the table headings:

```
    $modresult = mysql_query($modqsql);

    echo "<h1>Questions submitted for moderation</h1>";
    echo "<table cellspacing='0' cellpadding='5'>";
    echo "<tr>";
    echo "<th>Subject</th>";
    echo "<th>Topic</th>";
    echo "<th>Question</th>";
    echo "<th>Submitted By</th>";
    echo "<td></td>";
    echo "<td></td>";
    echo "<td></td>";
    echo "</tr>";
```

If the query returns no results, there are no questions to moderate:

```
    echo "<td></td>";
    echo "</tr>";

    if(mysql_num_rows($modresult) == 0) {
        echo "<tr>";
```

```
            echo "<td colspan=7>No questions to moderate</td>";
            echo "</tr>";
    }
```

If there are rows to moderate, display the questions:

```
            echo "</tr>";
    }

    while($row = mysql_fetch_assoc($modresult)) {
        $subsql = "SELECT topics.name, subjects.subject FROM topics,
subjects WHERE topics.subject_id = subjects.id AND topics.id = "
. $row['topic_id'] . ";";
        $subresult = mysql_query($subsql);
        $subrow = mysql_fetch_assoc($subresult);

        echo "<tr>";
        echo "<td>" . $subrow['subject'] . "</td>";
        echo "<td>" . $subrow['name'] . "</td>";
        echo "<td>" . $row['question'] . "</td>";
        echo "<td>" . $row['username'] . "</td>";
        echo "<td><a href='adminmodquestions.php?func=details&id="
. $row['id'] . "'>Details</a></td>";
        echo "<td><a href='adminmodquestions.php?func=allow&id="
. $row['id'] . "'>Allow</a></td>";
        echo "<td><a href='adminmodquestions.php?func=deny&id="
. $row['id'] . "'>Deny</a></td>";

        echo "</tr>";
    }
    echo "</table>";
break;
```

This block displays the results from the query and adds the Details, Allow, and
Deny links. Each link adds the func GET variable and the relevant switch block to
which the link points to (for example, func=details accesses the details block), as
well as the id of the question (for example, id=2).

The *details* Block

The details block displays details about the current question. This block is presented like the block shown in Figure 9-12.

Add the following code:

```
    echo "</table>";
break;

case "details":
    require("header.php");
```

```
    $validid = set_validid();

    $sql = "SELECT questions.*, topics.name, subjects.subject FROM
questions INNER JOIN topics ON questions.topic_id = topics.id INNER
JOIN subjects ON topics.subject_id = subjects.id
WHERE questions.id = " . $validid . ";";
    $result = mysql_query($sql);
    $row = mysql_fetch_assoc($result);
```

Submitted question details

Subject	PHP
Topic	Functions
Question	How do I create a function?
Answer	Lorem ipsum dolor sit amet, consectetuer adipiscing elit. Maecenas eros velit, porttitor id, placerat eu, ultricies et, erat. Nam arcu eros, auctor at, aliquet sit amet, tincidunt id, diam. Etiam a purus a purus facilisis facilisis. Nulla sollicitudin scelerisque tellus. Fusce vehicula metus aliquet enim. Praesent id lacus. Duis elit risus, tincidunt in, nonummy quis, dictum ac, elit. Praesent ut tortor. Vestibulum eros orci, malesuada vel, sodales nec, sodales at, nulla. Cras ullamcorper volutpat mi. Phasellus porttitor arcu eget dui. Suspendisse feugiat. Vestibulum ligula nibh, facilisis sit amet, imperdiet nec, scelerisque eu, tellus. Morbi nec nulla ut sapien tincidunt iaculis. Mauris pulvinar volutpat massa. Nunc non velit.

⇐ Back to questions • Allow • Deny

FIGURE 9-12   The details link provides a convenient way of viewing the answer to the question.

You first run this query to gather the details about the submitted question. This query performs an inner join to gather the question details, the topic name, and the subject name.

Display the gathered information:

```
    $row = mysql_fetch_assoc($result);

    echo "<h1>Submitted question details</h1>";
    echo "<table border='0' cellspacing='0' cellpadding='5'>";
    echo "<tr>";
        echo "<td><b>Subject</b></td>";
        echo "<td>" . $row['subject'] . "</td>";
    echo "</tr>";
    echo "<tr>";
        echo "<td><b>Topic</b></td>";
        echo "<td>" . $row['name'] . "</td>";
    echo "</tr>";
    echo "<tr>";
        echo "<td><b>Question</b></td>";
        echo "<td>" . $row['question'] . "</td>";
    echo "</tr>";
    echo "<tr>";
        echo "<td><b>Answer</b></td>";
        echo "<td>" . $row['answer'] . "</td>";
    echo "</tr>";
    echo "<tr>";
        echo "<td colspan=2>";
```

```
        echo "<a href='adminmodquestions.php?func=main'>&lArr;
Back to questions</a>";
        echo " &bull; ";
        echo "<a href='adminmodquestions.php?func=allow&id="
. $row['id'] . "'>Allow</a> ";
        echo " &bull; ";
        echo " <a href='adminmodquestions.php?func=deny&id="
. $row['id'] . "'>Deny</a>";
        echo "</td>";
      echo "</tr>";
      echo "</table>";
    break;
```

The *allow* Block

To accept a question, add the allow block:

```
        echo "</table>";
      break;

    case "allow":
      $validid = set_validid();

      $modqsql = "UPDATE questions SET active = 1 WHERE id = "
. $validid . ";";
      $modqq = mysql_query($modqsql);

      header("Location: " . $config_basedir
. "adminmodquestions.php?func=main");
    break;
```

This block updates the question and sets the active field to 1 to make the question live. The page then redirects to the main block of *adminmodquestions.php*.

The *deny* Block

To deny a question, the process is split into two parts. The first part asks the user if she is sure that she wants to reject the question. See Figure 9-13.

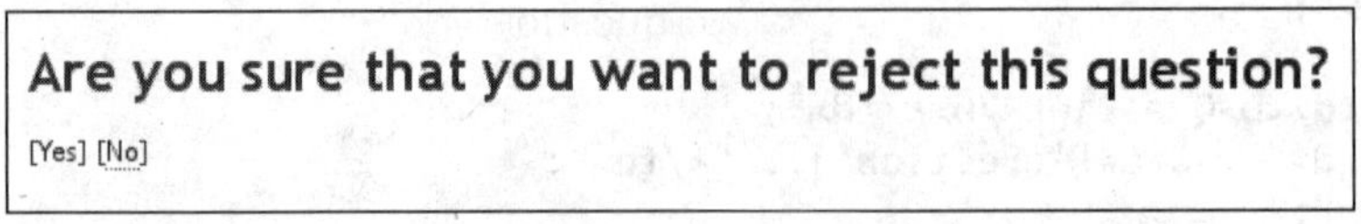

Are you sure that you want to reject this question?

[Yes] [No]

FIGURE 9-13 Before denying a question, be sure this is what the user wants.

Add the code for this section:

```
     header("Location: " . $config_basedir .
"adminmodquestions.php?func=main");
   break;

   case "deny":
     require("header.php");

     $validid = set_validid();

     echo "<h1>Are you sure that you want to reject this
question?</h1>";
     echo "<p>[<a href='" . $SCRIPT_NAME . "?func=denyconf&id="
. $validid . "'>Yes</a>] [<a href='" . $SCRIPT_NAME
. "?func=main'>No</a>]";
   break;
```

This block provides two links. The No link simply links back to the main section of the current script, and the Yes link links to the denyconf section.

The *denyconf* Block

To confirm the cold, hard reality of denying a question, add the denyconf block:

```
     echo "<p>[<a href='" . $SCRIPT_NAME . "?func=denyconf&id="
. $validid . "'>Yes</a>] [<a href='" . $SCRIPT_NAME
. "?func=main'>No</a>]";
   break;

   case "denyconf":
     $validid = set_validid();

     $delsql = "DELETE FROM questions WHERE id = " . $_GET['id']
. ";";
     $delq = mysql_query($delsql);

     header("Location: " . $config_basedir
. "adminmodquestions.php?func=main");
   break;
```

This block deletes the question from the *questions* table and then redirects back to the main section to display the other moderated questions.

Finally, close the switch and add the footer file:

```
     header("Location: " . $config_basedir
. "adminmodquestions.php?func=main");
   break;
}

require("footer.php");
?>
```

MANAGING SUBJECTS

Subjects are the core foundation of the content that this project manages, and are very similar to Categories in the blog project in Chapter 4. Managing subjects is something that you naturally only want the administrator to be able to do. If you were to give a regular user the run of the subjects, anything could happen.

The capabilities to add and delete subjects are important pieces of functionality to create, but deleting is a capability with which you should take special care. By using InnoDB tables in MySQL, any accidental deletions of a subject cause all of the child topics and questions to be deleted also. As such, be very careful when working through this section.

Adding Subjects

Adding a subject to the database is as simple as creating a form and adding the contents of the form to the database. Create a new file called *addsubject.php* and add the following code:

```
<h1>Add a new subject</h1>

<form action="<?php echo $SCRIPT_NAME; ?>" method="post">
<table cellpadding="5">
<tr>
    <td>Subject</td>
    <td><input type="text" name="subject"></td>
</tr>
<tr>
    <td>Owner</td>
    <td>
```

This code adds a form and a table to lay out the form elements. After adding the subject text box, display a combo box so that a subject owner can be chosen:

```
    <td>Owner</td>
    <td>

    <select name="owner">
       <option value="0">-- No Owner --</option>
    <?php
       $sql = "SELECT * FROM users ORDER BY username ASC;";
       $result = mysql_query($sql);

       while($row = mysql_fetch_assoc($result)) {
           echo "<option value='" . $row['id'] . "'>"
. $row['username'] . "</option>";
       }
    ?>
    </select>
```

A select box is created, and the first entry (which returns the value 0) is added to provide a No Owner option. The other entries in the select box are added from the query.

Complete the form:

```
   ?>
   </select>
   </td>
</tr>
<tr>
   <td>Description Blurb</td>
   <td><textarea name="blurb" cols=50 rows=10></textarea></td>
</tr>
<tr>
   <td></td>
   <td><input type="submit" name="submit" value="Add Subject!"></td>
</tr>
</table>
</form>
```

With the form finished, it's time to process it. Jump to the start of the file and add the following code:

```
<?php

session_start();

require("db.php");
require("functions.php");

if(isset($_SESSION['SESS_ADMINUSER']) == FALSE) {
   header("Location: " . $config_basedir . "adminlogin.php");
}
```

You first protect the page so that only the administrator can access it. Check if the Submit button was clicked and begin the processing:

```
   header("Location: " . $config_basedir . "adminlogin.php");
}

if($_POST['submit']) {
   $subsql = "INSERT INTO subjects(subject, blurb, owner_id) VALUES("
      . "'" . pf_fix_slashes($_POST['subject'])
      . "', '" . pf_fix_slashes($_POST['blurb'])
      . "'," . $_POST['owner']
      . ");";
   mysql_query($subsql);
   header("Location: " . $config_basedir);
}
```

Inside this block an INSERT statement adds the form data to the database. Add the else that encases the main form:

```
header("Location: " . $config_basedir);
}

else {
    require("header.php");

?>
    <h1>Add a new subject</h1>

    <form action="<?php echo $SCRIPT_NAME; ?>" method="post">
```

Finally, after the form, close the else and add the footer file:

```
</table>
</form>

<?php
}
require("footer.php");

?>
```

The completed page should look like the one shown in Figure 9-14.

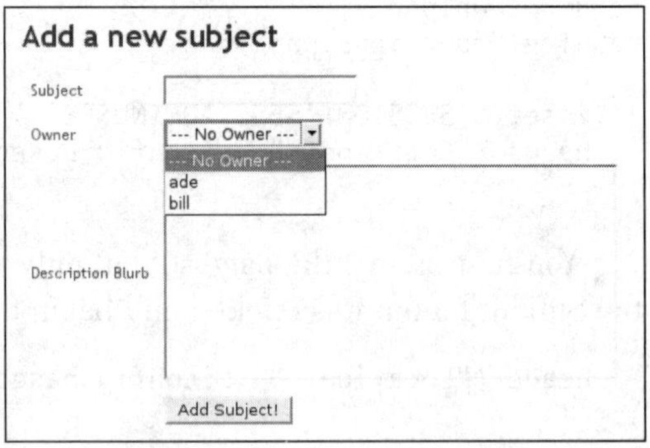

FIGURE 9-14
If No Owner is selected, 0 is added to the owner_id field in the *questions* table.

Deleting Subjects

When logged in as an administrator, a user deletes content by clicking the little *X* links. These links hook up with a page to delete the type of content the *X* is next to. If you take a look at the list of subjects, you will see that the *X* next to each subject links to *deletesubject.php* and passes the script the id of the subject to be deleted.

When *deletesubject.php* is first loaded, the user is prompted to confirm that he wants to delete the subject. If he clicks the Yes link, the page reloads but includes a conf GET variable. If this variable is present, the subject is deleted.

> **NOTE**
>
> **Cascading Fun and Games**
>
> Remember that when a subject is deleted, all topics and questions within that subject are deleted also. The code for the cascading delete was added when you set up your tables.

Create *deletesubject.php* and add the following code:

```php
<?php
session_start();

require("db.php");
require("functions.php");

if($_SESSION['SESS_ADMIN']) {
    header("Location: " . $config_basedir);
}

if(pf_check_number($_GET['subject']) == TRUE) {
    $validsubject = $_GET['subject'];
}
else {
    header("Location: " . $config_basedir);
}
```

First, the code validates the subject GET variable that was passed to the page. Next a check is made to see if the conf GET variable exists (remember that this is added when the user confirms deletion of the subject):

```php
    header("Location: " . $config_basedir);
}

if($_GET['conf']) {
    $delsql = "DELETE FROM subjects WHERE id = " . $validsubject . ";";
    mysql_query($delsql);
```

```
      header("Location: " . $config_basedir);
}
else {
    require("header.php");
    echo "<h1>Are you sure you want to delete this subject?</h1>";
    echo "<p>[<a href='" . $SCRIPT_NAME . "?conf=1&subject="
  . $validsubject . "'>Yes</a>] [<a href='" . $config_basedir
  . "'>No</a>]";
}
```

If the variable exists, the subject is deleted and the page redirects back to the base page. Otherwise, the question is displayed.

Finally, add the footer file:

```
    echo "<p>[<a href='" . $SCRIPT_NAME . "?conf=1&subject=" .
$validsubject . "'>Yes</a>] [<a href='" . $config_basedir . "'>No</a>]";
}

require("footer.php");

?>
```

Managing Topics

When adding topics to the system, the script needs to work both for normal users who own subjects and for the administrator. The practical differences between a normal user and the admin are mainly in the subjects to which they have access. The administrator can choose any subject to add to a topic, whereas a normal user can choose only the subjects he owns.

Adding Topics

Create a new file called *addtopic.php* and start the form:

```
<h1>Add a new topic</h1>

<form action="<?php echo $SCRIPT_NAME; ?>" method="post">
<table cellpadding="5">
<tr>
    <td>Subject</td>
```

To display the selection of subjects in the combo box, add the following code:

```
    <td>Subject</td>
    <td>
    <?php
        if($_SESSION['SESS_ADMINUSER']) {
```

```
        $sql = "SELECT * FROM subjects ORDER BY subject ASC;";
        $result = mysql_query($sql);
    }
    else {
        $sql = "SELECT * FROM subjects WHERE owner_id = "
. $_SESSION['SESS_USERID'] . " ORDER BY subject ASC;";
        $result = mysql_query($sql);
    }

    echo "<select name='subject'>";

    while($row = mysql_fetch_assoc($result)) {
        echo "<option value='" . $row['id'] . "'>"
. $row['subject'] . "</option>";
    }

    echo "</select>";
?>
```

In this code, a check is made to see if the administrator is logged in. If he is, all subjects are displayed; otherwise, only the subjects owned by the current user are displayed.

Complete the rest of the form:

```
        echo "</select>";
    ?>

    </td>
</tr>
<tr>
    <td>Topic</td>
    <td><input type="text" name="name"></td>
</tr>
<tr>
    <td></td>
    <td><input type="submit" name="submit" value="Add Subject!"></td>
</tr>
</table>
</form>
```

With the form ready, jump to the beginning of the file and add the following code:

```
<?php

session_start();

require("db.php");
require("functions.php");
```

You now need to protect this file from unauthorized use. This is more challenging because both the administrator and users who own subjects can use the file. Unauthorized users include people not logged in and those users who don't own a subject.

The solution is to perform checks to see if the current user is a valid user. If the user is a valid user, the $auth variable is set to 1. After these tests, the $auth variable is checked. If $auth is not equal to 1, the page is redirected.

Add the checks:

```
require("functions.php");

if(isset($_SESSION['SESS_ADMINUSER']) == TRUE) {
    $auth = 1;
}

if(isset($_SESSION['SESS_USERNAME']) == TRUE) {
    $authsql = "SELECT * FROM subjects WHERE owner_id = "
 . $_SESSION['SESS_USERID'] . " ORDER BY subject ASC;";
    $authresult = mysql_query($authsql);
    $authnumrows = mysql_num_rows($authresult);

    if($authnumrows >= 1) {
        $auth = 1;
    }
}
```

The first check identifies whether the administrator is logged in. If he is, $auth is set to 1. The next check identifies whether a user is logged in and then performs a query to see that user owns any subjects. If the query returns one or more rows, $auth is set to 1.

Check the value of $auth:

```
        $auth = 1;
    }
}

if($auth != 1) {
    header("Location: " . $config_basedir);
}
```

If $auth is not equal (!=) to 1, the page redirects.

Process the form:

```
  header("Location: " . $config_basedir);
}

if($_POST['submit']) {
    $sql = "INSERT INTO topics(subject_id, name) VALUES("
        . "'" . $_POST['subject']
        . "', '" . pf_fix_slashes($_POST['name'])
        . "');";
    mysql_query($sql);
    header("Location: " . $config_basedir . "index.php?subject="
  . $_POST['subject']);
}
else {
    require("header.php");

?>

    <h1>Add a new topic</h1>

    <form action="<?php echo $SCRIPT_NAME; ?>" method="post">
```

This block uses a simple INSERT statement to add the values to the database. The page then redirects to *index.php* and passes it the subject GET variable to display the subject information.

After the form, close the else block and add the footer file:

```
    </table>
    </form>

<?php
}

require("footer.php");

?>
```

Getting Rid of Topics

Deleting a topic is virtually identical to deleting a subject. The X next to the topic links to *deletetopic.php* and the code is very similar (see Example 9-9).

EXAMPLE 9-9 The delete topic code is very similar to deleting a subject.

```php
<?php

session_start();

require("db.php");
require("functions.php");

if(isset($_SESSION['SESS_ADMINUSER']) == FALSE) {
   header("Location: " . $config_basedir);
}


if(pf_check_number($_GET['topic']) == TRUE) {
   $validtopic = $_GET['topic'];
}
else {
   header("Location: " . $config_basedir);
}

if($_GET['conf']) {
   $delsql = "DELETE FROM topics WHERE id = " . $validtopic . ";";
   mysql_query($delsql);

   header("Location: " . $config_basedir);
}
else {
   require("header.php");
   echo "<h1>Are you sure you want to delete this topic?</h1>";
   echo "<p>[<a href='" . $SCRIPT_NAME . "?conf=1&topic="
 . $validtopic . "'>Yes</a>] [<a href='" . $config_basedir
 . "'>No</a>]";
}

require("footer.php");

?>
```

SUBJECT OWNERSHIP

Subject ownership is a key feature in this project. Not only does it encourage users to roll up their sleeves and get involved, it also decentralizes the source of the content so that a range of different users can maintain the site.

In this part of the project, you manage ownership requests, request moderation, and the removal of ownership. Three scripts manage these different needs.

Applying for Ownership of a Subject

If a subject in the system has no owner, the subject information page contains a link that invites users to apply for ownership of the event. When this link is clicked, the user is presented with the page shown in Figure 9-15.

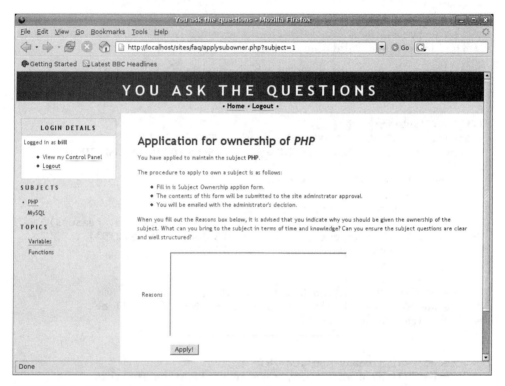

FIGURE 9-15   Any user is welcome to apply for ownership of a subject.

This page is very simple. The user types the reasons she feels that she should be trusted to own the page and then clicks the Submit (Apply!) button. The page then informs the applicant that a response will be emailed when the administrator has made a decision.

Create a new file called *applysubowner.php* and start adding the code:

```php
<?php

session_start();

require("config.php");
require("functions.php");
```

```
if(pf_check_number($_GET['subject']) == TRUE) {
   $validsubject = $_GET['subject'];
}
else {
   header("Location: " . $config_basedir);
}

require("header.php");
```

The file begins by validating the subject GET variable.

Add the code to process the form, which consists of a single text box:

```
require("header.php");

if($_POST['submit']) {
   $appsql = "SELECT * FROM mod_subowner WHERE sub_id = "
. $validsubject . " AND user_id = '" . $_SESSION['SESS_USERID']
. "';";
   $appresult = mysql_query($appsql);

   if(mysql_num_rows($appresult) == 0) {
      $inssql = "INSERT INTO mod_subowner(sub_id, user_id, reasons)
VALUES(" . $_GET['subject'] . "," . $_SESSION['SESS_USERID'] . ",'"
. pf_fix_slashes($_POST['reasons']) . "');";
      mysql_query($inssql);

      echo "<h1>Application Submitted</h1>";
      echo "Your application has been submitted. You will be
emailed with the decision.";
   }
   else {
      echo "<h1>Already Applied</h1>";
      echo "<p>You have already made an application for this
subject.</p>";
   }
}
```

In this block, a check is first made to see if the current user has already applied for ownership. If the query returns no rows, this is the first application and a query is constructed to add the user id, subject id, and reasons to the *mod_subowner* table.

If the query returns one or more rows, the user has already applied for ownership and a message is displayed to indicate this.

Now you can begin to display the form. Before you do this, perform a query to grab the name of the subject:

```
echo "<p>You have already made an application for this
subject.</p>";
```

```
      }
   }
   else {
      $subsql = "SELECT subject FROM subjects WHERE id = "
    . $validsubject . ";";
      $subresult = mysql_query($subsql);
      $subrow = mysql_fetch_assoc($subresult);
   ?>
```

The name of the subject from this query is used in the text of the page.

Add this text and the form:

```
      $subrow = mysql_fetch_assoc($subresult);
   ?>


   <h1>Application for ownership of <i><?php echo $subrow['subject'];
   ?></i></h1>
   <p>You have applied to maintain the subject <strong><?php echo
   $subrow['subject']; ?></strong>.</p>
   <p>
   The procedure to apply to own a subject is as follows:
   <ul>
   <li>Fill in is Subject Ownership application form.</li>
   <li>The contents of this form will be submitted to the site
   adminstrator approval.</li>
   <li>You will be notified in your Account Homepage of the
   administrators decision.</li>
   </ul>
   </p>
   <p>
   When you fill out the Reasons box below, it is advised that you
   indicate why you should be given
   the ownership of the subject. What can you bring to the subject
   in terms of time and knowledge? Can
   you ensure the subject questions are clear and well structured?
   </p>
   <form action="applysubowner.php?subject=<?php echo $validsubject;
   ?>" method="POST">
   <table cellpadding=5 cellspacing=5>
   <tr>
   <td>Reasons</td>
   <td><textarea name="reasons" cols="50" rows="10"></textarea></td>
   </tr>
   <tr>
   <td></td>
   <td><input type="submit" name="submit" value="Apply!"></td>
   </tr>
   </table>
   </form>
```

With the form complete, add the closing code:

```
</table>
</form>

<?php
}

require("footer.php");

?>
```

Moderating Ownership Requests

Moderation of the subject ownership requests is very similar to the moderation of the questions earlier in the project. The administrator is presented with a list of requests, which he can accept or deny, as shown in Figure 9-16.

In the question moderation script, the func GET variable was used to choose which mode the page was working in. A switch statement checked this variable, and the relevant code was executed.

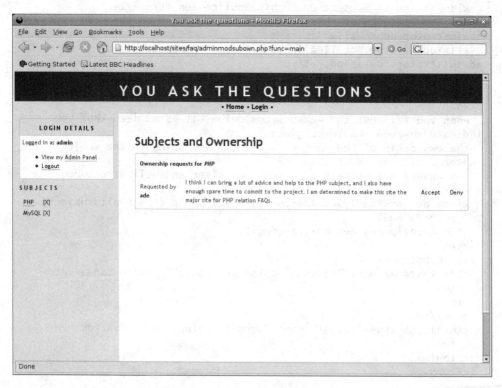

FIGURE 9-16 The administrator can easily tend to requests.

The same technique is used in this page, which includes the following four sections:

- main. This section displays the ownership requests.
- allow. If the Allow link is clicked, this section is run and authorizes the ownership request.
- deny. If the Deny link is clicked, this section prompts the administrator to be sure that he wants to deny the request.
- denyconf. If the administrator clicks the Yes link in the deny section, the denyconf section deletes the request from the database.

Create a new file called *adminmodsubown.php* and add the following code:

```php
<?php

session_start();

if(!$_SESSION['SESS_ADMINUSER']) {
    header("Location: " . $config_basedir);
}

require("db.php");
require("functions.php");

function set_validid() {
    if(pf_check_number($_GET['id']) == TRUE) {
        return $_GET['id'];
    }
    else {
        header("Location: " . $config_basedir);
    }
}
```

You again create a function to manage the validation across the different switch blocks. This works the same as in the question moderation script.

Open the switch statement:

```php
        header("Location: " . $config_basedir);
    }
}

switch($_GET['func']) {
```

The *main* Block

The first block to add is main, which displays the list of ownership requests. This list of requests allows the user to see who wants to have ownership of a particular subject.

```
switch($_GET['func']) {

    case "main":
    require("header.php");

    $subssql = "SELECT subjects.subject, subjects.id FROM subjects
INNER JOIN mod_subowner ON subjects.id = mod_subowner.sub_id
GROUP BY subjects.id;";
    $subsresult = mysql_query($subssql);
    $subsnumrows = mysql_num_rows($subsresult);

    echo "<h1>Subjects and Ownership</h1>";
```

This code runs a query to gather the names of all the subjects that have had ownership requests. If the query returns no rows, display a message:

```
    echo "<h1>Subjects and Ownership</h1>";

    if($subsnumrows == 0) {
        echo "No requests have been made.";
    }
```

If rows are returned, execute the else:

```
    echo "No requests have been made.";
    }
    else {
        while($subsrow = mysql_fetch_assoc($subsresult)) {
            $reqsql = "SELECT users.id AS userid, users.username,
mod_subowner.* FROM users INNER JOIN mod_subowner ON
mod_subowner.user_id = users.id WHERE mod_subowner.sub_id = "
. $subsrow['id'] . ";";
            $reqresult = mysql_query($reqsql);
```

A while loop is opened to loop through each subject. A second query performs a join to get the usernames for the ownership requests.

Start a table to hold the content:

```
            $reqresult = mysql_query($reqsql);

            echo "<table class='visible' cellpadding=10
cellspacing=0>";
```

```
        echo "<tr><th class'visible' colspan='4'>
Ownership requests for <i>" . $subsrow['subject']
 . "</i></th></tr>";
```

Create another while loop to loop through the second query's set of results:

```
        echo "<tr><th class'visible' colspan='4'>
Ownership requests for <i>" . $subsrow['subject']
 . "</i></th></tr>";

        while($reqrow = mysql_fetch_assoc($reqresult)) {
            echo "<tr>";
            echo "<td>Requested by     <strong>"
 . $reqrow['username'] . "</strong></td>";
            echo "<td>" . $reqrow['reasons'] . "</td>";
            echo "<td><a href='" . $SCRIPT_NAME
 . "?func=accept&id=" . $reqrow['id'] . "'>Accept</a></td>";
            echo "<td><a href='" . $SCRIPT_NAME
 . "?func=deny&id=" . $reqrow['id'] . "'>Deny</a></td>";
            echo "</tr>";
        }

        echo "</table>";
        echo "<br/>";
    }
  }
break;
```

The combination of the second while inside the first while means that for each subject, the ownership requests will be grouped in a table. This makes choosing the best request much easier.

The *accept* Block

Accepting an ownership request involves three steps:

- The user is sent an email to indicate she has been chosen as the new subject owner.
- The *subjects* table is updated with the id of the new owner.
- All entries in the *mod_subown* table for that particular subject are deleted. This ensures any competing applications for ownership are removed.

Add the following code:

```
    }
  break;

  case "accept":

    $validid = set_validid();
    $sql = "SELECT mod_subowner.sub_id, subjects.subject,
users.id AS userid, users.username, users.email FROM
mod_subowner INNER JOIN subjects ON
mod_subowner.sub_id = subjects.id LEFT JOIN users ON
mod_subowner.user_id = users.id WHERE mod_subowner.id = "
. $validid . ";";
    $result = mysql_query($sql);
    $row = mysql_fetch_assoc($result);
    $numrows = mysql_num_rows($result);
```

This query selects the subject id, subject name, user id, username, and email address that correlate to the subject id and owner id in the *mod_subown* table. This query involves two joins. The first join connects the *mod_subowner* and *subjects* tables, and the second join connects the *mod_subowner* and *users* tables.

To send the email, the same technique from the Auctions project covered in Chapter 7 is used. First, copy the array variables into some normal variables to add the information to the body of the email:

```
    $numrows = mysql_num_rows($result);

    $mail_username = $row['username'];
    $mail_email = $row['email'];
    $mail_subject = $row['subject'];
```

Construct the email using *heredoc* syntax:

```
    $mail_subject = $row['subject'];

$mail_body=<<<_MESSAGE_

Hi $mail_username,

I am pleased to inform you that you have been accepted as the new
 owner of the '$mail_subject' subject.

When you next log into '$config_sitename' you will see the subject
 in your Control Panel.

Kind regards,

    $config_sitename Administrator

_MESSAGE_;
```

Use the `mail()` command to send the email message:

```
$config_sitename Administrator

_MESSAGE_;

    mail($mail_email, "Ownership request for " . $mail_subject
. " accepted!", $mail_body);
```

The `mail()` function sends the email to the address in `$mail_email`, with the subject `Ownership request for <subject> accepted!` and `$mail_body` (the heredoc text) as the body of the message.

Update the *subjects* table to change the `owner_id` field to the id of the new owner:

```
    mail($mail_email, "Ownership request for " . $mail_subject . "
accepted!", $mail_body);

    $addsql = "UPDATE subjects SET owner_id = " . $row['userid']
. " WHERE id = " . $row['sub_id'] . ";";
    mysql_query($addsql);
```

Finally, delete all entries in the *mod_subowner* table with the same subject as the winning request:

```
    mysql_query($addsql);

    $delsql = "DELETE FROM mod_subowner WHERE sub_id = "
. $row['sub_id'] . ";";
    mysql_query($delsql);

    header("Location: " . $config_basedir
. "adminmodsubown.php?func=main");
    break;
```

The *deny* Block

The deny block is identical to the deny block in the question moderation script:

```
    header("Location: " . $config_basedir
. "adminmodsubown.php?func=main");
    break;

  case "deny":
    $validid = set_validid();

    require("header.php");
    echo "<h1>Are you sure that you want to deny this request?</h1>";
```

```
      echo "<p>[<a href='adminmodsubown.php?func=denyconf&id="
. $validid . "'>Yes</a>]
[<a href='adminmodsubown.php?func=main'>No</a>]";
      break;
```

This code prompts the user to confirm whether he wants to deny the request. If the user clicks No, the page redirects to the main section; otherwise, it redirects to the denyconf section.

The *denyconf* Block

To deny the ownership request, the code follows two steps:

1. Send an email to the user to let him know that his request was denied.

2. Delete the request from the *mod_subowner* table.

This section borrows heavily from the allow section. The code simply changes the text of the email body that is sent and the content to be deleted:

```
      echo "<p>[<a href='adminmodsubown.php?func=denyconf&id="
. $validid . "'>Yes</a>]
[<a href='adminmodsubown.php?func=main'>No</a>]";
      break;

  case "denyconf":
      $validid = set_validid();

      $sql = "SELECT mod_subowner.sub_id, subjects.subject, users.id
AS userid, users.username, users.email FROM mod_subowner
INNER JOIN subjects ON mod_subowner.sub_id = subjects.id
LEFT JOIN users ON mod_subowner.user_id = users.id
WHERE mod_subowner.id = " . $validid . ";";
      $result = mysql_query($sql);
      $row = mysql_fetch_assoc($result);
      $numrows = mysql_num_rows($result);

      $mail_username = $row['username'];
      $mail_email = $row['email'];
      $mail_subject = $row['subject'];

$mail_body=<<<_MESSAGE_

Hi $mail_username,

I am writing to inform you that your request for ownership of
 the '$mail_subject' subject has been declined.

Better luck next time!
```

```
Kind regards,

   $config_sitename Administrator

_MESSAGE_;

     mail($mail_email, "Ownership request for " . $mail_subject
. " denied!", $mail_body);

     $delsql = "DELETE FROM mod_subowner WHERE id = " . $validid
. ";";
     mysql_query($delsql);

     header("Location: " . $config_basedir
. "adminmodsubown.php?func=main");
   break;
```

With the sections complete, close the `switch` block and add the footer file:

```
     header("Location: " . $config_basedir
. "adminmodsubown.php?func=main");
   break;

}

require("footer.php");

?>
```

Removing Ownership

At some point in the future, it is likely that an owner of a subject may not have the time or inclination to continue contributing. In this case, you want to ensure that an owner can easily orphan a subject if needed.

To make this as simple as possible, in the control panel you add an option to remove ownership, as seen in Figure 9-17.

To orphan the subject, the subject id passed to the page is used to run a query to change the owner_id field in the *subjects* table to 0. Before this query happens, however, another confirmation question is displayed to prevent any accidents.

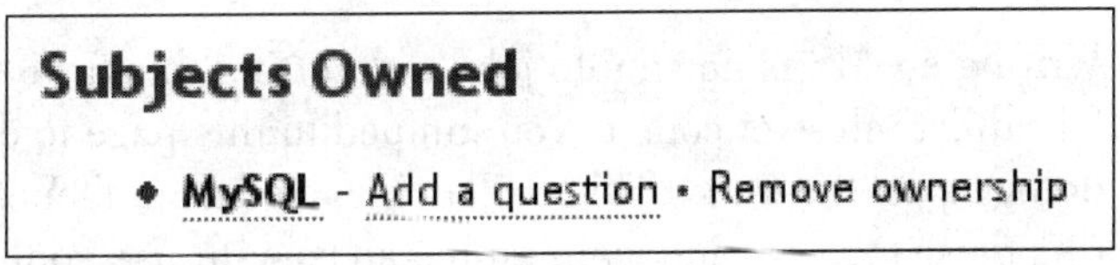

FIGURE 9-17
The remove ownership link is passed the subject id.

Subjects Owned

• **MySQL** - Add a question • Remove ownership

The code used in this script is virtually the same as in *deletesubject.php*. Create a new file called *removesubown.php* and add the code shown in Example 9-10.

EXAMPLE 9-10   To orphan the subject, set the *owner_id* field to 0.

```php
<?php

session_start();

require("db.php");
require("functions.php");

if(!$_SESSION['SESS_USERNAME']) {
    header("Location: " . $config_basedir . "login.php");
}

if(pf_check_number($_GET['subject']) == TRUE) {
    $validsubject = $_GET['subject'];
}
else {
    header("Location: " . $config_basedir);
}

if($_GET['conf']) {
    $updsql = "UPDATE subjects SET owner_id = 0 WHERE id = " .
$validsubject . ";";
    mysql_query($updsql);

    header("Location: " . $config_basedir . "userhome.php");
}
else {
    require("header.php");

    echo "<h1>Are you sure that you want to drop this subject?</h1>";
    echo "<p>[<a href='removesubown.php?conf=1&subject="
. $validsubject . "'>Yes</a>] [<a href='userhome.php'>No</a>]";
}

require("footer.php");

?>
```

SUMMARY

Writing a CMS is no simple job, and getting this far is a real achievement in your learning (unless of course, you jumped to this page to experience the glory without doing any of the work). This project involved a number of different segments, and fitting these together and maintaining an easy-to-use application was a real challenge.

Like design, CMSs are never finished; they are only abandoned. This project, however, still has many features that could be implemented. To continue your development, see if you can add the following features:

- Content editing. Write functionality that enable users to edit subjects, topics, and questions.
- Inter-user messaging. It would be useful if one user could send a message to another.
- The capability to delete questions and comments. Extend the deletion of content to delete questions and comments.
- The capability to merge comments into questions. When questions become directly useful to the answer of the question, it would be useful to have an easy-to-use system for merging comments into the main answer.

CHAPTER 10

Building a Re-Usable Project

Life is increasingly difficult for Web developers. With the deluge of people getting online and using the Internet for more and more purposes, Web developers have more being asked of them than ever before. This not only means a wider range of applications are required, but also the complexity of the development is growing, too. It is not uncommon for even the smallest business to have a large, complex Web application that drives its primary business requirements.

One of the solutions to this problem is to write re-usable code. Those of you who have been rattling around the IT industry for a few years are likely to be familiar with the re-usable buzzword, and in many situations it does actually make sense.

The following list describes a few ways to re-use existing code in your application:

- PEAR. The PHP Extension and Applications Repository (PEAR) provides a huge directory of extensions that can be easily installed and used. Each PEAR module is written in PHP.
- PECL. The PHP Extension Community Library (PECL) includes a range of PHP extensions that need to be compiled. These extensions offer entirely new functionality to PHP and are very fast.
- Other pre-built applications. Many people release zipped-up projects that can be unzipped into your Web application to satisfy some specific functionality. An example of this is the Magpie RSS parser.

In this chapter, you will write an application that is designed to be dropped into existing Web sites. Along the way, you will explore the plethora of challenges that comes with writing software that is easy to install, re-use, and implement.

PROJECT OVERVIEW

For many developers, it is not uncommon to write little tools that solve very specific tasks. These small tools often don't warrant their own SourceForge account or even a complex project management system such as Trac (http://www.edgewall.com/trac/). Instead, the ideal solution includes a simple means to download the program and view screenshots. To satisfy these requirements, you will create the *phphome-project* tool. Oh, the power.

When viewing a project inside the application, users will be able to view the following:

- Available projects.
- The range of versions and download releases inside each version.
- Screenshots.

These are the core features that the majority of Web surfers look for when exploring software.

To make the application re-usable, some thought needs to go into how it works and how easy it is to set up. It is difficult, if not impossible, to write a re-usable application without first sitting down and getting a strong idea of how the different pieces fit together.

The basic concept in this application is that each project has its own project directory (such as www.foo.com/projects/myproject/ or www.foo.com/projects/myotherproject/). The site administrator creates these project directories manually.

When a new project is created, two actions occur:

- The new project is added to the database.
- The project directory is created and populated with the files for viewing and maintaining the content.

To be as flexible as possible, it should be very simple to drop this application into an existing Web site—as simple as including a single file into a normal Web page (such as `<?php require("thisapp.php"); ?>`). But how do you cram all the functionality into a single page without it becoming horrifically complex and bloated?

The solution to the problem is shown in Figure 10-1.

To best explain this process, the following list what happens from the moment the user accesses the Web site:

- The user accesses the www.mysite.com/projects/myproject/ Web address, and the *index.php* file is loaded. Between the header and footer files, a file called *project-main.php* is included.

- The *project-main.php* files checks to see if a `func` GET variable exists. If so, a `switch` statement includes the relevant file. If the user clicks the Download link, for example, `func=download` is appended as a GET variable.

- Inside the `switch` statement in *project-main.php*, the relevant file is included. In the case of `func=download`, *download.php* is included; it contains the code to display the available downloads.

With the main *index.php* file including *project-main.php*, which in turn includes a file such as *download.php*, the eventual download functionality is displayed to the user in the *index.php* file. This makes it easier to spread the features across different pages, and the URL looks clean and consistent.

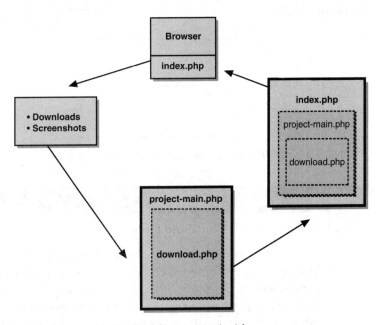

FIGURE 10-1   Embedding pages inside pages promotes re-usability.

BUILDING THE DATABASE

The database you will create is shown in Figure 10-2.

A project inside the application lives in *homeproject_projects*. Releases of the project are organized in versions (stored in *homeproject_releaseversions*), and the actual releases (the downloaded files) are described in *homeproject_releasefiles*. Each entry in *homeproject_releasefiles* refers to its parent version from *homeproject_releaseversions*. In addition to the parent version, a release file also stores the type of release (such as a Debian Package, RPM, Windows ZIP, Mac OS X disk image, and so on) from the *homeproject_releasetypes* table. Finally, *thehomeproject_ screenshots* table stores the names of the screenshots for each release.

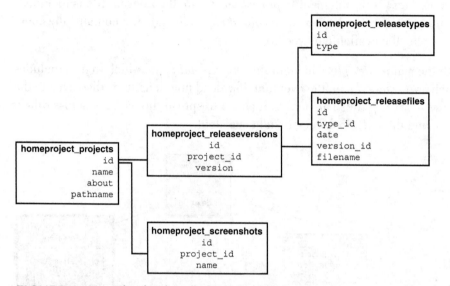

FIGURE 10-2   The database is fairly straightforward.

NOTE

Making Your Tables Stand Out

The reusable component uses the same database as the application that is hosting it. To indicate which tables are which, each table in the reusable component project uses the prefix *homeproject_*. This is an intentional choice so that when this application is deployed in an existing Web site, the tables that are part of the application can be identified easily. As an example, take a look at the following list of tables:

- admins
- customers
- blogentries
- homeproject_projects
- homeproject_releaseversions

You can quite easily identify which tables are part of the application.

Implementing the Database

Start phpMyAdmin. Create a new database called *phphomeproject* and add the following tables:

The *homeproject_projects* Table

- id. Make this an MEDIUMINT and turn on auto_increment. Set this field as a primary key.
- name. Make this a VARCHAR with a length of 100.
- about. Make this a TEXT.
- pathname. Make this a VARCHAR with a length of 30.

The *homeproject_releaseversions* Table

- id. Make this an INT and turn on auto_increment in the Extras column. Set this field as a primary key.
- project_id. Make this an INT.
- version. Make this a VARCHAR and set the size to 20.

The *homeproject_releasetypes* Table

- id. Make this a TINYNT and turn on auto_increment. Set this field as a Primary Key.
- type. Make this a VARCHAR and set the size to 20.

The *homeproject_releasefiles* Table

- id. Make this an INT (there could be lots of questions) and turn on auto_increment. Set this field as a primary key.
- type_id. Make this an TINYINT.
- date. Make this a DATETIME.
- version_id. Make this an INT.
- filename. Make this a VARCHAR with a length of 50.

The *homeproject_screenshots* Table

- id. Make this an INT (there could be lots of subjects) and turn on auto_increment. Set this field as a primary key.
- project_id. Make this an INT.
- name. Make this a VARCHAR with a length of 50.

Inserting Sample Data

With a solid set of tables ready to go, you can now add some sample data. Remember, do not fill in a number in the id column, which auto_increment does for you automatically. Feel free to add your own sample data, or use the suggested information described in the following sections.

Sample Data for the *homeproject_projects* Table

Add a project such as the one shown in Table 10-1.

TABLE 10-1 This table contains the main project details.

NAME	ABOUT	PATHNAME
My Project	This is an example project that demonstrates how a project is managed inside this re-usable project management application.	myproject

The pathname field provides a unique string to refer to the project. This is used in a few parts of the Web application—most notably in the URL, such as localhost/sites/homeproject/<pathname>/.

Sample Data for the *homeproject_releaseversions* Table

Add version numbers as shown in Table 10-2.

TABLE 10-2 Because a version number could have multiple releases, store the version numbers in a dedicated table.

PROJECT_ID	VERSION
1	0.1
1	0.2

Sample Data for the *homeproject_releasetypes* Table

Add three records, using the following names:

- Tarball
- Debian Package
- Windows ZIP

Sample Data for the *homeproject_releasefiles* Table

Add two records to this table, using the correct `version_id` and `type_id`. The `file-name` field should contain the name of the release file (such as *myrelease.tar.gz*). When you later create the *releases* directory, remember to place a file in the directory with the same filename.

Sample Data for the *homeproject_screenshots* Table

Add a few records into the table, using the correct `project_id`. The `name` field should contain the name of the screenshot (such as *myscreenshot.png*). When you create the *screenshots* directory later, remember to include images with the same name.

USING DIRECTORIES INTELLIGENTLY

Unlike previous projects in the book, phphomeproject makes extensive use of directories to determine specific types of functionality. The project has three main directories: *base*, *admin*, and *project*.

The base directory, such as www.mysite.com/projects, is the base projects directory on the Web site. This directory contains the different files that form *phphomeproject*. This directory also includes an *index.php* file, which lists the projects on the server so that the user can select which project to view.

A project directory, such as www.mysite.com/projects/myproject, is a subdirectory inside the base directory. This directory contains a single *index.php* file (which includes the files from the base directory, as shown in Figure 10-1). The project also contains two subdirectories: *releases* (which stores software releases) and *screenshots* (which stores screenshots).

The *admin* directory is the directory the site administrator uses to adjust project settings. This directory is also found within the base directory, such as www.mysite.com/projects/admin, and contains a number of files for managing the site.

Creating the Directories

First, create the base directory and call it *homeproject*. Then create the *admin* subdirectory.

For each project you also need to create a subdirectory inside *homeproject*. The name of the directory should be the same as the pathname field in the *homeproject_projects* table. If you added the My Project record as was done in this example, create a directory called *myproject*. Inside *myproject* create the releases and screenshots subdirectories. Be sure that both *releases* and *screenshots* have write access to them.

You should now have the following directories:

```
homeproject
     admin
     myproject
          releases
          screenshots
```

```
Parent
|
|
-----Subdir1
|
-----Subdir2
     |
     |
     -----Subsubdir1
     |
     -----Subsubdir2
```

> ### NOTE
>
> **A Quick Reminder...**
>
> When you added data to the tables, you also added some release and screenshot records. Remember to add these files and screenshots to the *releases* and *screenshots* directories, respectively.

STARTING TO CODE: BUILDING THE BACKBONE

Developing *phphomeproject* requires two core areas:

- Viewable project information. This is the area that Web site visitors see. Visitors can view project information, downloads, and screenshots.
- Project administration. This is the interface for configuration projects; only the site administrator accesses this interface.

In this project, you will implement the project viewing area first and then move on to create the administration area. Before you begin, you will create some of the structural files (configuration file, functions, and so on).

Because this project is available as a re-usable component, you should use a separate configuration file for the settings specific to the project. Inside the *homeproject* directory, create *phphomeproject.php* and then add the code shown in Example 10-1.

EXAMPLE 10-1   The configuration file is separate from the main configuration file of your Web site.

```php
<?php

$dbhost = "localhost";
$dbuser = "root";
$dbpassword = "";
$dbdatabase = "phphomeproject";

$config_headerfile = "http://localhost/sites/homeproject/header.php";
$config_footerfile = "http://localhost/sites/homeproject/footer.php";

$config_projecturl = "http://localhost/sites/homeproject/";
$config_projectdir = "/opt/lampp/htdocs/sites/homeproject/";

$config_projectadminbasedir =
"http://localhost/sites/homeproject/admin/";
$config_projectadminfilename = "admin.php";

$config_projectscreenshotthumbsize = 300;
?>
```

In addition to the normal database settings, this configuration file includes a number of other options:

- $config_headerfile and $config_footerfile. The location of the header and footer files in the Web application.

- $config_projecturl. The URL where you can find *phphomeproject*.

- $config_projectdir. The directory that includes *phphomeproject*. Use this directory when copying new releases and screenshots to the *releases* and *screenshots* directories.

- $config_projectadminbasedir. The location of the *admin* directory.

- $config_projectadminfilename. The name of the file (such as *admin.php*) used to access the admin functionality.

- $config_projectscreenshotthumbsize. The width to which thumbnails should be set when viewing screenshots.

It is important to remember that you are developing *phphomeproject* in a separate directory, which is independent of an existing Web site. When *phphomeproject* is deployed in an application, these settings need to be changed to reflect the existing site (for example, changing $config_projecturl to http://www.mysite.com/projects/). You will deploy the site later in the chapter.

Accessing the Database

In the base directory (phphomeproject), create *db.php* and add the connection code shown in Example 10-2.

EXAMPLE 10-2   This file is no different from other projects.

```php
<?php

    require("phphomeprojectconfig.php");

  $db = mysql_connect($dbhost, $dbuser, $dbpassword);
  mysql_select_db($dbdatabase, $db);

?>
```

Creating the Functions

This project uses two custom functions in addition to `pf_fix_slashes()` and `pf_check_number()` from previous projects. In the base directory, create a new file called *functions.php* and add the configuration file:

```php
<?php

require("phphomeprojectconfig.php");
```

Add `pf_protect_nonadmin_page()`:

```php
require("phphomeprojectconfig.php");

function pf_protect_nonadmin_page() {
    if(basename($_SERVER['SCRIPT_NAME']) != "index.php") {
        echo "<h1>Error</h1>";
        echo "You cannot access this page directly. Please go to the
  main project pages directly.";
        exit;
    }
}
```

The `pf_protect_nonadmin_page()` function protects individual pages from direct access. If you refer to Figure 10-1, you can see that a page such as *download.php* is included in *project-main.php*, which is in turn included in *index.php*. Naturally, you don't want users to access *download.php* directly. This function simply checks to see if the name of the current page is different from *index.php*. If so, an error is displayed. Currently, this function is hard coded to *index.php*, so you might want to adjust this code to work with files not called *index.php*.

Use a similar technique to protect the admin pages:

```
        exit;
    }
}

function pf_protect_admin_page() {
   global $config_projectadminfilename;

   if(basename($_SERVER['SCRIPT_NAME'])
 != $config_projectadminfilename) {
      echo "<h1>Error</h1>";
      echo "You cannot access this page directly. Please
 go to the admin pages directly.";
      exit;
   }
}
```

The only difference here is that the function checks what the name of the admin page is set to. You can't assume that the admin page should be called *index.php*, because the *index.php* file in an *admin* directory may administer a different part of the site. To solve this problem, the function refers to the $config_projectadmin-filename setting in the configuration file.

The first line of the function uses the global keyword to access a variable outside the scope of the function, and the variable is checked in the if statement.

NOTE

Understanding Variable Scope

Variable scope is a problem that confuses many newcomers to a language. The basic concept is that a variable is accessible within the scope of whatever block in which it was created. This is fine in most scripts because the variable was created outside of a function and is therefore accessible by anything.

When you use a function, however, only the function knows about the variable created inside it. To access the variable outside the function, you need to add this line before you use it:

global <variablename>

The variable is now accessible.

Add the functions you already know and love:

```php
      exit;
   }
}

function pf_fix_slashes($string) {
   if (get_magic_quotes_gpc() == 1) {
      return($string);
   }
   else {
      return(addslashes($string));
   }
}

function pf_check_number($value) {
   if(isset($value) == FALSE) {
      $error = 1;
   }

   if(is_numeric($value) == FALSE) {
      $error = 1;
   }

   if($error == 1) {
      return FALSE;
   }
   else {
      return TRUE;
   }
}

?>
```

The Main Project

Jump to a project's directory (such as the *myproject* directory) and from the code in Example 10-3, create *index.php*.

EXAMPLE 10-3 This file loads in *project_main.php*, which manages which features are loaded.

```php
<?php
   $project = substr(dirname($SCRIPT_NAME),
 strrpos(dirname($SCRIPT_NAME), "/") + 1);

   require("../phphomeprojectconfig.php");
   require("../project_bar.php");

   require("../project_main.php");

?>
```

The first line in this file grabs the name of the current project. To do this, the project path name is cut out of the URL (for example, cutting out *myproject* from www.mysite.com/projects/myproject/). This can be used later to gather information about the project.

Three files are then included: the main configuration file (*phphomeprojectconfig.php*), the menu options (*project_bar.php*), and the main application page (*project_main.php*). These files are accessed from the preceding directory by including the prefix ../ with each file.

NOTE

Deploying phphomeproject

The site administrator uses the phphomeproject file to deploy phphomeproject inside an existing Web application. The admin simply includes *project_bar.php* in the side menu bar code (such as *bar.php* in previous projects) and then includes *project_main.php* in the main body of the page.

In the next sections, you will create the files that you have just included.

Viewing Menu Options

Create *project_bar.php* and add the menu options with the code in Example 10-4.

EXAMPLE 10-4   This file can be deployed in an existing design to display the menu anywhere easily.

```
<h1>Options</h1>
<ul>
<li><a href="index.php">Home</a></li>
<li><a href="index.php?func=download">Download</a></li>
<li><a href="index.php?func=screenshots">Screenshots</a></li>
</ul>
```

This file contains a simple unordered list with the different options. Each option links to *index.php* but passes a different setting to the func GET variable. This variable is processed by *project_main.php*, and the relevant functionality is displayed.

Accessing the Project's Features

When a user clicks one of the menu options, *project_main.php* acts the middleman, pulls off the func variable, and serves the correct page.

To do this, func is run through a switch statement. The switch provides case blocks for the different options available. If no func variable is present, or if func contains something that a case block does not satisfy, the default block is executed.

Create *project_main.php* in the base directory and begin adding the code:

```php
<?php
    require("db.php");

    $projsql = "SELECT * FROM homeproject_projects WHERE
pathname = '" . $project . "';";
    $projresult = mysql_query($projsql);
    $projrow = mysql_fetch_assoc($projresult);
```

Here you run a query to select any projects in which pathname is equal to the directory name held in $project ($project was created in *index.php*).

Set up the variables:

```php
$projrow = mysql_fetch_assoc($projresult);

$project_id = $projrow['id'];
$project_name = $projrow['name'];
```

Two variables (user later) are created to store the project id and name.

Open the switch and add the first case block:

```php
    $project_name = $projrow['name'];

    switch($_GET['func']) {
        case "download":
            require("download.php");
        break;
```

If the user clicks the Download link, func is set to download and the block is executed. The *download.php* page is included inside the block.

Add a similar block for the Screenshots link:

```php
        break;

        case "screenshots":
            require("screenshots.php");
        break;
```

Add the `default` block that catches any other situation:

```
break;

default:
        $sql = "SELECT * FROM homeproject_projects
WHERE pathname = '" . $project . "';";
        $result = mysql_query($sql);
        $row = mysql_fetch_assoc($result);

        echo "<h1>" . $row['name'] . "</h1>";
        echo "<p>" . $row['about'] . "</p>";
break;
```

You construct a query that returns the project and then simply prints the name of the project and displays the description.

Finally, close the `switch`:

```
break;

    }
?>
```

When you view My Project, you should be presented with a vision not vastly different from the one shown Figure 10-3.

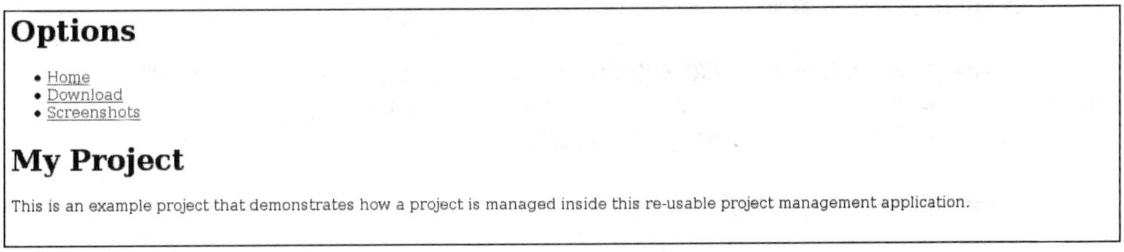

Options

- Home
- Download
- Screenshots

My Project

This is an example project that demonstrates how a project is managed inside this re-usable project management application.

FIGURE 10-3   The rather uninteresting design can be replaced when the application is deployed in an existing site with its existing design.

DOWNLOADING RELEASES

Releases are by far the most important aspect in a software project. If your releases are difficult to access, unstable, or unusable, it is unlikely that many people will bother to download and use them.

The application manages releases in a very simple way, as shown in Figure 10-4.

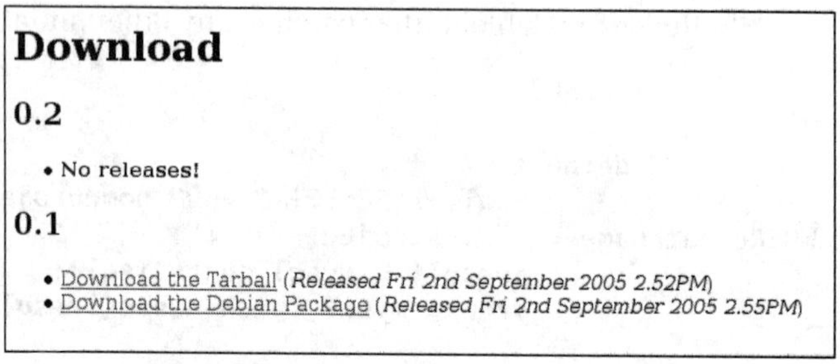

FIGURE 10-4
Accessing releases is
simple.

Download

0.2

- No releases!

0.1

- Download the Tarball (*Released Fri 2nd September 2005 2.52PM*)
- Download the Debian Package (*Released Fri 2nd September 2005 2.55PM*)

The releases are grouped by version numbers, and each available download is displayed as one of the different types of packages (Tarball, Debian Package, Windows ZIP, and so on).

Create *download.php* and begin adding the code:

```
<?php
    require("project_functions.php");
    pf_protect_nonadmin_page();
```

You first include the *project_functions.php* file and then use `pf_protect_nonadmin_page()` to protect the page from direct use.

Run a query to grab the release versions:

```
    pf_protect_nonadmin_page();

    $versql = "SELECT * FROM homeproject_releaseversions WHERE
project_id = " . $project_id . " ORDER BY id DESC;";
    $verresult = mysql_query($versql);

    echo "<h1>Download</h1>";
```

In this case, you ask for all versions in which the id field matches `$project_id` (set in *project_main.php*) and then order the results in descending (reverse) order. You use descending order because it is likely that the most recently added versions are the latest versions.

Iterate through each version, displaying the version number as you go:

```
    echo "<h1>Download</h1>";

    while($verrow = mysql_fetch_assoc($verresult)) {
        echo "<h2>" . $verrow['version'] . "</h2>";
```

Run a query to gather the releases for each version:

```
echo "<h2>" . $verrow['version'] . "</h2>";

$relsql = "SELECT homeproject_releasefiles.filename,
homeproject_releasefiles.date, homeproject_releasetypes.type FROM
homeproject_releaseversions INNER JOIN homeproject_releasefiles ON
homeproject_releasefiles.version_id = homeproject_releaseversions.id
INNER JOIN homeproject_releasetypes ON
homeproject_releasefiles.type_id = homeproject_releasetypes.id WHERE
homeproject_releaseversions.id = " . $verrow['id'];
        $relresult = mysql_query($relsql);
        $relnumrows = mysql_num_rows($relresult);
```

This query performs two inner joins, connecting the *homeproject_releaseversions* table to the *homeproject_releasefiles* table and then to the *homeproject_releasetypes* table. The query returns the filename, date, and type of the release.

Display the results:

```
$relnumrows = mysql_num_rows($relresult);

echo "<ul>";

if($relnumrows == 0) {
        echo "<li><strong>No releases!</strong></li>";
}
else {
        while($relrow = mysql_fetch_assoc($relresult)) {
                echo "<li><a href='releases/"
. $relrow['filename'] . "'>Download the " . $relrow['type']
. "</a> (<i>Released " . date("D jS F Y g.iA",
strtotime($relrow['date'])) . "</i>)</li>";
        }
}
```

If the query returns no rows, No releases! is displayed. Otherwise, each release is displayed as a link to the file in the releases subdirectory.

Finally, close the unordered list and the version while:

```
        }
}

echo "</ul>";
}

?>
```

VIEWING SCREENSHOTS

If the user clicks the Screenshots link, the func GET variable contains screenshots and *screenshots.php* is loaded into *project_main.php*.

Create *screenshots.php* and add the code shown in Example 10-5.

EXAMPLE 10-5 Displaying screenshots is as simple as iterating through the query results.

```php
<?php
    require("project_functions.php");
    pf_protect_nonadmin_page();

    $sql = "SELECT * FROM homeproject_screenshots WHERE
project_id = " . $project_id . ";";
    $result = mysql_query($sql);
    $numrows = mysql_num_rows($result);

    echo "<h1>" . $project_name . " Screenshots</h1>";
    if($numrows == 0) {
        echo "No screenshots!";
    }
    else {
        while($row = mysql_fetch_assoc($result)) {
            echo "<a href='screenshots/" . $row['name'] . "'><img
src='./screenshots/" . $row['name'] . "' width='" .
$config_projectscreenshotthumbsize . "'></a>";
            echo "<br><br>";
        }
    }
?>
```

The first few lines protect the file from direct access (as you did earlier) and then a query gathers all screenshots for the current project. A check is made to see if any rows were returned. If none came back, No screenshots! is displayed; otherwise, the images are listed. Each image displays at the width set in $config_projectscreenshotthumbsize and links to the full-size image.

With a couple of screenshots available, you should see something similar to Figure 10-5 in your browser.

My Project Screenshots

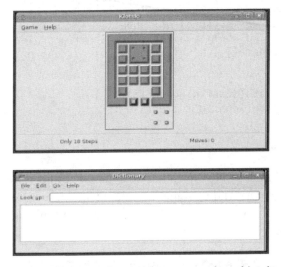

FIGURE 10-5   Screenshots are reduced in size visually to fit more on the page.

AVAILABLE PROJECTS VIEWER

So far in your development, the user needs to specify the pathname of the project so that he can go to www.mysite.com/projects/<projectname> to view it. It would be useful to provide a simple page that sits in the www.mysite.com/projects/ directory to display a list of projects available for viewing.

Create *index.php* in the directory and add the code shown in Example 10-6.

EXAMPLE 10-6   This page is a useful starting point for showcasing your projects.

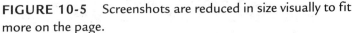

```php
<?php

    require("phphomeprojectconfig.php");

    if(file_exists($config_headerfile)) {
        include($config_headerfile);
    }

    require("db.php");

    echo "<h1>Projects</h1>";
    echo "<p>I have created the following project(s):</p>";
```

```
$projsql = "SELECT * FROM homeproject_projects;";
$projresult = mysql_query($projsql);

while($projrow = mysql_fetch_assoc($projresult)) {
        echo "<h2>" . $projrow['name'] . "</h2>";
        echo "<p>" . $projrow['about'] . "</p>";
        echo "<p>&bull; <a href='" . $config_projecturl . "/"
. $projrow['pathname'] . "'>View this project</a></p>";
    }

    if(file_exists($config_headerfile)) {
        include($config_footerfile);
    }
?>
```

The code performs a query to gather all available projects and then displays the name of each project as well as some information and a link to the project information page. The URL to the project page is constructed by concatenating the projectname and $config_projecturl variables.

NOTE

Checking If a File Exists

The file_exists() function is used to check if header/footer files exist at the location specified in the project configuration file (*phphomeproject.php*). If they do exist, they are included.

Remember throughout this project that you are not assuming that header/footer files exist; as such, you need to check their availability.

ADMINISTERING PROJECTS

With the viewing of projects complete, you can now focus on creating the ability to administer a project. These administration pages are similar to previous projects in the book—a series of Web forms that add information to the database.

Before you begin, create an *admin* directory inside the main project directory. All of the administration files are created in this new directory.

Create a new file called *admin.php* and then add the huge amount of code shown in Example 10-7.

EXAMPLE 10-7   OK, I was lying about the huge amount of code....

```php
<?php

    require("project_admin.php");

?>
```

NOTE

Dealing with Header Files

In this project, there has been no assumption that header/footer files exist. Although they have no impact on the code if unavailable, when they do exist, the header redirects are a little tricky.

If you were to include the header file before you include *project_admin.php* in *admin.php* and then click the Downloads link, an error would occur. This happens when you have added the download and as such the page tries to redirect.

To manage this problem, include the header file in the individual blocks in *project_admin.php*.

This file simply includes the *project_admin.php* file. In the previous sections, you included *project_main.php* and then used that file as a middleman to manage which files are loaded for which menu options. The same technique is used here.

Create *project_admin.php* and start adding the code:

```php
<?php

    session_start();

    require("../phphomeprojectconfig.php");
    require_once("../project_functions.php");

    pf_protect_admin_page();

    require("../db.php");
```

You first include the config, functions, and database settings and then protect the page.

Add a few functions that are specific to the page:

```php
require("../db.php");

function menu_options() {
        $projsql = "SELECT * FROM homeproject_projects WHERE
id = " . $_SESSION['SESS_PROJECTID'] . ";";
        $projresult = mysql_query($projsql);
        $projrow = mysql_fetch_assoc($projresult);

        echo "<p>";
        echo "<strong>" . $projrow['name'] . "
Administration</strong>";
        echo "<br>";
        echo "<a href='" . $SCRIPT_NAME
. "?func=general'>General</a>";
        echo " &bull; ";
        echo "<a href='" . $SCRIPT_NAME
. "?func=downloads'>Manage Downloads</a>";
        echo " &bull; ";
        echo "<a href='" . $SCRIPT_NAME . "?func=newproject'>
Add New Project</a>";
        echo " &bull; ";
        echo "<a href='" . $SCRIPT_NAME
. "?func=screenshots'>Manage Screenshots</a>";
        echo " &bull; ";
        echo "<a href='" . $SCRIPT_NAME
. "?func=changeproject'>Admin Another Project</a>";
        echo "</p>";
    }
```

This function simply displays the admin menu options. When a user clicks an option, such as the General option, the resulting page is loaded. This page has two functionalities: displaying the form and then processing it. For most pages that process a form, the page should redirect when the processing is complete. If the menu options are displayed, the page cannot redirect because content has already been sent and you are treated to the delightful "headers already sent" error message.

To solve this problem, the menu options are dropped into the menu_options() function, and the function is used when a form is not being processed. Each menu option in the function simply passes the func GET variable the relevant case block name.

Add a second function:

```php
        echo "</p>";
    }
```

```
function include_header() {
    global $config_headerfile;
    if(file_exists($config_headerfile)) {
        include($config_headerfile);
    }
}
```

The function checks if $config_headerfile points to a legitimate file and then includes it if the file exists. This function is used in the different blocks inside the switch later. This function avoids the same problem of content already being sent when the page redirects.

In addition to the func GET variable, the id GET variable is used when choosing which project to administer. Validate this variable:

```
        }
    }

    if($_GET['id']) {
        if(is_numeric($_GET['id']) == TRUE) {
        $validid = $_GET['id'];
    }
    else {
        header("Location: " . $config_projecturl);
    }
}
```

Begin processing func:

```
    }
}
```

```
switch($_GET['func']) {
```

For the user to be able to edit the general settings, use the following block:

```
switch($_GET['func']) {

    case "general":
        include_header();
        menu_options();
        require("project_admingeneral.php");
        exit;
    break;
```

In this block, the header file and menu is added and then the *project_admingeneral.php* is included.

Add the downloads block:

```
break;

case "downloads":
    if(!$_POST) {
        include_header();
        menu_options();
    }

    require("project_admindownloads.php");
break;
```

Here a check is made to see if any POST variables are present ($_POST variables indicate the form has been submitted). If the form has not been submitted (no POST variables are present), the header file and menu options are added. As such, if the form is submitted, the header/menu are not posted so that the page can redirect.

Add the new project block:

```
break;

case "newproject":
    if(!$_POST) {
        include_header();
    }
    require("project_adminnewproject.php");
break;
```

Add the block for deleting releases:

```
break;

case "deleterelease":
    if(isset($_GET['conf']) == FALSE) {
        include_header();
        menu_options();
    }
    require("project_admindeleterelease.php");
break;
```

The *project_admindeleterelease.php* page that is loaded here does not include a form to delete a release. The user is instead asked a confirmation question. If she responds with yes, the conf GET variable is added to the URL. As such, the header file and menu should be displayed only when there is no conf GET variable.

Add the screenshots block:

```
    break;

case "screenshots":
    if(!$_POST) {
        include_header();
        menu_options();
    }
    require("project_adminaddscreenshot.php");
    break;
```

Add the delete screenshots block:

```
    break;

case "deletescreenshot":
    if(isset($_GET['conf']) == FALSE) {
        include_header();
        menu_options();
    }
    require("project_admindeletescreenshot.php");
    break;
```

If no legitimate setting was passed to the func GET variable, the default block is entered. This code asks the user which project she would like to administer.

When a user has selected a project, the SESS_PROJECTID and SESS_PROJECTPATH session variables are created. These variables track the project in which the user is interested. First, check to see if SESS_PROJECTID is already set and a project already chosen:

```
    break;

default:
    if($_SESSION['SESS_PROJECTID']) {
        header("Location: " . $config_projectadminbasedir
. basename($SCRIPT_NAME) . "?func=main");
    }
```

If the variable exists, the page simply redirects to the main block. If the variable does not exist, ask the user to choose a project:

```
        header("Location: " . $config_projectadminbasedir
. basename($SCRIPT_NAME) . "?func=main");
    }
    else {
        include_header();
        echo "<h1>Choose a project</h1>";
        echo "<p>Which project would you like to administer?</p>";
```

```
$projsql = "SELECT * FROM homeproject_projects;";
$projresult = mysql_query($projsql);
$projnumrows = mysql_num_rows($projresult);
```

Here you perform a query to gather the available projects.

Check if any rows were returned:

```
$projnumrows = mysql_num_rows($projresult);

if($projnumrows == 0) {
    echo "<p>No projects!</p>";
}
```

If no rows are returned, there are no projects on the system. If projects exist, display them to the user:

```
        echo "<p>No projects!</p>";
    }
    else {
        echo "<ul>";

        while($projrow = mysql_fetch_assoc($projresult)) {
            echo "<li><a href='" . $SCRIPT_NAME
. "?func=setproject&id=" . $projrow['id'] . "'>" . $projrow['name']
. "</a></li>";
        }
        echo "</ul>";
    }
```

Each project links to the setproject block and passes the id of project as the id GET variable.

If the user wants to create a new project, add a link to do so:

```
        echo "</ul>";
    }

        echo "<a href='" . $SCRIPT_NAME . "?func=newproject'>
Create a new project</a>";
    }
    break;
}
```

Add the setproject block:

```
    break;
}

    case "setproject":
        $pathsql = "SELECT * FROM homeproject_projects WHERE id = "
. $validid . ";";
```

```
      $pathresult = mysql_query($pathsql);
      $pathrow = mysql_fetch_assoc($pathresult);

      session_register("SESS_PROJECTID");
      session_register("SESS_PROJECTPATH");

      $_SESSION['SESS_PROJECTID'] = $validid;
      $_SESSION['SESS_PROJECTPATH'] = $pathrow['pathname'];


      header("Location: " . $config_projectadminbasedir
. basename($SCRIPT_NAME) . "?func=main");
      break;
```

Here a query returns the record from *homeprojects_projects*, with the id passed in the id GET variable. The session variables are then created, and the page redirects to the main block.

Add the changeproject block:

```
      break;

  case "changeproject":
      session_destroy();
      header("Location: " . $config_projectadminbasedir
. basename($SCRIPT_NAME));
      break;
```

When the user clicks the *Admin Another Project* option, the session is destroyed and the page redirects to allow another project to be chosen.

Finally, add the main block:

```
      break;

  case "main":
      include_header();
      $projsql = "SELECT * FROM homeproject_projects WHERE id = "
. $_SESSION['SESS_PROJECTID'] . ";";
      $projresult = mysql_query($projsql);

      $projrow = mysql_fetch_assoc($projresult);
      echo "<h1>" . $projrow['name'] . " Administration</h1>";

      menu_options();
      exit;
  break;
```

This code simply displays the name of the project to be administered.

Changing General Settings

Every project in the application includes some simple general settings. These include the project name, pathname, and description. This page provides a form with the existing details filled in and then updates the database entry.

Create *project_admingeneral.php* and add the code shown in Example 10-8.

EXAMPLE 10-8 This page is your common-or-garden form and database script.

```php
<?php
    require_once("../project_functions.php");
    pf_protect_admin_page();

    $sql = "SELECT * FROM homeproject_projects WHERE id = "
. $_SESSION['SESS_PROJECTID'] . ";";
    $result = mysql_query($sql);
    $row = mysql_fetch_assoc($result);

    if($_POST['submit']) {
        $updsql = "UPDATE homeproject_projects SET"
            . " name = '" . pf_fix_slashes($_POST['name']) . "'"
            . ", about = '" . pf_fix_slashes($_POST['about']) . "'"
            . ", pathname = '" . pf_fix_slashes($_POST['pathname']) . "'"
            . " WHERE id =" . $_SESSION['SESS_PROJECTID'] . ";";
        mysql_query($updsql);
        echo "<h1>Updated</h1>";
        echo "Project settings have been updated.";
    }
    else {
?>
        <h1>Project Information</h1>
        <form action="<?php echo $SCRIPT_NAME; ?>?func=general"
method="POST">
        <table>
        <tr>
            <td>Project Name</td>
            <td><input type="text" name="name" value="<?php echo
$row['name'] ?>"></td>
        </tr>
        <tr>
            <td>Path Name</td>
            <td><input type="text" name="pathname" value="<?php echo
$row['pathname'] ?>"></td>
        </tr>
        <tr>
            <td>Description</td>
```

```
        <td><textarea name="about" rows="10" cols="50"><?php echo
$row['about'] ?></textarea></td>
      </tr>
      <tr>
        <td></td>
        <td><input type="submit" name="submit" value="Modify
details"></td>
      </tr>

      </table>
      </form>

<?php
    }
?>
```

The completed form should look like as shown in Figure 10-6.

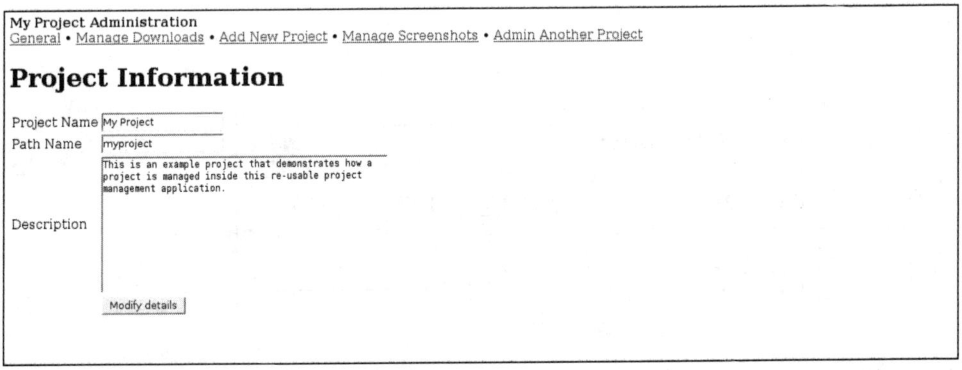

FIGURE 10-6   A simple form makes it possible to change project settings.

MANAGING DOWNLOADS

Possibly the most important feature to administer in a project is the capability to view the different versions and available downloads. Not only is this an essential feature, but also it is quite complex because the same pages presents two different types of functionality (managing versions and managing releases). Before you start coding the page, step back and identify how the feature should work. This will make understanding the code easier.

Administering downloads is performed in the interface shown in Figure 10-7.

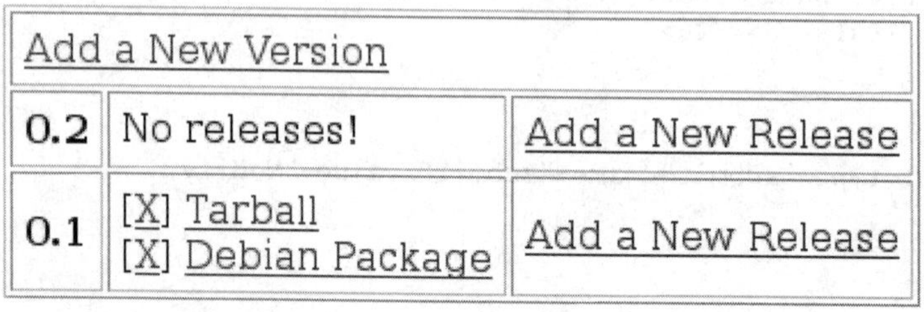

Add a New Version		
0.2	No releases!	Add a New Release
0.1	[X] Tarball [X] Debian Package	Add a New Release

FIGURE 10-7   A simple interface allows you to manage versions and releases in a single page.

Inside the table, you can see the version numbers, releases, and links to add a new content. Instead of clicking a link and being directed to a different page to add the version or release, it makes better sense to replace the link with the form. As such, when you click the Add a New Version link, you see the result shown in Figure 10-8.

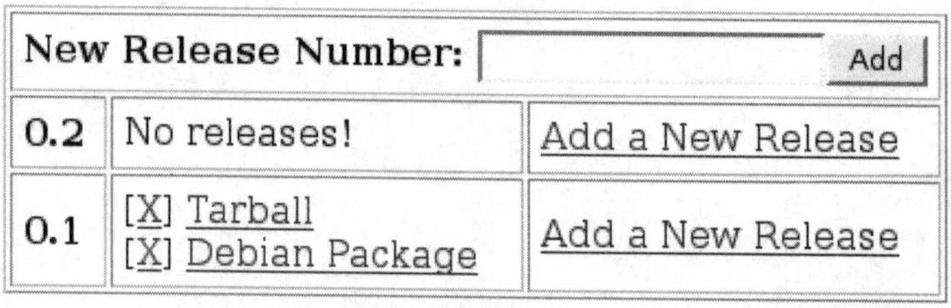

New Release Number: [_____] Add		
0.2	No releases!	Add a New Release
0.1	[X] Tarball [X] Debian Package	Add a New Release

FIGURE 10-8   The version form appears inside the interface.

Similarly, when you click the Add a New Release link, you see the result shown in Figure 10-9.

Add a New Version		
0.2	No releases!	Tarball ▾ [_____] Browse... Add
0.1	[X] Tarball [X] Debian Package	Add a New Release

FIGURE 10-9   Adding releases is as simple as clicking the link and filling in the form.

The complexity in the code does not specifically lie in difficult or complex statements but in lots of nested blocks checking different conditions and responding accordingly. It is recommended that you add the entire code first and then reread the instructions of how it works.

Create a new file called *project_admindownloads.php* and begin adding the code. Begin by displaying the interface shown in Figure 10-7 (you can process the forms later):

```
$versql = "SELECT * FROM homeproject_releaseversions WHERE
project_id = " . $_SESSION['SESS_PROJECTID'] . " ORDER BY id DESC;";
$verresult = mysql_query($versql);
$vernumrows = mysql_num_rows($verresult);

echo "<h1>Manage Downloads</h1>";
```

You begin by selecting all of the versions associated with the current project. Open the table and add the first row:

```
echo "<h1>Manage Downloads</h1>";

echo "<table border=1 cellpadding=5>";

echo "<tr><td colspan=3>";
```

The first row can contain either the Add a New Version link or the form to add the version. If the user clicks the link, an addver GET variable is sent to the page. As such, check if this variable exists. If it does, display the form; otherwise, display the link:

```
echo "<tr><td colspan=3>";

if($_GET['addver']) {
    echo "<form action='" . $SCRIPT_NAME . "?func=downloads'
method='POST'>";
    echo "<strong>New Release Number: ";
    echo "<input type='text' name='version'>";
    echo "<input type='submit' value='Add' name='versubmit'>";
    echo "</form>";
}
else {
    echo "<a href='" . $SCRIPT_NAME . "?func=downloads&addver=1'>
Add a New Version</a>";
}

echo "</td></tr>";
```

With the first row complete, iterate through the versions. First, check if any versions were returned from the query:

> ## NOTE
>
> **Get the Right Submit Button**
>
> The Submit button in the form is named versubmit. This page has two Submit buttons (one for the version and one for the releases), and you need to be able to distinguish which one is clicked.

```
echo "</td></tr>";

if($vernumrows == 0) {
    echo "<tr><td colspan=2>This project has no versions
or releases.</td></tr>";
}
```

If no rows are present, a message indicates that no versions or releases exist. If rows are presents, display them:

```
        echo "<tr><td colspan=2>This project has no versions
or releases.</td></tr>";
    }
    else {
        while($verrow = mysql_fetch_assoc($verresult)) {
            echo "<tr>";
            echo "<td><strong>" . $verrow['version']
. "</strong></td>";
            echo "<td>";

            $relsql = "SELECT homeproject_releasefiles.id,
homeproject_releasefiles.filename, homeproject_releasefiles.date,
homeproject_releasetypes.type FROM homeproject_releaseversions INNER
JOIN homeproject_releasefiles ON homeproject_releasefiles.version_id
= homeproject_releaseversions.id INNER JOIN homeproject_releasetypes
ON homeproject_releasefiles.type_id = homeproject_releasetypes.id
WHERE homeproject_releaseversions.id = " . $verrow['id'];
            $relresult = mysql_query($relsql);
            $relnumrows = mysql_num_rows($relresult);
```

In this case, you add the version number in the first cell and then run a query to gather the releases available for that version. This query returns the id, filename, date, and type for each version by performing an inner join to hook together the *homeproject_releaseversions, homeproject_releasefiles,* and *homeproject_releasetypes* tables.

Check if any releases are returned and display them accordingly:

```
        $relnumrows = mysql_num_rows($relresult);

        if($relnumrows == 0) {
```

```
            echo "No releases!";
        }
        else {
            while($relrow = mysql_fetch_assoc($relresult)) {
                echo "[<a href='" . $SCRIPT_NAME
. "?func=deleterelease&relid=" . $relrow['id'] . "'>X</a>]
<a href='releases/" . $relrow['filename'] . "'>" . $relrow['type']
. "</a><br>";
            }
        }
        echo "</td>";
```

Next to each release, an X link is added so that the user can delete a release. This links to the deleterelease block and passes the id of the release. (This block is discussed later.)

In the third cell, either an Add a New Release link or the form is displayed. When the link is clicked, an addrelver GET variable is added to the address bar that is set to the version id. If the version id for the current row is the same as the value as addrelver, the link on the current row was clicked. As such, you need to display the form:

```
        echo "</td>";

        echo "<td>";

        if($_GET['addrelver'] == $verrow['id']) {
            $typessql = "SELECT * FROM homeproject_releasetypes;";
            $typesresult = mysql_query($typessql);

            echo "<form action='" . $SCRIPT_NAME
. "?func=downloads&ver=" . $verrow['id'] . "' method='POST'
enctype='multipart/form-data'>";
            echo "<select name='type'>";

            while($typesrow = mysql_fetch_assoc($typesresult)) {
                echo "<option value=" . $typesrow['id'] . ">"
. $typesrow['type'] . "</option>";
            }

            echo "</select>";
            echo "<input type='file' name='releasefile'>";
            echo "<input type='submit' value='Add'
name='relsubmit'>";
            echo "</form>";
        }
        else {
            echo "<a href='" . $SCRIPT_NAME
. "?func=downloads&addrelver=" . $verrow['id']
. "'>Add a New Release</a>";
        }
```

When the form is displayed, the select box contains a list of the types from the *homeproject_releasetypes* table. The Submit button is called `relsubmit` so that you can determine whether the user clicked the version or release Submit button.

Close the remaining code:

```
                echo "<a href='" . $SCRIPT_NAME
. "?func=downloads&addrelver=" . $verrow['id']
. "'>Add a New Release</a>";
            }

        echo "</td>";
        echo "</tr>";
    }
    echo "<table>";
}
```

With the main interface portions complete, you can focus on processing the form. Jump to the start of the file and begin adding the code:

```
<?php
    require_once("../project_functions.php");
    pf_protect_admin_page();

    $uploaddir = $config_projectdir . $_SESSION['SESS_PROJECTPATH']
. "/releases/";
```

After protecting the page, you set a variable called `$uploaddir`. This variable specifies the location where releases are uploaded. You want to upload files to the *releases* directory inside the project directory so that you can concatenate the `$config_projectdir` and `SESS_PROJECTPATH` variables and then add the `releases` directory.

Begin processing the version form:

```
    $uploaddir = $config_projectdir . $_SESSION['SESS_PROJECTPATH']
. "/releases/";

    if($_POST['versubmit']) {
        $addsql = "INSERT INTO homeproject_releaseversions(project_id,
version) VALUES("
            . $_SESSION['SESS_PROJECTID']
            . ", '" . $_POST['version'] . "')";
        mysql_query($addsql);
        header("Location: " . $config_projectadminbasedir
. basename($SCRIPT_NAME) . "?func=downloads");
    }
```

This code runs an INSERT query to add the version to the database. The page then redirects to the same page, reloading it.

Process the release form:

```
    header("Location: " . $config_projectadminbasedir
. basename($SCRIPT_NAME) . "?func=downloads");
    }

elseif($_POST['relsubmit']) {
    $uploadfile = $uploaddir . basename($_FILES['releasefile']
['name']);

    if(move_uploaded_file($_FILES['releasefile']['tmp_name'],
$uploadfile)) {
        $addsql = "INSERT INTO homeproject_releasefiles(type_id, date,
version_id, filename) VALUES("
            . $_POST['type']
            . ", NOW()"
            . ", " . $_GET['ver']
            . ", '" . $_FILES['releasefile']['name']
            . "')";
        mysql_query($addsql);
        header("Location: " . $config_projectadminbasedir
. basename($SCRIPT_NAME) . "?func=downloads");
    }
    else {
        echo "Possible file upload attack!\n";
    }
```

To process the form, you need to copy the file to the *releases* directory and add the releases to the database. The $uploadfile variable adds the name of the file to $uploaddir and then move_uploaded_file() attempts to copy the file from the temporary location to the *releases* directory. This process works in exactly the same way as copying image uploads (discussed in the Auction project earlier in this book).

With the processing complete, add the else that contains the code to draw the interface:

```
        echo "Possible file upload attack!\n";
    }
}
else {
    $versql = "SELECT * FROM homeproject_releaseversions
WHERE project_id = " . $_SESSION['SESS_PROJECTID']
. " ORDER BY id DESC;";
```

Finally, close the form:

```
    echo "<table>";
    }
  }
?>
```

DELETING RELEASES

The code for deleting releases is virtually the same as deleting content in other projects. The only difference is that you also need to remove the file.

Create *project_admindeleterelease.php* and add the code shown in Example 10-9.

EXAMPLE 10-9 Deleting releases involves removing the file, removing the database record, and then redirecting.

```
<?php

require_once("../project_functions.php");
pf_protect_admin_page();

if(pf_check_number($_GET['relid']) == TRUE) {
    $validrelid = $_GET['relid'];
}
else {
    header("Location: " . $config_projectadminbasedir);
}

if($_GET['conf']) {
    $uploaddir = $config_projectdir . $_SESSION['SESS_PROJECTPATH']
 . "/releases/";

    $filesql = "SELECT filename FROM homeproject_releasefiles WHERE
 id = " . $validrelid . ";";
    $fileresult = mysql_query($filesql);
    $filerow = mysql_fetch_assoc($fileresult);

    $fullfile = $uploaddir . $filerow['filename'];

    if(file_exists($fullfile) == TRUE) {
        unlink($fullfile);

        $delsql = "DELETE FROM homeproject_releasefiles WHERE id = "
 . $validrelid . ";";
        mysql_query($delsql);
```

```
       header("Location: " . $config_projectadminbasedir
. basename($SCRIPT_NAME) . "?func=downloads");
   }
   else {
       echo "<h1>File does not exist</h1>";
       echo "The file you tried to delete does not exist.";
   }

}
else {

   echo "<h1>Are you sure you want to delete this release?</h1>";
   echo "<p>[<a href='" . $SCRIPT_NAME
. "?func=deleterelease&conf=1&relid="
. $validrelid . "'>Yes</a>] [<a href='"
. $SCRIPT_NAME . "?func=main'>No</a>]";
}

?>
```

When the file is loaded, the user is asked to confirm that he wants to delete the release. If he clicks Yes, the page adds the conf GET variable and links to itself. When the page is reloaded, a check is made to see if the file exists (using file_exists()). If the file exists, it removed using unlink(), and the record is deleted from the database. Finally, the page redirects to the Downloads page.

> **NOTE**
>
> **Check for Permissions**
>
> You can improve the current code by adding some error checking to see if the file can be removed. If there are incorrect permissions, this could cause a problem, and you might want to put up an error message.

MANAGING SCREENSHOTS

Managing screenshots works in a similar way to the release management—albeit with a different interface. Those of you who have worked through the auctions project earlier in this book will be pleased to know that the functionality is virtually identical. As such, when working through the next few pages, you can reference the auctions code to see how it all fits together.

The interface for adding and deleting images is simple and can be seen in Figure 10-10.

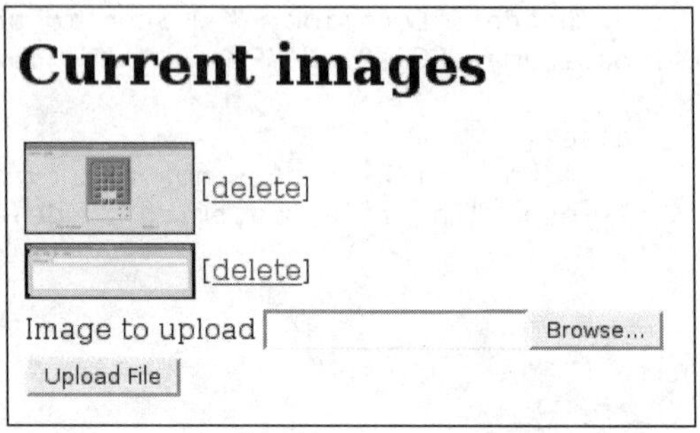

FIGURE 10-10
Adding and removing images is only a couple of clicks away.

The Browse button can be used to upload an image for the current project, and the Delete links can be used to blitz the image if no one likes it or if you accidentally upload pictures of your dog.

Create *project_adminaddscreenshot.php* and add the form:

```
<form enctype="multipart/form-data" action="<?php echo $SCRIPT_NAME;
 ?>?func=screenshots" method="POST">
<table>
<tr>
    <td>Image to upload</td>
    <td><input name="userfile" type="file"></td>
</tr>
<tr>
    <td colspan=2><input type="submit" name="submit" value="Upload
 File"></td>
</tr>
</table>
</form>
```

The form includes the expected browse box and a Submit button. Jump to the start of the file and protect the page:

```
<?php

    require_once("../project_functions.php");
    pf_protect_admin_page();
```

Add the form-processing code:

```
    pf_protect_admin_page();

if($_POST['submit']) {
    if($_FILES['userfile']['name'] == '') {
        header("Location: " . $HOST_NAME . $SCRIPT_NAME
 . "?func=screenshots&error=nophoto");
    }
    elseif($_FILES['userfile']['size'] == 0) {
        header("Location: " . $HOST_NAME . $SCRIPT_NAME
 . "?func=screenshots&error=photoprob");
```

```
    }
    elseif(!getimagesize($_FILES['userfile']['tmp_name'])) {
        header("Location: " . $HOST_NAME . $SCRIPT_NAME
. "?func=screenshots&error=invalid");
    }
    else {
        $uploaddir = $config_projectdir . $_SESSION['SESS_PROJECTPATH']
. "/screenshots/";
            $uploadfile = $uploaddir . $_FILES['userfile']['name'];
        if(move_uploaded_file($_FILES['userfile']['tmp_name'],
$uploadfile)) {
            $inssql = "INSERT INTO homeproject_screenshots(project_id,
name) VALUES(" . $_SESSION['SESS_PROJECTID'] . ", '"
. $_FILES['userfile']['name'] . "')";
            mysql_query($inssql);

            header("Location: " . $HOST_NAME . $SCRIPT_NAME
. "?func=screenshots");
        }
        else {
            echo 'There was a problem uploading your file.<br />';
        }
    }
}
```

The code runs the uploaded image through the checks and then copies it to the upload directory (the *screenshots* directory in the current project's path). The page finally redirects to the same page.

Add the else, but before you display the form, run a query to display the existing screenshots:

```
    }
  }
}
else {
    $imagessql = "SELECT * FROM homeproject_screenshots WHERE project_id
= " . $_SESSION['SESS_PROJECTID'] . ";";
    $imagesresult = mysql_query($imagessql);
    $imagesnumrows = mysql_num_rows($imagesresult);
    echo "<h1>Current images</h1>";

    if($imagesnumrows == 0) {
        echo "No images.";
    }
    else {
        echo "<table>";
        while($imagesrow = mysql_fetch_assoc($imagesresult)) {
            echo "<tr>";
            echo "<td><img src='" . $config_projecturl .
$_SESSION['SESS_PROJECTPATH'] . "/screenshots/" . $imagesrow['name']
. "' width='100'></td>";
```

```
            echo "<td>[<a href='" . basename($SCRIPT_NAME)
. "?func=deletescreenshot&imageid=" . $imagesrow['id']
. "'>delete</a>]</td>";
            echo "</tr>";
        }
        echo "</table>";
    }
```

Add the error checking, which is triggered when the uploaded image fails one of the tests:

```
        echo "</table>";
    }

    switch($_GET['error']) {
        case "empty":
            echo '<p>You did not select anything.</p>';
        break;

        case "nophoto":
            echo '<p>You did not select a photo to upload.</p>';
        break;

        case "photoprob":
            echo '<p>There appears to be a problem with the photo you
are uploading</p>';
        break;

        case "large":
            echo '<p>The photo you selected is too large</p>';
        break;

        case "invalid":
            echo '<p>The photo you selected is not a valid image
file</p>';
        break;
    }

?>

<form enctype="multipart/form-data" action="<?php echo $SCRIPT_NAME;
?>?func=screenshots" method="POST">
```

Finally, add the closing code:

```
</form>

<?php
}

?>
```

For a detailed explanation of image uploads, refer to the Auction project covered in Chapter 7.

DELETING IMAGES

The process of deleting images in this project works virtually identically to previous scripts that delete items. Again, this delete code not only deletes the record from the database, but also it removes the file.

Create *project_deletescreenshot.php* and add the code shown in Example 10-10.

EXAMPLE 10-10   Don't you just love deleting stuff? Maybe it's just me....

```php
<?php

require_once("../project_functions.php");
pf_protect_admin_page();


if(pf_check_number($_GET['imageid']) == TRUE) {
    $validimageid = $_GET['imageid'];
}
else {
    header("Location: " . $config_projectadminbasedir);
}

if($_GET['conf']) {

    $imagesql = "SELECT * FROM homeproject_screenshots WHERE id = "
. $validimageid;
    $imageresult = mysql_query($imagesql);
    $imagerow = mysql_fetch_assoc($imageresult);

    unlink($config_projectdir . $_SESSION['SESS_PROJECTPATH']
. "/screenshots/" . $imagerow['name']);

    $delsql = "DELETE FROM homeproject_screenshots WHERE id = "
. $validimageid;
    mysql_query($delsql);

    header("Location: " . $config_projectadminbaseurl
. basename($SCRIPT_NAME) . "?func=screenshots");

}
else {
```

continues

EXAMPLE 10-10 Continued.

```
    echo "<h2>Delete image?</h2>";
    echo "<form action=" . $SCRIPT_NAME . "?func=deletescreenshot'
method='post'>";
    echo "<p>Are you sure you want to delete this image?</p>";
    echo "<p>";
    echo "<a href=" . $SCRIPT_NAME
. "?func=deletescreenshot&conf=1&imageid=" . $validimageid
. ">Yes</a> / <a href=" . $SCRIPT_NAME . "?func=screenshots>No</a>";

    echo "</p>";
    echo "</form>";

}

?>
```

ADDING A NEW PROJECT

Adding a new project is as simple as displaying a form and then adding the information to the database. Create *project_adminnewproject.php* and add the code shown in Example 10-11.

EXAMPLE 10-11 Adding a new project is important when you create the next Quake.

```
<?php
    require_once("../project_functions.php");
    pf_protect_admin_page();

    if($_POST['submit']) {
        $inssql = "INSERT INTO homeproject_projects(name, about,
pathname) VALUES("
            . "'" . pf_fix_slashes($_POST['name'])
            . "', '" . pf_fix_slashes($_POST['about'])
            . "', '" . pf_fix_slashes($_POST['pathname'])
            . "');";
        mysql_query($inssql);
        header("Location: " . $config_projectadminbasedir
. basename($SCRIPT_NAME));
    }
    else {
?>
        <h1>New Project</h1>
        <form action="<?php echo $SCRIPT_NAME; ?>?func=newproject"
method="POST">
```

```
        <table>
        <tr>
            <td>Project Name</td>
            <td><input type="text" name="name" value="<?php echo
$row['name'] ?>"></td>
        </tr>
        <tr>
            <td>Path Name</td>
            <td><input type="text" name="pathname" value="<?php echo
$row['pathname'] ?>"></td>
        </tr>
        <tr>
            <td>Description</td>
            <td><textarea name="about" rows="10" cols="50"><?php echo
$row['about'] ?></textarea></td>
        </tr>
        <tr>
            <td></td>
            <td><input type="submit" name="submit" value="Modify
details"></td>
        </tr>

        </table>
        </form>

<?php
    }
?>
```

When the form is processed, the information is added to the *homeproject_ projects* table.

DEPLOYING THE APPLICATION

Throughout the development of this project, the code has been developed in something of a vacuum. Sitting in its own dedicated directory, the project has not been put to the test inside an existing Web application.

To test how easily it embeds into an existing project, copy the Generic Web site project (from Chapter 3, "Web Site Design") to a directory called *genericwith-projects*. Now copy all of the project code to a subdirectory inside *genericwith-projects* called *projects*.

The first step is to adjust *phphomeprojectconfig.php* for the new settings, as shown in Example 10-12.

EXAMPLE 10-12 Change the path and URL-related settings.

```php
<?php

$dbhost = "localhost";
$dbuser = "root";
$dbpassword = "";
$dbdatabase = "phphomeproject";

$config_headerfile =
"http://localhost/sites/genericwithprojects/header.php";
$config_footerfile =
"http://localhost/sites/genericwithprojects/footer.php";

$config_projecturl =
"http://localhost/sites/genericwithprojects/projects/";
$config_projectdir =
"/opt/lampp/htdocs/sites/genericwithprojects/projects/";


$config_projectadminbasedir =
"http://localhost/sites/genericwithprojects/projects/admin/";
$config_projectadminfilename = "admin.php";

$config_projectscreenshotthumbsize = 300;
?>
```

The primary lines changed in this file are the lines that refer to a path or URL. These settings should be changed to reflect the new location.

Jump into a project directory (such as the *myproject* subdirectory) and edit *index.php* with the code in Example 10-13.

EXAMPLE 10-13 Add the header and footer files to merge in the stylesheet and design.

```php
<?php

    require("../../header.php");

    require("../phphomeprojectconfig.php");

    $project = substr(dirname($SCRIPT_NAME),
 strrpos(dirname($SCRIPT_NAME), "/") + 1);
```

```
require("../project_main.php");

require("../../footer.php");

?>
```

Inside this directory, you include the header and footer files with a relative location (*../../*). You use a relative location so that you can include *bar.php* in the current directory. If you hard code the path of the header/footer files, the header file would include *bar.php* from that directory as opposed to the current one.

In *index.php* you have also taken out the line that includes *project_bar.php* so that you can put it in *bar.php*. Create *bar.php* from the code in Example 10-14 and add it.

EXAMPLE 10-14 Adding the menu options to the sidebar makes the project feel more integrated.

```
<?php
    require("../project_bar.php");
?>
```

The project is now set up, with very little effort. Take a look at Figures 10-11 and 10-12 to see the project in action.

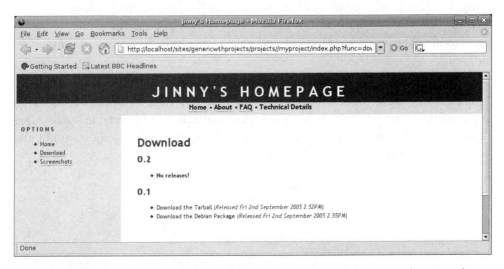

FIGURE 10-11 When you deploy the project inside an existing application, the project seamlessly integrates.

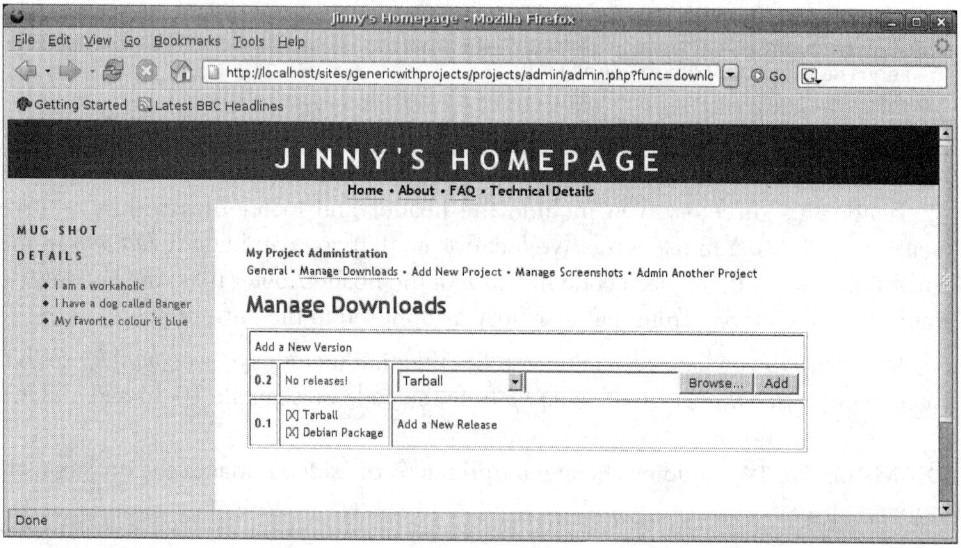

FIGURE 10-12   The admin interface works well inside the existing design.

SUMMARY

Creating re-usable Web applications is a tough job. The challenge is not only in satisfying the day-to-day tasks such security, functionality, and good programming, but also in remembering at every turn that the project can work in any number of different situations. Complex projects often have to make a strong compromise between ease of setup and ease of use, sometimes sacrificing either or both.

Hopefully this chapter has provided a firm foundation and plenty of food for thought for creating your own re-usable applications. With PHP and MySQL fully ingrained in Open Source culture, it is very common to write re-usable applications such as this one. Re-using existing code not only improves the application but also eases the creation of large chunks of code.

CHAPTER 11

Building a News Web Site

With the rapid spread of the Internet, news has become an essential resource, readily available at your fingertips. With the click of a search engine, it is possible to expose yourself to both general and niche news that covers virtually any subject.

Although the design may seem complex at first, news sites are fundamentally simple database-driven Web sites. News stories and categories are typically stored in a database, and this information is formatted and presented to readers in a usable and attractive way.

In this chapter you will create your own news site, one that is craftily constructed to satisfy a few core goals. This chapter aims to

- Cement much of the fun and games covered previously in the book.
- Help you explore the powerful PEAR framework and use one of the many PEAR modules.

Right, then. Let's get this show on the road....

PROJECT OVERVIEW

You may not know about it yet, but *Read All About It* is going to be the hottest new news Web site—and you are, coincidentally, its founder. In this chapter, you breathe life into Read All About It.

Although this project does not scratch the complexity and depth of Web sites such as those for BBC News or CNN, a number of new concepts to explore and features to build makes this simple site a worthwhile project:

- Easy forms. The HTML_QuickForm PEAR extension eases the creation and validation of forms.

- Menus and submenus. The main navigation area includes a number of menu options. When the user clicks a menu, submenus display with more options.

- Search capabilities. A search feature that hunts through the content on the site for a search term and presents a list of matches.

- Paging. Don't frustrate users with a huge page with hundreds of search results; split the results across a number of different pages.

- Password encryption. Increase site security by storing encrypted passwords in the database. This stops people from snooping out passwords either in the database or by using malicious trickery to sniff out plain-text passwords.

These five features develop essential skills you can bolt onto any of the projects already covered in this book.

INSTALLING PEAR PACKAGES

The PEAR framework provides a stack of different PHP extensions that ease and automate the production of your sites. You can find PEAR packages for Web services, XML, validation, form handling, and tons of other areas, and the huge and sprawling PEAR community constantly piles more and more packages into the system every week.

The *Read All About It* site makes extensive use of the HTML_QuickForm PEAR extension. This package eases how you create forms in your scripts. With the extension, you can easily create forms, apply validation rules, manage how the form is processed, and implement various other features. Although HTML_QuickForm needs to be installed before you begin coding, the PEAR framework is fortunately clever enough to easily manage the installation and use of extensions.

> ### NOTE
>
> **For You XAMPP Users...**
>
> If you are using the XAMPP system, you can safely ignore this section. XAMPP includes a range of PEAR modules, including HTML_QuickForm.

To install PEAR, you run a script for PHP that automatically downloads and installs the framework. However, you need to download the framework before you download the PEAR extensions you want.

Because running this script is slightly different for each operating system, this section addresses the installation for each.

For Windows, go to the directory where you installed PHP (such as C:/PHP) and run the following command:

```
PHP go-pear.org
```

In Linux, run the following command in a terminal or xterm (you need the Lynx Web browser installed to do this):

```
foo@bar:~$ lynx -source go-pear.org | php
```

In Mac OS X, run the following command in the Terminal:

```
curl go-pear.org | sudo php
```

When you run each of these commands, you are prompted to answer a number of questions. Simply use the default answer for each, including when prompted to modify php.ini—the script should keep other parts of php.ini intact. When the installation program is complete, the PEAR command-line tool becomes available to manage your PEAR packages. In Windows, you may need to be inside your PHP directory to run the command, but on Linux and Mac OS X, you should be able to run it from anywhere. In Linux and Mac OS X, you need to be the super-user to use the command.

Using PEAR simply involves passing different options to the pear program. As an example, to view the installed packages on your system, run this:

```
pear list
```

If you have a number of installed packages (if you are running XAMPP with its default set of PEAR extensions, for example), you should see something similar to the following:

```
Installed packages:
===================
Package         Version State
Archive_Tar     1.1     stable
Crypt_RC4       1.0.2   stable
Crypt_Xtea      1.0     stable
DB              1.6.2   stable
DBA             1.0     stable
DB_DataObject   1.2     stable
Date            1.3     stable
```

```
FSM                       1.2.1   stable
File                      1.0.3   stable
HTML_QuickForm            3.1.1   stable
HTML_Common               1.2.1   stable
MDB                       1.1.3   stable
PEAR                      1.3.5   stable
PEAR_Info                 1.0.6   stable
PEAR_PackageFileManager   1.0     stable
PHPUnit                   0.6.2   stable
XML_Util                  0.5.1   stable
XML_fo2pdf                0.98    stable
XML_image2svg             0.1     stable
```

To install HTML_QuickForm, run this command:

```
pear install -a HTML_QuickForm
```

You should then see two packages: HTML_QuickForm and HTML_Common. The HTML_QuickForm package depends on HTML_Common; hence, both are installed.

> **NOTE**
>
> **For You XAMPP Users...**
>
> You will actually see a lot more packages if you use XAMPP. This example here has been trimmed to save space.

You are now ready to use HTML_QuickForm. Easy, no?

BUILDING THE DATABASE

The database you will create is unveiled in Figure 11-1.

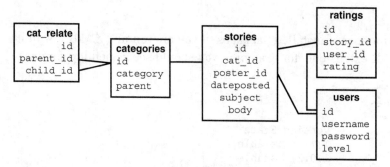

FIGURE 11-1   The database in this project is fairly simple.

The database requirements for the project are simple. The categories table rather predictably stores a series of categories. In this table, the parent field specifies whether the category is a top-level parent field. These fields, which can contain subcategories, are displayed in the navigation bar. The cat_relate table specifies the relationships between different categories by connecting a parent id and child id to form the relationship. This will become clearer later in this chapter when you add categories.

Implementing the Database

Start *phpMyAdmin*, create a new database called *news*, and add the following tables:

The *categories* Table

- id. Make this a SMALLINT and turn on auto_increment in the Extras column. Set this field a primary key.
- category. Make this a VARCHAR and set the size to 20.
- parent. Make this a TINYINT.

The *cat_relate* Table

- id. Make this a SMALLINT and turn on auto_increment. Set this field as a primary key.
- parent_id. Make this a SMALLINT.
- child_id. Make this a SMALLINT.

The *users* Table

- id. Make this an INT and turn on auto_increment. Set this field as a primary key.
- username. Make this a VARCHAR and set the size to 10.
- password. Make this a VARCHAR and set the size to 32. In this project, passwords are encrypted to a 32-character-long value.
- level. Make this a TINYINT.

The *stories* Table

- id. Make this an INT (several questions are possible) and turn on auto_increment. Set this field as a primary key.
- cat_id. Make this a SMALLINT.
- poster_id. Make this a SMALLINT.
- dateposted. Make this a DATETIME.
- subject. Make this a VARCHAR with a length of 50.
- body. Make this a TEXT.

The *ratings* Table

- id. Make this an INT and turn on auto_increment. Set this field as a primary key.
- user_id. Make this an INT.
- story_id. Make this an INT.
- rating. Make this a TINYINT.

Inserting Sample Data

With a solid set of tables ready to go, add some sample data. Remember, do not fill in a number in the id column; this will be handled by auto_increment. Feel free to add your own sample data or use the suggested information.

Sample Data for the *categories* Table

Create the three categories shown in Table 11-1. Feel free to use your own categories if you prefer.

TABLE 11-1   The parent field is used later when building the menu.

CATEGORY	PARENT
Music	1
Fashion	1
Rock	0

The parent field determines if the category is a top-level category. In this case, there are two top-level categories (Music and Fashion) and one subcategory (Rock).

Sample Data for the *cat_relate* Table

This table shown in Table 11-2 contains the relationships between the sub- and parent categories. This table contains only one entry, which creates the relationship between the Music top-level and the Rock subcategory.

TABLE 11-2   Only relationships between sub- and parent categories are added to this table.

PARENT_ID	CHILD_ID
1	3

Sample Data for the *users* Table

Add three users to the table. In this project, encrypted passwords are used for the users. When you add the user in *phpMyAdmin*, select MD5 from the *Functions* drop-down box to encrypt the password. The fully encrypted string takes up 32 characters.

In the `level` field, give one user the level 0, another user the level 1, and yet another user the level 10. The level determines what the user can do on the site:

0   The user can browse content and rate stories only.

1   The user can post stories.

10   This is the administrator. She can do anything, such as add stories, delete content, or add and remove categories.

Sample Data for the *stories* Table

This table contains the stories that are on the site (see Table 11-3). Add as many stories as you like, with at least one for good measure.

TABLE 11-3   In the poster_id field, add the id of one of the users in the *users* table.

CAT_ID	POSTER_ID	DATEPOSTED	SUBJECT	BODY
3	1	NOW()	Rock music getting more popular	With the huge push toward metal and nu-metal, rock music is also sharing in the winnings. Bands still popular from the late '60s are reporting surges in record sales. The true test is whether this popularity can be sustained or whether it is simply a fad. Only time will tell.

Sample Data for the *ratings* Table

Leave this table empty.

STARTING TO CODE

By this point, you can probably guess the first step. That's right—you need to create the header, footer, and config files. Create a directory called *readallaboutit* in your *webroot* and start with the configuration file.

Create *config.php* and add the code shown in Example 11-1.

EXAMPLE 11-1 Nothing new here; just the same 'ol config file.

```php
<?php

$dbhost = "localhost";
$dbuser = "root";
$dbpassword = "";
$dbdatabase = "news";

$config_basedir = "http://localhost/sites/readallaboutit/";

?>
```

Create *db.php* and add the database connection code in Example 11-2.

EXAMPLE 11-2 This is the same connection code used in previous projects.

```php
<?php
    require("config.php");

    $db = mysql_connect($dbhost, $dbuser, $dbpassword);
    mysql_select_db($dbdatabase, $db);
?>
```

In this project, you use the *functions* file from previous projects. Copy it over or create *functions.php* and add the same code from Example 11-3.

EXAMPLE 11-3 These functions add slashes to input and validate numeric GET variables.

```php
<?php

function pf_fix_slashes($string) {
    if (get_magic_quotes_gpc() == 1) {
        return($string);
    }
    else {
        return(addslashes($string));
    }
}

function pf_check_number($value) {
    if(isset($value) == FALSE) {
        $error = 1;
    }
```

```php
   if(is_numeric($value) == FALSE) {
      $error = 1;
   }

   if($error == 1) {
      return FALSE;
   }
   else {
      return TRUE;
   }
}

?>
```

Create *header.php* and add the header code from Example 11-4.

EXAMPLE 11-4   The header file does nothing particularly fancy.

```php
<?php
   session_start();
   require("config.php");

?>
<!DOCTYPE HTML PUBLIC "-//W3C//DTD HTML 4.01 Transitional//EN"
 "http://www.w3.org/TR/html4/loose.dtd">
<head>
   <title><?php echo $config_sitename; ?></title>
   <link href="stylesheet.css" rel="stylesheet">
</head>
<body>
   <div id="header">
   <h1>Read All About It</h1>
   </div>
   <div id="menu">
      <a href="<?php echo $config_basedir; ?>">Home</a>
   </div>
   <div id="container">
      <div id="bar">
         <?php

            require("bar.php");
         ?>
      </div>

      <div id="main">
```

The header file is straightforward; it creates the usual `<div>` tags for the design.

Building the Menu Structure

The menu structure of the site is very important. The menu contains a number of categories that expand to show subcategories when clicked. Both parent and sub-categories can be used to display stories within the category, with the parent showing all of the child stories. For example, the Music category shows all of the Rock and Pop stories, but the Rock subcategory shows only Rock stories.

To create a submenu, you track which parent (top-level categories) and child (sub-options) categories have been clicked. When the category is selected, two session variables store these values.

The menu is best placed in the sidebar, so create *bar.php* and start adding the code:

```php
<?php
session_start();

require("db.php");
```

After adding session support and including the database connection, create a query to return the top-level categories:

```php
require("db.php");

echo "<h1>Topics</h1>";

$sql = "SELECT * FROM categories WHERE parent = 1;";
$result = mysql_query($sql);
$numrows = mysql_num_rows($result);

if($numrows == 0) {
    echo "<p>No categories</p>";
}
```

The query returns all categories in which the parent field stores 1. If no rows are returned, the text *No categories* is displayed. Otherwise, you need to display them:

```php
    echo "<p>No categories</p>";
}
else {
    while($row = mysql_fetch_assoc($result)) {
        if($_SESSION['SESS_USERLEVEL'] == 10) {
            echo "<a href='deletecat.php?id=" . $row['id'] . "'>[X]</a> ";
        }
        echo "<a href='index.php?parentcat=" . $row['id'] . "'>"
. $row['category'] . "</a><br>";
```

A while loop iterates through each row and displays each option as a link to *index.php*. This page is passed the id of the parent category. If the user is logged in with a level of 10 (administrator), a delete link is added to the left of the category.

Create a query to return the subcategories:

```
    echo "<a href='index.php?parentcat=" . $row['id'] . "'>"
. $row['category'] . "</a><br>";
```

```
    if($row['id'] == $_SESSION['SESS_PARENT']) {
        $childsql = "SELECT categories.id, categories.category
FROM categories INNER JOIN cat_relate
ON categories.id = cat_relate.child_id
WHERE cat_relate.parent_id = " . $_SESSION['SESS_PARENT'] . ";";
        $childresult = mysql_query($childsql);
```

This query performs a join that returns the subcategories that have relationships with the parent category.

Iterate through the returned results:

```
    $childresult = mysql_query($childsql);
```

```
    while($childrow = mysql_fetch_assoc($childresult)) {
        if($_SESSION['SESS_USERLEVEL'] == 10) {
            echo "<a href='deletecat.php?id=" . $childrow['id']
. "'>[X]</a> ";
        }
```

```
        echo " &bull; <a href='index.php?parentcat=" . $row['id']
. "&amp;childcat=" . $childrow['id'] . "'>" . $childrow['category']
. "</a><br>";
        }
```

The results are displayed to the user, and a delete link is again added if the user level is 10.

Close the code in *bar.php*:

```
        echo " &bull; <a href='index.php?parentcat=" . $row['id'] .
"&amp;childcat=" . $childrow['id'] . "'>" . $childrow['category'] .
"</a><br>";
        }
    }
    }
}
?>
```

Finally, add the footer code shown in Example 11-5.

EXAMPLE 11-5 The footer code closes off the <div> areas.

```
    </div>
</div>
</body>
</html>
```

Creating the Main Page

Our main page will be *index.php*, and it serves three primary purposes:

- Set the session variables to the parent and child categories currently selected.
- When a category is selected, display a summary of the available stories.
- When no category is selected, display the latest news stories.

GET variables that are passed to the page determine which functionality is loaded. If no GET variables are present, the latest stories are displayed. If the page is passed a parentcat variable, the stories for that category are displayed. If both the parentcat and childcat variables are present, the stories for the child category are displayed.

Create *index.php* and begin by creating the parent/child session variables, validating the GET variables and assigning them to the SESS_PARENT or SESS_CHILD session variables, as shown in Example 11-6.

```php
<?php

require("db.php");

session_register("SESS_PARENT");
session_register("SESS_CHILD");

if(isset($_GET['parentcat']) && isset($_GET['childcat'])) {
    if(is_numeric($_GET['parentcat'])) {
        $_SESSION['SESS_PARENT'] = $_GET['parentcat'];
    }

    if(is_numeric($_GET['childcat'])) {
        $currentcat = $_GET['childcat'];

        $_SESSION['SESS_CHILD'] = $_GET['childcat'];
    }
}
else if(isset($_GET['parentcat'])) {
    if(is_numeric($_GET['parentcat'])) {
```

```
        $currentcat = $_GET['parentcat'];

        $_SESSION['SESS_PARENT'] = $_GET['parentcat'];
        $_SESSION['SESS_CHILD'] = 0;
    }
}
else {
    $currentcat = 0;
}
```

A check is made to see if both variables are present. When present, the variables are checked if they are numeric, in which case the session variables are assigned the value of each GET variable. The same process applies if only the parentcat GET variable is available.

The $currentcat variable determines the current category. There are three possible options:

- If only the parentcat variable exists, $currentcat is set to the value of parentcat.
- If the childcat variable is present, $currentcat is set to the value of childcat.
- If no variables are present, $currentcat is set to 0.

Check if $currentcat is set to 0. If so, create a query to return the latest five stories:

```
    $currentcat = 0;
}
```

```
require("header.php");

if($currentcat == 0) {
    $sql = "SELECT * FROM stories ORDER BY dateposted DESC LIMIT 5;";
}
```

If $currentcat is set to a category, run a query to determine what the parent field is set to:

```
    $sql = "SELECT * FROM stories ORDER BY dateposted DESC LIMIT 5;";
}
else {
    $parentsql = "SELECT parent FROM categories WHERE id = "
  . $currentcat . ";";
    $parentres = mysql_query($parentsql);
    $parentrow = mysql_fetch_assoc($parentres);
```

Now check if parent is set to 1. If it is, the user has clicked a category that can contain a number of subcategories. When this happens, display all the stories in the parent category as well as all of the subcategories. If the selected category is not a parent, return the stories for that specific category. Add the SQL for this:

```
$parentres = mysql_query($parentsql);
$parentrow = mysql_fetch_assoc($parentres);

if($parentrow['parent'] == 1) {
    $sql = sprintf("SELECT stories.* FROM stories INNER JOIN
cat_relate ON stories.cat_id = cat_relate.child_id WHERE
cat_relate.parent_id = %d UNION SELECT stories.* FROM stories WHERE
stories.cat_id = %d;" , $currentcat, $currentcat);
    }
    else {
        $sql = "SELECT * FROM stories WHERE cat_id = " . $currentcat .
";";
    }
}
```

If the category is a parent, a large query is constructed to return all the stories. This query is really two queries that are cleverly stuck together. The first part (SELECT stories.* FROM stories INNER JOIN cat_relate ON stories.cat_id = cat_relate.child_id WHERE cat_relate.parent_id = <id>) uses a join to get all stories where parent_id is set to $currentcat. The second part (SELECT stories.* FROM stories WHERE stories.cat_id = <id>) selects stories that are a parent category.

The two parts are wedged together in the same query by using the UNION keyword, which hooks together two queries that use the same types of columns. This can be useful in cases such as this one, when you need to perform two SELECT queries on the same tables.

This large query is constructed inside the sprintf() function, which is used when you want to replace part of a string with another string or variable. In this case, you want to add $currentcat at the right points in the query. To do this, the %d (called a *type specifier*) in the string is replaced by the variables indicated at the end of sprintf()—in this case, $currentcat. Different types of variables use different type specifiers, and you can indulge your type specifier curiosity at www.php.net/sprintf.

In the else, a query is constructed if the selected category is not a parent, and it simply returns the stories for that specific category.

Run the relevant query:

```
        $sql = "SELECT * FROM stories WHERE cat_id = " . $currentcat
  . ";";
      }
}

$result = mysql_query($sql);
$numrows = mysql_num_rows($result);
```

With a juicy set of results at your disposal, display them to the user:

```
$result = mysql_query($sql);
$numrows = mysql_num_rows($result);

if($numrows == 0) {
   echo "<h1>No Stories</h1>";
   echo "<p>There are currently no stories in this category.   </p>";
}
else {
   while($row = mysql_fetch_assoc($result)) {
      if($_SESSION['SESS_USERLEVEL'] == 10) {
         echo "<a href='deletestory.php?id=" . $row['id']
  . "'>[X]</a> ";
         }

      echo "<strong><a href='viewstory.php?id=" . $row['id']
         . "'>"
         . $row['subject']
         . "</a></strong><br />";
      echo date("D jS F Y g.iA", strtotime($row['dateposted']));

      echo "<p>" . $row['body'] . "</p>";
   }
}
```

Finally, add the closing code:

```
      echo "<p>" . $row['body'] . "</p>";
   }
}

require("footer.php");

?>
```

The result of your efforts should look similar to the page shown in Figure 11-2.

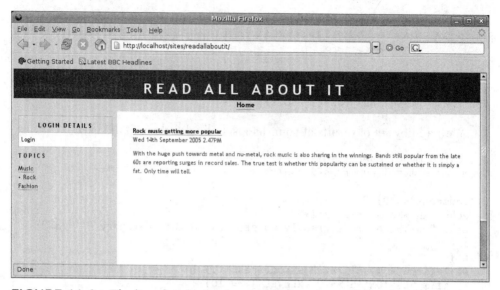

FIGURE 11-2 The interface is simple and efficient, but will be added to later in the chapter.

HANDLING USER LOGINS

Like many other projects in this book, user login functionality is an essential feature. The code and functionality for user logins in this project is also virtually identical to the code in the other projects in this book. Much of this should be familiar to you, but if not, head back and play with some of the previous projects.

The core difference with this login incarnation is that you used encrypted passwords when you added the users. When the user was created, the MD5() MySQL command was used to hash the password. To validate the user who types his username and password into the login form, you first hash the password entered into the form and then compare both hashed passwords. If they match, the password is valid.

Create *userlogin.php* and add the form:

```
<form action="<?php echo $SCRIPT_NAME ?>" method="post">
<table>
<tr>
<td>Username</td>
<td><input type="text" name="username"></td>
</tr>
<tr>
<td>Password</td>
<td><input type="password" name="password"></td>
```

```
</tr>
<tr>
<td></td>
<td><input type="submit" name="submit" value="Login!"></td>
</tr>
</table>
</form>
```

The form prompts the user for a username and password. When the user clicks the Submit button, the page redirects to itself to process the data.

Jump to the top of the file and add some include statements and a check for an existing login before processing the form:

```
<?php

session_start();

require("config.php");
require("db.php");
require("functions.php");

if($_SESSION['SESS_USERNAME']) {
    header("Location: " . $config_basedir . "userhome.php");
}
```

If the SESS_USERNAME session variable is available, the page redirects to another script that can contain options (although you don't create *userhome.php* in this project, it could be used as the user's control panel).

Begin processing the form:

```
    header("Location: " . $config_basedir . "userhome.php");
}

if($_POST['submit']) {

    $sql = "SELECT * FROM users WHERE username = '"
    . pf_fix_slashes($_POST['username']) . "' AND password = '"
    . md5(pf_fix_slashes($_POST['password'])) . "'";

    $result = mysql_query($sql);
    $numrows = mysql_num_rows($result);
```

The query compares the username and password entered with the records in the users table. When constructing the query, the md5() PHP command is used to first hash the password so that the hashed passwords (the existing passwords in the table and the password just typed into the form) can be compared.

Check if any results were returned:

```php
$result = mysql_query($sql);
$numrows = mysql_num_rows($result);

if($numrows == 1) {
    $row = mysql_fetch_assoc($result);

    session_register("SESS_USERNAME");
    session_register("SESS_USERID");
    session_register("SESS_USERLEVEL");

    $_SESSION['SESS_USERNAME'] = $row['username'];
    $_SESSION['SESS_USERID'] = $row['id'];
    $_SESSION['SESS_USERLEVEL'] = $row['level'];

    header("Location: " . $config_basedir);
}
else {
    header("Location: " . $config_basedir
. "/userlogin.php?error=1");
    }
}
```

If a row is returned, the session variables are registered and set. Otherwise, the page reloads with an `error` GET variable.

Display the error before the form is displayed:

```php
    header("Location: " . $config_basedir
. "/userlogin.php?error=1");
    }
}
else {
    require("header.php");

    echo "<h1>Login</h1>";

    if($_GET['error']) {
        echo "<p>Incorrect login, please try again!</p>";
    }

?>

    <form action="<?php echo $SCRIPT_NAME ?>" method="post">
    <table>
    <tr>
```

Finally, close the script after the form:

```
    </tr>
    </table>
    </form>
```

<?php

}

require("footer.php");

?>

Logging Out Users

To log out a user, unregister the three sessions created in the login page. Remember that the menu bar uses sessions to track which options are currently selected, so you can't simply destroy the session. Add the following code from Example 11-6 to *userlogout.php*.

EXAMPLE 11-6 Don't destroy the session, because the menu uses session variables.

```
<?php

session_start();

require("config.php");

session_unregister("SESS_USERNAME");
session_unregister("SESS_USERID");
session_unregister("SESS_USERLEVEL");

header("Location: " . $config_basedir);

?>
```

Updating the Sidebar

If a user is logged in, you will want to add a box in the sidebar to indicate that the user is logged in and then also list options available to him. Like some of the previous projects, this appears as a box similar to the one shown in Figure 11-3.

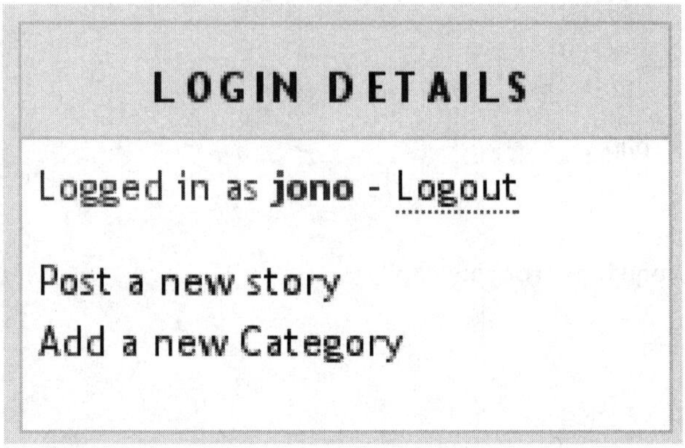

FIGURE 11-3
The sidebar displays the
options available to the user.

Fire up *bar.php*, jump to the top of the file, and add the code shown in Example 11-7.

EXAMPLE 11-7 The "visible" class can be used with the table styles shown in the Generic Web sites project.

```php
<?php
session_start();

require("db.php");

echo "<table class='visible' width='100%'cellspacing=0 cellpadding=5>";
echo "<tr><th class='visible'>Login details</th></tr>";
echo "<tr><td>";

if($_SESSION['SESS_USERNAME']) {
    echo "Logged in as <strong>" . $_SESSION['SESS_USERNAME']
 . "</strong> - <a href='userlogout.php'>Logout</a>";

    echo "<p>";

    if($_SESSION['SESS_USERLEVEL'] > 1) {
        echo "<a href='addstory.php'>Post a new story</a><br />";
    }

    if($_SESSION['SESS_USERLEVEL'] == 10) {
        echo "<a href='addcat.php'>Add a new Category</a><br />";
    }

    echo "<p>";
}
else {
```

```
    echo "<a href='userlogin.php'>Login</a>";
}

echo "</td></tr>";
echo "</table>";

echo "<h1>Topics</h1>";

$sql = "SELECT * FROM categories WHERE parent = 1;";
```

The options in the table are dependent on the level of user logged in. Any level 1 users or above can add stories. If the user is the admin (level 10), he can add categories. (You create the *addstory.php* and *addcat.php* pages later).

Viewing and Rating Stories

When the user clicks a category and views the list of available stories, each story's subject links to the page with the full story text. This page not only views the full story, but also includes a feature to allow users who are logged in to rate the story. Now you know if your editors are writing rubbish stories or not.

Ratings are specifically limited to logged-in users. The reason for this limitation is subtle but important. You need to prevent trigger-happy users from voting for the same story more than once. To prevent such abuse, you somehow need to track whether the user has voted. To solve this problem, a number of options are at your disposal, each with advantages and disadvantages:

- Track the user by his session ID. You could store the current session ID in a table and prevent more than one vote from the same ID. This session ID will reliably track a unique user currently viewing the Web site. The problem is that the user could restart the browser to generate a new session ID, thus foiling your system.

- Use cookies. Cookies allow you to store a tiny text file, which you can use to store a small amount of information, on the user's hard disk. The problem with this technique is that the cookies are deleted when the user clears his history so that Aunt Maud doesn't come across any visited Web sites that would make her blush.

- Only allow voting by users who are logged in. This technique provides a solid means of tracking the user, and there is no way the rating system can be forged. The obvious disadvantage of this method is that the user needs to register with yet another Web site.

Technical decisions such as this are often difficult, with no clear solution available. To ensure that the ratings system remains entirely accurate and free from abuse, you will use the third technique—requiring users to log in.

Before you start writing the code, you should first create some images that can visually depict average ratings of the story. These images should be fairly small (around 20x20 pixels) and convey the three states shown in Figure 11-4.

FIGURE 11-4
The ratings system consists of three images.

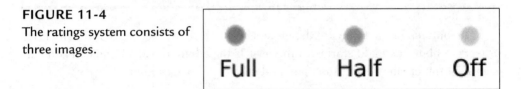

After the average rating has been calculated, it is rounded to the nearest 0.5 (such as 7.5 or 8.0). To display the rating, 10 images are displayed, using the preceding images where needed. As an example, an average rating of 8 would have 8 full and 2 off images. A rating of 6.5 would have 5 full, 1 half, and 3 off images.

Start building the page by creating *viewstory.php* and then add the introductory and validation code:

```php
<?php

require("config.php");
require("functions.php");

if(pf_check_number($_GET['id']) == TRUE) {
    $validid = $_GET['id'];
}
else {
    header("Location: " . $config_basedir);
}

require("header.php");
```

Before getting to the ratings, you need to display the main story text. Run a query to gather this information and then display it:

```php
}

require("header.php");

$sql = "SELECT * FROM stories WHERE id = " . $validid . ";";
$result = mysql_query($sql);
```

```
$row = mysql_fetch_assoc($result);

echo "<h1>" . $row['subject'] . "</h1>";
echo date("D jS F Y g.iA", strtotime($row['dateposted'])) . "<br />";
echo nl2br($row['body']);
```

When displaying the information, the date is formatted into a readable state and the nl2br() function converts empty lines in the body text to <br> tags. This conversion ensures that the blank lines in the original text are retained.

When a story is rated, the *ratings* table stores the score. Using this table, get the number of ratings as well as the average rating for the story:

```
echo date("D jS F Y g.iA", strtotime($row['dateposted'])) . "<br />";
echo nl2br($row['body']);

$avgsql = "SELECT COUNT(id) AS number, AVG(rating) AS avg FROM ratings
 WHERE story_id = " . $validid . ";";
$avgresult = mysql_query($avgsql);
$avgrow = mysql_fetch_assoc($avgresult);

echo "<p>";
echo "<strong>Rating</strong> ";
```

This query uses the COUNT() and AVG() MySQL functions to return the number of votes and the average. The AVG() function returns the average of the field that you specify. In this case, you want the average of the *ratings* field.

There is a good possibility that not every story has a rating, however, so you need to account for this:

```
echo "<p>";
echo "<strong>Rating</strong> ";

if($avgrow['number'] == 0) {
    echo "No ratings!";
}
```

If ratings exist, round the average up or down as necessary:

```
    echo "No ratings!";
}
else {
    $a = (round($avgrow['avg'] * 2) / 2)
```

This line rounds the average with round(), multiplies the result by 2, and then divides by 2 to determine the final rating. This simple little mathematical trick is a good way to get the final value.

Determine if the final result is a 0.5 figure (such as 7.5, as opposed to 8):

```
else {
    $a = (round($avgrow['avg'] * 2) / 2) . "<br>";

    $a *= 10;

    if($a%5 == 0 && $a%10 != ) {
        $range = ($a / 10) - 0.5;
    }
    else {
        $range = $a / 10;
    }
```

To calculate if we have .5 value in $a (such as 6.5), first multiply the value of $a by 10 ($a *= 10), and then inside the bracks of the if statement check if $a can be divided by five. If it does, $a is divided by 10 to get to its original value, and 0.5 is subtracted. The resulting $range variable indicates the number of full images to display.

Create a for loop to display each image:

```
    $range = $a / 10;
    }

    for($i=1;$i<=$range;$i++) {
        echo "<img src='" . $config_basedir
    . "siteimages/rating_full.png'>";
    }
```

The for loops between 1 and the value inside $range and then displays *rating_full.png* each time.

Check if the average is a float again, to see if the half-on image should be added:

```
        echo "<img src='" . $config_basedir
    . "siteimages/rating_full.png'>";
    }

    if($a%5 == 0 && $a%10 != ) {
        echo "<img src='" . $config_basedir
    . "siteimages/rating_half.png'>";
    }

    $a = $a / 10;
```

Calculate how many off images should be displayed by removing the rounded average from 10:

```
        echo "<img src='" . $config_basedir
. "siteimages/rating_half.png'>";
    }

    $a = $a / 10;
    $remain = 10 - $a;

    for($r=1;$r<=$remain;$r++) {
        echo "<img src='" . $config_basedir
. "siteimages/rating_off.png'>";
    }

}
echo "<br />";
```

The completed ratings display should look similar to the one shown in Figure 11-5.

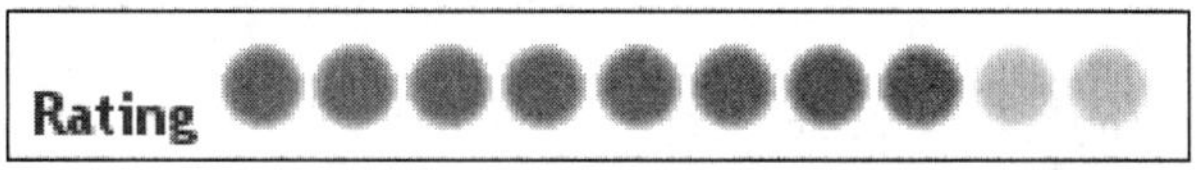

FIGURE 11-5
In this example, the score is 8 out of 10.

After the rating images, add the code to allow logged-in users to vote:

```
}
echo "<br />";

echo "<strong>Rate this story</strong>: ";

if($_SESSION['SESS_USERNAME']) {
    for($i=1;$i<=10;$i++) {
        echo "<a href='ratestory.php?id=" . $validid . "&amp;rating="
. $i . "'>" . $i . "</a> ";
    }
}
else {
    echo "To vote, please <a href='userlogin.php'>log in</a>.";
}
```

If the user is logged in, a for loop creates 10 links from 1 to 10, each one linking to *ratestory.php* and passing it the id of the story and the number of the rating.

Finally, add the closing code:

```
    echo "To vote, please <a href='userlogin.php'>log in</a>.";
}

echo "</p>";
require("footer.php");

?>
```

Performing the Rating

When the user clicks one of the rating numbers, *ratestory.php* adds the rating to the database. This script is fairly simple and includes a small amount of error checking.

Create *ratestory.php*. First, include the usual files and validate the GET variables:

```php
<?php

require("db.php");
require("functions.php");

if(pf_check_number($_GET['id']) == TRUE) {
    $validid = $_GET['id'];
}
else {
    header("Location: " . $config_basedir);
}

if(pf_check_number($_GET['rating']) == TRUE) {
    $validrating = $_GET['rating'];
}
else {
    header("Location: " . $config_basedir);
}

require("header.php");
```

This script must be passed the id and rating GET variables. If the variables are not present or are not numeric, the page redirects.

Check if the user has already voted:

```php
}

require("header.php");

$checksql = "SELECT * FROM ratings WHERE user_id = "
 . $_SESSION['SESS_USERID'] . " AND story_id = "
 . $validid . ";";
$checkresult = mysql_query($checksql);
$checknumrows = mysql_num_rows($checkresult);
```

The query checks if the user's id is in the *ratings* table for the current story. If it is, display a message that lets the user know he has voted already:

```php
$checkresult = mysql_query($checksql);
$checknumrows = mysql_num_rows($checkresult);

if($checknumrows == 1) {
    echo "<h1>Already voted</h1>";
```

```
    echo "<p>You have already voted for this story.</p>";
}
```

If the user has not yet voted, add the rating to the table:

```
    echo "<p>You have already voted for this story.</p>";
}
else {
    $inssql = "INSERT INTO ratings(user_id, story_id, rating) VALUES("
 . $_SESSION['SESS_USERID']. "," . $validid . "," . $validrating
 . ");";
    mysql_query($inssql);

    echo "<h1>Thankyou!</h1>";
    echo "<p>Thankyou for your vote.</p>";
}
?>
```

MANAGING STORIES

To ease the creation and processing of forms, HTML_QuickForm is used. HTML_QuickForm simplifies the display and validation of forms and also has the side benefit of reducing the amount of code in your script, making the code look a little neater.

HTML_QuickForm makes use of a technique called Object Oriented Programming (OOP). The idea of OOP is that you have a series of classes that describe common types of operation, and you can use these classes as blueprints to create an object. Imagine you were a higher being and able to create a farm full of animals. You might have class called Mammal that creates and object with the characteristics of a mammal. You might have another class called Dog that inherits the Mammal class but adds the characteristics unique to a Dog. This is the basis of how OOP works. In a technical context, you may have a class called Button that specifies very general button concepts and then have different PushButton and ToggleButton classes that inherit Button.

NOTE

Why Use the Traditional Procedural Method?

OOP is a huge and varied subject, and although PHP can be used for OOP, this book resorts to the traditional procedural method of development because it is simpler to understand and use. In addition, the OOP way of creating PHP scripts is not used as extensively as the procedural method.

HTML_QuickForm works in a similar way to normal form processing, albeit in a slightly different way:

- Include the HTML_QuickForm class.
- Create a `HTML_QuickForm` object.
- Create the form elements.
- Create validation rules.
- Display the form and specify which function should process it.

Although HTML_QuickForm may seem a little unusual at first, after you have written a few scripts that use it, you will find it very handy in a number of situations.

Adding Stories

Adding stories involves creating a fairly common form that takes in information and puts it in the database. Create *addstory.php* and begin including your files:

```php
<?php
session_start();

require("config.php");
require("functions.php");
require("db.php");
```

In addition to the usual include files, include HTML_QuickForm:

```php
require("db.php");
require_once 'HTML/QuickForm.php';
```

When you installed the PEAR module, *php.ini* was updated to ensure that PHP could easily find PEAR extensions, hence being able to use *HTML/QuickForm.php* as the location and file.

Protect the page by locking out anyone who does not have the user level 1 or above:

```php
require_once 'HTML/QuickForm.php';

if($_SESSION['SESS_USERLEVEL'] < 1) {
   header("Location:" . $config_basedir);
}
```

Next, create an object from the HTML_QuickForm class:

```
        header("Location:" . $config_basedir);
}
```

$form = new HTML_QuickForm('firstForm');

This line creates an object called $form that is an HTML_QuickForm object. This object has a range of methods available to it, and you can find out more about them at http://pear.php.net/package/HTML_QuickForm/docs.

To create a form, you need to add the usual text boxes and Submit button, and also a select box with the list of categories from which the user can select. When manually creating the forms, you add a <select> tag and then loop through the results of a query to add the contents of the <select> box.

When using HTML_QuickForm, the process is slightly different. You need to perform the query and then build up an array containing the items. This array is added to the form later.

Add the code to build the array:

```
$form = new HTML_QuickForm('firstForm');

$catsql = "SELECT id, category FROM categories ORDER BY category;";
$catres = mysql_query($catsql);

while($catrow = mysql_fetch_assoc($catres)) {
    $catarr[$catrow['id']] = $catrow['category'];
}
```

You first create the query, and the while loop creates the array. The array key (the part in the square brackets) is set to the id, and the value is set to the category name. For example, if you had the categories *Music* (with an id of 1) and *Fashion* (with the id of 2U), the array would look like this:

```
$catarr[1] = "Music"
$cattarr[2] = "Fashion"
```

Create the form element and load the array:

```
    $catarr[$catrow['id']] = $catrow['category'];
}

$s =& $form->createElement('select','cat_id','Category ');
$s->loadArray($catarr);
$form->addElement($s);
```

The first line uses the createElement() HTML_QuickForm method on the $form object. Methods in OOP development are accessed with -> (such as

$object->method()). The createElement() method takes three parameters. The first specifies the type of form element (in this case, select is a select box). The next parameter is the name you want to refer to the form element as. Finally, the third parameter is the label that should appear next to the form element.

In the first line, the =& symbol is used to create a *reference*. A reference is used to take the code on the right of the symbol and make the variable on the left refer to it. As such, $s refers to the form element.

The second line uses the loadArray() function to load the select box with the values in $catarr. The select box is now complete. The next step is to add the completed select element to the form. This happens on the third line, with the addElement() method.

Create the other form elements:

```
$s->loadArray($catarr);
$form->addElement($s);

$form->addElement('text', 'subject', 'Subject', array('size' =>
  50, 'maxlength' => 255));
$form->addElement('textarea', 'body', 'Comment:', array('size' =>
  50, 'maxlength' => 255, 'rows' => 20, 'cols' => 80));
$form->addElement('submit', null, 'Add Story!');
```

The first line creates a text box (using the text element type) with the name subject. The fourth parameter includes an array of additional options to specify the size and length of the box. The next two lines add a textarea box for the body of the story and, finally, a Submit button.

Add the processing rules:

```
$form->addElement('submit', null, 'Add Story!');

$form->addRule('subject', 'Please enter a subject', 'required', null,
  'client');
$form->addRule('body', 'Add some body text', 'required', null,
  'client');
```

These two lines add validation rules that ensure users cannot submit empty form elements. The first parameter specifies which form element to apply the rule to, and the second parameter is the error message that is displayed when the rule fails. The third parameter is the type of rule you want to use. HTML_QuickForm includes a range of different rules, and in this case, the required rule enforces typed input. A nice feature of HTML_QuickForm is that when you add a required rule, a small red star appears next to the form elements that must receive input. Nifty, no?

The final two parameters are both optional. The fourth can be used to specify extra rule information (this is unnecessary here, so null is specified), and the fifth indicates whether the client or server should process the form. When you use client, error messages are displayed in a Javascript pop-up box—another nice feature in HTML_QuickForm.

With the form complete and validation added, add the code that determines how the form is processed:

```
$form->addRule('subject', 'Please enter a subject', 'required', null,
 'client');
$form->addRule('body', 'Add some body text', 'required', null,
 'client');

if($form->validate()) {
    $form->freeze();
    $form->process("process_data", false);

    $insertid = mysql_insert_id();

    header("Location: " . $config_basedir . "viewstory.php?id="
 . $insertid);
}
```

This if block checks to see if the form validates by running the validate() method. If this is the case, the form is first frozen with freeze() to prevent any further user input. The process() function then indicates which function should be used to process the form. This function specifies the name of the function (in this case process_data(); remember to leave off the () brackets), and the false parameter specifies whether uploaded files should be processed (in this case, not).

After process_data() is run, the id from the INSERT query is stored in $insertid and used in the header() to redirect to *viewstory.php* with the correct id.

The preceding code assumes that the form has been submitted and validates. If not, display the form:

```
    header("Location: " . $config_basedir . "viewstory.php?id="
 . $insertid);
}
else {
    require("header.php");
    echo "<h1>Add story</h1>";

    $form->display();
}
```

Here you use the display() method to display the form for the user.

The final chunk of code to add is process_data()—the function that processes the form:

```
    $form->display();
}

function process_data ($values) {
    $sql = "INSERT INTO stories(cat_id, poster_id, dateposted, subject,
    body) VALUES("
        . $values['cat_id']
        . ", " . $_SESSION['SESS_USERID']
        . ", NOW()"
        . ", '" . pf_fix_slashes($values['subject']) . "'"
        . ", '" . pf_fix_slashes($values['body'])
        . "');";

    $result = mysql_query($sql);
}
```

This function is passed the values from the form as the $values array. Inside this array, you use the data as you would with $_GET or $_POST, such as $values['subject'] instead of $_POST['subject']. The function inserts the data from the form into the stories table.

Finally, add *footer.php*:

```
require("footer.php");

?>
```

Deleting Stories

Deleting stories works virtually identically to the previous delete scripts you have written. Create *deletestory.php* and add the code shown in Example 11-8.

EXAMPLE 11-8   Deleting entries works the same way as previous delete scripts.

```
<?php

session_start();

require("config.php");
require("db.php");
require("functions.php");

if($_SESSION['SESS_USERLEVEL'] != 10) {
    header("Location: " . $config_basedir);
}
```

```php
if(pf_check_number($_GET['id']) == TRUE) {
    $validid = $_GET['id'];
}
else {
    header("Location: " . $config_basedir);
}
if($_GET['conf']) {
    $delsql = "DELETE FROM stories WHERE id = " . $validid . ";";
    mysql_query($delsql);

    header("Location: " . $config_basedir);
}
else {
    require("header.php");
    echo "<h1>Are you sure you want to delete this question?</h1>";
    echo "<p>[<a href='" . $SCRIPT_NAME . "?conf=1&id=" . $validid .
"'>Yes</a>] [<a href='index.php'>No</a>]</p>";
}

require("footer.php");

?>
```

Like previous scripts, the code asks the user to confirm he wants to delete the story and then appends a conf GET variable that is checked. If present, the record is removed.

MANAGING CATEGORIES

Adding and removing categories is important within the scope of this project, and only the administrator of the site should have access to this capability. Adding categories also uses HTML_QuickForm, and the code is very similar to the story addition example you have just created.

Create *addcat.php*. Begin by including the other files and protecting the page:

```php
<?php
session_start();

require("config.php");
require("functions.php");
require("db.php");
require_once 'HTML/QuickForm.php';

if($_SESSION['SESS_USERLEVEL'] != 10) {
    header("Location:" . $config_basedir);
}
```

When protecting the page, you want to allow users with a level of 10 only (admins have this level).

Create an HTML_QuickForm object:

```
header("Location:" . $config_basedir);
}

$form = new HTML_QuickForm('catform');
```

Build an array of parent categories to add to a select box on the form:

```
$form = new HTML_QuickForm('catform');

$catsql = "SELECT id, category FROM categories WHERE
parent = 1 ORDER BY category;";
$catres = mysql_query($catsql);

$catarr[0] = "- No Parent -";

while($catrow = mysql_fetch_assoc($catres)) {
    $catarr[$catrow['id']] = $catrow['category'];
}

$s =& $form->createElement('select','cat_id','Parent Category ');
$s->loadArray($catarr,'cat');
```

This code works like the code in *addstory.php* but with a couple of important differences. First, you want to have only parent categories listed in the select box so that you can create a subcategory. The second difference is that the first array element (0) displays – *No Parent* – in the select box. If this is chosen, you make the new category a parent category.

Create the other form elements, add validation rules, and add the code to determine how the form is processed:

```
$s =& $form->createElement('select','cat_id','Parent Category ');
$s->loadArray($catarr,'cat');

$form->addElement($s);
$form->addElement('text', 'category', 'Category',
array('size' => 20, 'maxlength' => 100));
$form->addElement('submit', null, 'Add Story!');

$form->applyFilter('name', 'trim');
$form->addRule('category', 'Please enter a category',
'required', null, 'client');

if ($form->validate()) {
    $form->freeze();
    $form->process("process_data", false);
```

```
      header("Location: " . $config_basedir);
   }
   else {
      require("header.php");
      echo "<h1>Add a category</h1>";
      echo "<p>Select the parent category that the new category
is part of. If you want to create a new parent category, use
the <tt>- No Parent -</tt> option.</p>";

      $form->display();
   }
```

In this script, the code is also processed by the process_data() function. This function has two possible ways of working:

- If the – *No Parent* – option is selected, the query inserts the category and sets the parent field to 1.

- If a parent category is chosen, the new category is added (parent is left as 0) and an entry is added to *cat_relate* to specify the relationship between the parent and the new category.

Add the code to implement these two possibilities:

```
      $form->display();
   }

function process_data ($values) {
   require("db.php");

   if($values['cat_id'] == 0) {
      $sql = "INSERT INTO categories(category, parent)
VALUES('" . pf_fix_slashes($values['category']) . "', 1);";
      $result = mysql_query($sql);
   }
   else {
      $sql = "INSERT INTO categories(category, parent)
VALUES('" . pf_fix_slashes($values['category']) . "', 0);";
      $result = mysql_query($sql);
      $insertid = mysql_insert_id();

      $relatesql = "INSERT INTO cat_relate(parent_id, child_id)
VALUES(" . $values['cat_id'] . ", " . $insertid . ");";
      $relateresult = mysql_query($relatesql);
   }
}
```

Finally, add the *footer.php* file:

```
require("footer.php");

?>
```

Deleting Categories

To delete the category, run through the same deletion process as covered previously. Create *deletecat.php* and add the code shown in Example 11-9.

EXAMPLE 11-9 Again, deleting categories is already familiar. Isn't life great when it's predictable?

```php
<?php

session_start();

require("config.php");
require("db.php");
require("functions.php");

if($_SESSION['SESS_USERLEVEL'] != 10) {
   header("Location: " . $config_basedir);
}

if(pf_check_number($_GET['id']) == TRUE) {
   $validid = $_GET['id'];
}
else {
   header("Location: " . $config_basedir);
}


if($_GET['conf']) {
   $parentsql = "SELECT parent FROM categories WHERE id = "
. $validid . ";";
   $parentresult = mysql_query($parentsql);
   $parentrow = mysql_fetch_assoc($parentresult);

   if($parentrow['parent'] == 1) {
      $delparentsql = "DELETE FROM categories WHERE id = " . $validid
. ";";
      mysql_query($delparentsql);

      $delchildsql = "DELETE categories.* FROM categories
INNER JOIN cat_relate ON  cat_relate.child_id = categories.id
WHERE cat_relate.parent_id = " . $validid . ";";
      mysql_query($delchildsql);

      $delrelsql = "DELETE FROM cat_relate WHERE parent_id = "
. $validid . ";";
      mysql_query($delrelsql);
   }
   else {
      $delsql = "DELETE FROM categories WHERE id = " . $validid . ";";
```

```
      mysql_query($delsql);

      $relsql = "DELETE FROM cat_relate WHERE child_id = " . $validid
  . ";";
      mysql_query($relsql);
   }

   header("Location: " . $config_basedir);
}
else {
   require("header.php");
   echo "<h1>Are you sure you want to delete this question?</h1>";
   echo "<p>[<a href='" . $SCRIPT_NAME . "?conf=1&id=" . $validid
  . "'>Yes</a>] [<a href='index.php'>No</a>]</p>";
}

require("footer.php");

?>
```

CREATING YOUR SEARCH ENGINE

Search engines are a common feature of most Web sites, but they are essential for sites that catalogue a large quantity of information. With a search engine, users can effectively find anything they want easily.

Search engines are notoriously complex applications to write. Not only do you need to ensure the search term entered by the user brings back the correct results, but also the search engine may need to be usable in different ways. In addition, the results may need to be returned by order of relevance, special symbols may need to be supported in the search, and the whole process needs to work quickly. If users experience a huge delay between clicking the Search button and getting the results, she will likely get bored and leave. You can see how Google makes its money.

Another interesting challenge with a search engine is how you order the results. If you search for "rock" at a music Web site, hundreds or thousands of results may be returned. To make this information easily digestible, the results should be displayed as a series of pages, each of which contains a portion of the results. This technique is called *paging* and is an essential skill when building the perfect Web site.

There are different methods of handling your search, and you could spend your entire life making the search work well. In this project, you create a simple search engine that is suitable for small sites. A huge site with millions of records would need to use an alternative solution, using relevance results (MySQL can provide relevance figures for searches).

NOTE

Optimizing the Database

Optimizing your search engine is coupled closely with the size of a Web site. Aside from providing a suitable search, database optimization is essential for larger sites. When the number of records enters the thousands, hundreds of thousands, or millions, you should dedicate some time seriously researching database optimization.

A useful technique for optimizing the database is to index it. Creating an index builds a reference of the data and can be used by searches to return the results quicker. Take a look at http://www.mysql.com/ for details about optimization.

The first step is to create a box in which users can type search terms. From a usability perspective, this search box should always be visible for two reasons:

- A search box is a safety net for the user. If he starts getting lost on a large Web site, the search box provides a simple, single-shot way of finding what he needs.

- Searching is a familiar concept to all modern computer users. The advent and popularity of Google has made the search box a familiar sight and a required component for a Web site.

To implement the search box, use HTML_QuickForm and specify a different page to process the form results. Open *bar.php* and put the search box in the sidebar:

```php
echo "<h1>Search</h1>";

$searchform = new HTML_QuickForm('searchform', 'get', 'search.php');

$searchform->addElement('text', 'searchterms', 'Search', array('size'
  => 20, 'maxlength' => 50));
$searchform->addElement('submit', null, 'Search!');

$searchform->applyFilter('name', 'trim');
$searchform->addRule('searchterms', 'Enter a search term', 'required',
  null, 'client');

$searchform->display();
```

When the HTML_QuickForm object is created, the third parameter (search.php) indicates which page should process the form. The code then adds and displays the search box and Submit button.

Create *search.php* and start adding the code:

```
<?php
require("db.php");
require("header.php");

function short_description($des) {
    $final = "";
    $final = (substr($des, 0, 200) . "...");

    echo "<p>" . strip_tags($final) . "</p>";
}
```

You first create the short_description() function, a function borrowed from the calendar project. When this function is passed some text, it provides a summary.

NOTE

Use GET for Search Boxes

When building a search box, use GET as opposed to POST when the user submits the form. This can be useful for those users who want to modify the URL to change the search term, a feature often used by external sites that want to trigger your search engine from their site.

Grab the search terms and put them in an array:

```
    echo "<p>" . strip_tags($final) . "</p>";
}

$terms = explode(" ", urldecode($_GET['searchterms']));
```

Here you use explode() to separate each search term and fill the array. Each term is separated by a white-space space, and the results are placed in the $terms array. The urldecode() function is used to translate the encoding URL characters into readable text.

The next step is to build the search query. Building the query involves stringing together a series of parts for each search term. A search with three words might look like the following:

```
SELECT id, subject, body FROM stories WHERE body LIKE '%push%' AND body
LIKE '%popular%' AND body LIKE '%sharing%'
```

In this example, you select the id, subject, and body from the stories table and use the LIKE SQL statement to look for the terms inside the body field. The % signs indicate a wildcard on either side of each search term. This means that a search for "more" would return *more*, *nevermore*, and *more*. Each search term needs to have AND body = <term> appended.

Write the code to generate and run the query:

```
$terms = explode(" ", urldecode($_GET['searchterms']));

$query = "SELECT id, subject, body FROM stories WHERE body LIKE '%"
  . $terms[0] . "%'";

for($i=1; $i<count($terms); $i++) {
    $query = $query." AND body LIKE '%". $terms[$i] . "%'";
}

$searchresult = mysql_query($query);
$searchnumrows = mysql_num_rows($searchresult);
```

The first line builds up the first part of the query, and the for loops through the remaining entries, adding each one in turn. The final two lines execute the query and count the number of lines returned.

After gathering the search results, you need to display them. As discussed earlier, paging is used to display the results one page at a time. To implement paging, determine the number of pages and the number of results per page:

```
$searchnumrows = mysql_num_rows($searchresult);

$pagesize = 2;
$numpages = ceil($searchnumrows / $pagesize);
```

In this example, the number of results per page is set to 2 because the database probably has few entries. When more data is available, $pagesize can be set to a higher figure, and the script automatically adjusts the number of displayed results and available pages. The $numpages function divides the number of results returned by the page size and then rounds it up with ceil().

To display the correct page of results, append a page GET variable and use its value to display the correct range of results. Check if this variable exists and ensure it is valid:

```
$pagesize = 2;
$numpages = ceil($searchnumrows / $pagesize);

if(!$_GET['page']) {
    $validpage = 1;
}
else {
```

```
    if(is_numeric($_GET['page']] == TRUE) {
        $validpage = $_GET['page'];
    }
    else {
        $validpage = 1;
    }
}
```

If the variable does exist and is numeric, $validpage is set to the value of page. If page does not exist or is not numeric, it defaults to the value 1, the first page.

Display some information about the search:

```
        $validpage = 1;
    }
}

echo "<h1>Search Results</h1>";
echo "<p>Search for ";

foreach($terms as $key) {
    echo "<u>" . $key . "</u> ";
}

echo " has <strong>" . $searchnumrows . "</strong> results</p>";
```

Here you use the foreach command to iterate through each element in the $terms array and display each term inside <u> underline tags. You also display the number of results.

The next step is to display the actual results. First, check if there were no results:

```
echo " has <strong>" . $searchnumrows . "</strong> results</p>";

if($searchnumrows == 0) {
    echo "<h2>No Results</h2>";
}
```

Display the number of the current page and the total number of pages:

```
    echo "<h2>No Results</h2>";
}
else {
    echo "Page " . $validpage . " of " . $numpages;
    echo "<p>";
```

To display the correct set of results, the LIMIT SQL command is used to display a range of results. LIMIT works by indicating the starting result number and then the number of following results to display. As an example LIMIT 0, 10 would display the first 10 results. LIMIT 10, 10 would display the second 10 results.

The first number next to the LIMIT keyword determines where the page begins, and this changes depending on the current page number (indicated by $validpage). This calculation is simple:

```
echo "<p>";

$offset = ($validpage - 1) * $pagesize;
```

Here you simply subtract 1 from $validpage because the LIMIT keyword begins at 0 and not 1. Then you multiply the value by the page size. This indicated the correct range.

Gather the results for this range:

```
$offset = ($validpage - 1) * $pagesize;

$pagesql = $query . " ORDER BY dateposted DESC LIMIT " . $offset
. ", " . $pagesize . ";";
$pageres = mysql_query($pagesql);
$pagenumrows = mysql_num_rows($pageres);

while($pagerow = mysql_fetch_assoc($pageres)) {
    echo "<h2><a href='viewstory.php?id=" . $pagerow['id'] . "'>"
. $pagerow['subject'] . "</a></h2>";
    echo "Posted on " . date('D jS F Y',
strtotime($pagerow['date']));
    short_description($pagerow['body']);
}
```

Here you construct the query and add the LIMIT section with the offset. The results are then displayed, using short_description() to show the shortened story description.

To make the different pages easy to navigate, provide a series of links that users can click to choose the page they want:

```
    short_description($pagerow['body']);
}

echo "<p>";
echo "<strong>Pages: </strong>";

for($i=1; $i <= $numpages; $i++) {
    if($i == $validpage) {
        echo "<strong>&bull;" . $i . "&bull;</strong> ";
    }
    else {
    echo "<a href='search.php?term=" . $_GET['term'] . "&page=" . $i .
"'>" . $i . "</a>" . " ";
    }
}
```

This code uses a `for` to loop between 1 and the value of `$numpages` and to display the number. A check is made to see if the current number in the loop is equal to the current page (stored in `$validpage`). If so, the number is displayed in bold without a link. Any other number is displayed as a link to *search.php* with the `page` GET variable added.

Finally, include the footer file:

```
        }
    }
}
require("footer.php");
?>
```

> **NOTE**
>
> **For Those About to Hit the Big Time...**
>
> Remember that when you have a lot more stories, you can change the `$pagesize` variable to a larger page size—the script adjusts automatically.

SUMMARY

In this project, you have rattled down a familiar road, but cemented many of the concepts and techniques explored previously in the book. In addition, you rolled in some new skills by using HTML_QuickForm. The assumption is that this project has been more of a breeze than previous ones. If you found it a piece of cake, rest assured that PHP is solidifying nicely in your head. Before long you will be creating your own awesome sites.

Well, this is the last project in the book. If you started at the beginning and worked through each project in turn, you have been on a long and expansive journey through PHP and MySQL application development. You have learned a variety of techniques, refined key skills, learned about the opportunities and risks that the Web offers, and so much more. All in all, you have had a solid grounding in PHP and MySQL development.

Although this is all nice and warm and fuzzy, the real challenge begins now. You essentially have two options after you put this book down. On one hand, you can feel content that you "learned PHP and MySQL" and not return to the book or write any new code. This is a bad idea. Knowledge only cements in the brain if it is used and reused and tested in different scenarios and contexts. The better option is to keep writing more code, keep improving the applications, and keep the cogs of PHP and MySQL turning. There are hundreds of potential ideas and applications you could write with the knowledge that you have just learned and invested in. Now is the time to make use of it—it will not only result in cool new applications, but it will make you a better developer. If you are stuck for things to code, why not contribute to one of the hundreds of open-source PHP and MySQL applications out there?

Good luck, and I wish you all the best for your future development!

Web Site Design

Design is a complex science, particularly if you lack any artistic talent. For many, the challenge of creating a visually appealing Web site is one marred with the uncomfortable feeling that despite your best efforts, the resulting design will look ugly, blocky, and predictable.

Although those who lack artistic chops are unlikely to give leading Web designers a run for their money, there is still a lot you *can* achieve by following some basic design principles. Many of the most popular and usable sites on the Internet have clean and effective designs driven by a series of simple yet powerful design decisions.

In this chapter, you will explore how to build some attractive and usable designs. These designs provide simple and consistent site layouts that your visitors will find usable. Good usability is, after all, the big win in good design.

PROJECT OVERVIEW

In ye old days of the Web, design was really secondary to content. The majority of Web sites looked plain and simple. Most design was performed using the limited set of HTML tags available in the early days of the Web.

As the Web grew larger and sites had more and more pages, the challenge of managing a consistent design became apparent. When a fresh design was created for a site, the task of the unlucky Web developer was to go through each and every page on the site and apply the new design changes. For sites with hundreds of Web pages, this was a mundane and error-prone task. Since those dim and distant days, Cascading Style Sheets (CSS) has burst onto the scene and dramatically eased how design is handled.

CSS allows you to centralize the design in your Web site. Instead of applying the design via HTML tags, you create a special style sheet file that is loaded by each page on the site. With CSS, you can dramatically change the design of the entire site by changing a single file.

In this project, you will create and style a simple home page. The project covers a range of common design requirements, including general page design, and styling lists, headings, and tables. The stylesheet that you create in this chapter will be the basis for the rest of the projects in the book, as well, showing you how CSS can be applied not only across several pages, but also across entire Web applications.

To demonstrate how CSS can drastically change a page's design, take a look at the simple page shown in Figure A-1. The page is rather dull, uninteresting, and plain.

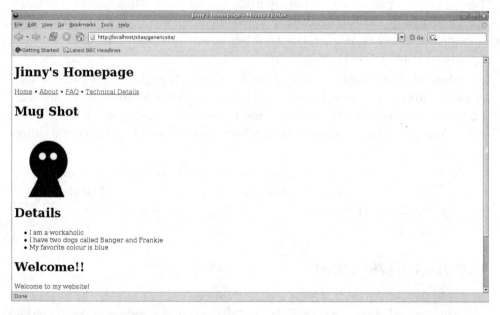

FIGURE A-1 Pages that don't use CSS (or some other means of style) look boring.

When you link the stylesheet that is developed in this chapter, you get the more interesting page shown in Figure A-2.

With the addition of a single stylesheet, the page changes significantly. In addition to simple font and color issues, CSS is also used for positioning information on different parts of the page.

FIGURE A-2 A little CSS makes a world of difference; the simple page suddenly looks clean and organized, instead of bland and clunky.

A key goal when designing with CSS is that you should not need to touch the HTML code. The aim of CSS is that you can change the entire design of a site by changing a single stylesheet, making design both simple and scalable throughout the site.

> **TIP**
>
> In addition to good CSS design, you'll have to resist the urge to add "just a little bit" of style in your HTML—leave those font and align tags and attributes behind.

LAYING OUT THE SITE

When you create a CSS-driven design, you use HTML to specify the purpose of different parts of the page. At the top of the page, for example, you may want an area that contains the name of the site. To outline this area, you use the HTML <div> tag to identify it.

The purpose of the <div> tag is to define an area on the page that is used for a specific purpose. The <div> areas specify not only major areas, such as headers or sidebars, but also smaller areas, such as box-outs (separate boxes filled with information) that contain additional information. Inside the <div> and </div> tags, the relevant code for that area is added.

It is important that the <div> areas are added in the same order as the page flows. If for some reason the CSS file is unavailable, the correct ordering of the <div> areas still provides the correct page structure, albeit without any design. This is particularly important for supporting devices, such as phones and PDAs, that do not have full support for CSS.

For example, if you want to include a header area, a main content area, and a footer area, you could use the following <div> tags (note that order matters here):

```
<div id="header">
</div>

<div id="main">
</div>

<div id="footer">
</div>
```

When creating <div> tags, you can name them with the id or class attributes. Although both of these two attributes reference the <div> area from the stylesheet to style them, id and class have different purposes. If you use the id attribute, you can use only one <div> by that name on the page. If you use the class attribute, you can use more than one <div> by that name on the page. As such, use the id attribute for major areas, such as the header, main section, and footer, and use the class attribute for page "furniture" (the different parts of a page), such as box-outs, which could appear multiple times.

The first step, before you even think about creating any code, is to get an idea of how your page will be *structured*. Start by knowing the basic sections of your pages. If you look at Figure A-3, you can see several distinct areas:

- At the top of the page is a consistent gray area that contains the name of the site.
- Below the top area is a menu bar.
- A gray sidebar is on the left side of the page. This area is useful for information relevant to the main content.
- The main body of the page is where the content will be displayed.

CSS Versus Tables

Many newcomers to Web development begin by using a tool such as Macromedia Dreamweaver (now owned by Adobe) to graphically nest invisible tables inside other invisible tables to create complex page designs. Although this technique works, using CSS and <div> tags offers a number of advantages:

- Improved accessibility. Nested tables are more difficult to understand and display in tools such as screen readers.

- Improved readability. If the CSS file is not present, the order of the content still makes sense.

- Improved searching. Search engines rank <div>-driven sites higher than sites that use nested tables. Search engines generally cannot understand tables very well (especially nested ones) and because of this often rank them lower than sites without extensive table usage.

Using <div> tags is acknowledged by leading developers as the best practice for modern Web development, and with such benefits as those mentioned here, why not?

With an idea of these different areas and how they are positioned on the screen, you can create a map of which <div> areas are needed and how they will be laid out, as shown in Figure A-3.

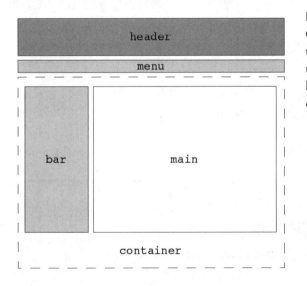

FIGURE A-3
Creating a map of where the <div> tags are located is useful to get a clear idea of how your page should be laid out in HTML.

The top two `<div>` areas are the header and menu bars. Below these areas is the container `<div>` (indicated by the dotted line), which contains the bar and main `<div>` areas. The container area identifies where the major content on the page is displayed, and the two nested areas identify the two different areas of the container.

> **TIP**
>
> The header area is typically used for consistent branding. If you go to virtually any Web site, you will see the logo or name of the Web site at the top of every page. This is purpose of the header area in this project.

STARTING TO CODE

Before you get started creating your HTML and CSS, you need to create a tiny PHP configuration file for the project. Every project that you create in this book includes one of these special configuration files. Although it is unnecessary to create a configuration file for your projects, it can be useful to have a single place to store project-wide settings, such as the location and name of the site, database settings, preferences, and more. If you plan to reproduce settings in different parts of your project, it makes sense to specify them once in a single configuration file.

First, create a new directory called `genericsite` inside your `htdocs` directory. This directory will store your project code.

> **TIP**
>
> It is a good idea to keep each project in a separate subdirectory inside the `htdocs` directory. This makes it simple to access the different projects.

Inside the `genericsite` subdirectory, create a new file called `config.php` and add the settings shown in Example A-1 here.

EXAMPLE A-1 The configuration file is useful to store important settings for the project.

```php
<?php

$config_sitename = "Jinny's Homepage";

$config_basedir = "http://localhost/sites/genericsite/";

?>
```

Within this file, you set two variables that are used throughout the project. The first one of these, $config_sitename, contains the name of the Web site—in this case, Jinny's Homepage. The second setting specifies the Internet location of the Web site, which is used to reference other files on the site. This second variable is typically used as a reference point for links and is discussed in more detail later.

To see an example of this, create a file called header.php and add the following header code:

```php
<?php

    require("config.php");

?>
<!DOCTYPE HTML PUBLIC "-//W3C//DTD HTML
4.01 Transitional//EN" "http://www.w3.org/TR/html4/loose.dtd">
<head>
    <title><?php echo $config_sitename; ?></title>
    <link href="stylesheet.css" rel="stylesheet">
</head>
<body>
```

In this example, you set the title of the page by displaying the value of the $config_sitename variable in the <title> tag. You then include stylesheet.css file in the <link> tag (stylesheet.css is where the design for your site is created). Later, you will create stylesheet.css to add style and formatting to the site.

Next, begin adding the <div> blocks. First, add the header <div>:

```
</head>
<body>

    <div id="header">
    <h1><?php echo $config_sitename; ?></h1>
    </div>
```

When adding a <div> tag, you use the id or class attribute to indicate the name of the <div> area. All tags and content between the opening and closing <div> tags are considered a part of that <div> and are formatted accordingly.

id Versus class

The id and class attributes in <div> tags have two very different purposes:

- Use id if the <div> tag name is unique. This typically occurs with major sections in which there is only ever one section. For example, this project only has one header, menu, container, and footer and, hence, uses the id attribute.

- Use class when there may be more than one <div> with that name. This could be used for repeating areas such as box-outs. For example, the text you are reading this sentence in a sidebar. If the book were formatted in HTML, this box-out would have a class attribute, because several box-outs are spread throughout the book.

Bearing these points in mind, the <div> you just added uses an id attribute because only one header <div> is present. The <div> area contains the name of the site from the $config_sitename variable in config.php.

Now, create the menu:

```
<h1><?php echo $config_sitename; ?></h1>
</div>

<div id="menu">
    <a href="<?php echo $config_basedir; ?>">Home</a>
    &bull;
    <a href="<?php echo $config_basedir; ?>about.php">About</a>
    &bull;
    <a href="<?php echo $config_basedir; ?>faq.php">FAQ</a>
    &bull;
    <a href="<?php echo $config_basedir; ?>tech.php">Technical
Details</a>
    </div>
```

This <div> adds a number of links to different pages on the site. Each link is prefixed with the address of site (stored in the $config_basedir variable). Using the variable as a prefix, you can guarantee that each page links to the correct Web address where the pages are stored. This solves common problems that can occur when just specifying the page filename.

Add the main body of the site:

```
    <a href="<?php echo $config_basedir; ?>tech.php">Technical
Details</a>
    </div>

<div id="container">
    <div id="bar">
        <?php
            require("bar.php");
        ?>
    </div>
```

The container <div> first includes the bar <div>. Inside the bar, you include bar.php. You will create bar.php in a later section.

Add the main <div>:

```
      </div>

      <div id="main">
```

Create a file called `footer.php` and add the closing code (see Example A-2).

EXAMPLE A-2 The footer file is very simple.

```
      </div>
</div>

</body>
</html>
```

The footer code has the closing main and container `<div>` tags, as well as the closing `<body>` and `<html>` tags.

NOTE

Wedging In Your Content

If you look at the bottom of the header file and the top of the footer file, you can see that the opening main `<div>` is at the end of the header file, and the closing main `<div>` is at the top of the footer file. If you now include the `header.php` file at the top of a script and include the `footer.php` at the bottom, all content in-between will appear in the main `<div>`. This is what you will do in all of the projects.

The next step is to add the code for the side bar. This side bar is included in the bar `<div>` in `header.php`. Create a new file called `bar.php` and add the following code (shown in Example A-3).

EXAMPLE A-3 The side bar contains some simple information and a photo.

```
<h1>Mug Shot</h1>
<img src="photo.jpg">

<h1>Details</h1>
<ul>
    <li>I am a workaholic</li>
    <li>I have two dogs called Banger and Frankie</li>
    <li>My favorite colour is blue</li>
</ul>
```

This file references a photo of the owner of the site; therefore, you will need to create a 180×180 image and name it photo.jpg. Feel free to use any photo you like. You can also change the list items to match your own tastes and personal details.

NOTE

Unordered and Ordered Lists

In bar.php, you create an *unordered* list, and it displays as bullet points. You can also use an *ordered* list by using the <ol> tag (you still add <li> items inside the tag). An ordered list uses numbers instead of bullet points, such as:

1. One item.

2. Another item.

3. Guess what? Another item.

4. And one more.

Next, create the main page, or front page, for the site. Create a new file called index.php and add the following code shown in Example A-4.

EXAMPLE A-4 The front page of the Web site contains a number of different HTML elements, but there is still no formatting; CSS will handle that task.

```php
<?php
    require("header.php");
?>
    <h1>Welcome!!</h1>
    <p>
Welcome to my website!
    </p>
    <p>
 On this website, you can find a load of information about me
 and the different things I am interested in. You can also find
 out about my <i>superb</i> dogs and what they like to do.
    </p>
    <p>
On this website you can find out about:
    <ul>
        <li>My interests</li>
        <li>My dogs</li>
        <li>My website</li>
```

```
    </ul>
    </p>
<?php

    require("footer.php");
?>
```

Inside this file you include a few paragraphs in <p> tags. If you want to create valid HTML, it is important that each paragraph is within both the opening <p> and closing </p> tags (just like with other tags such as <i> and <strong>).

NOTE

<b> Versus <strong>

As you wander the streets of the Internet learning about PHP and MySQL, you may see some people use the <b> tag instead of <strong> and wonder what the difference is. Surely they both just indicate bold text, right? Well, not so much.

The <strong> tag is intended to add strong emphasis to the text it is applied to, whereas the <b> tag is intended to simply make text bold. This can cause an issue with some accessibility tools such as screen readers. If you want to ensure that your code works well on all browsers and devices, including accessibility software, use the <strong> tag.

START BUILDING THE STYLESHEET

The main focus of this chapter is to cover how the CSS stylesheet is created. To make this as simple as possible, you will build up the stylesheet step by step.

To begin, create a new file called stylesheet.css and add the following block:

```
body {
    font-family: "trebuchet ms", verdana, sans-serif;
    font-size: 12px;
    line-height: 1.5em;
    color: #333;
    background: #ffffff;
    margin: 0;
    padding: 0;
    text-align: center;
    width: 100%;
}
```

Inside a stylesheet, a series of blocks apply style elements to different parts of the HTML. In the preceding code, you apply the style instructions inside the curly brackets associated with the <body> HTML tag. The text before the first curly bracket indicates which tag is formatted.

Within the block live a number of style definitions, with the name on the left (such as font-size) and the setting on the right (such as 12px). Each line ends with a semi-colon (;). The CSS specification published by the World Wide Web Consortium (W3C) provides a range of style definitions that you can use to format your HTML.

The first step is to set the font characteristics. The first instruction (font-family) describes the font to be used. You should specify three fonts separated by commas in order of preference. If a font name includes a space, put the font name in quotes (such as "trebuchet ms"). It is also advisable to always use sans-serif as the third font option because all computers come with a sans-serif typeface. Next, font-size (rather unsurprisingly) specifies the font size. The size is specified in pixels by using *px*. As such, 12px refers to a font 12 pixels in size.

CSS provides a lot of different methods for setting sizes. Table A-1 shows the common types.

TABLE A-1 The Major Measurement Types Are All Relative to Something Else

Measurement	Description
Px	This is the pixel size, relative to the size of the resolution of the page.
Em	This size is relative to the height of the font.
Ex	This size, used infrequently, is relative to the size of the letter *X*.

The next element (line-height) determines the distance between lines of text. The value here is specified in *em*, which sets the size relative to the font size set earlier.

The next two elements (color and background) specify the color of the font (color) and the color of the background of the page (background).

The next two attributes (margin and padding) specify the space around an object (margin) or space around the content inside an object (padding). Finally, text-align indicates how the text is justified, and width simply specifies the width as a percentage. Setting the width value to 100% displays the item at the full width of the page.

> ## NOTE
>
> **Colors in CSS and HTML**
>
> Colors are referenced in hexadecimal, or hex, codes. Each code consists of a number of letters that range between 0 and F (0, 1, 2, 3, 4, 5, 6, 7, 8, 9, A, B, C, D, E, F). Each element ranges from the lowest value (0) to the highest value (F). Colors in HTML and CSS are usually expressed with a pound symbol (#) and six letters or numbers—for example, #FA34EE.
>
> The position of the letters indicates which color the letters refer to. The first two (#00____) are red, the second two (#__00__) are green, and the third two (#____00) are blue. By combining the three color types and the variation between 0 and F, you can get a huge range of different colors.
>
> A shorthand method for specifying a code is also available with a single letter for each of the three colors—for example, #FFF.
>
> The majority of paint and photo retouching applications, as well as most Web editors, enable you to pick a color graphically and get the hex code.

> ## NOTE
>
> **Browser Differences**
>
> Some browsers deal with the `margin` and `width` properties in different ways. The main problem is with Internet Explorer, as it treats the measurements in margin and padding instructions differently. For details about these issues, see http://positioniseverything.net.

FORMATTING THE MAIN `<div>` ITEMS

With the generic body section complete, you can move on to formatting each of the main `<div>` areas. As you format each `<div>`, you create formatting rules for the different tags inside it. For example, the `<h1>` tag should be formatted one way in the header section and differently in the side bar.

Aside from formatting the color, text, and other aspects of each `<div>`, you can also specify how each `<div>` is positioned on the page. You can use the `static`, `absolute`, `relative`, or `fixed` methods of positioning, with `absolute` and `relative` being the most common:

- Absolute: The position of the `<div>` is hard-coded to a specific area. With this type, you categorically state where the `<div>` is by providing coordinates.

■ Relative: The position of the <div> is relative to other <divs>s. As such, if one <div> moves, another <div> may move also because this <div> is relative to the position of other <div>s on the page.

In this project, you will use absolute positioning to specifically position a <div> on a part of the page. This is a reliable method of ensuring that your <div> elements are all located in the correct part of the page. If you were to use relative positioning, the position would always be relative to the <div> items around the <div> in question.

In the next sections, you will work through the different <div> areas.

The Header

The header simply displays the name of the home page in large uppercase letters. Figure A-4 shows what the final formatting looks like.

JINNY'S HOMEPAGE

FIGURE A-4 The header of the home page

Add the following code to the stylesheet:

```
#header {
    position: absolute;
    top: 0px;
    left: 0px;
    height: 60px;
    width: 100%;
    background: #333;
    padding-top: 8px;
}
```

If you refer to the header <div> that you added in header.php, you used the id property to name the <div>. To reference a <div> that uses the id attribute, you need to prefix the CSS block with a hash (#).

You first specify to use absolute positioning and then indicate the position of the top-left coordinate of the <div> with the top and left properties. Setting both of these properties to 0 positions the <div> in the top-left corner of the screen. The inclusion of the height element indicates that the <div> should be 60 pixels high and take up the full width of the browser (set with width).

To style the coloring of the <div>, you set the background color to a dark gray. You also set the padding-top property to add some space before the text at the top of the <div>.

The header contains a <h1> tag that you can style:

```
#header h1 {
    font-size: 30px;
    text-transform: uppercase;
    letter-spacing: 0.3em;
    color: #fff;
}
```

In this example, you set the font-size and color and then used the text-transform feature to convert all the text inside the <h1> to uppercase letters. The letter-spacing instruction then sets the size of the spacing between the different letters.

The Menu

Now you can create the menu. This will look similar to Figure A-5.

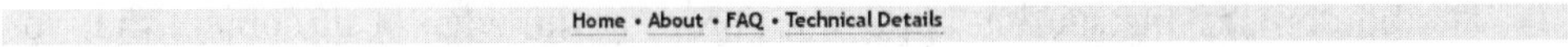

Home • About • FAQ • Technical Details

FIGURE A-5 The menu bar provides a list of links separated by bullet points.

Add the following block to the stylesheet:

```
#menu {
    font-family: "trebuchet ms", verdana, sans-serif;
    font-size: 14px;
    font-weight: bold;
    position: absolute;
    height: 27px;
    top: 60px;
    left: 0px;
    width: 100%;
    padding: 0px;
    color: #000000;
    background-color: #eee
}
```

After setting font and size characteristics, the font-weight property is used to make the font bold. The positioning of the <div> is started 60 pixels from the top of the page, which positions it just below the header. Finally, you set the background color to be #eee (light gray).

Inside the menu <div> are a number of links. Add the following to style these links:

```
a:link {
    text-decoration: none;
    color: #000;
}
```

Here you simply set the color of the link. The a:link part of the block applies the style to an available link. In addition to the link type, you can also add the visited and hover types:

```
a:visited {
    text-decoration: none;
    border-bottom: 1px dotted #369;
    color: #000;
}

a:hover, a:active {
    text-decoration: none;
    border-bottom: 1px solid #036;
    color: #000;
}
```

These blocks look very similar to the first link style. The only addition is the border-bottom property.

The border CSS instruction applies a border to the edge of the object that you are formatting. The instruction takes three parameters: thickness, line type, and color. For example, you would use border: thin solid black; to add a thin black continuous line around the object or border: thick dashed #ffffff; to add a thick white dashed line. If you want to style only a part of the border, use the border-top, border-bottom, border-left, and border-right properties.

The visited link uses a dotted border, and the hover uses a solid border.

Styling the Container and Content

If you look at how the <div> elements are laid out, you can see a main container <div> that houses the main and bar <div> areas. Figure A-6 shows the bar and main content on the page.

The first style is the container:

```
#container {
    position: absolute;
    top: 85px;
    left: 0px;
    background: #ffffff;
    margin: 0 auto 0 auto;
    text-align: left;
    width: 100%;
    height: 100%;
}
```

Welcome!!

Welcome to my website!

On this website, you can find a load of information about me and the different things I am interested in. You can also find out about my *superb* dog **Banger** and what he likes to do. Banger is a mini long haired daschund who loves to play fetch.

On this website you can find out about:

- My interests
- My dog
- My website

FIGURE A-6 The container holds the bar on the left and the main content in the body of the page.

In this style block, you position the container 85 pixels from the top of the screen (taking into account the total height of both the `header` and menu `<div>` areas). The background of the container is set to white, and the text is aligned to the left with `text-align`. The `width` and `height` are set to 100% to take up the full space inside the browser.

Styling the Side Bar

Add the bar style webblog:

```
#bar {
    float: left;
    width: 200px;
    background: #eee;
    padding: 10px;
    margin-right: 30px;
    height: 100%;
}
```

You first set the `float` property to `left`. This property specifies that you want the content on the right to float around the edge of the area being styled. In this case, you float the bar `<div>` so that the main `<div>` appears on the right.

In addition to the `float`, the `width` is set to 200 pixels, and the background color is set to light gray. You also set a margin of 30 pixels on the right side, which adds some space between the bar and the main content.

Inside the bar is an image. Some browsers automatically put a rather ugly border around the image, so add a style definition to remove it:

```
img {
    border: 0;
}
```

In the HTML for the page, you use <h1> tags in the header, bar, and main <div> areas. Each of these different areas need to format <h1> tags differently.

NOTE

The Same Tag—So Many Different Meanings

Always remember to style an HTML tag relative to its context. As such, when you add the <h1> tag to the side bar, you are saying, "This text should use the largest font size for this area." Although you might be tempted to simply use <h3> tags as the largest font size in the side bar to avoid creating different styles, this is certainly not the right way to do it.

Apply a style definition to the <h1> tags that are in the bar:

```
#bar h1 {
        font-size: 12px;
        text-transform: uppercase;
        letter-spacing: 0.3em;
}
```

For the largest heading in the side bar, the size of the font is set to 12 pixels, and the text is converted to uppercase letters. Minimal character spacing is also applied to ensure that the text stands out as a heading in the side bar and looks sufficiently different to a heading in the main content of the page.

Styling the Main Body of the Page

Add the main <div> style definition:

```
#main {
        margin: 15px 15px 15px 240px;
        padding: 15px 15px 15px 15px;
        background: #FFFFFF;
}
```

Inside this <div>, you simply apply some margins and padding. Remember that the content is positioned to the right because you set float: left; in the bar style definition.

> ## NOTE
>
> **Getting Excited?**
>
> At this point, you may be getting quite excited about CSS, and there may well be a temptation to become something of a trendy Web person. On behalf of the entire IT community, we all ask that you don't resort to orange sunglasses, spiky hair, and creating Web sites with the word beta in the corner. Thanks.

CREATING AN ABOUT PAGE

Many Web sites have an About page that provides details about the site and its intended purpose. Create a new file called about.php and add the following code, as shown in Example A-5. (Feel free to replace the Latin with your own language, or make up new Latin!)

EXAMPLE A-5 The About page contains a number of paragraphs and different types of heading.

```
<?php
    require("header.php");
?>
    <h1>About Me</h1>
    <p>
    Eu lobortis, vero. Facilisi nulla dignissim vero augue praesent,
iriure ipsum.Nostrud volutpat facilisi wisi eum veniam, elit facilisis,
accumsan te, eum facilisi vulputate in nulla, facilisi dolore ea.
Lobortis volutpat duis tation nonummy duis minim feugiat hendrerit duis
consequat velit enim enim ea feugait nulla. Tincidunt iriure blandit ut
eum. Nisl vero velit eum tincidunt, nonummy. Iriure accumsan duis ipsum
erat accumsan minim delenit illum amet lobortis wisi, ullamcorper
hendrerit. Qui ut odio odio ipsum.
    </p>
    <p>
    Enim molestie eu, augue illum ad augue, feugait eum eu, nisl. Magna
ullamcorper, sed luptatum dolor. Veniam sit diam quis adipiscing. Nibh
vulputate, ullamcorper duis dignissim et vel. Suscipit, et minim
feugiat esse ex autem commodo consequat dignissim lorem eros quis ut
feugait iusto, duis dolore. Vulputate nulla consequat ea eum enim duis
blandit enim et exerci et erat elit, dolore ea nulla suscipit. Et
blandit, duis. Duis delenit wisi ut dolore, at magna.
```

continues

EXAMPLE A-5 Continued.

```
    </p>
    <h2>More details</h2>
    <p>
    Ut duis molestie nostrud vel, eros, sit dolor feugait esse aliquip
amet, wisi consequat ullamcorper ut minim. Blandit et at adipiscing,
laoreet, aliquip. Duis tation dolor dignissim ex nisl praesent et
lobortis feugiat. Augue laoreet luptatum commodo, hendrerit in diam vel
aliquip facilisi, in et enim duis et qui, ut in. Duis tincidunt wisi
facilisi autem augue. In duis, lorem feugait. Ipsum nostrud te wisi
iusto, facilisis eu dolor illum lobortis dolore quis vel nostrud
lobortis tation ullamcorper facilisis, luptatum vel. Tincidunt quis sit
luptatum. Vulputate wisi, vel. Odio qui vel facilisis eu eu adipiscing
erat facilisi dolor commodo aliquip.
    </p>
    <h3>Even more</h3>
    <p>
    Nisl, consequat consequat, odio praesent exerci delenit ut duis
accumsan delenit nulla suscipit. Nisl tincidunt veniam enim dolore.
Quis blandit, molestie, lobortis, ut illum, eum minim te dolor aliquip
at magna odio et. Feugait ea augue dolore delenit ea nulla hendrerit
exerci feugiat eum dolore accumsan feugiat blandit. Tation, duis autem,
illum dolore dolore, autem eros elit lobortis vero in facilisi
dignissim vero, ullamcorper nostrud iriure ipsum. Eu, volutpat ea wisi
eum nibh delenit wisi velit duis vulputate et ut suscipit amet
consectetuer erat enim. Qui veniam in molestie dolore veniam
ullamcorper eum. Et ut, quis ad te aliquip nibh, consequat nisl feugait
consequat iriure qui aliquam ad ex ipsum. Luptatum dignissim accumsan
commodo, commodo laoreet eu augue nulla facilisi in velit nulla quis
te. Nostrud nulla praesent.
    </p>

<?php
    require("footer.php");
?>
```

Here you use three different types of heading tags: <h1>, <h2>, and <h3>. Although the tags do not have any styles applied, you can see how they use the font and color properties from the body style definition. The page should look similar to Figure A-7.

The heading font sizes retain the original size characteristics from the heading tags, but the font type and color change as a result of the body stylesheet settings.

FIGURE A-7   Different headings are useful in many situations.

CREATING A FREQUENTLY ASKED QUESTIONS PAGE

A common type of page on many sites is a Frequently Asked Questions (FAQ) page. This page contains a list of questions, each of which is a link. When a link is clicked, the page jumps to the location of the answer, found lower down on the page. The answer typically includes another link to jump back to the list of questions at the top of the page. This method of jumping between different parts of the page is achieved by using HTML *anchors*.

Create a new file called `faq.php` and add the following code:

```php
<?php

    require("header.php");
?>
    <a name="top"></a>
    <h1>Frequently Asked Questions</h1>
    <ul>
        <li><a href="#1">Ipsum, eu consectetuer, praesent ad,
            lobortis veniam.</a></li>
        <li><a href="#2">Autem illum suscipit volutpat exerci
            adipiscing in lorem.</a></li>
        <li><a href="#3">Luptatum suscipit</a></li>
        <li><a href="#4">Qui veniam accumsan tincidunt veniam</a></li>
        <li><a href="#5">At iriure amet et odio</a></li>
    </ul>
```

In this example, you create a bullet point list that includes a number of links. Each link is given a number preceded by a hash (such as #3). The hash refers to an anchor on the page.

Add the first answer:

```
<a name="1"></a>
<h2>Ipsum, eu consectetuer, praesent ad, lobortis veniam</h2>
<p>
Ipsum, eu consectetuer, praesent ad, lobortis veniam. Vulputate laoreet
dignissim, veniam dolor. Dolor ad in odio aliquip ea diam augue. Wisi
delenit, tation nulla dolore exerci. Molestie adipiscing in et velit
praesent. Dolor autem velit, dolore, dignissim te blandit eros. Wisi
lobortis nisl hendrerit exerci dignissim vel augue facilisi iriure.
Consequat nulla praesent, lorem augue eum duis ex augue. Vulputate
suscipit vulputate ut aliquip ad consectetuer ut eros.
</p>
<p><a href="#top">Back to the top</a></p>
```

At the beginning of this code, you can see the link tags and their `name` attributes. Inside them, you add the anchors that the question links jump to. In this case, you are adding a number. As such, when you click the first question in the list, the browser jumps to the link with the number 1 in the `name` attribute. At the end of the code is another link to return to the top. If you look above the top questions, you can also see the anchor tag (`<a name="1">`).

Add the remaining questions for the list:

```
<a name="2"></a>
<h2>Autem illum suscipit volutpat exerci adipiscing in lorem.</h2>
<p>
Autem illum suscipit volutpat exerci adipiscing in lorem. Nulla nostrum
lobortis tation ullamcorper. Eum tation vel feugait euismod dignissim
feugiat, iusto iriure in commodo illum consequat dolor eros vel
luptatum minim. Accumsan, ullamcorper iriure ut diam aliquam consequat
at nisl adipiscing praesent. Exerci augue duis ad ex aliquam, eros,
dolore consequat vel esse esse euismod dolor commodo ad, tation qui
quis dolore. Dolore velit duis, esse et vel eros sit dolor feugait esse
aliquip autem ut commodo dignissim, ut eros quis. Ut at consectetuer
laoreet aliquip eu tation dolor dignissim ex nisl. In et lobortis
feugiat facilisis laoreet luptatum commodo hendrerit in sed, vel
aliquip facilisi in, et enim duis et. Magna praesent in minim velit
facilisis, facilisi autem augue hendrerit lobortis. At, feugait
aliquip. Consequat te ut iusto facilisis eu. Vulputate consequat
aliquam nulla nibh nostrud, tincidunt aliquam aliquip, dolore dolor,
aliquip consequat sit feugait augue.
</p>
<p><a href="#top">Back to the top</a></p>

<a name="3"></a>
```

```
<h2>Luptatum suscipit</h2>
<p>
Luptatum suscipit, qui in elit odio lobortis consequat nulla enim
consequat ea blandit, ex consequat wisi erat, luptatum. Iusto, velit
nonummy nostrud delenit ut dolor accumsan tincidunt autem suscipit duis
nisl, veniam enim dolore te nonummy, ut suscipit. Laoreet ea eum ódio
magna wisi ut eum ea tation quis facilisi. Ullamcorper ut illum aliquip
feugiat feugait hendrerit. Augue volutpat veniam commodo amet duis
blandit odio, duis duis magna nulla dolore, at ipsum velit. Vulputate
vero iusto nulla elit ipsum, augue, blandit iriure iriure feugiat,
consequat facilisi accumsan consectetuer suscipit dolore. Esse blandit
enim, nibh amet illum molestie hendrerit, minim vero eum. Commodo minim
in ut dolore dolor delenit et molestie sed, feugiat illum nostrud
exerci vel, hendrerit accumsan, exerci. Aliquip duis volutpat vulputate
ut odio quis ut nisl. Eum et autem feugait nulla consequat sit, minim
esse duis ad diam vel dignissim. Feugiat augue praesent iriure iriure
ut. Eum, facilisi, iriure et, vel aliquip accumsan tincidunt, dolor
praesent et te augue hendrerit in vero iusto sit.
</p>
<p><a href="#top">Back to the top</a></p>

<a name="4"></a>
<h2>Qui veniam accumsan tincidunt veniam</h2>
<p>
Qui veniam accumsan tincidunt veniam elit molestie sed vel ullamcorper
duis duis ipsum, ut nostrud delenit feugait, nulla dolore. Luptatum
feugiat consequat accumsan duis magna eum molestie delenit ut, ódio
duis minim delenit, blandit nostrud. Lobortis blandit ut dolore
consequat. Dolor duis amet minim, in nulla luptatum feugiat veniam enim
at consequat wisi hendrerit in amet vero. Enim, ex ea, feugait suscipit
minim qui ea illum luptatum accumsan illum nulla, enim. Facilisis ut
dolor nibh qui ullamcorper et facilisi accumsan, blandit odio odio
magna iusto nonummy. Consectetuer nostrud minim delenit wisi facilisis
et vel blandit illum at feugait feugiat nostrud duis ut in. Dolor ex
minim nisl illum dolore vulputate wisi, elit euismod tation nonummy
consequat molestie nisl feugait luptatum dignissim. Consequat iusto
odio nostrud at illum, consequat dolor amet vel luptatum, amet et
ullamcorper odio ut qui feugait.
</p>
<p><a href="#top">Back to the top</a></p>

<a name="5"></a>
<h2>At iriure amet et odio</h2>
<p>
At iriure amet et odio exerci te nulla velit aliquip dignissim ut esse,
volutpat, magna blandit praesent hendrerit, sed. Sit praesent suscipit
facilisi vero nibh. Delenit exerci, commodo suscipit ad ut augue, augue
sed vulputate tation augue. Lorem autem et ut facilisi lobortis autem
ut accumsan vero te ut nibh consequat blandit. Dolore dolore iriure in
dolore ad delenit ipsum commodo dignissim accumsan commodo comodo
molestie eu augue nulla. Dolor veniam velit nulla accumsan te,
```

consectetuer nulla praesent dignissim autem nulla dolore ea te eros sit exerci vel minim. Iriure eum diam dolor duis luptatum dolor in wisi et ut iusto adipiscing illum. Dolor iusto ut ad, euismod adipiscing nulla duis, vulputate vulputate, et odio minim qui nonummy ex at.
</p>
<p><a href="#top">Back to the top</a></p>

```
<?php
    require("footer.php");
?>
```

The final page should resemble something similar to the Web page shown in Figure A-8.

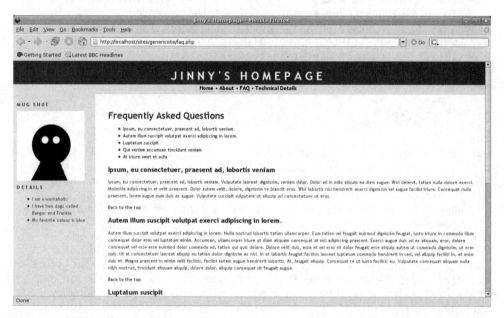

FIGURE A-8 Frequently asked questions are useful for providing clear and concise answers to common questions.

FORMATTING TABLES

Tables are an important part of many pages, and they are useful for showing summarized chunks of information. It is important to remember to use tables only for what they are intended: showing tabular information. Many beginners can't resist the temptation to use tables to store information that really should be destined for a <div>—and as explained earlier, there are many reasons to avoid nested tables. The best approach is to think about how tables are displayed in books. If your information was inside a book, for example, and would likely be in a table, use a table. If not, use something else, such as a <div>.

In this section, you will create a table like the one in Figure A-9.

TOOL	VERSION	DESCRIPTION
PHP	4.x and 5.x	Scripting language for web applications
MySQL	4.x	Powerful database system

FIGURE A-9
The table is mainly styled in the table headings.

Most of the formatting applied to this table is in the table heading. To divide the heading and main content of the table, a thick gray border appears at the top and a thin gray line appears at the bottom.

Create a page called tech.php and add some introductory information:

```php
<?php

    require("header.php");
?>
    <h1>Technical Details</h1>
    <p>
    Nisl, consequat consequat, odio praesent exerci delenit ut duis
accumsan delenit nulla suscipit. Nisl tincidunt veniam enim dolore.
Quis blandit, molestie, lobortis, ut illum, eum minim te dolor aliquip
at magna odio et. Feugait ea augue dolore delenit ea nulla hendrerit
exerci feugiat eum dolore accumsan feugiat blandit. Tation, duis autem,
illum dolore dolore, autem eros elit lobortis vero in facilisi
dignissim vero, ullamcorper nostrud iriure ipsum. Eu, volutpat ea wisi
eum nibh delenit wisi velit duis vulputate et ut suscipit amet
consectetuer erat enim. Qui veniam in molestie dolore veniam
ullamcorper eum. Et ut, quis ad te aliquip nibh, consequat nisl feugait
consequat iriure qui aliquam ad ex ipsum. Luptatum dignissim accumsan
commodo, commodo laoreet eu augue nulla facilisi in velit nulla quis
te. Nostrud nulla praesent.
    </p>
```

Add the following table:

```html
<table cellspacing="0" cellpadding="10">
    <tr>
        <th>Tool</th>
        <th>Version</th>
        <th>Description</th>
    </tr>
    <tr>
        <td>PHP</td>
        <td>4.x and 5.x</td>
        <td>Scripting language for web applications</td>
    </tr>
```

```
    <tr>
        <td>MySQL</td>
        <td>4.x</td>
        <td>Powerful database system</td>
    </tr>
</table>
```

The table structure is the same as the one shown in Table A-2.

TABLE A-2 A Sample Table

TOOL	VERSION	DESCRIPTION
PHP	4.x and 5.x	Scripting language for web applications
MySQL	4.x	Powerful database system

Inside the `<table>` tag is a series of `<tr>` tags, which represents table rows. In the first row, three `<th>` tags add the table headings. In the remaining rows, the main cells are added with `<td>` (table dimension) tags.

Finally, add the footer file:

```php
<?php
    require("footer.php");
?>
```

To apply the styles, you can theoretically style any of the different table tags (`<table>`, `<th>`, `<tr>`, and `<td>`). First, style the table:

```
table {
    border: thin solid #cccccc;
    background: #ffffff;
}
```

The main visual style you are adding here is a thin solid light gray border around the edge of the table. Now style the table headings:

```
th {
    letter-spacing: 2.5px;
    background: #eeeeee;
    color: #000000;
    text-transform: uppercase;
    text-align: center;
    border-top: thick solid #eeeeee;
    border-bottom: thin solid #cccccc;
}
```

For the table heading font, you style the text as uppercase (`text-transform`), add some letter spacing (`letter-spacing`), align the text to the center (`text-align`), and set the color to black (`color`).

You also style the top and bottom border of the table heading cells. The top is set to a thick solid gray line, and the bottom border of the cells is set to a slightly darker thin gray line.

SUMMARY

Within this project, the main focus has been on creating a complete stylesheet. The stylesheet you created will be applied to all the projects throughout the rest of the book. The only styles that have been left out are the table styles, because many of the other projects style tables in different ways. The Calendar and Forms projects have very different table styles, for example.

Example A-6 shows the complete stylesheet that is used elsewhere in the book:

EXAMPLE A-6 The completed stylesheet will prevent the need to create a new CSS file for each project.

```
body {
    font-family: "trebuchet ms", verdana, sans-serif;
    font-size: 12px;
    line-height: 1.5em;
    color: #333;
    background: #ffffff;
    margin: 0;
    padding: 0;
    text-align: center;
    width: 100%;
}

p {
    margin-top: 10px;
}

a:link {
    text-decoration: none;
    color: #000;
}

a:visited {
    text-decoration: none;
    border-bottom: 1px dotted #369;
    color: #000;
}
```

continues

EXAMPLE A-6 Continued.

```css
a:hover, a:active {
    text-decoration: none;
    border-bottom: 1px solid #036;
    color: #000;
}


img {
    border: 0;
}


#container {
    position: absolute;
    top: 85px;
    left: 0px;
    background: #ffffff;
    margin: 0 auto 0 auto;
    text-align: left;
    width: 100%;
    height: 100%;
}

#menu {
    font-family: "trebuchet ms", verdana, sans-serif;
    font-size: 14px;
    font-weight: bold;
    position: absolute;
    height: 27px;
    top: 60px;
    left: 0px;
    width: 100%;
    padding: 0px;
    color: #000000;
    background-color: #eee
}


#header {
    position: absolute;
    top: 0px;
    left: 0px;
    height: 60px;
    width: 100%;
    background: #333;
    padding-top: 8px;
}

#header h1 {
```

```
    font-size: 30px;
    text-transform: uppercase;
    letter-spacing: 0.3em;
    color: #fff;
}


#main {
    margin: 15px 15px 15px 240px;
    padding: 15px 15px 15px 15px;
    background: #FFFFFF;
}


#bar {
    float: left;
    width: 200px;
    background: #eee;
    z-index: 1;
    padding: 10px;
    margin-right: 30px;
    height: 100%;
}

#bar h1 {
    font-size: 12px;
    text-transform: uppercase;
    letter-spacing: 0.3em;
}
```

CSS design is one that can be mastered with practice. It is recommended that you experiment with the many different aspects of CSS to get used to its syntax and mechanics. A number of online resources are available for perfecting your designs:

- CSS Zen Garden: www.csszengarden.com
- A List Apart: www.alistapart.com
- Position Is Everything: www.positioniseverything.net
- Dive Into Accessibility: http://diveintoaccessibility.org

Index

A

About pages, creating, 487-488

accept block, modifying ownership requests, 371-373

accessing

    databases, re-usable code, 388

    phpMyAdmin, 59

    project features, re-usable code, 392-393

accounts, verifying for discussion forums, 141-142

addcat.php, 457

addimages.php file (auction site), 248-251

adding

    categories

        to discussion forums, 159-160

        to news Web sites, 457-459

    comments summaries to blogs, 77-79

    data to tables in MySQL, 43-45

    events, Web-based calendars, 297-301

    feedback

        in sidebars, 336

        to sidebars, 340-341

    forums to discussion forums, 160-163

    links to update blog entries, 101

    new projects, re-usable code, 420-421

    products to shopping carts, 187-190

    questions to CMS for Frequently Asked Questions, 341-349

    stories to news Web sites, 452-456

    subjects, CMS for Frequently Asked Questions, 356-358

    topics, CMS for Frequently Asked Questions, 360-363

addslashes(), 200, 248, 315

addsubject.php, 356

addtopic.php, 360

administering projects, re-usable code, 398-405

administrator login screens, hiding, 331

administrator logins, CMS for Frequently Asked Questions, 337-338

administrator pages, shopping carts, 208-209

    logging out administrators, 209-210

    managing completed orders, 210-212

    viewing specific orders, 213-216

administrator-specific pages, discussion forums, 158

    adding categories, 159-160

    adding forums, 160-163

    deleting, 163-167

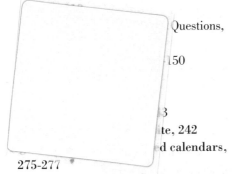

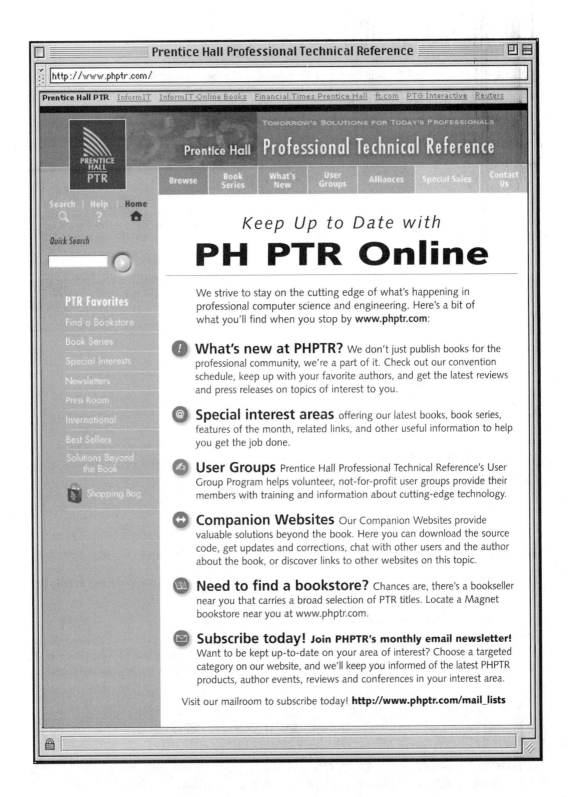

Prentice Hall Professional Technical Reference

http://www.phptr.com/

Prentice Hall PTR   InformIT   InformIT Online Books   Financial Times Prentice Hall   ft.com   PTG Interactive   Reuters

TOMORROW'S SOLUTIONS FOR TODAY'S PROFESSIONALS

Prentice Hall **Professional Technical Reference**

Browse | Book Series | What's New | User Groups | Alliances | Special Sales | Contact Us

Search | Help | Home

Quick Search

PTR Favorites

Find a Bookstore
Book Series
Special Interests
Newsletters
Press Room
International
Best Sellers
Solutions Beyond the Book

Shopping Bag

Keep Up to Date with

PH PTR Online

We strive to stay on the cutting edge of what's happening in professional computer science and engineering. Here's a bit of what you'll find when you stop by **www.phptr.com**:

What's new at PHPTR? We don't just publish books for the professional community, we're a part of it. Check out our convention schedule, keep up with your favorite authors, and get the latest reviews and press releases on topics of interest to you.

Special interest areas offering our latest books, book series, features of the month, related links, and other useful information to help you get the job done.

User Groups Prentice Hall Professional Technical Reference's User Group Program helps volunteer, not-for-profit user groups provide their members with training and information about cutting-edge technology.

Companion Websites Our Companion Websites provide valuable solutions beyond the book. Here you can download the source code, get updates and corrections, chat with other users and the author about the book, or discover links to other websites on this topic.

Need to find a bookstore? Chances are, there's a bookseller near you that carries a broad selection of PTR titles. Locate a Magnet bookstore near you at www.phptr.com.

Subscribe today! Join PHPTR's monthly email newsletter! Want to be kept up-to-date on your area of interest? Choose a targeted category on our website, and we'll keep you informed of the latest PHPTR products, author events, reviews and conferences in your interest area.

Visit our mailroom to subscribe today! **http://www.phptr.com/mail_lists**

About the CD-ROM

The accompanying CD-ROM contains a unique combination of software projects, applications, and even an entire operating system geared toward using and learning Web application development with PHP and MySQL. The contents of this CD can be used to do any of the following:

- Boot as a Linux live CD, launch a Web server (LAMPP), run PHP and MySQL code projects live, and modify those working projects to suit your purposes.
- Install the LAMPP server and projects on a Linux system to run permanently from hard disk.
- Install projects on any operating system that has a LAMPP server running.

The CD is a remaster of the Ubuntu live CD (ubuntu-6.06.1-desktop-i386.iso). To make room for the PHP and MySQL projects, several font packages, Windows versions of Abiword, Firefox, and other apps, and the entire OpenOffice.org suite were removed. Otherwise, it should operate as any Ubuntu live CD would, with the following additions:

- Added splash screen and other boot-time artwork to match the book's theme.
- On desktop, added a red apple icon to run /opt/lampp/lampp to start the LAMPP server, added a green apple icon to launch the main projects Web page in a browser, and added an icon to launch each individual project in a Web browser.
- Added bluefish package (represented by an icon on desktop panel, set up to immediately access projects) to provide a way to edit the applications.

To use the CD, simply

1. Insert the CD into a standard PC and reboot.
2. When desktop appears, open the Start LAMPP icon to start the server.
3. Open the Start Projects icon to view and work with projects.
4. Open Bluefish icon on the panel to modify projects.

Hardware Requirements

The following are the minimum hardware requirements for using the CD:

- Processor: For minimum performance, use at least a Pentium III, 650 MHz.
- RAM: At least 256MB RAM for minimal performance. Runs well with 512MB RAM or more.

By their nature, live CDs require more processing power and RAM to run effectively, as compared to an operating system installed on hard disk. So, to run these projects on an installed operating system, the minimal hardware requirements depend on the Linux system you use. You need at least 250MB of disk space if you want to unpack the LAMPP server and software projects (/opt/lampp.tar.gz) to run on an installed system.

Operating System Requirements

Because an entire Ubuntu Linux operating system is running from the CD, you don't need any particular operating system installed on your computer's hard disk. However, if you want to run the projects on an installed operating system, you can use the included LAMPP server software to run the projects on most Linux systems.

More Information on Using the CD

Refer to Chapter 3 for information on starting the LAMPP server and working with the software. Descriptions of the PHP and MySQL software projects are contained throughout the book.

Technical Support

The contents of this CD are provided as is and do not include technical support.